International Studies

This book provides a much-needed classroom text in international studies that is genuinely interdisciplinary in its approach.

International Studies focuses specifically on five core disciplines—history, geography, anthropology, political science and economics—and describes them in relation to one another, as well as their individual and collective contributions to the study of global issues. The expert authors also emphasize the continuing importance of area studies within an interdisciplinary and global framework, applying its interdisciplinary framework to substantive issues in seven regions: Europe, East Asia and the Pacific, South and Central Asia, sub-Saharan Africa, the Middle East and North Africa, Latin America and North America. This new edition has been completely updated and substantially revised with two new chapters on Media, Sovereignty and Cybersecurity, and Sustainable Development.

This disciplinary and regional combination offers a useful and cohesive framework for teaching students a substantive and comprehensive approach to understanding global issues.

Stanley Toops is an associate professor of Geography and International Studies at Miami University, Ohio, USA.

Mark Allen Peterson is a professor of Anthropology and International Studies at Miami University, Ohio, USA.

Walt Vanderbush is chair and associate professor of Global and Intercultural Studies at Miami University, Ohio, USA.

Naaborle Sackeyfio is assistant professor of Global and Intercultural Studies at Miami University, Ohio, USA.

Sheldon Anderson is a professor of History at Miami University, Ohio, USA.

International Studies

An Interdisciplinary Approach to
Global Issues

Fifth Edition

Stanley Toops, Mark Allen Peterson,
Walt Vanderbush, Naaborle Sackeyfio
and Sheldon Anderson

Routledge
Taylor & Francis Group

NEW YORK AND LONDON

Fifth edition published 2022
by Routledge
605 Third Avenue, New York, NY 10158

and by Routledge
2 Park Square, Milton Park, Abingdon, Oxon OX14 4RN

Routledge is an imprint of the Taylor & Francis Group, an informa business

First edition published by Westview 2007
Fourth edition published Routledge 2017

Library of Congress Cataloging-in-Publication Data
Names: Toops, Stanley, author. | Peterson, Mark Allen, author. | Vanderbush, Walt, author. |
Sackeyfio, Naaborle, author. | Anderson, Sheldon R., 1951– author.
Title: International studies : an interdisciplinary approach to global issues / Stanley Toops,
Mark Allen Peterson, Walt Vanderbush, Naaborle Sackeyfio and Sheldon Anderson.
Description: New York, NY : Routledge, 2022. |
Includes bibliographical references and index.
Identifiers: LCCN 2021013606 (print) | LCCN 2021013607 (ebook) |
ISBN 9780367463434 (hardback) | ISBN 9780367463441 (paperback) |
ISBN 9781003028314 (ebook)
Subjects: LCSH: International education. | Interdisciplinary approach in education.
Classification: LCC LC1090 .T73 2022 (print) |
LCC LC1090 (ebook) | DDC 370.116–dc23
LC record available at https://lccn.loc.gov/2021013606
LC ebook record available at https://lccn.loc.gov/2021013607

ISBN: 9780367463434 (hbk)
ISBN: 9780367463441 (pbk)
ISBN: 9781003028314 (ebk)

DOI: 10.4324/9781003028314

Typeset in Goudy
by Newgen Publishing UK

Access the companion website: www.routledge.com/cw/Toops

Contents

PART THREE
Contemporary Global Issues   **263**

About the Authors

Stanley Toops is an associate professor of Geography and International Studies at Miami University, Ohio, USA. He has taught International Studies for 30 years. Toops is the co-editor of *Understanding Contemporary China*, 5th edition (2017) and co-author of *The Routledge Atlas of Central Eurasian Affairs* (2012).

Mark Allen Peterson is a professor of Anthropology and International Studies at Miami University, Ohio, USA. He is the author of *Connected in Cairo: Growing Up Cosmopolitan in the Modern Middle East* (2011) and *Anthropology and Mass Communication: Media and Myth in the New Millennium* (2003). He has published more than 40 scholarly articles on globalization and localization, modernity, media and consumption. He has conducted fieldwork in Egypt, India and the United States.

Walt Vanderbush is chair and associate professor of Global and Intercultural Studies at Miami University, Ohio, USA, where he previously served as the Director of Latin American Studies. His research has been primarily in the areas of Latin American Political Economy and US–Latin American relations, including a co-authored book, *The Cuban Embargo: Domestic Politics of American Foreign Policy* (2005), as well as a range of journal articles and book chapters. Those journal outlets have been both political science and interdisciplinary in nature, including *New Political Science*, *Foreign Policy Analysis*, *International Studies Perspectives*, and *International Studies Quarterly*.

Naaborle Sackeyfio is an assistant professor of Global and Intercultural Studies at Miami University, Ohio, USA. She has taught a range of courses incorporating many aspects of Political Science and International Studies. Her scholarship explores energy/resource politics, sustainable development, gender and economic empowerment in Africa. She is the author of *Energy Politics and Rural Development in Sub-Saharan Africa: The Case of Ghana* (2017), which explores energy and development through an interdisciplinary lens. She has authored a number of journal articles forthcoming in *New Political Science*, *African and Asian Relations* and a book chapter with Routledge.

Sheldon Anderson is a professor of History at Miami University, Ohio, USA. He co-authored the previous editions of this textbook.

Figures

Maps and Tables

Maps

Tables

Preface

International Studies (ITS) at Miami University, and at many other colleges and universities, has evolved over several decades from a melding of political science, area studies and world languages into a true interdisciplinary approach to current global affairs. Through the vision of Dean Stephen Day and ITS Director William Hazleton in the early 1990s, the ITS program at Miami expanded its curriculum and hired new faculty members with joint appointments in ITS and geography, history, anthropology, and political science. The ITS program now serves hundreds of majors, and over 500 non-majors take the ITS introductory course every year.

One of the great challenges of teaching interdisciplinary International Studies is finding readings that recognize the importance of disciplinary histories and commitments while emphasizing the importance of analytical conversations between them such that each complements the blind spots of the others. When we were a small major with a handful of faculty, we managed this problem by lecturing in one another's classes, and sharing pedagogical strategies and resources. But in time we became victims of our own success, with hundreds of majors and a growth in faculty, many of them in temporary positions. To maintain our interdisciplinary focus, we decided to write a text that emphasizes an interdisciplinary analysis of issues of regional and global importance. The first part of this book covers the way each discipline—history, geography, anthropology, economics, and political science—contributes to understanding and solving world problems. Part Two examines various regions of the world—North America, Europe, East Asia and the Pacific, South and Central Asia, Sub-Saharan Africa, the Middle East and North Africa, and Latin America—while stressing the diversity within these regions and the interconnections among them. Part Three includes essays that analyze contemporary global issues through an interdisciplinary lens. These can be used for discussion coinciding with Part Two of the book.

The authors recognize that the interdisciplinary nature of international studies will draw teachers from various areas of expertise into unfamiliar academic realms. This book is designed to give them a construct with which to teach international studies and an approach to enhance students' understanding of the complexities of the modern world.

This is the fifth edition of the book. The new edition features up-to-date information on each region of the world and new global issues chapters in Part Three. Each chapter is accompanied by a map and a list of recommended readings, films, and websites. There is a glossary of keywords, which appear in bold throughout the text.

The text also comes with online teaching resources, including course objectives, syllabi, and assignments that have proven effective in the classroom over many years. Please visit: www.routledge.com/9780367463441

The authors of the text have published extensively in their respective disciplines, and each has a different regional and linguistic expertise. Dr. Stanley Toops is one of the foremost US geographers of the Uyghur region of northwest China. He is fluent in Chinese and conversant in Uyghur, and he has written articles and chapters on geography, tourism, and population in China and Central Asia. Recent works include an atlas of Central Eurasia and an edited collection on China. Dr. Toops was primary author for the chapters on geography, East Asia, South Asia, and the essays on climate change and sustainable development. Dr. Walt Vanderbush is an expert on Latin American political economy, as well as US–Latin American relations and US foreign policy. Fluent in Spanish, he has done original research individually and collaboratively in Mexico, Cuba and the Caribbean. He is the primary author of the chapters on political science and Latin America. Dr. Mark Allen Peterson has published groundbreaking work on Middle Eastern and South Asian media and globalization. He is fluent in Arabic, Hindi and Urdu. Dr. Peterson was primary author for the chapters on anthropology and the Middle East, as well as the essays on international terrorism, the refugee crisis, and global issues in media. Dr. Naaborle Sackeyfio specializes in energy and resource politics, gender equality and sustainable development with a regional focus on sub-Saharan Africa. She has published work on energy politics and rural development in Ghana and is studying African migrant incorporation in Japan. She is the primary author of the chapters on economics and Africa.

The authors owe a debt of gratitude to many people. First, this book owes a tremendous debt to Sheldon Anderson and Jeanne Hey, who conceived the project and served as its co-authors and co-editors on many of the earlier editions. We also thank our many colleagues past and present in International Studies at Miami, Melanie Ziegler, Carl Dahlman, Charles Stevens, Dilchoda Berdieva, and Kathryn LaFever, for their suggestions on updating the book. Stanley Toops thanks Mark, Walt, and Naaborle for their invaluable work, Simone Andrus for her contributions to his chapters, librarians Jenny Presnell and Katie Gibson for references, and students Daniel Kyale, Kristy Fortman, Adanma Ogboo, Hannah Koonce, Ana Contessa, Lisa Dershowitz, and Michael Browne for their work on the maps and tables. Sheldon Anderson would like to thank his family—Kristie, O Maxwell, Lauren, and Mongo—for their patience and support as he worked on previous editions of the book. Walt Vanderbush thanks Elena Albarrán for her very helpful comments after reading an early draft of the Latin America chapter. Walt would also like to thank Caroline McClellan for all of her support and patience during the writing process. Naaborle Sackeyfio offers gratitude to Stanley Toops and Mark Peterson for the opportunity to contribute to this collaborative effort to highlight unique perspectives and interdisciplinary strengths that are invaluable to students of international studies or politics and so thanks them both for this timely endeavor. In addition to his co-authors, Mark Allen Peterson thanks James Bielo, John Cinnamon, Cameron Hay-Rollins, Linda Marchant, Geoff Owens, Susan Paulson, Dawna Peterson, Douglas Rogers, Christa Salamandra, Daniel Varisco, and Jessica Winegar for their comments on various drafts of chapters. Thanks to Miami University's GIS coordinator, Robbyn Abbitt, who edited the maps.

Introduction

The global pandemic. International terrorism. Proliferation of weapons of mass destruction. An international refugee plight on an unprecedented scale. Transnational economic inequities. A planetary environmental crisis. Our world is faced with extraordinary challenges that are beyond the capacity of any one country to solve. The global issues require deep, thorough analysis if they are to be successfully resolved. This is the mission of International Studies.

Why Do International Studies?

Why take an interdisciplinary approach to global issues? The answers are found in the increasing interdependence of people, nations, and institutions at all levels of human society. Human interdependencies date back millennia, at least to the rise of trade links between Sumer and the Indus Valley Civilization in the third millennium BCE. Five hundred years ago, Europeans broadened their commercial contacts with Africa and Asia, and began a system of exploitation, colonization and world wars that brought the regions of the world together in an unprecedented process of globalization. The Industrial Revolution in the nineteenth century and the high-tech revolution in the late twentieth century have brought many of us to the point today where a phone call is possible between someone riding a train in Peru and a climber standing atop Mount Everest. An Indian doctor can read an X-ray for a patient sitting in a physician's office in Topeka. A Russian can buy a car built in South Korea, Germany, Italy, Japan, or the United States. Although most people in the world could not locate Bangladesh on a **map**, the cap they wear might have been made there.

Never before has the world been so integrated. Politics, markets, culture, the media, and information are no longer local but global. The ripple effect of local events on wider regions has grown exponentially in the last century; a century ago events in one part of the world often went unnoticed in another. Today, the proliferation of information through the Internet, cell phones, print media, and television allows people on opposite sides of the globe to experience events simultaneously. What happens on Tokyo's stock exchange has an instantaneous effect on other markets as they open throughout the day. The extent of the destruction of the tsunami that hit Japan in 2011 and the earthquake that shook Italy in 2016 was known to the world within hours. The effects of terrorist attacks are amplified because the media disseminate the chaos of the moment and engender the fear that follows. Suicide attackers often make videos for posting on the Internet after they have struck, which maximizes the sense that these murderers will stop at nothing to claim innocent people's lives. Beginning in 2011, the so-called Arab Spring of pro-democratic revolts in Tunisia, Egypt, and Libya, among others, was spurred on by Internet and cell phone connections, as was the growth of the Islamic State (IS) in northern Syria and Iraq.

DOI: 10.4324/9781003028314-1

The boom in world commerce since World War II is unprecedented. World exports totaled $61 billion in 1950, expanding to $25 trillion by 2015. In 1960 trade amounted to 17.5 percent of the world's GDP. In 2015 the percentage had grown to 45 percent (el-Ojeili and Hayden 2006, 60; World Bank 2016). International financial and business transactions happen instantaneously on electronic networks. The possibility of a default by the Greek government in 2011 sent shock waves through international markets. Millions of foreign workers send money home using secure global-banking services. Products move around the world on airplanes, ships, trains, and long-range trucks, often without human hands touching the containers. There are about 100,000 airplane departures from approximately 9,000 different airports daily and over 60,000 large merchant vessels plying the high seas (www.marinetraffic.com).

This increasing interdependence is usually called globalization, an "intensification of worldwide social relations which link distant localities in such a way that local happenings are shaped by events occurring many miles away and vice versa" (Giddens 1990, 64). Weapons of mass destruction, global climate change, interconnected and fragile trade and financial systems, armed conflict, burgeoning populations, humanitarian crises, pandemics, and global poverty are among the many international problems that demand the attention of scholars, policymakers, and citizens. Never before has it been so important to find solutions to these problems, and never have these complex issues been harder to grasp. An interdisciplinary approach is essential to fully understanding the historical, geographical, political, cultural, and economic dimensions of these global challenges.

The complexities of the modern age and the interconnectedness of global people, events, and processes are so strong that a break from traditional methods of research and inquiry is required. Foreign-policy makers and educators are becoming increasingly aware of the deficiencies of strict disciplinary approaches to the globalization processes and international affairs today. By *disciplinary* we mean approaches connected to the traditional academic disciplines of history, political science, economics, geography, and anthropology. Instead, international studies offers an integrative, comprehensive, and interdisciplinary approach to issues of global importance.

This book breaks new ground by introducing five disciplines applicable to international studies and addressing regional and global issues through an interdisciplinary approach. Four of the five disciplines considered here are social sciences, whereas the fifth, history, tends to fall in the humanities. While history does not pretend to be a science, a complete understanding of current international affairs is impossible without knowing the historical context. Historians play a vital role in resolving international conflicts by writing objective historical accounts free of polemic and propaganda. But the advent of the Internet and the rapid flow of information from sources of dubious reliability have created new challenges. Different memories or interpretations of past events are at the heart of many international conflicts. For example, the controversy between the United Nations and Iran over Tehran's quest for nuclear power has its roots in Iran's resentment of British imperialism and US intervention in Iran's struggles to develop economic independence during the Cold War. And Japanese–Chinese friction often revolves around the brutal Japanese occupation of China during World War II. At the heart of these tensions is the way historical memory is manipulated to create a national identity. Many Chinese continue to view the Japanese as imperialists, whereas Japanese remember themselves as progressives and missionaries who brought the benefits of civilization to supposedly backward people.

Geography's role in international studies is to analyze space, regions, and environments. The physical geographer studies the processes of the natural environment; the human geographer is concerned with human interaction with the physical world. Geographers' evidence includes demographic statistics, climate studies, health records, and communication networks. The map is a special tool that geographers use in their analyses of the earth and people's interactions with it.

Geographic study goes to the heart of such international problems as population density, the spread of disease, water shortages, environmental degradation, border conflicts, population flows, use of space, and transportation networks. Hundreds of millions of migrants annually move from one region to another, millions even making leaps from one continent to another, bringing new customs, expectations, and political agendas. Diseases, blights, and bugs travel on the thousands of ships, airplanes, trains, and automobiles moving around the globe daily. Delicate regional ecologies are subject to alien invaders that hitch rides on long-distance transports. The world waits on edge for invisible strains of flu, drug-resistant tuberculosis, and other deadly diseases transferred on the global highways. Global warming, water and air pollution, soil erosion, and desertification know no political boundaries and are best understood through geography's contribution to an interdisciplinary analysis.

Political science analyzes the power relationships between peoples and the institutions used to mediate their competing interests. Political scientists often employ case studies to identify the variables that explain political behavior, trying to determine if past models are applicable to present cases. Questions of international import are ultimately tied to those who have the power to solve them. Democratic development, international institutions, international relations, and international conflict and conflict resolution are within the purview of political science as it relates to international studies.

Some political scientists have moved from paradigms that seemed to explain international power relationships in the past, such as hegemony and dependence theory, to **complex interdependence**, which the interdisciplinary approach of international studies seeks to explain. Political relationships are more complicated today because globalization has created greater "power for the powerless" (Havel 1985). For example, international human-rights organizations and the media can disseminate information on a government's political practices that is difficult to control. The Chinese regime is desperately trying to regulate Internet sites that criticize its undemocratic practices. Political scientists are keenly interested in whether China can maintain political repression while participating in a globalized economy.

The global information network can also undermine the power of liberal democratic governments, which can be criticized for the influence of money in politics, the disparity between rich and poor, and racial discrimination. Easy access to information also foments identity politics, which can divide societies into cultural or political groups that oppose each other and make democratic compromise and cooperation nearly impossible. The street protests in Egypt in 2013 attest to the power of social media to rally supporters. Internet commerce also undermines national legal systems. For example, it is illegal in Germany to sell Adolf Hitler's *Mein Kampf*, but it became one of Amazon.com's top-ten sellers in Germany in 1999 (Friedman 2000, 37).

Anthropology examines the role of culture: the way humans give importance to similarities and differences in environments, economic systems, ideologies, political systems, and languages that shape identities, values and actions. People understand and explain the world in different ways, and these different understandings shape the ways that peoples create, maintain and interact across social and political borders. Anthropologists seek to make concrete the elusive concept of **culture**, a learned system of meanings through which people orient themselves in the world.

Global cultural transfers put pressure on local customs and traditions. Richer countries once dominated these transfers, but cultural flows have never gone in only one direction. The world's consumption of McDonald's burgers and Hollywood films is often cited as an example of the effect of globalization on local eating habits and artistic expression, but Indian Bollywood movies, South Korean cars, low priced goods from China, and workers moving from one country to another are also causing profound challenges to local cultures. Indians may be eating Tex-Mex, but Texans are eating curry, too—often cooked by Indians who've relocated. Anthropology urges us to look also at the flip side of globalization—*localization*—the process through which people appropriate commodities, services, and ideas that enter their communities from outside, transforming them and making them their own.

Although some scholars highlight a "clash of civilizations" (Huntington 1996) that globalization engenders, others argue that the world is actually experiencing an integration of civilizations that brings peoples closer together. Understanding the cultural elements of behavior is an essential component of a broad international studies education. In this increasingly mobile world, cultural clashes, cultural sharing, and cultural changes are happening faster now than ever before.

Economists study the production, distribution, and consumption of goods and services. **International economics** concerns financial relations, trade regimes, and economic development. Economists deal with the most basic yet most complex problems facing any society. For example, what strategies promote economic growth and provide for basic human needs and economic opportunities? Are there any fundamental economic rights, such as medical care, housing, and food?

One of the hot economic debates in the world today pits globalists against economic nationalists. The globalists, or liberal economists, advocate free and unfettered economic relations between states as a means to increase the wealth and prosperity of all people in all nations. Some even argue that war is less likely between open-market economies because the economic costs to an aggressor are too high. Economic nationalists argue that the world's free-trade regime lowers wages and causes unemployment for workers in developed economies. They also point to the increasing economic disparity between the rich and the poor, both within and between countries. Small businesses in every country struggle to compete against the world's giant corporations, which can often provide cheaper goods and services and consistently meet demand at lower cost to the consumer. But in some industries small businesses may be more nimble at utilizing or inventing productive technologies than bigger corporations.

The second half of the book introduces seven regions of the world: North America, Europe, East Asia, South Asia, Africa, the Middle East, and Latin America. Some scholars have criticized the area-studies approach because Westerners arbitrarily constructed these regional labels. For example, if we think of the so-called Middle East as an area composed mainly of Arab peoples, it also has to include northern Africa as well as southwestern Asia. Iran and Turkey are bookends of the region, but neither of these countries is Arab.

The authors are fully aware of the limitations of a regional approach to international affairs. However, even in an era of globalization, thinking about the world in terms of geopolitical regions remains useful for several reasons. First, dividing the world into regions offers a way to manage enormous amounts of information about environments, people, and social relations. Trying to understand international issues in terms of the over 200 countries and recognized dependent areas in the world—each with its unique history, environment, economy, and political and cultural systems—is beyond the scope of any scholar or analytical approach. Trying to attend to every country can lead to a failure to see the forest for the trees.

Second, thinking regionally allows us to aggregate information common to groups of peoples and countries in order to see big pictures. Each region exhibits some common political, economic, linguistic, religious, or historical currents. Most Europeans have a Christian heritage, similar cultural norms, and social democratic political systems. Latin Americans are mostly Catholic, speak either Spanish or Portuguese, have many similar economic challenges, have struggled to establish stable democracies and draw on a history of interventions from the United States. Although Westerners devised most of the world's continental designations and national borders, peoples in these regions have constructed their regional identities as well.

The authors have made conscious efforts to illustrate the diversity within the regions as well as their interconnectedness. There are no walls dividing these regions, but many bridges linking them together. Globalization along the electronic highway, sea lanes, rails, and roads has blurred old regional categories. Understanding the political, economic, historical, geographic, and cultural differences both within and among these areas is the essence of international studies inquiry.

Thinking about the world regionally can also serve as a useful heuristic device that helps us avoid ethnocentric and region-specific thinking. For example, in the US people tend to see issues of global terrorism through the lens of Islamic terrorism, because this has become particularly important to US national security. The major terrorism issue in the US is right-wing terrorists. By making a point of looking at international issues in terms of every region, we discover terrorism in Latin America, Asia, and Africa. Terrorism is certainly not a Muslim or Middle Eastern activity, although too much of the Western press might arrive at that conclusion. Al Qaeda and Islamic State (IS) are not representative of mainstream society in any Muslim region of the world. That said, terrorist organizations are at the top of the global agenda because of their responsibility for the September 11, 2001, attacks in the United States, as well as for the urban bombings in Madrid in 2004 and London in 2005, and in Paris and Brussels in 2015 and 2016. Islamic anger has also been blamed for the murder of Dutch filmmaker Theo van Gogh for allegedly defaming Islam and for widespread demonstrations throughout the world in reaction to a Danish newspaper's printing of satirical cartoons of the prophet Muhammad.

Globalization creates a new context within which terrorism—a centuries-old political tool—occurs in the modern world. Indeed, globalization creates a new context within which all political activity operates. First, events themselves are publicized instantaneously, repeatedly, and globally. Modern terrorists know that their acts will gain worldwide attention. Second, all political organizations, including terrorist ones, benefit from the Internet's global reach. Personal computers and global networks make fund-raising, recruiting, and disseminating information easier than ever before. Third, and in a different vein, globalization and technology also give terrorists and other groups access to points of view different from their own group's ideology. Finally, law enforcement uses the instruments of globalization to monitor and capture potential terrorists and other criminals.

Scholars, politicians, and ordinary people have desperately searched for answers to the terrorist threat emanating from a tiny minority of the fundamentalist Muslim community. A geographer might find answers in the demographic explosion of an unemployed, frustrated, and angry younger population. A historian might place terrorism in the continuum of a long history of conflicts between the Middle East and Western imperialists. A political scientist might approach the problem through the lens of the Israeli–Palestinian conflict, illegitimate borders, or the authoritarian regimes and lack of democracy in the Middle East. An economist might emphasize the poverty in the Middle East or the region's frustration with the challenges of modernization and economic development. An anthropologist might ask what kinds of cultural symbols are employed by terrorist organizations to recruit people willing to kill and die for a cause—and why these ideologies attract a relatively small number of people. International studies, unlike any singular discipline, draws on *all* of these disciplines in an integrated way for answers that can lead to solutions.

Adopting the Interdisciplinary Approach

An interdisciplinary approach to global issues requires the application of basic methodological and theoretical assumptions of several disciplines to the understanding of an issue. It seeks a holistic approach that borrows the strengths of all the constituent disciplines.

Because we often think about global issues in terms of real or potential conflict, political science often seems the most relevant discipline. Political science assumes that all social units are political—not only countries but families, communities, enterprises, alliances, and all others.

They are political in that their members organize and disagree around issues of resource allocation, behavioral norms, and ownership of authority. Political science teaches us to put conflict at the center of understanding an issue, and seeks to analyze relations of conflict and power.

Political science urges us to ask the question: How is power distributed and used to manage conflict? Following the political science approach means locating stakeholders in an event or situation, determining what each has at risk, and analyzing how relations of power are distributed and used to manage conflict.

The economic approach supplements these descriptions by offering effective explanatory mechanisms for the behaviors of the stakeholders in a given situation. Economics assumes that all social units act rationally, and that individuals, groups, and states will always seek to maximize their gains and minimize their losses as best they can, given their understanding of the situation.

The economic approach seeks to understand the behavior of stakeholders in a situation—and predict how they will act in the future—by describing what each stakeholder risks and what they stand to gain. An economic perspective prompts us to ask: What are the costs and benefits of particular courses of action for the various stakeholders?

Anthropology offers an important series of correctives for this political-economic framework. First, anthropology reminds us that knowledge of how the system works can differ according to different perspectives, so that what appears irrational from an analytical point of view may appear quite rational to actors operating according to different cultural logics. Second, anthropology suggests that in addition to power and wealth, social actors may view principles and values as significant. A social actor might act quite rationally to maximize *symbolic* capital (values, principles, religious beliefs) or *social* capital (status, reputation, honor, belonging) in addition to, or even instead of, economic (wealth) and political (power) capital. Anthropology urges us to ask: What do these events mean to the peoples involved in them, and how do these beliefs and values shape their interactions?

Geography and history add important dimensions to analysis of global issues by expanding the scope of inquiry to consider the past, and environmental capacities and constraints. Geography assumes the importance of the relationships between groups of people and the places where they live. It emphasizes the description and analysis of the relations between people, space, and environment, and urges us to broaden our analysis from the actors in a conflict to broader contexts: population shifts, environmental changes, ecological impacts. It also calls on us to look at constraints that might not occur to us when looking strictly at the actions of the people involved. How might a dam built in one country create further problems for the nations downriver? Are there enough consumers to make a free-market solution feasible? How can international groups be resettled if their traditional lands can no longer support them because of environmental degradation? Many apparently political conflicts have important spatial and environmental contexts. Geography, then, urges us to ask: How do space and environments shape events?

History adds a temporal context that is crucial for understanding contemporary conflicts and even more important for developing solutions. The historical approach reminds us that every people has a past, and they draw on that past to understand who they are, and to explain and interpret current events. History seeks to create chronological description and analysis of events in the development of a people or institution, including explanation of, and commentary on, those events. Historical approaches thus teach us to ask: How did things get to where they are now?

This set of key questions brings together the five international studies disciplines described in this book.

Table 0.1 International Studies

POLITICAL SCIENCE
- **Key Assumption**: All social units organize around and disagree about issues of resource allocation, behavioral norms and ownership of authority.
- **Project**: Description and analysis of relations of conflict and power.
- **Key Question**: *How is power distributed and used to manage conflict?*

ECONOMICS
- **Key Assumption**: All social units seek to maximize their gains and minimize their losses to the best of their ability (given their understanding of the situation.)
- **Definition**: Describing what each stakeholder risks and what they stand to gain in any given situation.
- **Key Question**: *Who are the stakeholders, and what are the costs and benefits of particular courses of action for the various stakeholders?*

ANTHROPOLOGY
- **Key Assumption**: All human social action makes sense when understood within its own contexts.
- **Definition**: Description and analysis of the shared, learned systems of meaning that members of societies use to orient themselves in the world and to render human action predictable.
- **Key Question**: *What do these events and issues mean to the peoples involved in them and how do these beliefs and values shape their interactions?*

GEOGRAPHY
- **Key Assumption**: Every group of people lives in a place and interacts with the features of that place.
- **Definition**: The description and analysis of the relations between people, space, and environment.
- **Key Question**: *How do space and environments shape events?*

HISTORY
- **Key Assumption**: Every people has a past, and they draw on that past to understand who they are, and to explain and interpret current events.
- **Definition**: Chronological description and analysis of events in the development of a people or institution, including explanation of or commentary on those events.
- **Key Question**: *How did things get to where they are now?*

Twenty-first-century challenges, such as terrorism, sustainable economic development, poverty, pollution, global warming, nuclear proliferation, human rights, pandemics, and interstate and civil conflicts do not stop at national boundaries or disciplinary categories. The notion that any global challenge can be studied or solved with the lenses and tools of one discipline is outdated. This book aims to help students begin to think in an integrated and critical way, relying on valuable perspectives from many disciplines but moving beyond disciplinary boundaries toward complex explanations and understanding.

References

el-Ojeili, Chamsy, and Patrick Hayden. 2006. *Critical Theories of Globalization*. New York: Palgrave.

Friedman, Thomas. 2000. *The Lexus and the Olive Tree: Understanding Globalization*. New York: Anchor Books.

Giddens, Anthony. 1990. *The Consequences of Modernity*. Stanford, CA: Stanford University Press.

Havel, Václav. 1985. "The Power of the Powerless." In *The Power of the Powerless: Citizens Against the State in Central-Eastern Europe*, edited by John Keane, 23–96. Armonk, NY: M. E. Sharpe.

Huntington, Samuel P. 1996. *The Clash of Civilizations and the Remaking of the World Order*. New York: Simon & Schuster.

World Bank. 2016. www.worldbank.org.

Part One

The Disciplines of International Studies

Chapter 1

The Past in the Present
Historical Interpretation in International Studies

The word **history** comes from the Greek (ἱστορία) meaning "inquiry". In current language, a history means a narrative, helping us to understand what happened and why it happened. In Chinese, history is 历史(lishi). "Li" refers to a chronicle, the traditional version of the character shows sheaves of grain counted from season to season. "Shi" is a narrative, a writing, the character shows a stack of books bound together. So, from Greek, we have an inquiry and, from Chinese, a writing of a chronicle. Historical inquiry combines all of the disciplines of international studies. Historians use geographical, economic, political, cultural, and any other relevant sources—regardless of their disciplinary category—to create an accurate portrayal of the past. History teaches students to evaluate evidence, consider contradictory interpretations, and construct coherent narratives. History is a useful way to understand human experiences and the patterns of change within society.

The study of history, in contrast to other disciplines in international studies, is part of the humanities. Economics, anthropology, geography, and political science are generally thought of as social sciences; anthropology and geography also have elements of the natural sciences. History has connections to the social sciences, many colleges and universities link history to the social sciences. In international studies, we study the histories of countries, global events, and people to gain an understanding of current issues around the world.

What Is History?

In 2003, author Bill Bryson wrote a thin volume called *A Short History of Nearly Everything*. On the one hand, the irony in Bryson's title is obvious, but on the other, there is a commonly held notion that history is everything that has happened in the past. That would be a very long book indeed. The past disappears if no one remembers it or passes it along. History is a written, oral, or visual reconstruction and interpretation of past human endeavors based on available sources.

Students often use the slang phrase "you're history" in the same way they think about history, that it is something over and done with. The historian's task is to revisit the past again and again, scrutinize histories for their veracity, and use new sources of information to verify, add to, or revise them.

The *Oxford English Dictionary* has several definitions of history. "The branch of knowledge that deals with past events; the formal record or study of past events, esp. human affairs." "A written narrative constituting a continuous chronological record of important or public events" (OED, 2020). History does utilize sources, often sources that are written, but the sources can also be spoken, of people's memories of past events. History deals with when and what happened, but also why it happened.

The ancient Greeks and Chinese both wrote histories of their worlds. Herodotus (484–425/ 414 BCE) was credited for being the Father of History by the Roman writer Cicero. Herodotus

DOI: 10.4324/9781003028314-3

wrote *The Histories* about the wars of Greeks and the Persians, recounting perspectives from both Persians and Greeks. Herodotus was from Halicarnassus, a city populated by Greeks and Persians (what is now Bodrum in Turkey). As a young man, Herodotus travelled around the Mediterranean. Sima Qian (145–84 BCE) wrote the *Records of the Grand Historian* which covered two thousand years of history of China up to his time. He was from Shaanxi province north of the capital of Chang'an (modern day Xi'an) of the Han Dynasty. Sima traveled around China as a young man and was sent to the lands west of China with a military expedition. Sima became a Confucian scholar and, like his father Sima Tan, the historian of the imperial court. Both of these early historians reviewed sources, both traveled around their worlds, both wrote early histories of their peoples and "neighbors" and both completed systematic investigations of the past events of their times. Sima Qian did not write about Greece and Persia. Herodotus did not write about China (Martin 2010). Historians today may be able to write about both Europe and Asia. Some historians today might have command of both Greek and Chinese languages and familiarity with both *The Histories* and *Records of the Grand Historian* in the original languages. Most historians would probably specialize in a history of a particular time and place, for example the ancient Mediterranean or ancient China.

There is no agreed-upon record of the past. Historians can come to some consensus on what was a major event and when it took place, such as natural disasters, economic depressions, or wars, but they differ on questions of **causation**, interpretation, and significance. History resembles a criminal trial: detectives compile evidence, and prosecutors use it to reconstruct the crime. Defense lawyers then call witnesses to revise that version of history. The reasonable-doubt standard for conviction always applies to any history.

Historians usually remembered the exploits of major political and religious leaders, such as Alexander the Great of Macedonia in the fourth century BCE or Emperor Charlemagne in the late eighth century CE. Written histories were often tales of war and imperial victories or defeats. Family histories traced the lineage of important historical figures, for example, the dynastic succession of ancient Roman or Chinese emperors, or the popes of the Catholic Church. Bureaucracies and legal standards were built on keeping records of past practices.

Until the late twentieth century, political history dominated the profession. From Thucydides' *History of the Peloponnesian War* in the fifth century BCE to Edward Gibbon's late-eighteenth-century *History of the Decline and Fall of the Roman Empire*, most historians studied the political fortunes of the most powerful members of society, most of them men. Many histories were panegyrics to glorify and justify the rule of the dominant political classes. The history of religion and ideas provided the spiritual and philosophical foundations of temporal power. Historical accuracy played a secondary role to the narrative's didactic purpose.

Influenced by the humanism and rational thinking of Renaissance and Enlightenment scholars, as well as by the rapid technological changes of modern industrial society, some nineteenth-century historians in the West championed a new empirical approach to history. Karl Marx devised a political-economic theory of history based on the "scientific" truth of class conflict (Figure 1.1). German historian Leopold von Ranke claimed to write history "*wie es eigentlich gewesen ist*," or history "as it really was." Von Ranke and fellow positivists tried to inject the scientific method into the process of writing history. They called for histories based on empirical evidence and historical objectivity. Reference notes cued the reader to the documents used to prove the truth of the history. To reflect this change in the approach to studying history, many history departments shifted from the humanities to the social sciences during the twentieth century.

The Rankean model came under increased fire after World War II, when **revisionist history** began to question the "scientific truth" of history. Revisionists claimed, often correctly, that conventional histories about the past were myths intended to foster a sense of national unity

Figure 1.1 Karl Marx.
Source: Library of Congress.

and national pride. They revealed that many stories of the past manipulated historical facts and ignored non-dominant perspectives. In the United States, revisionists laid bare the lies that the Johnson and Nixon administrations told about the Vietnam War. Civil-rights advocates demanded a truer version of the past to reflect the dismal treatment of minorities in American history. In Europe, historians exposed the brutality of imperial rule, state violence against working classes, and, in light of the Holocaust, Europe's endemic anti-Semitism and fascist tendencies. Historians examine and re-examine new evidence to reframe the past, or to confirm previous accounts (Arnold, 2000).

Today, **postmodernist historians** deny the existence of any objective histories. They argue that the past cannot be recovered and that no narrative can be an accurate reflection of what actually transpired. Like impressionist and expressionist art, they consider history to be a partial and particular depiction of reality as the creator creates it or the audience perceives it. Observed from different angles and distances, and under different kinds of light, the image changes.

Postmodernists emphasize the cultural mediation of historical memory; in some ways, they argue, historical narratives reveal more about the author's beliefs and cultural milieu than history "as it really was." Historians are the filter through which the past is constructed. They bring their own personal, national, or class biases to the trade. They are carried along by the stream of human history, and they influence the cultural context and are influenced by it. Even video and film documentation is dependent on the framing, camera angle, and editing. Scenes can be staged, and in this age of computer imaging, entirely contrived. Because history is merely a representation of the past and is continually shaped and reshaped, postmodernists argue, there can be no objective historical truth.

Professional historians know this, but they still make a good-faith effort to use all relevant sources and write balanced narratives that come as close to the truth about the past as possible. Reliable histories depend on the skill and thoroughness of historians, the cogency of their logic, and conscious subordination of the biases that they bring to their work. Sources take good historians where they may not want to go. Writers who start with a premise, fit the sources to prove it, and ignore contrary evidence are more interested in polemical than historical discourse. The resolution of international disputes often depends on histories and historians dedicated to accurate renditions of the past.

Historians and Their Tools

The historian's task is to garner all available relevant sources to construct a plausible story of the past. Historians scour archives, libraries, museums, and other repositories of documents and artifacts. They often gather data through interviews, although the passage of time limits their utility. Journalists are historians too, but short-term deadlines limit their access to relevant evidence. Historians benefit by drawing on a wider range of sources, although the clues to the historian's case are always incomplete.

Historical data are often divided into two, somewhat subjective, categories. **Primary sources** include artifacts, diaries, letters, memoirs, e-mails, autobiographies, interviews, official documents, visual images, coins, stamps, demographic statistics, economic records, and polls. Primary sources are written by people and still show the biases and perspectives of the writer (Presnell 2019). Primary sources are direct evidence about the past from someone involved in the past event, without an intermediary's interpretation. Theoretically, primary sources are raw objective data that are untainted by bias or the knowledge that historians will use them to construct a history. There is a fine line between primary and secondary sources, however, because it is often difficult to know what motives people had for leaving sources behind. For example, did the minute taker of an important foreign-policy planning session give an honest rendering of the meeting, or did that person intend to exaggerate the wisdom of the participants? Like a prosecuting attorney, the historian must search for other corroborating evidence to find the truth and decide which primary sources are most reliable.

Letters and diaries may seem to be direct and objective links to the past, but the authors often write them knowing that historians will read them later. Autobiographies are also written for posterity; authors are unlikely to provide critical self-examination of their lives. Eyewitness accounts, a staple in the journalist's trade, provide very different pictures of a single event. The historian is well aware of the irony in the witness-stand pledge to "tell the truth, the whole truth, and nothing but the truth." There is no such thing. Taken at face value, statistics appear to be the most objective of all primary sources. But as any sociologist knows, statistics are only as good as the data from which they are derived. And even the most accurate statistics can be skewed to fit a political agenda.

Secondary sources are oral or written narratives derived from primary sources. Secondary sources are interpretations that draw on primary sources (Presnell 2019). The authors of newspaper articles, journal articles, and books gather sources to interpret what happened in the past. Secondary sources include books such as *Vietnam: A New History* (Goscha 2016), journal articles such as "The Ming Rejection of the Portuguese Embassy in 1517" (Fujitani 2016), websites such as *Wonders of the African World* (PBS) or films such as *Citizen Kane* (Welles and Mankiewicz 1941). The distinction between primary and secondary sources is muddled when a historian writes a history of histories, often called a **historiography**. In that case, previous histories become the author's primary sources.

Historians must make judgments about the reliability of their source material. Both historians and political scientists try to find patterns in the past, but historians are more skeptical about categorizing behaviors and using models to make predictions about the future (Arnold 2000; Presnell 2019).

Politics, Power, and History

The victors in power struggles have passed down most of recorded history. The politically powerful have greater access to written, oral, and visual media. Histories often glorify political leaders, praise heroic exploits on the battlefield, or emphasize a particular group's cultural and scientific accomplishments. Political agendas filter out dissonant historical evidence. The "triumphal" version of American history includes Christopher Columbus's "discovery" of America (as though no one lived in the Western Hemisphere; Figure 1.2), the unique democratic character of the American form of government (what about the Netherlands, France, or the United Kingdom?), and the "benevolent" US expansion into the American West and abroad (ask Native Americans). This history typically exaggerates the peculiar democratic and righteous character of the American people and downplays the country's slaveholding past, imperialism, and ethnic cleansing of America's native peoples.

Figure 1.2 Landing of Christopher Columbus in the Caribbean.

Source: Library of Congress.

The history of the oppressed has always existed, but until recently their stories have been excluded from the dominant cultural discourse. It was only in the last half of the twentieth century that "history from below" became mainstream. Revisionist histories have become common; now historians study Native Americans, colonized peoples, women, the working classes, and other groups hidden from view in the old political histories of "dead white guys."

Histories of the "defeated" can be just as biased as those of their oppressors, however. Some historians have exaggerated the peace-loving character of Native American or African peoples before Europeans corrupted their cultures. Some Afrocentrists have shaped the historical record to argue that Egyptians and other African peoples were more advanced than the Greeks or Romans, or they have downplayed the lively African slave trade before the arrival of European slavers. Some labor historians portray working-class leaders as intelligent, nonviolent, altruistic champions of the people, and factory owners as inherently greedy, inhumane, and exploitative. Victims of oppression do themselves no service by exaggerating their political and cultural achievements and distorting the historical record. No other group will believe myths based on historical falsehoods.

When leaders distort the historical record to suit their political aims, tragedy often results. The French were fully appreciative of American military assistance in World War I, but their military histories stressed the sacrifices and heroism of the French forces for winning the war, and the success of trench warfare in defending Paris. These histories downplayed the role of American soldiers in turning the military balance in favor of the Allies in 1917. Acting upon these false assumptions about why they had won the war, the French built the massive Maginot Line along the French–German border. This costly, sophisticated line of defensive fortifications did not save France from the German onslaught in 1940.

Soviet scholars ran a historical enterprise that was dedicated to "predicting the past." In other words, the past had to be cast in a way that squared with Marx's theory of history as class struggle. Thus peasant revolts were part of an inexorable struggle against the aristocratic classes, and the middle classes were deemed keepers of an inherently oppressive democratic-capitalist system. After his death in 1924, Lenin was permanently encased in a glass mausoleum for all Soviet citizens to view for eternity. Although Marx had focused on classes rather than individuals to explain historical progress, paradoxically there was room for sainthood in "scientific" Soviet history. Russians are now divided about whether to bury Lenin.

The leaders of the Soviet Communist Party could do no wrong; even Soviet leader Nikita Khrushchev's "secret speech" in 1956, in which he exposed Joseph Stalin's crimes, did not result in a serious revision of Soviet history. The system survived by hiding the Party's culpability (Khrushchev included) for the ruthless suppression of any opposition, the collectivization that resulted in mass starvation in the 1930s, and the incarceration and murder of hundreds of thousands of innocent people during the Great Purges. The last Soviet leader, Mikhail Gorbachev, allowed a policy of *glasnost* (openness) in the late 1980s that finally released Russian historians from 70 years of lies and distortions. Once Gorbachev revealed the falsehoods of Soviet history, the system could not survive. The Chinese Communist leadership today knows that they must control their version of the past lest they meet the same fate as the Soviet Union.

Some historians credit nuclear deterrence for keeping the peace between the United States and the Soviet Union during the **Cold War**. There is no evidence in newly released documents from Soviet and US archives, however, that either side contemplated a first strike except in response to a direct conventional military attack on a friend or ally. Will the deterrent principle prevent nuclear powers India and Pakistan from going to war again? If we believe nuclear weapons prevent war, some countries may try to build their own deterrent nuclear arsenal. Nuclear proliferation could be the result. In the age of weapons of mass destruction, the stakes are obviously too high for the public to tolerate the willful use of inaccurate histories to make and justify policy decisions.

History and International Conflicts

The current state of international affairs cannot be understood without a thorough comprehension of the way history is constructed. Contradictory versions of the past are at the heart of the most intractable international conflicts today. Collective memories are often fostered to serve national political goals. **Nationalist histories** are usually not concerned with individual rights and responsibilities; rather, they tend to champion one nation over another and often elicit demands for retribution to right past injustices. Such histories became important to nations seeking independence from colonial control during the nineteenth and twentieth centuries; see Map 1.1 for an image of when these struggles took place worldwide. This "our group has done no wrong" version of the past is a major obstacle to political compromise.

For example, some Irish Catholics interpret the centuries-old British presence in Ireland as imperial conquest rather than settlement. Many Irish Catholics still blame the British for the loss of their land, the potato famine (Figure 1.3), and the lingering poverty in the Northern Irish Catholic community. Oliver Cromwell, the Union Jack, and the English crown are reminders of British imperialism and frustrated national expression. In contrast, Northern Irish Protestants driving through Belfast might take a nostalgic look at the giant cranes of the defunct dry dock where the *Titanic*, a symbol of the modern economic progress and relative wealth of their community, was built in the early twentieth century. The presence of British political institutions in Northern Ireland is a comforting reminder to them of their close links to the British Empire.

Diametrically opposing versions of history are used to justify Israeli or Arab claims on Palestine. Israelis reference the Hebrew Bible to make the "we were here first" argument. That is ancient history to Arabs, who argue that their presence in Palestine over the last 1,200 years is a more legitimate historical claim. Arab Muslims, Jews, and Christians lived in the area for centuries before European Jewish immigrants began arriving in significant numbers after World War I. Israel has won the three wars against Arab states since partition in 1947, prompting many Israelis to shrug and say that might makes right. Israelis celebrate the birth of the new Israeli state in 1948, while Palestinians term it the *nakba* (catastrophe).

Most Israeli and Palestinian history books give different versions of the Palestinian flight to the West Bank and Gaza Strip in 1947 and 1948. The Israelis certainly terrorized some of the Palestinian community into leaving the UN-designated area of Israel, as Palestinians maintain, but many Arabs left of their own accord. Whether or not Palestinians have a right to return to their homes in Israel hinges on this historical debate, which contributed to the failed peace process of the late 1990s. The tragedy of the Arab–Israeli conflict is that both sides have legitimate historical claims to Palestine (Figure 1.4).

Similarly, Russian President Vladimir Putin justified taking Crimea from Ukraine in 2014 because of Russia's presence there for centuries. Soviet Premier Nikita Khrushchev ceded the region to the Ukrainian Soviet Socialist Republic in 1954, never imagining that the Soviet Union would break up, leaving Crimea in an independent Ukrainian state. China goes back centuries to claim the "historic waters" of the South China Sea, and to the so-called "eleven-dash line" drawn by the nationalist Chinese government in 1947. China's assertion of this maritime border far beyond mainland China ignores similar historical arguments made by Vietnam and the Philippines, and contradicts the UN Convention on the Law of the Sea.

Historians make semantic choices that often reveal bias. Palestinians might refer to their suicide bombers as martyrs on a political, military, and religious mission, while Israelis label them criminals and mass murderers. Nationalist Serbs embrace their militias in Bosnia during

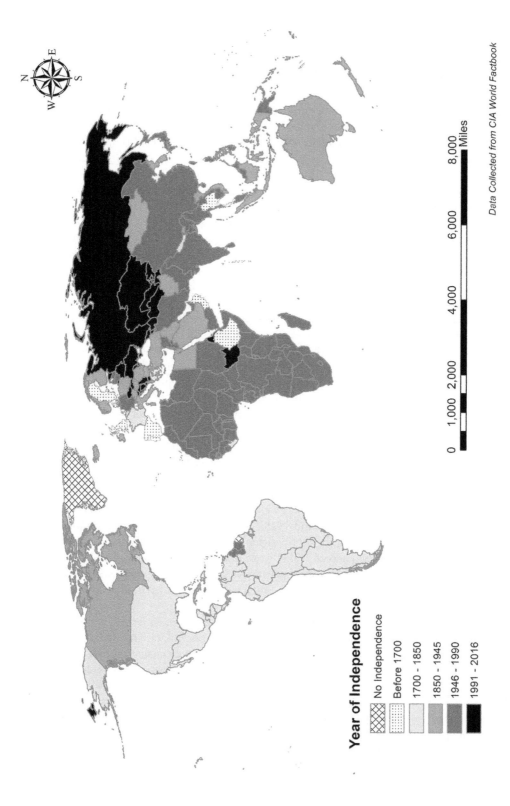

Map 1.1 Year of Independence.

Figure 1.3 Irish woman during the famine begging for help from American ships.

Source: Library of Congress.

the Yugoslav Civil War in the 1990s as heroic defenders of the nation, not rapists or mass murderers. The Nicaraguan Contra rebel group fought the leftist Sandinista government in the 1980s. They were paramilitary remnants of the thuggish deposed dictatorship of Anastasio Somoza, but President Ronald Reagan gave them the moniker "freedom fighters." Some observers claim that the **janjaweed** bands operating against the indigenous populations in the

Figure 1.4 The Temple Mount in Jerusalem is a disputed holy site for both Jews and Muslims.
Source: Library of Congress.

Darfur region of western Sudan are government supported; the government prefers to call them "rogue bandits."

When nationalists are confronted with criticism of their people, they react with denial and verbal attacks on other peoples. They view history as an inexorable struggle of nation against nation and, therefore, criticism of one's own history as treasonous. Serbian nationalists point out that Croatians and Bosnian Muslims committed mutual atrocities during the war. This is true enough, but that does nothing to exonerate Serbian criminals.

India and Pakistan use opposing versions of history to stake their claims to Kashmir. When the British granted independence to India in 1947, the state fell into communal strife between Muslims and Hindus. Two new Islamic states of West and East Pakistan (today Pakistan and Bangladesh, respectively) emerged, leaving hundreds of thousands dead and millions of people displaced. Whether Muslim-majority Kashmir should be part of these Islamic states or part of India depends on the details of the complicated processes by which rajahs turned over their states to these newly formed nations more than 60 years ago. Pakistan and India have fought three wars since then, and low-level fighting over Kashmir continues. Both states have nuclear weapons, making the area one of the most dangerous threats to regional and world peace. Historical dissonance persists over which side was the aggressor and how many people were forced to leave their communities.

Defense of the nation becomes synonymous with defense of the national myth. At the end of the twentieth century, an Indian education minister mandated a revisionist version of Indian history texts to recast former Muslim rulers of India as uncivilized, brutal despots. In 2003, a US author published a much-acclaimed book that some Indians believed maligned the reputation of a seventeenth-century Hindu king. Former Prime Minister Atal Bihari Vajpayee warned foreign authors not to "play with our national pride. We are prepared to take action against the foreign author in case the state government fails to do so" (Dalrymple 2005, 62).

"History is a nightmare from which I am trying to awake," lamented Stephen Dedalus, an Irish character in James Joyce's *Ulysses*. Joyce's Haines, an Englishman, understood the plight of the Irish: "I can quite understand that an Irish man must think like that, I dare say. We feel in England that we have treated you rather unfairly. It seems history is to blame" (Joyce [1922] 1984, 38). It is a sign of a mature democratic society when scholars enjoy the freedom to criticize their own people for crimes against humanity. Germans have conducted a thorough examination of the Holocaust and other atrocities committed in their name by the Third Reich. The South African Truth and Reconciliation Commission has tried to reconstruct the crimes of the South African apartheid regime in an effort to move race relations and democracy forward. Confronted with a mountain of physical evidence of the mass murder of Bosnian Muslims by Serbs in Srebrenica in 1995, the new democratic government in Belgrade has hunted down and prosecuted the perpetrators. In contrast, authoritarian regimes imprison or kill their critics, rather than seek absolution for past crimes committed by the state.

What Is Good History?

If all history is subjective, how can we trust any rendition of the past? The recent worldwide expansion of written and electronic media now puts thousands of different sources at one's fingertips. Much to the chagrin of history teachers, students can cull sources from websites of unknown credibility.

Obviously, some sources are more trustworthy than others. The historical field, like medicine or law, has professional historical associations and professional journals. For example, the American Historical Association publishes the *American Historical Review*, and the Society for Historians of American Foreign Relations publishes *Diplomatic History*. Articles are refereed by other historians. Reputable publishing houses and university presses put prospective books through a similar vetting process.

Some university presses will even operate at a loss to ensure that important new research is published, even if the work is not marketable to a general audience. Histories published by a reputable university press are generally more reliable than private television productions, the popular press, blogs, or other websites of doubtful reliability. Universities and research centers in the free world hire historians on the basis of their professional training and prior publishing record. These institutions afford scholars the opportunity to write without fear of political reprisal or pressure to turn a profit.

Popular histories are less accurate narratives of the past, but they have a great capacity to influence public opinion. If authors must convince an editor of the marketability of their work, they will be tempted to embellish the story. A question often posed regarding historical novels and movies is whether or not they are historically accurate. It is a fair question if one recognizes that the producer will add dramatic effect whether or not it has any connection to the known historical record. Movies such as *Titanic*, *Lincoln*, and *Twelve Years a Slave*, or novels such as *The Da Vinci Code*, attract mass audiences because they combine realism with a captivating, if not entirely accurate, version of past events.

Theories of History

Historians construct theories of the past to explain and understand the human condition. Theories guide the historian's method, approach, and sources. For example, Western historians have tried to explain Europe's rise to global ascendancy in the last five centuries. Some theorize that the key factor was Europe's advantageous geographical and climatic position, or the **balance of power** among European states that spawned intense scientific and technological competition, or Europeans' navigational skills and resistance to disease. Others emphasize Christianity and an interpretation to understand the Bible and subdue the world. Historians use available evidence to test these hypotheses, although theory will often determine the direction of their research.

The historical debate about the origins of humans between evolutionists and those who believe in intelligent design hinges on the testability of these respective approaches. Evolution can be verified or disproven through observation, but intelligent design is a belief that cannot be subjected to the rigors of the historical method. Intelligent design is not provable.

Some people think of history as **providential** (Benjamin 2007). From this perspective, meaning in life derives from the belief that a higher power is operating in the world, if not always in explicable ways. God must have had some reason for unleashing the hurricane that devastated New Orleans in 2005, or the catastrophic flooding in Louisiana, or the earthquake in central Italy in 2016. Some people believe that God has given their nation a special mission to fight evil (often another nation), promote global freedom, or spread their religion and culture. This view, like other determinist theories of history, reduces the importance of individual free will and responsibility. Most professional historians leave the question of divine intervention and the meaning of life to philosophers and theologians, and instead concentrate on the historical events they can observe.

Another way to make sense of the past is a **progressive** view of history. In the early nineteenth century, German philosopher Georg Hegel wrote that as new ideas challenged old traditions, a new synthesis would result to develop better political, economic, and social structures. In other words, through education and rising standards of living, people can rid society of past wrongs such as slavery, war, and inequality, and learn to live in peace and harmony. This is an essential element of Western thought, and it provides the rationale for universal education and liberal democracy. Marxism is also a progressive view of history. The end of history will be a utopian, classless society in which all people will "make according to their ability and take according to their needs."

A more pessimistic **theory of history** is that the past is cyclical. In other words, there are discernible patterns in the past that are likely to repeat themselves. In the history of capitalism, for example, economies have cycles of growth and recession. Some realists argue that any new rising power will challenge the power of the older, and a military clash is likely. Those who adhere to this view of history foresee an inevitable Sino–American conflict over dominance in Asia.

These theories of history bring some **rationality** and meaning to our daily lives. We are most uncomfortable with the randomness of historical events. When we read of a murder in the newspaper, we may be comforted to find out that the perpetrator knew the victim. No one wants to contemplate walking down the street and being killed by a stranger. Random violence has no meaning, and there is no way to avoid it. Terrorists can create a disproportionate fear in people, although we have a greater chance of getting hit by lightning than dying in a terrorist act. Over 3,000 people simply went to work on September 11, 2001, and died in the terrorists' attacks. Highway deaths worldwide vastly dwarf the terrorists' death toll, but people's fears of dying in a car crash are not great enough to create the political will to do much about it.

Casinos have capitalized on people's desires to believe in logic and patterns of the past. Roulette wheels now have a "history board" informing potential players of the numbers and colors that have hit in the last several hours. Suppose, for example, that "red seven" has not come up all day. By what mathematicians call the *law of independent trials*, red seven has no better odds of hitting on the next or any subsequent spin of the wheel than does any other number, including those that have already come up, perhaps even several times. Nonetheless, people passing by the history board impulsively plunk their money down on red seven on the expectation that it is due to come up.

Historians try to identify some patterns in the past to help understand the present, but historians do not agree about which variables caused events. Causation is one of the trickiest problems in writing about the past, and historians' conclusions can have far-reaching effects on future policies. If Germany were mainly responsible for the catastrophe of World War I, then the Germans should have paid with an even harsher treaty than Versailles. If one believes that US containment policy caused the fall of Soviet communism, not Soviet Premier Mikhail Gorbachev's bold new foreign policies, then American leaders might exaggerate US power to influence world politics in any way it wants. The essential question in the war on terror is this: Did US policies cause September 11, or did the terrorists merely hate the United States because it is free? How historians answer these questions has a direct impact on the way we think about the present. The dilemma for policymakers is that historians have many different answers to the same questions.

Historians often elevate their particular focus on the past to create a theory of causation. Environmental historians might emphasize climate, environment, geography, and natural resources to explain human development (Diamond 2003, 2005, 2019). Political historians study power relationships and the influence of leaders' decisions on social systems and people's lives. Marxists believe that economic relationships are the main determinants of human history, while intellectual historians raise the significance of ideas to cause change. International studies not only employs an interdisciplinary approach to global issues but also recognizes that many independent or interdependent forces can influence human behavior and cause historical events.

Are There Lessons of History?

An old history essay question asks students to compare and contrast certain events, implying that there are discernible patterns of history from which to draw lessons. People often express the belief that "history tells us" to make a particular choice, but the relationship among the past, present, and future is a conundrum, a puzzle with many missing pieces. Geographers can help us understand where we stand and where we are going, but history cannot always tell us what will happen along the way or if or when we will get there. Human agents can alter history in unforeseen ways, and events take accidental turns that are dependent on random occurrences.

Policymakers frequently invoke historical analogies to make and justify decisions, in the belief that history teaches particular lessons. Yet historians and philosophers are not so sure. Hegel said that what we learn from history is that we do not learn from history. Aphorisms such as "history repeats itself" or "those who do not remember the past are condemned to repeat it" (Santayana 1905, 284) are based on the notion that history is something we can know and build predictive models from.

Historical analogies provide clarity, rationality, and logic to current affairs, and historians often contribute to the idea that history teaches great lessons by declaring that certain works are "definitive" or "the last word." Obviously, decision making requires comparison to previous policy successes and failures, but historical analogy drawn from unique events can lead policymakers down a dark alley. Erroneous presumptions about what happened in the past constrain an accurate analysis of and creative thinking about the present.

Definitive lessons of history are impossible to derive from different accounts and interpretations of the past. Many scholars have debated the causes of World War I, but what lessons do policymakers draw if there is disagreement about how and why the war started? Economists would make a killing in the stock market if **economic history** allowed them to predict the ups and downs of the stock exchanges.

Policymakers are often blinded by their beliefs about the past that may not have any application for the present. For example, American policymakers during the Cold War consistently used the appeasement of Hitler before World War II to argue against accommodation with the Soviet Union, which they cast as a similarly aggressive, **totalitarian** dictatorship. The United States acted on the erroneous assumption that if Vietnam fell to the Communists, the dominos in Asia would fall like the East European countries had to the Nazis in the late 1930s. The failure in Vietnam created another "lesson of history" that warned against armed intervention into civil conflicts, with devastating consequences in places like Yugoslavia and Rwanda in the 1990s. In the run-up to the United States' war in Iraq in 2003, the George W. Bush administration argued that if the United States could successfully occupy Germany and Japan after World War II, it could surely handle the occupation of Iraq, a much smaller country. That historical analogy turned out to be wrong, as well.

Historical events, unlike scientific experiments, can never be replicated. History often yields analogies for decision makers that are more dangerous than using no history at all. Historian Barbara Tuchman cautioned, "The trouble is that in human behavior and history it is impossible to isolate or repeat a given set of circumstances" (Tuchman 1981, 249).

An example

To study the history of Vietnam, the historian assembles a wide range of material in Vietnamese, English, French, and Chinese. If you do not know Vietnamese or French, you first must study these languages. The Vietnamese word for history is lịch sử. For primary sources, you would contact the Ministry of Foreign Affairs in Hanoi to visit the National Archives. One might seek to establish connections with the Department of History at University of Social Sciences and Humanities, Vietnam National University, Ho Chi Minh City. The National Archives has an archive of colonial records and an archive of Democratic Republic of Vietnam (north) in Ha Noi; the archive of the Republic of Vietnam (south) is in Ho Chi Minh City. The application must be in Vietnamese. Depending on the topic, you will need a letter of introduction from your supervisor / chair / boss as well as a support letter from a Vietnam supervisor (could be a university or research center). You may be able to access some records, but you need to have an idea of the topic, place, and time of these records. If you want the French Colonial records, some are available at the Archives nationales d'outre-mer in Aix-en-Provence, France (www.archivesnationales.culture.gouv.fr/anom/en/Presentation/Empires-coloniaux-francais-10.html). They have the records of the French High Commission in Saigon (1948–1954) as well as residents-superior in Tonkin (north) and Annam (central). They do not have the archives of Cochinchina (south) (1859–1954); those are in Hanoi. If you want to know what happened in the south between 1859 and 1954, you must go to Hanoi. If you are interested in the 1950s–1970s and US involvement in Vietnam, you should contact the National Archives of the US in College Park, Maryland (www.archives.gov/research/vietnam-war).

In the US, we speak of the Vietnam War, while in Vietnam, the war is simply the American War. Historians may call it the Second IndoChina War (the First IndoChina War was between the Vietnamese and the French). Read secondary sources such as Goscha (2016) or Karnow (1983). Watch the Ken Burns PBS documentary *The Vietnam War* (2017). Read the novel *The Sympathizer* by Viet Thanh Nguyen (2015), a Pulitzer Prize winner. The protagonist is a communist spy in the South Vietnamese army. Read *In Retrospect: The Tragedy and Lessons of Vietnam* by Robert McNamara (1995). McNamara was the US Secretary of Defense during the war, perhaps there are some lessons of history. Read articles about Vietnam in *The New York Times* or *The Washington Post* from those years. Tim O'Brien has a fascinating novel about the US in Vietnam. He was a soldier in the US Army. He writes: "But this is true too, stories can save us." (O'Brien 1990, 225). You can talk to my brother-in-law who was in the US Navy, my friend who was in the US Army in Vietnam, or my uncle who was in the US Air Force. When you go to Vietnam, make some friends and talk to them as well. Any of them over 60 may well remember the war, even though they would be but a child. Any under 45 will have no memory of a war, just its aftermath. Formulate your ideas and write to the historians and archives. Go to the archives, bring your pencils, papers, notebook, laptop. Begin your research.

Realize that our perceptions are different. In Ho Chi Minh City, the War Remnants Museum (http://warremnantsmuseum.com/) has exhibits profiling the US–Vietnam conflict. There are helicopters and armaments, photos and memories, artifacts and history. In Washington DC, there is the Vietnam Veterans Memorial (www.nps.gov/vive/index.htm) which includes a wall listing the names of 58,318 American service personnel who died in the conflict, the "Three Servicemen Statue" reflecting three men who served and the "Vietnam Women's Memorial" reflecting the women who served mostly as medical personnel. The wall is chronological from 1955 to 1975, showing the few who died at the beginning and then becoming larger through the war. Compare two different views of the conflict in two different memorials (Figures 1.5 and 1.6).

Figure 1.5 War Remnants Museum, Ho Chi Minh City.

Source: S. Toops.

Figure 1.6 Vietnam Veterans Memorial, Washington, DC.

Source: S. Toops.

Conclusion

Although past histories cannot provide blueprints for the future, a thorough grounding in contemporary world history is essential for understanding current global issues, and honest and accurate histories are indispensable for human progress and reconciliation of international conflicts. The issues confronting future generations are simply too important to ignore past history.

Many international conflicts today cannot be resolved without agreement about what happened in the past, from Japan acknowledging its aggression in the Far East in the 1930s to Israel admitting that many Palestinians were forced from their homes when the state of Israel was created after World War II. Professional historians are charged with writing histories that are as true to the facts as possible, and to act as critics of those who warp the story of the past for political or economic gain.

A thorough reading of history is an essential part of a comprehensive understanding of the world today. All of the other social sciences of international studies are based on an accurate picture of the past. Political scientists use case studies to develop theories of political behavior. Likewise, economists examine previous trends to analyze the present and hypothesize about the best economic policies. Anthropologists are essentially observers of people and their social behaviors. Finally, geographers depend on accurate measurements of spaces and environments to explain current affairs. "But remember from here on in, history has its eyes on you" (Miranda 2016).

References

Archives nationales d'outre-mer. 2020. www.archivesnationales.culture.gouv.fr/anom/en/Presentation/Empires-coloniaux-francais-10.html (Accessed July 1, 2020).

Arnold, John. 2000. *History: A Very Short Introduction*. New York: Oxford University Press.

Benjamin, Jules. 2007. *A Student's Guide to History*. 10th ed. New York: St. Martin's Press.

Burns, Ken and Lynn Novick. 2017. *The Vietnam War* (PBS) www.pbs.org/kenburns/the-vietnam-war/

Bryson, Bill. 2003. *A Short History of Nearly Everything*. New York: Broadway Books.

Dalrymple, William. 2005. "India: The War over History." *New York Review of Books*, April 7.

Diamond, Jared. 2003. *Guns, Germs, and Steel*. New York: Spark Publishers.

———. 2005. *Collapse: How Societies Choose to Fail or Succeed*. New York: Viking Press.

———. 2019. *Upheaval: Turning Points for Nations in Crisis*. New York: Little, Brown and Company.

Fujitani, James. 2016. "The Ming Rejection of the Portuguese Embassy of 1517." *Journal of World History* 27 (1) 87–102.

Goscha, Christopher. 2016. *Vietnam: A New History*. New York: Basic Books.

Herodotus (Tom Holland trans.). 2015. *The Histories*. New York: Viking.

Joyce, James. [1922] 1984. *Ulysses*. New York: Garland Publishing.

Karnow, Stanley. 1983. *Vietnam: A History*. New York: Viking.

Levesque, Stephane. 2008. *Thinking Historically: Educating Students for the Twenty-first Century*. Toronto: University of Toronto Press.

Martin, Thomas, Herodotus, and Sima Qian. 2010. *Herodotus and Sima Qian: The First Great Historians of Greece and China*. Boston: Bedford /St. Martins.

McNamara, Robert. 1995. *In Retrospect: The Tragedy and Lessons of Vietnam*. New York: Times Books.

Miranda, Lin-Manuel. 2016. *Hamilton: An American Musical* (vocal score). Los Angeles: Warner.

National Archives. 2020. www.archives.gov/research/vietnam-war (accessed July 1, 2020).

Nguyen, Viet Thanh. 2015. *The Sympathizer*. New York: Grove Press.

O'Brien, Tim. [1990] 2009. *The Things They Carried*. Boston: Houghton Mifflin Harcourt.

Oxford English Dictionary. 2020. www.oed.com.

Presnell, Jenny. 2019. *The Information-Literate Historian*. 3rd ed. New York: Oxford University Press.

Public Broadcasting Service. 2020. *Wonders of the African World*. www.pbs.org/wonders/ (accessed July 1, 2020).

Santayana, George. 1905. *The Life of Reason. Volume I. Reason in Common Sense*. New York: Scribner.

Sima, Qian (B. Watson trans.). 1993. *Records of the Grand Historian*. New York: Columbia University Press.

Tuchman, Barbara W. 1981. *Practicing History: Selected Essays*. New York: Knopf.

Welles, Orson and Herman Mankiewicz. 1941. *Citizen Kane* (video). Warner Brothers.

Westfall, Richard S. 1993. *The Life of Isaac Newton*. New York: Cambridge University Press.

Further Reading

Books

Anderson, Sheldon. 2008. *Condemned to Repeat It: "Lessons of History" and the Making of U.S. Cold War Containment Policy*. Lanham, MD: Lexington Books.

Burke Peter, ed. 2001. *New Perspectives on Historical Writing*. 2nd ed. University Park, PA: Pennsylvania State University Press.

Carr, Edward H. 1961. *What Is History?* New York: Vintage Books.

Collingwood, R. G. 1946. *The Idea of History*. Oxford: Oxford University Press.

Gardiner, Juliet. 1988. *What Is History?* London: Humanities Press International.

Green, Anna, and Kathleen Troup, eds. 2016. *Houses of History: A Critical Reader of Twentieth-Century History and Theory*. 2nd ed. Manchester, UK: Manchester University Press.

Hoffer, Charles, and William W. Stueck. 1994. *Reading and Writing American History: An Introduction to the Historian's Craft*. Lexington, MA: D. C. Heath.

Howard, Michael. 1991. *The Lessons of History*. New Haven, CT: Yale University Press.

Jordanova, Ludmilla. 2019. *History in Practice*. 3rd ed. New York: Bloomsbury Academic.

Storey, William Kelleher. 2020. *Writing History: A Guide for Students*. 6th ed. Oxford: Oxford University Press.
Winks, Robin W., ed. 1969. *The Historian as Detective: Essays on Evidence*. [1st ed.]. New York: Harper & Row.

Journals

American Historical Review. www.historians.org/publications-and-directories/american-historical-review
Cold War History. www.tandfonline.com/loi/fcwh20
Diplomacy and Statecraft. www.tandfonline.com/loi/fdps20
Diplomatic History. academic.oup.com/dh
Journal of Contemporary History. journals.sagepub.com/home/jch
Journal of World History. www.uhpress.hawaii.edu/t-journal-of-world-history.aspx

Films

Citizen Kane (1941). Orson Welles, director.
Judgment at Nuremberg (1961). Stanley Kramer, director.
Rashomon (1950). Akira Kurosawa, director.
The Thin Blue Line (1988). Erroll Morris, director.
Triumph of the Will (1934). Leni Riefenstahl, director.

Websites

American Historical Association. www.historians.org/teaching/links
International Interdisciplinary Organization of Scholars. networks.h-net.org/
Society for Historians of American Foreign Relations. www.shafr.org
World History Association. www.thewha.org
WWW Virtual Library: International Affairs. www2.etown.edu/vl/

Chapter 2

Peoples, Places, and Patterns
Geography in International Studies

What Is Geography?

At the 2012 National Geographic GeoBee, President Obama said, "The study of geography is about more than just memorizing places on a map. It's about understanding the complexity of our world, appreciating the diversity of cultures that exists across continents." **Geography** is a core discipline of international studies about where and why. The roots of the word *geography* (γεωγραφία) are Greek. *Geo* means "earth," while *graphy* refers to "writing." Hence geography is writing about or a description of the earth. In another culture with roots in antiquity, the Chinese, the word for geography is *dili* (地理). *Di* refers to "earth," while *li* refers to "pattern or arrangement." So, in Chinese, *dili* means the patterns on or of the earth. Geography, then, is a detailed description of both the earth and its identifiable patterns. To understand those patterns requires thorough analysis and deep understanding rather than superficial description.

"Geography is the study of where natural environments and human activities are found on Earth's surface and the reasons for their location" (Rubenstein et al. 2013, 2). From this definition, we see that geography is a study of the activities of people as well as a study of the earth itself. The disciplines of history and anthropology study people too, but what distinguishes geography from these other disciplines is that geography considers the arrangement of these activities across the earth. Where and why do activities occur? At its core, geography answers the question of where: Geographic inquiry analyzes the arrangement of people and their activities across the earth and searches for explanations of those patterns.

Geography has two main areas of study: physical and human. Physical geography examines the natural environment, focusing on topics such as soil, climates, plants, and animals. Subfields of physical geography include climatology, geomorphology, and resource geography. Human geography studies the activities of people, focusing on topics such as industries, cities, cultures, and transportation. Subfields of human geography include political geography, economic geography, and cultural geography. For international studies, our considerations of states, cultures, resources, and economies require an understanding of geography.

Development of Geography

Geography is an ancient field of study. The classical Greeks, as well as the classical Chinese, studied the geography of their respective known worlds. The Greek Eratosthenes (c. 275–195 BCE), who directed the library at Alexandria, Egypt, wrote a book entitled *Geography*. Greek theory posited that the lands to the south would be hotter than the temperate climes of Greece and thus uninhabitable. The oldest example of Chinese geographical work is the *Tribute of Yü*, written down around 500 BCE. This tale surveys the Chinese empire, dividing the empire into nine provinces and annotating the peoples and resources. After the fall of the Roman Empire in

DOI: 10.4324/9781003028314-4

476 CE, geography as a discipline did not develop in Europe. Much knowledge was actually lost in the West but preserved by the Arabs. Under the patronage of the Caliph in the eighth century, the Greek and Roman geographies were translated into Arabic. During the Renaissance, Europeans relearned the geography of the Greeks through encounters with the Muslims. The age of discovery in the 1600s spurred a new awakening of European geographic thought (Short 2020; Martin 2005). Although the parallels of latitude were well known in navigation, the lines of longitude could not be adequately measured. The invention of the marine chronometer in 1759 by John Harrison allowed for accurate east–west measurements (Sobel 1995).

Modern geography as a science developed through the twentieth century. By the 1990s, geography educators (college and secondary) in the United States conceptualized the discipline as embodying a number of concepts. Space, region, and environment are key components to understanding geography in international studies (GESP 2012), as discussed in the next section.

For international studies, the utility of understanding geography can be illustrated through examples. For example, we can examine the structure of population patterns around the world. We can analyze global population trends in terms of their effects on the earth's environment. Although China has a much larger population than the United States, its ecological impact is similar. We can examine Chinese culture and its responses to globalization. Modern scientific geography is based on scientific reasoning, linking human and physical geography (GESP 2012).

Components of Geography

The history of geography points to three main components of a geographical way of thinking: (1) space, (2) region, and (3) environment. **Space** includes the locations of people. **Regions** are mental constructs with which people identify. **Environment** consists of human interaction with our natural surroundings. Geography's role in international studies is to answer the questions of spatial location, regional identity, and issues of human–environment relations (Johnston 2010). Let's examine the concepts of space, region, and environment more thoroughly.

Space

The study of space in geographic analysis is composed of location, spatial interaction, and spatial organization. **Location** is the essential element; it answers the question, where? Locations can be nominal, relative, and absolute. A *nominal location* is a name attached to a place, such as Oxford, Ohio. A *relative location* reveals a direction relative to other locations: north or south, east or west. For example, Ohio is west of New York and east of California; or Ohio is in the Midwestern United States. Finally, an *absolute location* expresses mathematical precision, such as latitude and longitude, which is an intersection of mathematical coordinates (Rubenstein 2020). Chicago, Illinois, is at 41° 52' N Lat, 87° 37' W Long. The designation of east (E) or west (W) longitude is essential, because 41° 52' N Lat, 87° 37' E Long would put one near Bosten Lake in northwestern China. Likewise, the designation of north (N) or south (S) latitude indicates regions north or south of the equator, respectively.

Spatial interaction involves analyzing flows, interdependence, and underlying structures. Why and how do people, resources, and ideas move? As an example, the geography of energy in an international context is the geography of localized resources of pipelines, straits, and great distances between producing and consuming areas. Oil reserves are increasingly inaccessible. The spatial pattern and arrangement of oil has impacts on cultures, economies, politics, and histories, not just geography (Rubenstein et al. 2013). For example, the oil in Kazakhstan in

Central Asia is located on the Caspian Sea. That oil is an important resource for Kazakhstan. To reach the global market, the route to a seaport could pass south to Iran, east to China, north to Russia, or west to Azerbaijan and Georgia. Given the current political climate, which of these routes is better for the United States? What do you think?

The study of **spatial organization** reveals how people have delineated various territories. International boundaries are one form of spatial organization. In the Pacific Ocean, small islands take on territorial significance as claims extend 200 miles out from shore. International boundaries and national jurisdiction entail an organization of space. Businesses focus on certain market areas. For example, how and why do US businesses try to get into the Asian market and vice versa (de Blij 2012)?

Hong Kong (Figure 2.1) is a good example of spatial organization and spatial interaction. Hong Kong means "fragrant harbor" in Chinese. Hong Kong was a British colony until 1997 and is now a Special Administrative Region of the People's Republic of China. Hong Kong is a major center for Asian trade. Spatial interaction is a key reason for the existence and success of Hong Kong. Current geopolitical difficulties may mean a different situation for Hong Kong in the future, yet the actual location is the same.

For international studies, space is of critical concern. Where are the political hot spots in the world? Where are the oil reserves located? Where is the focus of international trade or migration? Of course, knowing where these phenomena are located is a first step; the next is to examine the ramifications of these locations.

Figure 2.1 Hong Kong. The harbor is the reason for Hong Kong.

Source: S. Toops.

Region

A region is a concept people use to differentiate one area from another. Geographers identify two types of regions: formal and functional. Formal regions include language communities, agricultural fields, the Bible Belt, the Midwest, the South, Europe and Asia, the Middle East, and zip code and area code regions. Functional regions include hunting territories, realms of empire, grazing areas, zones of trading activities, newspaper readership regions, river basins (watersheds), commuting corridors, and airspaces (Price et al. 2020).

How do geographers classify these regions? A **formal region**, also known as a **uniform region**, is an area in which selected physical or human characteristics are present throughout the region. Its identity could be a certain climate, specific landforms, or a shared language or religion. A region's characteristics can also be technically defined: per capita income, literacy rate, televisions per capita, or hospital beds per capita. Regions can reflect organizational areas such as congressional districts, prefectures, provinces, or special economic zones. They can have everyday usage such as the South, the Midwest, or the Middle East. And usage of regional terms tells as much about the observer as the region. For example, much discussion about Iraq assumes similarity throughout the country. A regional analysis, however, points to a northern area with a mostly Sunni Kurd population, a southern area with a mostly Shia Arab population, and a central area with a mostly Sunni Arab population. Understanding the regional cultural geography of Iraq is a first step to understanding the character of the country (Sutton 2017).

A **functional region** is an area in which an activity has a network, a focal point, or a node. A river system or a trading system has a network of activity that inscribes a region. The issue here is one of dynamism through connections or linkages. Commuter areas and newspaper readership areas are examples of functional regions. The bounds of these regions change daily with new connections established between the focal center and the consumers or market. The range of a television signal, a radio broadcast, a political idea, or the extent of governmental control all determine a functional region (Rubenstein 2020).

For international studies, we consider broad world regions such as North America, Europe, East Asia, South Asia, Africa, the Middle East, and Latin America (as in this book). Each of these has a territory but the boundaries may well overlap. Each is a formal region in the sense that there are established characteristics such as language, culture, history, and economy that help to define each world region. At the same time, there are functional networks active in each region. The nodes of the regions are leading global cities. In East Asia, global cities are Beijing, Shanghai, Singapore, and Tokyo; in South Asia, Mumbai and Delhi; in the Middle East, Dubai and Jerusalem; in Latin America, Mexico City and São Paulo; in North America, New York City and Los Angeles; in Africa, Johannesburg and Cairo; in Europe, London, Paris, Zürich, and Moscow (Short 2020).

Within these world regions, however, there are strong regional differences. In Africa, many different cultural, economic, and political identities hold sway. In South Africa, for example, Zulu, Xhosa, Khoi-San, Sotho, and Afrikaner provide a diverse cultural mosaic. Asia, because of its size, is very differentiated. We can identify strong cultural distinctions among Uzbekistan, China, India, and Indonesia as countries respectively from Central Asia, East Asia, South Asia, and Southeast Asia. European identity also varies but it is coalescing somewhat due to the European Union. The Middle East may be mostly Arab, but Jewish, Turkish, and Persian peoples are quite significant to the area politically, economically, and culturally. In contrast, North America and Latin America have less variation. The English language dominates in North America, and most people speak Spanish or Portuguese (but not Latin) in Latin America.

Zürich, Switzerland (Figure 2.2) is a good example of region and place. Two million people live in the metropolitan area; of that, 400,000 are in the central city. In terms of economic geography, the city is a global center for finance because of the Swiss banking policy and low

Figure 2.2 Zürich. The largest city and financial center of Switzerland. Major churches, such as Grossmünster on the right and Fraumünster on the left, show Zürich's wealth of history and culture.

Source: S. Toops.

corporate tax rates. Interestingly, this financial center was the home of Lenin in exile, where he wrote *Imperialism: The Highest Stage of Capitalism* in 1916. Zürich is a hub for Swiss railway, road, and air traffic. In terms of political geography, Bern, not Zürich, is the capital of Switzerland. By the 1300s, Zürich joined other cantons to form a Swiss confederacy. Switzerland has maintained its neutrality since the early 1800s. In terms of cultural geography, the locals here speak German at home, though most Swiss are multilingual, speaking French, Italian, and English also. Zürich was a focus for the Protestant Reformation in the 1500s, yet many people here are Catholic. Grossmünster Church was a major center for the Protestant Reformation and Fraumünster Church has stained glass windows by Marc Chagall. Theaters, museums, and churches provide the base of the cultural life of the city. In terms of physical geography, the city grew up on the banks of the Limmat River where it flows into Lake Zürich. Mountains and hills covered with forests enclose the city. In sum, Zürich is a cultural and economic center for Switzerland and a financial center for the world.

The borders between these regions are more aptly called transition zones. The zone between North and Latin America is blurred in California, New Mexico, and Texas. As Turkey endeavors to enter the European Union, the distinction between Europe and the Middle East fades. Egypt and Sudan have strong roots in the Middle East and Africa. South Sudan has broken off from Sudan and established a new state. Pakistan and Indonesia are Asian but have cultural identities resonant with the Middle East. Russia straddles the divide between Asia and Europe (Short 2020).

Istanbul (Figure 2.3) lies at an intersection of regions. This largest city of Turkey is where Asia and Europe meet. The Bosporus, a strait connecting the Black Sea to the Mediterranean Sea, divides the city. Much of the city's population lives on the European side, home to the Byzantine sites of the Hippodrome (300 CE) and Hagia Sophia (532 CE), and the Ottoman sites of Topkapi Palace (1453 CE) and the Sultan Ahmet Mosque (1606 CE). On the Asian side of the Bosporus are rail links to Ankara and the rest of the country. Today we may think of Turkey

Figure 2.3 Istanbul. Asia is in the background, Europe is in the foreground, and in between is the Bosporus, the historical divide between Europe and Asia.

Source: S. Toops.

as part of the Middle East, but the cultural heritage of the Turks is in Central Asia. Region is indeed a mental construct.

Environment

International studies involves an understanding of the environment. Humans modify and react to the natural environment. Global environmental processes produce climates, soils, biotic communities (biomes), minerals, and landforms. The physical geographer studies the processes of the natural environment, while the human geographer is concerned more with the human interaction than with these physical processes.

Some countries have more resources than others, some have larger populations, and some have milder climates. All of these attributes of a country relate to the physical environmental processes at work there. A common observation is that people tend to congregate in flatter areas with access to freshwater, in climates not too hot or too cold, but with access to resources, such as plants, animals, or minerals. An analysis of population distribution around the earth would entail an understanding of climate, soils, biomes, minerals, and landforms. Simple spatial questions such as where is it flat and well-watered usually indicate the locations of denser populations. Major concentrations of population are in (1) South Asia with India, Pakistan, and Bangladesh (1.97 billion); (2) East Asia with China, South Korea, and Japan (1.64 billion); (3) Sub-Saharan Africa with Nigeria and Ethiopia (1.09 billion); and (4) Europe with the

United Kingdom, Germany, France, and Russia (747 million). Population is concentrated on the Yellow and Yangtze Rivers of China, the Ganges River of India, and the Rhine of Europe, but also along the coasts of Japan, Bangladesh, and the United Kingdom. Location (space) is a part of the geographic attribute of a country, but so is the environment (Rubenstein et al. 2013).

People and their environment are mutually interactive, each influencing the other. This contemporary view has replaced traditional conceptions going back to the ancient Greeks that the environment exerts a controlling influence over people: for example, people in cold climates can only act in a certain fashion while people in warm climates act in another fashion. This concept of **environmental determinism** is rejected by contemporary geography because of the inaccuracies of using the environment to predict how a group of people will behave. Plains in temperate climates with grasslands exist in Russia, Mongolia, and the United States. And yet the human geographies of cultures, economies, and polities of the plains of Russia, Mongolia, and the United States have all developed quite differently. Environmental determinist views still crop up. Robert Kaplan's *The Revenge of Geography* (2012) examines global politics from a relatively conservative view of the world, that somehow geography ordains European dominance in world politics. People have agency, however, and are not bound by what the land offers.

Another modern view is that people can control their environment. We can make dams, move the earth, control the waves, farm crops, raise animals, build factories, and construct cities, all without regard to environmental concerns. This, however, is **human determinism**. This belief in human determinism has led us to build great dams in the former Soviet Union, China, and the United States to tame mighty rivers. The damming of the Amu Darya (River) in Uzbekistan has led to the desiccation of the Aral Sea. The damming of the Colorado River in the United States does provide Los Angeles with water and Las Vegas with electricity, but the Colorado River no longer reaches the ocean. The Three Gorges Dam on China's Yangtze River, the biggest dam in the world, has caused problems such as a reservoir plagued by garbage, sewage, and algae. Huge floods in 2020 were not held back by this huge dam, perhaps a series of smaller dams would be more useful. In 2020 the big rains downstream of this dam inundated much of the central Yangtze valley (Gan 2020). The huge weight of the water in the reservoir has also increased the risk of earthquakes and landslides. More power has been generated, but at what cost? Another view beginning in the nineteenth century is that of **environmental possibilism**. While there are some physical limits to human actions, people have various options to adapt to the physical environment. We can choose many possibilities. The physical environment does not determine what we can do but it can limit what we can achieve. Norwegians can grow bananas in a hothouse, but it is easier and cheaper for Norwegians to buy bananas from Africa. We can modify the environment using our technology, but we need to do so sensitively. Otherwise, there will not be a habitable earth for future generations (Rubenstein 2020).

A good example of human–environmental interaction is the Hunza Valley in northern Pakistan (Figure 2.4). Glaciers lie high above the valley. The water used for irrigation comes down from the glaciers. Local residents, Hunzakuts, cut channels into the rugged mountains to bring the water to the fields. This is much more efficient than bringing water up from the river. This irrigation system has been vital to the continued productivity of the valley.

Resources are key components in the environment. When humanity became aware of itself and its needs, people became capable of identifying resources. The term **resource** refers primarily to the functions that an object or substance may perform. A rock was simply an inanimate object until someone came along and used the rock to dig for roots or to hunt. Out of the material world, human needs and ingenuity have fashioned resources. Without human evaluation and appraisal, a rock remains a rock. Culture and technology play a major role in the determination of what a resource is. We use coal for heating but also as a basis for petrochemicals, dyes, and fibers. Yet coal was just another rock until the Industrial Revolution.

Figure 2.4 Hunza, Pakistan. The Hunza Valley is irrigated from the glaciers in the surrounding mountains.
Source: S. Toops.

Resources are either nonrenewable or renewable. **Nonrenewable resources** are materials or energy that have finite amounts. Their continued use leads to exhaustion. Some nonrenewable resources are recyclable in that these materials (primary minerals) can be removed from the waste heaps humanity has created and used again. Your local recycling center makes use of aluminum, plastic, and paper. Other nonrenewable resources such as fossil fuels are not recyclable. They can be used only once; they are destroyed by their use (Rubenstein et al. 2013).

Renewable resources are consumed, but they can be restored; there are two types: continuous flow and short-term renewable. *Continuous-flow resources* approach inexhaustibility because they are direct products of the actions of the sun, the earth, or the moon. Tidal power, solar power, hydropower, and geothermal power are all examples of continuous flow resources. The flow of rivers can power turbines to generate electricity. *Short-term renewable resources* are sustainable in that they can be continued with careful management. These include the usage of timber, soil, crops, or water. Water can be reused in heating and cooling processes (Price et al. 2020).

In international studies, we seek to understand the physical inventory of the earth and how we use its natural resources. Geography helps us to understand the human use of the earth and its resources. Our future depends upon the wise use of these resources.

To summarize, the basic components of geography—space, region, and environment—figure prominently in the essential geographic questions today. A key issue for geography is how we delineate space. A map of the world showing states (political territories) evokes a different perception than a map of the world showing rivers. As a matter of practical research, when we study pollution problems on rivers, do we frame our analysis in terms of states or watersheds? Geographers study how places and regions differ from one another. How can policies be implemented in a world fragmented socially and environmentally? Being able to explain the nature of this variability is a key challenge for geography. How has the earth been transformed by human action? Humans have altered the earth, its air, and its water on scales ranging from the global to the local. Globally, our industries inject carbon dioxide into the atmosphere in massive amounts. Locally, we create new urban environments in which we live, work, and play. Local pollution translates into global climate change. Space, region, and environment all provide concepts for the big questions in geography (Cutter et al. 2002).

Here is an example of a geography (Figure 2.5). I (Stanley Toops) grew up on a farm in Iowa with about 160 acres of a corn, soybean, wheat, cattle, and hog operation. The location of the farm is in southeast Iowa about 2 miles from Missouri and 55 miles from Illinois, part of the Mississippi River watershed. Rainfall is about 40 inches per year; the soil is good black loam, rich in humus. Native vegetation is tall-grass prairie. A nuclear family of parents and five children worked the land using tractors and combines. Brands of the farm machinery included John Deere, Allis-Chalmers, International, and Belarus. The Belarus tractor was made in the Soviet Union. Much of the corn and soybeans were fed to cattle and hogs. The livestock were sold at auction and then turned into steaks and chops. The corn, soybeans, and wheat were sold to the grain elevator operator and then trucked to the Mississippi, where the grain was put on a barge for further shipment domestically or overseas. Some of the corn, wheat, and soybeans were exported to the Soviet Union and China.

There is a spatial and environmental geography to this Midwestern region. The scenery is replicated throughout the Midwest. Even on a farm in Iowa, the international connections linked that plot of land to China and the Soviet Union through the trade of corn, wheat, and tractors. The author grew up here; so, this location is home—a place filled with memories and meaning, beyond a node in the food chain. This particular family farm is no more. The land was

Figure 2.5 Farm in Iowa. A piece of land, a farm, a home, a place, a geography.

Source: S. Toops.

sold to a neighbor who had a cash grain operation of over 1,000 acres. Yet the scene remains in memory for a time.

Maps: Tools for International Studies

Like numbers, writing, speeches, music, or pictures, maps are a form of communication that expresses ideas about the world. The map is a specialized picture of mathematical precision, a multifaceted tool that provides a concrete understanding of the relationships that locations have with other locations. Knowledge of a map's versatility can help one gain a thorough understanding of our world. Ken Jennings, the record-breaking *Jeopardy* game-show champion, traces a history (and geography) of maps from ancient times to the twenty-first-century digital formats of GIS and GPS in *Maphead* (Jennings 2011). Maps are fascinating tools for international studies.

Map Fundamentals

Maps convey spatial relationships. To use maps effectively requires some knowledge about the fundamentals of their preparation.

Scale. Scale is the relationship between the length of an object on a map to the length of that object in the real world. Most maps of the entire world can only show a portion of the myriad detail. Such maps of the world are small scale, perhaps 1:4,000,000 (which is a very small number). At this ratio, one inch on the map represents a distance of 4,000,000 inches, which adds up to more than 63 miles in the real world. A map of a city can show more detail because it covers less area. Such a map may have a scale of 1:25,000. This is a large-scale map. In this case, one inch on the map represents 25,000 inches, or about 0.4 miles, in the real world (de Blij 2012).

Centering and orientation. Maps can be centered on any point on the earth. Maps produced in the eighteenth century were centered on Paris or London. The prime meridian, at 0° longitude, runs through Greenwich in London. Many maps of the world produced in the United States may have the American continents at the center. Maps centered on the Pacific or on the Atlantic convey a different view of the world. Maps 2.1 and 2.2 are centered on Europe and Africa rather than the Pacific (Sutton 2017).

Projection. All maps involve some distortion of the earth's surface. The world is a three-dimensional object. To flatten the spherical globe to a plane means some characteristic—distance, direction, shape, or area—is sacrificed. Distortion is always present in world maps and other small-scale maps; in some cases, the distortion is quite severe. Some **projections** have elongated shapes or distorted areas. Many atlases and cartographic products will use equal-area projections; in this way, the distribution of items across the earth is kept accurate even though shapes may be altered. The practicalities are such that a flat map is more easily used, yet keep in mind that the world is a sphere (Sutton 2017).

Here are two types of map projections. The *Mercator projection* (Map 2.1), developed in 1569, preserves shape and orientation, and the lines of latitude and longitude are at right angles. The Mercator projection was developed for navigation and is excellent for that purpose. However, as can be seen on the Mercator projection, the sizes of land masses in high-latitude areas are severely distorted. Greenland looks similar in size to South America. In reality, South America is 8.6 times the size of Greenland. Thus, the Mercator should not be used to show distribution of space. In contrast, consider the *Robinson projection* (Map 2.2). This projection is oval, thus achieving a more global (rounder) esthetic. The Robinson projection preserves many spatial relationships, particularly in the middle to low latitudes. South

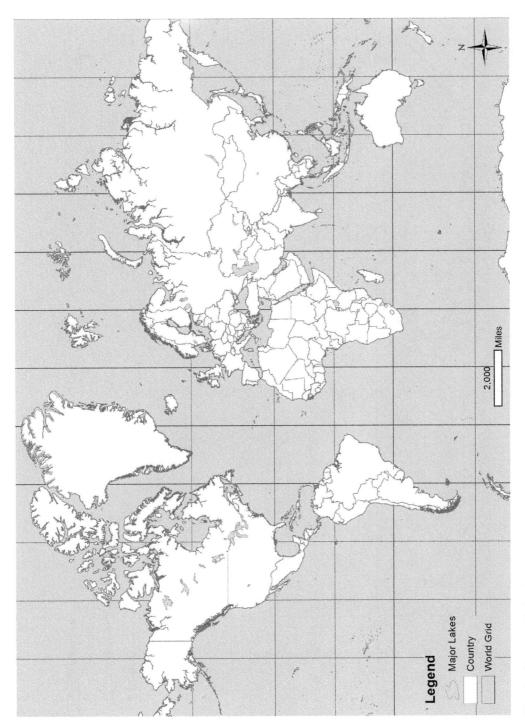

Map 2.1 Mercator Projection.

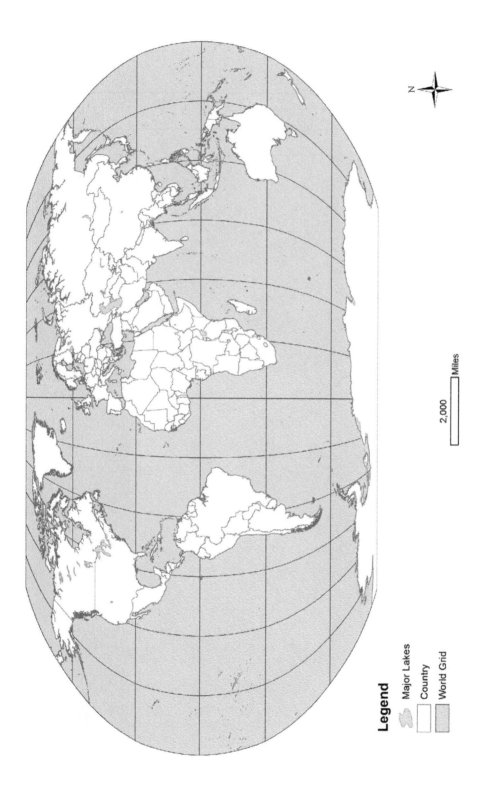

Map 2.2 Robinson Projection.

Legend

Major Lakes

Country

World Grid

2,000 ⊓ Miles

America is indeed much larger than Greenland when viewed on the Robinson projection. Overall, the Robinson, while not specifically accurate, represents the spatial distributions more clearly (Rubenstein et al. 2013).

A specialized type of geographic product is a **geographic information system**, or GIS. The scale and projection are matched completely and digitally so that layers of information, such as physical or human attributes, are known for each and every location. With remotely-sensed imagery from satellites and computer facilities, a large amount of detail is available on a GIS. Much analysis in geography today utilizes GIS and remote sensing (Gewin 2004). Satellite technology gives us an excellent method to view complex information about our earth. Environmental issues such as the impacts of floods in Bangladesh or deforestation in the Amazon can all be analyzed using remote sensing and GIS (Sheehan 2000).

Map 2.3 is an example of a *thematic map*. The theme of this map is the population growth rate of various countries in 2016. This thematic map is an example of a *choropleth* map: *choro* means "area" and *pleth* means "multitude" in Greek. In a choropleth map, areas are shaded in proportion to a statistical variable. In this particular example, countries of high, medium, low, or negative population growth are assigned a different shade. A spatial analysis would indicate that the areas of high growth—over 2.1 percent—are clustered together, mostly in sub-Saharan Africa. Countries with lower rates of growth are mostly in Europe. We can see regional or spatial patterns of population growth around the world with this map. From a policy perspective, if we are considering family planning programs, we can use this map to highlight the locations of higher-growth countries for analysis. Similarly, we can identify the countries that have negative growth and then examine the demographic situation in these countries. The interdisciplinary approach of international studies uses geography and maps to analyze population issues.

Lying with Maps

A picture may be worth a thousand words, but maps can be used to misinform and as propaganda. The propagandist uses maps to manipulate political opinion (Monmonier 2014). Maps are used as icons to stake out a national territory. India, Pakistan, and China all claim Kashmir. Maps in each of those countries show Kashmir to be the rightful territory of that country. In global atlases such as *Goode's World Atlas* these territories are marked to show the different claims (Sutton 2017).

Another issue open to manipulation and misinformation is projection. The Mercator projection, which shows direction accurately and thus is very useful for navigation, distorts the true size of the polar areas, making the upper-latitude areas appear very large. Propagandists such as the right-wing John Birch Society used Mercator projections to alert the West to the significance of the Communist threat posed by the Soviet Union.

Map design is another useful tool for the propagandist. The Nazis designed their propaganda maps to show Germany surrounded by enemies (the United Kingdom, France, and the Soviet Union). In one example, the outline of Germany is compared with that of the British Empire, with territories including Canada and India. With a map showing the British Empire covering over a quarter of the world's land area, Nazi Germany tried to make the case that the British Empire was the greater imperial threat. Map colors can be used to stir emotions and manipulate opinions: yellow might show warning, red might show danger, or green or blue might be used for a friendly country. Red for Russia, yellow for China, and green for the United States and Europe portrayed the Western view of the Cold War. From outer space, of course, the earth is mostly blue ocean (Monmonier 2014).

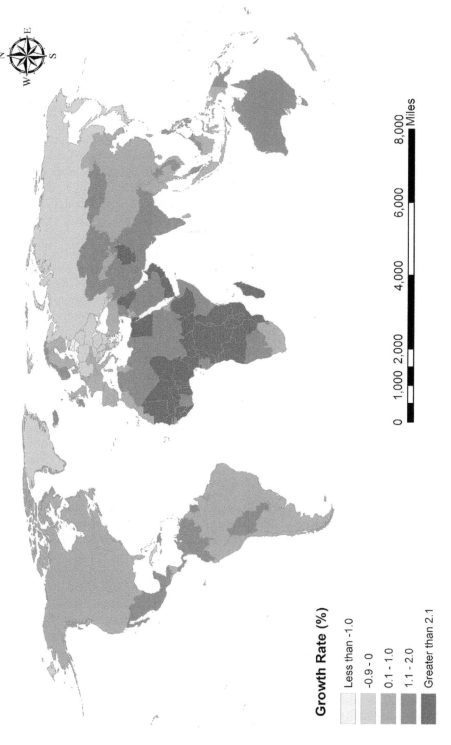

Data collected from CIA World Factbook

Growth Rate (%)

Less than -1.0

-0.9 - 0

0.1 - 1.0

1.1 - 2.0

Greater than 2.1

Map 2.3 Population Growth Rate 2016.

The colors on a map can describe more than political views. In *Tom Sawyer Abroad*, Tom and Huck Finn set out in a hot air balloon from Missouri to Europe. Huck Finn remarks that they must still be in Illinois and not yet in Indiana. Tom asks why. Because Indiana is pink and Illinois is green.

HUCK: What's a map for? Ain't it to learn you facts?
TOM: Of course.
HUCK: Well, then, how's it going to do that, if it tells lies? That's what I want to know.

A more useful knowledge of maps may aid both Huck and Tom in their excursion abroad (Twain 1894).

Conclusion

Space, region, and environment are used often in international studies. Courses in human geography—such as political geography or economic geography, which emphasize the spatial element—are important for international studies. Another group of courses is the geography of certain world regions, such as the geography of Europe, Latin America, and Asia. A third set of courses concerns the environment and physical elements such as natural resources, ecology, and climatology. There are also courses on geographic methodologies, maps, geographic information systems (GIS), and remote sensing that would prove helpful in international studies. The study of international relations must be built upon recognition of geographical concepts.

For international studies, geography is critical in a number of endeavors. International studies graduates often work in business, government, education, and nongovernmental organizations (NGOs). In the business world, retailers, banks, and firms engaged in international business rely upon location analysis to seek new markets, suppliers, labor, and raw materials. Transportation and travel sectors utilize geographic analysis as well. GIS analysis is a common career-entry path. In government, geographical skills are practical for many in international studies. In the United States, such departments and agencies as agriculture, census, commerce, NASA, state, defense, intelligence, mapping, and interior employ spatial, environmental, and regional analysis. International organizations such as the United Nations, the World Health Organization, UNESCO (the United Nations Educational, Scientific, and Cultural Organization), and the World Trade Organization use geographical methods to gather and analyze spatial, regional, and environmental knowledge. NGOs hire international studies graduates for their skills in geography, economics, languages, politics, history, and anthropology.

As we've discussed, the main components of geography are space, region, and environment (Johnston 2010). A combined concern for these components distinguishes geography from history, political science, economics, and anthropology. Geography's role in international studies is to analyze space, regions, and environments of the earth. The map is a special tool that geography applies in its analysis of the earth. As people struggle to understand their role in a world characterized by instant global communications, shifting geopolitical relationships, and growing evidence of environmental change, we come to realize that geography needs to be rediscovered (Murphy 1998). Without geography, we are nowhere.

A 2016 survey of 1,200 young adults on geography and current events sponsored by the National Geographic Society and the Council on Foreign Relations found that while the respondents could answer basic questions, the average score on the 75 questions was 55 percent. Two-thirds could not identify Indonesia as a Muslim-majority nation. Most did have a good understanding of environmental issues. Knowledge of global affairs certainly has an impact on political or economic decisions by people (Little 2016). Murphy (2018) discusses the spaces and places far and near, from the grand scale of Africa to the complex geopolitics of Ukraine, elucidating why we need geography.

The events of the Indian Ocean tsunami of December 26, 2004, illustrate the utility of geography. An English schoolgirl was vacationing with her parents in Phuket, Thailand, when she noticed the ocean suddenly receding in the distance. She recalled the lesson from her geography class: a tsunami is preceded by a noticeable fall or rise in water level (de Blij 2012). There was just enough time to alert about 100 people of the impending wave and to move to higher ground. Those who followed her advice survived. Of those who stayed behind, none survived. Geography does indeed matter.

References

Cutter, Susan L., Reginald Golledge, and William L. Graf. 2002 "The Big Questions in Geography." *The Professional Geographer* 54: 305–17.

de Blij, Harm. 2012. *Why Geography Matters: More Than Ever*. 2nd ed. New York: Oxford University Press.

Gan, Nectar. July 31, 2020. "China's Three Gorges Dam Is One of the Largest Ever Created. Was It Worth It?" *CNN*. www.cnn.com/style/article/china-three-gorges-dam-intl-hnk-dst/index.html

GESP (Geography Education Standards Project), American Geographical Society of New York, Association of American Geographers, National Council for Geographic Education, and National Geographic Society. 2012. *Geography for Life: National Geography Standards*. 2nd ed. Washington, DC: National Geographic Research and Exploration.

Gewin, V. 2004. "Mapping Opportunities." *Nature* 247: 376–77.

Jennings, Ken. 2011. *Maphead: Charting the Wide, Weird World of Geography Wonks*. New York: Scribner.

Johnston, R. J. 2010. "Geography and International Studies." In *The International Studies Encyclopedia*, edited by Robert A. Denemark. Chichester, UK: Blackwell.

Kaplan, Robert D. 2012. *The Revenge of Geography: What the Map Tells Us About the Coming Battle Against Fate*. New York: Random House.

Little, Becky. September 13, 2016. "Most Young Americans Can't Pass a Test on Global Affairs—Can You?" National Geographic.com. www.nationalgeographic.com/news/2016/09/survey-geography-foreign-relations-americans-students/

Martin, Geoffrey J. 2005. *All Possible Worlds: A History of Geographical Ideas*. New York: Oxford University Press.

Monmonier, Mark. 2014. *How to Lie with Maps*. 2nd ed. Chicago: University of Chicago Press.

Murphy, Alexander B. 1998. "Rediscovering the Importance of Geography." *The Chronicle of Higher Education*, October 30.

Murphy, Alexander B. 2018. *Geography: Why It Matters*. Medford, MA: Polity.

Obama, Barack. 2012. *National Geographic GeoBee*. Washington, DC: National Geographic Society. www.nationalgeographic.org/video/edu-obama-question/

Price, Marie, Martin Lewis, William Wyckoff and Lester Rowntree, 2020. *Globalization and Diversity: Geography of a Changing World*. 6th ed. Upper Saddle River, NJ: Prentice Hall.

Rubenstein, James M. 2020. *The Cultural Landscape: An Introduction to Human Geography*. 13th ed. Upper Saddle River, NJ: Pearson Education.

Rubenstein, James M., William H. Renwick, and Carl T. Dahlman. 2013. *Introduction to Contemporary Geography*. Upper Saddle River, NJ: Pearson Education.

Sheehan, Molly O'Meara. 2000. "Gaining Perspective." *World Watch* (March/April): 14–24.

Short, John Rennie. 2020. *World Regional Geography*. New York: Oxford University Press.

Sobel, Dava. 1995. *Longitude*. New York: Walker.

Sutton, Christopher, ed. 2017. *Goode's World Atlas*. 23rd ed. Skokie, IL: Rand McNally.

Twain, Mark. [1894] 1996. *Tom Sawyer Abroad*. New York: Oxford University Press.

Further Reading

Books

Castree, Noel, Alisdair Rogers, and Douglas Sherman, eds. 2005. *Questioning Geography: Fundamental Debates*. Malden, MA: Blackwell.

Clifford, Nicholas J., Sarah L. Holloway, Stephen P. Rice, and Gill Valentine, eds. 2009. *Key Concepts in Geography*. 2nd ed. Thousand Oaks, CA: Sage.

de Blij, Harm. 2009. *The Power of Place: Geography, Destiny, and Globalization's Rough Landscape*. New York: Oxford University Press.

Dodds, Klaus. 2000. *Geopolitics in a Changing World*. Harlow, UK: Prentice Hall.

Haass, Richard. 2020. *The World: A Brief Introduction*. New York: Penguin Press.

Hite, Kristen A. and John L. Seitz. 2012. *Global Issues: An Introduction*. 6th ed. Malden, MA: Wiley-Blackwell.

Johnston, R. J., Peter J. Taylor, and Michael J. Watts, eds. 2002. *Geographies of Global Change: Remapping the World*. 2nd ed. Malden, MA: Blackwell.

Rogers, Alisdair, and Heather A. Viles, eds. 2003. *The Student's Companion to Geography*. 2nd ed. Malden, MA: Blackwell.

Journals

Annals of the Association of American Geographers. www.aag.org/cs/publications/journals/annals

Eurasian Geography and Economics. www.tandfonline.com/loi/rege20

Geographical Journal. onlinelibrary.wiley.com/journal/10.1111/(ISSN)1475-4959

Political Geography. www.journals.elsevier.com/political-geography/

Professional Geographer. www.tandfonline.com/loi/rtpg20

Films

Power of Place: World Regional Geography (1996). BBC and Annenberg/CPB Project.

Is Wal-Mart Good for America? (2004). Frontline: PBS Home Video.

Diarios de Motocicleta (Motorcycle Diaries) (2005). Walter Salles, director. United States: Universal.

The Story of the Weeping Camel (2003). Byambasuren Davaa, director. [München]: Hochschule für Fernsehen und Film München.

Whale Rider (2003). Tim Sanders, director. Culver City, CA: Columbia TriStar Home Entertainment.

Websites

American Association of Geographers. www.aag.org/

International Geographical Union. www.igu-net.org

Miami University, Department of Geography. miamioh.edu/cas/academics/departments/geography/

National Geographic Society. www.nationalgeographic.com/

Perry-Castañeda Library Map collection. www.lib.utexas.edu/maps/

Chapter 3

Anthropology and Intercultural Relations

Understanding the web of connections that links people around the world involves more than the study of environments, historical change, economies, and power. It requires studying the ideas by which people make sense of these processes. However integrated communities become through globalization, their models of how the world works continue to be shaped by different environments, histories, economic systems, ideologies, political systems, and languages. These differences in how people understand the world lead to different ways of acting and behaving in it.

Anthropologists, the scientists who study human similarities and differences, call these differences in belief and behavior *culture*. Culture involves the socially mediated human capacity to differentiate, to categorize the world of experience according to what is important to pay attention to, and what is not, and to assign meanings to the categories created.

What this means, says Michael Herzfeld (2001, 1) of Harvard University, is that cultural anthropology is the comparative study of common sense. **Common sense** is that set of unstated assumptions we share with others in our community that we can most rely on in making sense of the world around us. It is what we accept to be true without questioning or analyzing it. Common sense does not need explanation because it *is* the explanation—we guarantee the truth of something by saying that it is just common sense. The problem for international social relations is that different communities have different common senses that work equally well in their respective physical and social environments. As economic, political, and environmental processes bring into contact people who operate according to different common senses, **cultural misunderstandings** occur. A thorough understanding of the international community requires an ability to learn and deal with **intercultural relations**: the flows of symbols across the global landscape, facilitated by transnational migration, new information technologies, and global markets, which can lead to creativity and innovation but also to misunderstanding and conflict.

Cultural Misunderstandings in an International Milieu

In a globalizing world, both communities and the common senses constructed within them become increasingly complex, and the likelihood of cultural misunderstanding increases. For example, Robert, an American executive, was brought into the Egyptian office of his company to increase efficiency. One day, he asked Ahmad, his top manager, when an important report would be finished. "You'll have it Monday, *insh'allah* [if God wills]," Ahmad told him.

"I don't want to hear excuses," Robert replied. "I expect to see that report on my desk Monday whether God is willing or not." Shocked, Ahmad left the office and shared the incident with many fellow employees, who were equally upset. A work slowdown ensued, frustrating Robert's efforts to improve efficiency. When corporate managers arrived from the regional headquarters to see how things were going under Robert's management, a delegation of employees met them

DOI: 10.4324/9781003028314-5

to complain about Robert's "sacrilegious" attitudes. It took weeks for the whole thing to get straightened out.

At the heart of the problem was a set of misunderstandings about what was meant by the term *insh'allah*. To Robert, Ahmad saying he would get the report Monday "if God wills it" was tantamount to him saying that he might not deliver the report on time. It supported a larger conviction he had that Egyptians generally failed to take personal responsibility for things and that this led to inefficiency and to a failure of entrepreneurial spirit.

To Ahmad, Robert's statement was an attempt to enforce an American secularism on people who recognize the sovereignty of God in all domains of life. The phrase is so common in everyday life among Egyptians—both Muslim and Christian—that most don't notice when they are using it. Ahmad intended to work hard on the report, and if he were to miss the deadline because of his own actions, he knew he would deserve criticism. But he also knew that he could be hit by a car and hospitalized and therefore fail because of things beyond his control.

Insh'allah operates in everyday Egyptian speech like clauses in business contracts that excuse companies from liability in the cases of "acts of God." It is not intended as a denial of personal responsibility but a reminder that humans are not in control of the universe. In the view of many employees, Robert's order was blasphemous because it amounted to claiming that they had more power over the world than God.

As the discussions continued, the Egyptians were surprised to discover what Robert had really meant. Didn't he know, they asked, that Egyptians have always had a strong entrepreneurial spirit, that Arabs were writing fairy tales with merchants as heroes when Europe was still mired in a feudal economy and spinning stories about knights and princesses? Successful entrepreneurs are admired for their cleverness and skill in recognizing and taking advantage of opportunities, but most Egyptians also believe that their successes and failures are allowed or disallowed by God. Even the cleverest entrepreneur can lose cargo to a shipwreck or have an important contract lost in a plane crash.

Robert was likewise disturbed to find that most of what the Egyptians thought of him came from stereotypes of arrogant, unprincipled bosses they acquired watching American soap operas and sitcoms. He warned his employees that these stereotypes were no more accurate than the ones he held about Middle Eastern fatalism, the notion that what happens to people is a matter of destiny rather than personal initiative. As an evangelical Christian, Robert actually agreed with Ahmad's perspective about God being in charge. He told the Egyptians that the incident had led him to think about how clearly he was carrying the principles he professed in church through to his office life. Once he understood the Egyptians, he came to respect their use of *insh'allah*. He adopted it himself, and his use of it gave him more credibility with Egyptian workers as he established clearer rules about employee responsibilities and professional conduct.

Both Robert and Ahmad had depended on their common sense to interpret what was happening. Common sense acted as a kind of cultural logic that helped them to generate behaviors and to interpret each other's actions. But since each held to a different common sense rooted in a different way of viewing the world, they initially failed to understand one another.

Cultural misunderstandings do not only occur at the interpersonal level, though. Common sense governs people's actions at all levels of social life, including large-scale political projects. Cultural misunderstandings in realms of policy are all too common. Anthropologist William Beeman, who served as a consultant to the Carter administration, points out that policymakers often rely on common-sense myths about the world even when these are out of sync with empirical realities and fail to accomplish policy goals. For example, he argues that the US State Department operates on the basis of a coherent, consistent model of the world that serves as a common-sense basis for policymaking. In this worldview, he writes, "the normal conduct of foreign policy consists of the elite leaders of nation-states meeting in seclusion discussing matters of power and economics chiefly in the context of a bipolar struggle" (previously in a Cold War context, now with regard to the "war on terror") (Beeman 2003, 680). He argues that while this view of the world is consistent with US historical experience and continues to work well when dealing with European nations, many of the failures of US foreign policy elsewhere—regardless of whether the administration is Democratic or Republican—stem from policymakers having a view of the world that is sometimes out of sync with reality and not shared by policymakers in many other parts of the world, who often have quite different views of how the world works.

For example, Iranian officials tend to work with a substantively different worldview, one in which Iran is an honest, just, and moral nation surrounded by hostile enemies. These enemies seek to destroy Iran's cultural and moral purity, not only through military threat but by the seduction of false ideologies like communism or open-market capitalism. This worldview is consistent with Iranian history, pre-Islamic Persian mythology, and contemporary Shiite Islamic doctrine, but it is not always correct, and it is rarely useful in formulating policies for dealing with foreign powers, including the United States. Moreover, Iranian assumptions about how international communication should proceed are just the opposite of American assumptions. Americans tend to be egalitarian in interpersonal communications but insist on the superior position of the United States in formal international communications. Iranian culture anticipates careful attention to hierarchy in interpersonal communication but expects that nation-states will treat one another as equals in international relations.

Beeman (2003) argues that in US–Iranian relations, neither side is able to generate foreign policy that produces desired results from the other because they do not understand how the world looks from the other's viewpoint, nor do they understand one another's styles of communication. Instead, after more than 30 years in which every overture or threat by either country produces results quite different from what their politicians' common sense expects, each country accuses the other of being crazy or evil.

From business to politics and in every other sphere of international relations, culture plays a crucial role. Attention to culture is therefore an essential element in understanding international situations.

What Is Culture?

To be human is to need to live in a world of meanings. To be able to act effectively in the universe, humans must construct models of how the world works, values that help them decide what goals are worth pursuing, and plans of action to help them achieve those goals. Yet all humans do not live in the *same* world of meanings. Groups of humans generate and elaborate different systems of meanings, and to the extent that these systems are shared, they define groups as communities. Individuals in communities create their own unique ways of acting, but they do so within the horizon of meanings defined by the community. **Culture**, then, is this learned system of meanings through which people orient themselves in the world so that they can act in it. Culture can therefore be said to be symbolic, shared, learned, and adaptive.

Culture Is Symbolic

Humans live in a physical world, and they understand and manipulate that world through symbols. Everything humans produce has a symbolic aspect—from words to gestures to clothes to housing to complex technologies. A **symbol** is *something* that stands for *something else* to *someone* in *some respect*. The use of words in language is a good example. A word such as *horse* is a "something" (the technical word is *signifier*) that stands for something else (its *referent*)—in this case, a particular animal—to speakers of English.

Figure 3.1 An example of the human world of meanings: people everywhere care for their dead with elaborate symbolism, as in this funeral in Moldavia.

Source: Doug Rogers.

When we define a symbol as a signifier standing for a referent to someone *in some respect*, we are drawing attention to special features possessed by symbolic systems. One of the most important is that signs usually have no intrinsic or essential relationship to their referent. There is nothing in the phonetic sounds of the words *horse, hassan, equus,* or *cheval* that connect them with the particular animal to which all these signs refer. Their relationship is **arbitrary**—we know the meaning of the word only if we've grown up in a community that shares the knowledge of which signifiers refer to which referents (Figure 3.1).

To say that a symbol means something only to a *someone* is to emphasize that culture is expressive. Our words, our actions, and our artifacts communicate things to others about us. Not only what we say but how we say it—intonation, volume, and pitch—communicates important information about us and what we may be thinking, feeling, or about to do. The same is true of the kinds of clothing we wear, how we cut our hair, how close we stand to people, and how we eat our food. Even the most practical of actions possesses a symbolic, communicative element. It is because we share a common set of understandings about what symbols mean that we can understand and predict one another's actions, and so cooperate as a community.

Culture Is Shared

Culture, then, involves shared understandings of symbols and their meanings that allow us to communicate, to cooperate, and to predict and understand one another's actions. Yet while culture is shared, it is not equally distributed among all the peoples of a society. Different distributions of cultural knowledge usually serve to produce and maintain differences in social positions such as gender, race, caste, or class. But in highly complex and diverse societies, differences can also distinguish people on the basis of education, occupation, or even leisure. In most societies, rights, responsibilities, and control over resources are unequally distributed to people on the basis of these social categories. The mobilization of cultural symbols to create, sustain, or resist such social inequities is called **ideology**.

Shared culture includes knowledge of history and also the whole realm of convention and belief we call tradition. Slavery is part of a shared history in the United States, but what it means to people differs according to their social positions and other aspects of their belief systems. These areas of similarity and differentiation intertwine in complex ways. Because of this, specific symbols may have very different meanings to different people within the same general culture. The tearing down of statues of Confederate leaders in the US or of King Leopold in Belgium by the #BlackLivesMatter movement, are enactments of the profound differences in people's understandings of the meanings of race, power, and the continuing legacies of slavery and colonialism.

Because culture is shared but unequally distributed, every society must have mechanisms to deal with two processes: the generation of similarity and the organization of difference (Wallace 1961). The **generation of similarity** involves those institutions and processes that teach and reinforce common beliefs, values, orientations, and models for action among members of a community. Family, school and peer groups, and mass media, among others, generally serve as key institutions for enculturating members of a society into the most deeply and widely held cultural symbols. But shared, uniform beliefs and values are not necessary for many cooperative activities. People from many different backgrounds can share a train in a multi-ethnic tube station in London; they simply need to know the rules for riding the Underground. Institutions concerned with the **organization of difference** include most political and social organizations with the power to regulate behavior and reward or punish behaviors, from schools and police to tribal institutions.

These beliefs about similarity and difference, about what is acceptable behavior and what is not, about what makes someone one of "us," and what makes them "other," powerfully shape intercultural behavior at every level, and influence legal, and political actions that influence global flows of people, goods, technologies and ideas.

Culture Is Learned

The fact that not all cultural knowledge is equally shared by all members of a society draws our attention to the fact that we do not simply possess culture by virtue of being born into a society, we learn our culture as we live, work, and grow. Which aspects of our society's total cultural repertoire we learn depends to a large extent on our unique experiences growing up. Yet those experiences are in turn shaped by society. Insofar as we are raised in similar ways and pass through similar institutions (like hospitals, schools, weddings, and funerals), we share common sets of cultural knowledge, values, and assumptions. Insofar as our experiences differ—because of unusual family structures, differences in wealth, and exposure to different areas of society—our cultural knowledge is different.

The processes by which members of a society pass on culture to new generations is called **enculturation**. One aspect of enculturation is **formal learning**, the acquisition of cultural knowledge that takes place within institutions specifically designed for this purpose, such as schools, apprenticeships, and on-the-job training. Each society has institutions that exist primarily to pass on to children specific knowledge and skills needed as adult members of that society.

Formal learning makes up only a small part of enculturation, however. Most enculturation takes place through processes of **informal learning**—the learning we engage in simply by watching, listening, and participating in everyday activities. Consider how you learned to speak, your taste in clothes, or your eating habits. These things are usually learned through observation, imitation, and gauging the responses of those around us (Figure 3.2).

Our deepest cultural learning often shapes our bodies and unconscious behaviors: how we speak, how we move, how we eat, how close we are comfortable standing next to people. This kind of enculturation is called **embodiment**. An example of embodiment is accent. As we learn the language of our community, we train our whole vocal apparatus to easily and automatically

Figure 3.2 Most enculturation involves informal learning—the learning we engage in simply by watching, listening, and participating in everyday activities.

Source: Cameron Hay.

produce a certain range of sounds. When we try later to learn a second language, we often find it difficult to produce all the sounds, resulting in a foreign accent. Even though we are physically capable of making the same sounds as any other human, we have trained our bodies so as to privilege certain sounds over others. Similar embodied patterns can be shown to exist for proximity, gesture, how we walk or sit, what we wear (or don't), and many other elements of our everyday life. Embodied culture is especially important because it feels completely natural to us. It is not only difficult to change, it is difficult for us even to become aware of.

Culture Is Adaptive

And yet, culture is not only capable of changing, it is always in a process of change. Enculturation does not refer only to the process whereby children become socially adept members of a community. Cultural learning is a lifelong process because cultural systems adapt to changing environmental, economic, political, and social conditions. All cultural systems change over time in response to shifts in context. Cultures change as they adapt to internal or external pressures. Cultures do not, however, all adapt to the same pressures in the same ways, nor do there seem to be stages that all cultures pass through.

Culture adapts to changing conditions in a number of ways. Creativity is a fundamental human trait, and all societies have mechanisms for generating innovation from within. At least equally important is the capacity of communities to borrow cultural innovations from other societies and adapt them to their needs. The **diffusion** of ideas, technologies, and practices occurs through direct contact, such as migration or conquest, as well as through indirect contact, such as trade and mass media.

It is important to recognize that culture does not cease to be culture because it borrows and adapts. When the Plains Indians adopted the horse and the rifle from Spanish conquerors, traders, and settlers, they completely transformed their society. They did not, however, become Spaniards. Today it is not uncommon to see McDonald's franchises in Cairo or New Delhi and interpret them to be evidence of an emerging global culture, or globalization, a process some have even referred to as *McDonaldization*. But the McDonald's of Egypt is not the McDonald's of the United States. In the United States, McDonald's is a low-status, inexpensive, and convenient restaurant designed to serve frantically busy lifestyles, low budgets, and the desire for places children can go with their parents. In Egypt, McDonald's is a high-priced, high-status restaurant that delivers food, caters for parties, and is a favorite place for young cosmopolitan Egyptians to hang out. Although the restaurants share most of the same elements, those characteristics mean very different things in their different contexts. Understanding how apparently identical things can have very different meanings in different contexts is an important aspect of international studies.

Levels of Culture

The poster for a program on multicultural education in Washington, DC, in 1989 represented culture in a way that would make any anthropologist cringe. It showed a series of identical stick figures, each wearing a different hat, such as a sombrero, a beret, and a feather headdress. The implication was that we are all basically the same, all fundamentally human, but we put on cultural differences like so many different hats.

There are many problems with such a conceptualization. The use of identical bodies to symbolize our underlying similarities belies the important role culture plays in shaping those bodies, through marriage rules, dietary practices, and routines of physical activity. The reduction of cultural difference to matters of style—something we can put on and take off—ignores the deep-seated, pervasive, and complex beliefs people hold about such things as family, faith, patriotism, and race—things that are very difficult to put on and take off.

And yet, there is something to this depiction. Cultural difference is *expressed* largely through overt behaviors such as dress and idiomatic phrases. One way to resolve this discrepancy between overt behaviors and underlying meanings is to imagine culture as existing at three levels: (1) a level of everyday practices, (2) an underlying level of reasons and logical explanations for those practices, and (3) a level of underlying assumptions about how the world works that are usually taken for granted. All of these combine to make up the common sense by which we deal with everyday life.

Cultural Practices

Cultural practices refers to the everyday actions through which people in a particular community get through their day. It is the work we do, the things we say, the tools we use, the physical spaces we occupy and the ways we live and work in them, the things we buy, the ways we behave around other people, the entertainment we enjoy, the prayers we say. Cultural practices are the surface of culture, the artifacts we produce and use, and the actions of everyday life. Because observable practices often involve material space and objects—business cards, seating arrangements, clothing, gifts, types of food—specialists in intercultural communication sometimes call this level *artifact*. Saying *insh'allah* in Egypt, presenting business cards with a bow in Japan, and having men and women eat separately in India are all cultural practices. But merely knowing about these cultural practices, and accepting or going along with them, does not reveal the deeper issues of faith, respect, or honor that generate them.

Cultural Logics

Cultural logics are the underlying mechanisms that generate meaningful human action, including routine cultural practices like those described above. Anthropologists have generally recognized two forces at work. On the one hand, people act according to ideas they have in their heads. They have goals, values that make the goals worthwhile, and strategies for achieving these goals. These do not seem to take the form of scripts and rules so much as sets of logics that generate consistent behaviors. On the other hand, people's cultural logics are always organized in part by real-world conditions. If culture is to offer us a meaningful model of reality, it must be sufficiently true to reality to work on an everyday basis. Nature, and our technological adaptations to it, enable and constrain forms of human action.

This is true even of culture logics like magic, which violate many other peoples' common sense. Writing of the use of magic in shipbuilding by Trobriand Islanders, Bronislaw Malinowski pointed out that magic and technology are always complementary systems of knowledge. To sail hundreds of miles across the ocean in an open boat requires sophisticated boatbuilding and navigational technology, and among the Trobrianders, excellent shipbuilders and sailors are celebrated for their skills. But even the best-built ship with the most skillful sailors can be destroyed by a sudden, severe storm. In such a case, Trobrianders believe it is the magic that sees them through. By their success in the face of the otherwise uncontrollable forces of nature, Trobrianders also recognize and respect those with particularly powerful magical skills (Malinowski 1992).

Because cultural logics are almost always self-consistent, they have ways to explain the failures of the practices they generate. Magicians have explanations as to why their magic failed, just as dentists have explanations as to why even those who brush their teeth twice a day still get cavities. Whether we believe these explanations is usually determined more by our faith in the cultural logic, and the authority of the person explaining it to us, than any objective truth of the matter.

Worldview

Although no cultural system ever forms a fully integrated whole, anthropologists have a great deal of evidence to support the notion that there are deep, systematic patterns that join logics together. The most encompassing level of cultural integration is usually called a **worldview**. Worldview refers to assumptions people have about the structure of the universe. A worldview is a model of reality that people use to orient themselves in the world. A worldview usually consists of fundamental principles and values that organize and generate cultural logics. These may include such propositions as the following:

- The world is made up of individuals who make choices.
- Most people's lives are shaped by circumstances beyond their control.
- There are supernatural beings who may answer my prayers or petitions.
- Everything in the universe can be explained by material operations in the universe.
- All living things have souls.

These propositions are rarely stated in such bald terms by members of communities where they are held as shared assumptions, even though they often underlie many different forms of social action. In most societies, worldviews are articulated through myth, religion, drama, and art. Collectively, these comprise domains of **expressive culture**, those institutions through which we show ourselves to ourselves. Most societies include specialists in expressive culture—writers, artists, poets, theologians, performers, ritual specialists, and others—who articulate and elaborate the society's worldview in various symbolic forms (Figure 3.3).

A worldview is often described as an encompassing picture of reality. The term worldview suggests that this level of cultural integration affects the ways people see the world. These visual

Figure 3.3 Rituals are part of expressive culture, in which worldviews are articulated and elaborated in symbolic forms.

Source: John Cinnamon.

metaphors are not accidental. Seeing is a widely used metaphor for understanding in many cultures, and worldview is often described as a set of tinted lenses that color our perceptions of reality. This metaphor helps us understand how two people can approach the same reality yet understand it and respond to it differently. A person who believes that human life is made up of a series of individual choices will generally apply this worldview in order to understand a story even if it is being told by someone who understands life to be outside human control. Someone who believes in malevolent spiritual forces will look for evidence of their presence in events that someone without this belief would shrug off as bad luck or poor choices.

Worldviews are important tools through which human beings make sense of the world around them. It is important, however, to avoid seeing worldviews as prisons that lock us into a single way of seeing the world. Many early formulations of worldview did just that. Some anthropologists and linguists argued that people learned a particular language and worldview simultaneously, and that when this enculturation process was complete, people were locked into their worldview. The argument was that, for example, people whose languages contained no word for green literally did not see the color green (they saw shades of blues and yellows), while people whose languages included words for many shades of green saw forests and grass in richer ways than those who had just one word.

Empirical studies of language and perception have clarified our understanding of worldview. As we encounter the world around us, our worldview makes certain ways of seeing and dealing with reality *easier* than others. For example, one series of studies with color chips showed that people with few color words in their vocabulary had no trouble categorizing subtle differences in color (Brown and Lenneberg 1954). Although they might use the words available to them, *blue* and *yellow*, to categorize various shades of green, if pressed they could give metaphorical descriptions like "the color of a broadleaf" or "the color of grass." The general conclusion of these experiments was that humans see the same reality but they divide it up into different categories. They routinely use these categories for dealing with the world, but they remain capable of creative, outside-the-box thinking. These studies also suggest that when faced with something new, we routinely try to understand the world in familiar terms. When these familiar ways of seeing the world don't work, we are capable of creatively discovering new ways of dealing with things outside our experience.

Intercultural Relations

These discoveries have important implications for intercultural relations and cultural change. The easiest way to imagine culture is to imagine a people living within a geographically defined area and sharing a common language, a common worldview, and a common repertoire of cultural logics and practices. Unfortunately for social theory, this easy way of thinking about culture is not the reality for most of the world's peoples, and for many of them it never has been. People encounter one another through trade, migration, and warfare, as well as through mediated forms of communication such as the circulation of technologies, art, books, and movies. This process is called cultural diffusion. Cross-cultural encounters can have powerful transformative effects on both social systems and on individuals, and any theory of culture needs to be able to account for this.

One way in which cultural diffusion operates is to provide opportunities for communities to innovate and expand their cultural repertoires without particularly acknowledging the origins of their cultural innovations. For example, the Nuer people of the Sudan were originally monotheistic. As they brought wives into their tribes from neighboring Shilluk and Dinka tribes, the wives taught their own myths and rites to their children. Gradually, Nuer religion came to accept the existence of lesser gods operating under the authority of the greater God. By the time E. E. Evans-Pritchard (1940) came to study them in the 1930s, they took their polytheism for granted. Most societies develop through such processes of diffusion. Ralph Linton (1936) wrote a now-classic article in which he pointed out that almost every artifact and cultural practice an American employs in daily life is appropriated from some foreign origin. Whether something is appropriated but has no symbolic connection to its origin (for example, the fact that pajamas come to us from South Asia is irrelevant to understanding their use and meanings in contemporary North America), or whether a practice's origin is part of its meaning (like the authenticity of imported ethnic art works), is an important aspect of understanding globalization.

But intercultural relations are never only about societies. They are always also about people. As labor migrants, tourists, soldiers, and **refugees**, people move with increasing frequency across cultural boundaries, from communities where they know the rules to places where very different practices, logics, and worldviews are in play. The term **culture shock** is often used to describe the unpleasant, even traumatic, feeling people get when the rules and understandings by which they have organized their lives no longer apply.

How do people deal with culture shock? There are several ways. Some people might hold on tightly to the worldview and logics they grew up with and believe the people among whom they now live are wrong, foolish, or even immoral. Often, they surround themselves with artifacts and people from their own community. To deal with their new host culture, they focus on pragmatic knowledge of local cultural practices. Take the case of John, an American businessman who spent two to four months each year doing business in Japan. John made a conscious effort to learn customary Japanese business practices as tools to get his job done. He learned to bow and present a business card, to give and receive gifts, and other important elements of doing business in Japan without ever making the effort to understand the deeper logics underlying these practices. He never tried to learn the language beyond a few greetings, to read translated Japanese novels, or to watch dubbed movies. He kept up on news about Japan but only through newspapers and television from the United States. John was shocked when, after five years as his company's Japanese liaison, he was transferred to another part of the world and Greg, a newly hired sales representative, got his job. The chief difference between them was that Greg seemed to appreciate many aspects of Japanese society. He had studied the language in college (although he did not speak it well), he read the illustrated novels Japanese call *manga*, and he kept up with Japanese news through the English edition of the Japanese newspaper *Asahi Shimbun*. Most importantly, Greg got a feel for the logics that generate Japanese practices rather than simply trying to memorize them as rules. As a result, he was comfortable in situations where John was uncomfortable or bewildered. Japanese clients were likewise more comfortable with Greg, who usually knew when to follow formal rules and when the rules changed.

An increasing number of people around the world live for long periods of time in host communities and become at least partially enculturated. The practices of the host community become increasingly normal, and they get a glimpse of the cultural logics that generate these practices. Susan, a teacher from the United States who taught for 13 years at an Egyptian private school, learned to dress conservatively, covering her shoulders and wearing skirts that fell below the knees. She also grew accustomed to the deference with which students treated her as a teacher. She grasped some of the underlying logics of life in Egypt, where one's behavior is a reflection of one's family, and where good people are expected to govern their lives so as to contribute to social stability. Dressing conservatively and speaking with deference to those in higher positions had nothing to do with her feelings; they were about respecting the feelings of others. When she returned to the United States and began teaching at a school in Florida, she suffered reverse culture shock. But gradually she came to recall the crucial role of individuality in the North American worldview and to understand that the Florida students' practices and modes of dress were about expressing their individual feelings and personalities. Susan gradually came to feel that she understood and was comfortable with both worldviews.

Not everyone is so fortunate. Oscar, a Venezuelan, and Peggy, his American wife, have lived with their three children in four different countries as they've followed Oscar's career in the oil industry. They speak Spanish at home, and their children have attended British and American schools during their postings. As his college years approached, Victor, the oldest, began to express worries about who he was and where he would go as an adult. He likes the lifestyle in the United States but feels the people are "ignorant and narrow, seeing everything in black and white." His American accent, modes of dress, and tendency to miss nuances of people's behavior set him apart in Venezuela. "It's like, wherever I live I'm a foreigner," he said. Victor's plight is that although he has linguistic and educational tools for success, he is unable to comfortably orient himself in the world. A significant part of culture is its capacity to help us generate **identity**, a sense of being part of a group through shared commonalities of belief and feeling. In many cases, it is subtleties of surface practices that generate this sense of being part of a community— being around others who speak, dress, and behave more or less as you do.

Studying Culture: The Anthropological Perspective

As even this brief overview suggests, culture is a pervasive aspect of human life that touches on everything we do. In the United States, culture is particularly studied by cultural anthropologists as part of a larger inquiry into human nature. Broadly speaking, anthropology is the empirical study of what it means to be human. Whereas most social sciences are defined by their subject matter, anthropology is not. History studies people's records of their past. Political science examines relations of power. Geography studies the relations of people to their environments (and vice versa). Economics studies the ways people produce, distribute, and consume goods and services. Since all of these are human activities, an anthropologist may well study any or all of these.

Lacking a bounded subject matter, anthropology is defined instead by a common perspective, a particular way of looking at human activities. This anthropological perspective can be said to be comparative, holistic, empirical, evolutionary, and relativistic.

Comparative Perspective

It is normal for people to believe that the ways they behave are natural. Heterosexual, American men don't usually express affection for each other through touching. The idea that men might show friendship through handholding, patting, or sleeping in one another's laps seems unnatural. Yet such displays are common in many parts of the world. For most Europeans and North Americans, the idea of a soup made of dog or guinea pig is repulsive, yet these are enjoyed thoroughly in parts of Asia and South America, respectively. Elsewhere in the world there are peoples for whom beef or pork are just as repulsive.

Because all people tend to assume their ways of life are natural, the only way one can study culture is through a **comparison** of cultural systems that shakes up this sense of normalcy, showing that what we assumed was natural and essential is actually cultural and historically contingent. Anthropology is therefore deeply concerned with understanding the similarities and differences among cultural systems.

Holistic Perspective

A second important aspect of the anthropological perspective is the capacity to understand human societies as complex systems with many interwoven elements. Rather than trying to reduce the complexity of social action by concentrating on one aspect of human action—like religion, social institutions, language, art, drama, or agriculture—anthropologists assume that all these aspects of human society are interconnected and that these interconnections can be discovered and described.

An example of this kind of **holism** can be found in the work of J. Stephen Lansing in Bali. Lansing was in Indonesia studying Balinese temple religion in 1983 when the island was going through an agricultural evolution. Indonesian and Western agronomists had introduced new breeds of rice, chemical fertilizers, pesticides, and other technologies as part of Asia's green revolution. Many of these techniques had enjoyed enormous success elsewhere in Asia. But in Bali, one of the world's leading rice producers, crop yields actually fell after these techniques were introduced.

Lansing was able to demonstrate that these problems were due in part to a failure to understand the complexity of Balinese society. At the peak of the volcanic island is a great crater lake and also the temple of Dewi Danu, the goddess the Balinese say created the island. At particular times during the year, according to detailed ceremonial calendars, priests open canal gates that flood a series of canals—but not all canals. Farming communities are organized around canal gates throughout the island, and the ceremonial calendars govern how irrigation takes place. Because farmers in different parts of the island are engaged in different stages of activity at different times, the cycle not only aids efficient rice production but also works around the life cycles of ducks, eels, and frogs, which consume insects that would otherwise eat the grain and which also form a significant protein source for the Balinese (Lansing 1991).

Lansing's work demonstrates not only that agriculture, social organization, and religion are intertwined, but that the separation of life into these distinct domains is not always relevant or useful. To the Balinese, agriculture, community, and religious rituals are all part of the same life and are not easily separable. Western agricultural experts, coming from a very different worldview, had a difficult time seeing the world from a Balinese perspective, even when the Balinese perspective yielded better harvests.

Empirical Perspective

A holistic perspective requires anthropologists to enter into the communities they study in order to gather information about everyday life. Anthropology is therefore an **empirical** science whose data are derived from direct observation and data collection by anthropologists living with the people they study. Anthropologists call what they do **fieldwork**, a term that may include a wide variety of methods, including interviewing, mapping, taking censuses, charting genealogies, and collecting stories and media produced by the people they are studying (Figure 3.4). For the most part, these methods are encompassed within the broader anthropological method they call participant observation. **Participant observation** refers to long-term engagements with a host community in which the anthropologist enters into the everyday life of the community, insofar as the hosts in that community permit.

Evolutionary Perspective

Once, anthropologists tended to assume that social systems were stable except when they were acted on by outside forces. They wrote of communities in a kind of eternal present tense as if they could capture once and for all the culture of a society. Empirical research has since demonstrated that stability is not normal for social systems. Contemporary anthropologists try to stay cognizant of the fact that all communities are in continual processes of historical change as they adapt to population pressures, environmental changes, wars, famines, new technologies, and other phenomena. This is not something new; it is inherent in social systems.

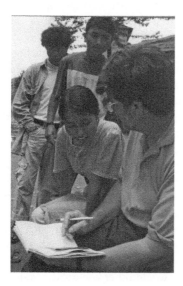

Figure 3.4 Fieldwork: Anthropologist James Hamill collects information from his hosts in Nepal.
Source: H. Sidky.

Arguing that all cultures continuously evolve by adapting to change—that they are in **evolution**—is not an argument for "survival of the fittest" thinking. Many times, a society changes to meet urgent pressures of war, famine, plague, or sudden economic change in ways that are not viable over the long term or that lead to other urgent crises down the road. As culture change recedes into history, it becomes possible for scholars to make judgments about how communities benefited from or were harmed by their particular adaptations and why their adaptations took the form they did.

An evolutionary perspective cautions anthropologists not to take stability for granted. This might seem obvious, but how many times do you hear news stories that explain cultural practices in terms of tradition? When the Taliban regime imposed the wearing of a full body and face covering called a **burqa** on all Afghani women, it was not imposing traditional dress. In most Pashtun villages before Taliban rule, girls wore no head covering until they began menstruating, then they adopted a head scarf. They assumed the *burqa* only after they were married. In imposing the *burqa* on every human female in Afghanistan without regard to class, age, or marital status, the Taliban regime was creating an entirely new cultural institution, forcing change on villagers as much as on urban women who didn't wear the veil. The evolutionary assumption reminds anthropologists that traditions have histories. When we find a practice our hosts understand to be traditional, the anthropological question is always, why *this* tradition *now*? What does it mean to people in the contemporary community, and what functions does it serve?

Relativistic Perspective

Perhaps the most controversial—and misunderstood—aspect of the anthropological perspective is the notion of **relativism**. In order to draw meaningful conclusions about human behavior from the comparison of these different societies, as well as to gather data about these societies fairly, anthropologists assume that all human societies offer data of the same type. This means that anthropologists cannot make advance judgments about the practices of the peoples they are studying.

From any given perspective, a whole range of behaviors practiced by others will appear repugnant. To most Americans, eating dog or guinea pig, the veiling of women, female (but not male) circumcision, penis bifurcation, arranged marriages, and myriad other practices around the world may seem disgusting, immoral, or oppressive. Yet common American practices such as premarital sex, eating pork, private ownership of land, male circumcision, making pets of dogs, talking to strangers about intimate family problems (including millions of strangers through television talk shows), and putting criminals to death are just as disgusting, immoral, or oppressive in the eyes of many other peoples. Often different beliefs and practices are used to define humans into larger categories, such as religious systems—for example, see the distributions of major religions in Map 3.1. The goal of anthropology is to understand the functions of these cultural practices, the roles they play in social systems, and their meanings to those who take them for granted rather than to privilege one system of meaning over another.

This does not mean that anthropologists do not have strong feelings about many of the practices they study. The commitment to relativism is not an abrogation of moral and ethical judgments. It is a commitment to recognizing that humans are capable of collectively generating innumerable creative solutions to the problems that beset life and to understanding how and why they work in a particular time and place. It is a commitment to learn *from* people, not only *about* them.

One way to understand relativism in anthropology is to divide it into three types. **Methodological relativism** is the principle that, to be comparative, anthropologists must treat all social practices as data of the same type, that is, as institutions that serve particular social

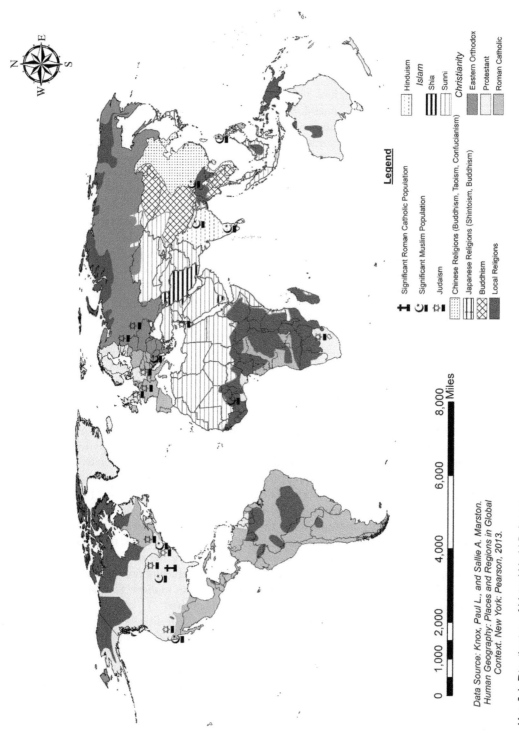

Data Source: Knox, Paul L., and Sallie A. Marston.
Human Geography: Places and Regions in Global
Context. New York: Pearson, 2013.

Map 3.1 Distribution of Major World Religions.

functions in specific times and places and that are embedded in complex webs of meanings. Practices, logics and worldviews are facts to be recorded and analyzed, not evaluated or judged. **Theoretical relativism** is an assumption, much tested and held by most anthropologists, that all human actions make rational sense when understood in their own contexts. This is often mistaken for **philosophical relativism**, a position that claims, in essence, that whatever people do is right for them. Few, if any, anthropologists would claim to adhere wholeheartedly to this philosophy. No anthropologist believes infanticide or genocide are okay—only that they are understandable. But because anthropologists do not hurry to judgment about cultural practices that many others may condemn out of hand, they are sometimes accused of taking a position of philosophical relativism.

Conclusion

The anthropological perspective offers at least five key insights for international studies. First, anthropology emphasizes the importance of culture in explaining human actions at every level of society, from the interpersonal to the international. The concept of culture reminds us that people's symbolic worlds are just as real as the material conditions in which they live; in fact, people only apprehend the empirical world through learned models of reality. While all peoples may respond to economic pressure and military power, we cannot begin to make accurate predictions about *how* they will respond unless we have a thorough understanding of their cultural realities.

Second, anthropology urges a more sophisticated approach to cultural boundaries. Rather than writing about culture as a shifting, eminently practical set of resources for making sense of the complex worlds in which people live, many contemporary approaches to international studies tend to write about cultures when they mean communities or societies, or to imagine that culture is somehow contained by the lines on a map that demarcate the borders of states. The anthropological perspective can offer an important corrective to these tendencies to imagine nation-states as the only important locus of culture and identity or to confuse symbolic systems with social groups (Figure 3.5).

Third, anthropology urges us to remember that there are usually more than two points of view. Imagining the world in binaries is a deeply rooted part of the American and Western European shared cultural heritage. We divide the political world into left and right, the economic world into socialist and free markets, we look for two sides to every story, and so forth. When we are faced with multiple perspectives on issues, we often lump them together into two opposed views. But differences between perspectives that seem trivial to us may be matters of life and death for those who hold them.

Fourth, anthropology encourages us to think small. Dictators, presidents, ministers, ayatollahs, and military commanders are not the only political actors who matter in the world. Political policies designed to bring dictators to heel may affect hundreds of thousands of people who have no say in how their states are run. Economic plans for increasing overall national economic growth may end up benefiting only a small percentage of the population while increasing poverty among the majority. Military strategies designed to quickly overcome militant groups may so devastate bystanders as to create more people willing to join such groups. Rooted in on-the-ground empirical observation, anthropology encourages us to recognize the unintended outcomes of international actions on communities beyond their intended targets— and to consider how these will reshape the worldviews of members of these communities and so their future encounters with us.

Finally, anthropology emphasizes that international studies is always ultimately about people. It urges students to learn *from* people, not just about them. It urges us to recognize that the

Figure 3.5 As cultures increasingly come into contact with each other through economic globalization, there is little evidence that a shared worldview is coming into existence. Rather, we find an increasing organization of diversity.

Source: Mark Allen Peterson.

generation of similarities and differences is part of the human condition and to seek to understand difference rather than fearing or dismissing it.

The contemporary world is a world of encounters across national, social, and cultural borders. Understanding culture is crucial to understanding human behavior at every level, from the individual to the nation-state, in an increasingly globalized world.

References

Beeman, William O. 2003. "Iran and the United States: Postmodern Culture Conflict in Action." *Anthropological Quarterly* 76 (4): 671–91.

Berlin, Brent, and Paul Kay. 1969. *Basic Color Terms: Their Universality and Evolution.* Berkeley: University of California Press.

Brown, Roger W., and Eric H. Lenneberg. 1954. "A Study in Language and Cognition." *Journal of American Social Psychology* 49: 454–62.

Evans-Pritchard, E. E. 1940. *The Nuer: A Description of the Modes of Livelihood and Political Institutions of a Nilotic People.* London: Clarendon Press.

Herzfeld, Michael. 2001. *Anthropology: Theoretical Practice in Culture and Society.* London: Blackwell.

Kay, Paul, and Chad K. McDaniel. 1978. "The Linguistic Significance of Basic Color Terms." *Language* 54: 610–46.

Lansing, J. Stephen. 1991. *Priests and Programmers: Technologies of Power in the Engineered Landscape of Bali.* Princeton, NJ: Princeton University Press.

Lenneberg, Eric H., and John M. Roberts. 1956. *The Language of Experience: A Study in Methodology.* Baltimore, MD: Waverly Press.

Linton, Ralph. 1936. "One Hundred Percent American." *The American Mercury* 40: 427–29.

Malinowski, Bronislaw. 1992. *Magic, Science and Religion and Other Essays.* Westport, CT: Greenwood Press.

Wallace, Anthony F. C. 1961. *Culture and Personality.* New York: Random House.

Further Reading

Books

Agar, Michael. 1996. *Language Shock: Understanding the Culture of Conversation.* New York: Harper.

Besteman, Catherine, and Hugh Gusterson, eds. 2005. *Why America's Top Pundits Are Wrong: Anthropologists Talk Back.* Berkeley: University of California Press.

Farmer, Paul. 2004. *Pathologies of Power: Health, Human Rights, and the New War on the Poor.* Berkeley: University of California Press.

Gonzalez, Roberto J., ed. 2004. *Anthropologists in the Public Sphere: Speaking Out on War, Peace, and American Power.* Austin: University of Texas Press.

Greenhouse, Carol J., Elizabeth Mertz, and Kay B. Warren, eds. 2002. *Ethnography in Unstable Places: Everyday Lives in Contexts of Dramatic Political Change.* Durham, NC: Duke University Press.

Koga, Yukiko. 2016 *Inheritance of Loss: China, Japan and the Political Economy of Redemption after Empire.* Chicago: University of Chicago Press.

Journals

Anthropological Quarterly. aq.gwu.edu

Anthropology News. www.anthropology-news.org

Anthropology Today. onlinelibrary.wiley.com/journal/10.1111/(ISSN)1467-8322

Cultural Survival. www.culturalsurvival.org

Sapiens. www.sapiens.org

Films

First Contact (1984). Bob Connolly and Robin Anderson, directors. Filmaker's Library, https://video.alexanderstreet.com/channel/ethnographic-video-online-foundational-films.

The Goddess and the Computer (1988). J. Stephen Lansing and Andre Singer, directors. Documentary Educational Resources, www.der.org.

In and Out of Africa (1993). Ilisa Barbash and Lucien Taylor, producers. Berkeley Media, www.berkeleymedia.com.

Transnational Fiesta: 1992 (1993). Paul Gelles and Wilton Martinez, producers. Berkeley Media, www.berkeleymedia.com.

Trobriand Cricket: An Ingenious Response to Colonialism (1976). Gary Kildea and Jerry Leach, producers. Berkeley Media, www.berkeleymedia.com.

Websites

Anthropology. zeroanthropology.net

Cultural Survival. www.culturalsurvival.org

Human Relations Area Files. www.yale.edu/hraf/index.html

Public Anthropology. www.publicanthropology.org

Savage Minds: Notes and Queries in Anthropology. savageminds.org

Chapter 4

Economics and International Development

The world is composed of 195 states whose overriding objectives are primarily economic and implicitly political. Economic priorities center on how resources will be allocated in the most efficient manner, while political issues are grounded in representation; and how individual and collective interests coalesce into outcomes that are desired within a country, nation or state. As global economic institutions bring states into heightened interconnectivity, an ongoing set of economic transactions (in which the means of production are privately owned) and watershed events have upended prospects for unfettered growth and development. The **Great Economic Crisis**, for example created ripple effects that reverberate today. As a sharp downturn in the world economy that began in the United States in 2008, the crisis had devastating and worldwide ramifications with millions losing their life savings and homes owing to a housing market crisis. More than a decade later, the context for current and ongoing conflicts in some of the world's hotspots are rooted in economic uncertainties created from this upheaval, which in turn created political and socioeconomic splinters within states. The United Kingdom voted to leave the European Union in the historic "Brexit" of 2019, which formally went into effect in early 2020. The world's largest economy, the United States, in 2016 elected controversial businessman Donald Trump as president based largely on a promise to restore jobs for working-class Americans. Similarly, Poland, Hungary, France, Brazil and many more countries have surprised political observers with a pivot to populism. Identity politics, demographic changes, migration movements offer some explanation, but what factors explain these shifts? This chapter examines defining aspects and perspectives of economics that informs the trajectory of international development using examples across the world's regions. It begins with a broad exploration of what economics is, examining the contending worlds of development, globalization and the market-oriented dynamics in an increasingly interdependent world. Following these sections, sustainability and emerging challenges related to economics and ecological development are discussed.

What Is Economics?

How do social scientists describe and understand what happened to world trade and finance in the years leading up to the global downturn? What are some underlying assumptions of economics that expose the contours of fault lines that have emerged since the Great Recession of 2008? How do governments decide what policies to enact to lessen the effects of the crisis, to shorten its duration, or to reverse its effects? How do we measure whether or not those policies are effective? **Economics** is the social science that studies, describes, models, and makes projections about the production, distribution, and consumption of goods and services. It does so by examining how the use of scarce resources satisfies individual and societal needs and wants; and how the mechanisms governing supply and demand in turn informs the allocation of these scarce resources.

DOI: 10.4324/9781003028314-6

In most contemporary definitions of economics, the meaningful unit of analysis is some individual actor seeking utility or pleasure by gratifying needs and wants, although the unit might also be a corporation, institution, or state. While wants are presumed to be unlimited, human beings have only limited resources to satisfy them. In the dominant contemporary economic theories, "rational" individuals seek to maximize utility by expending the fewest resources (or costs) to obtain a need. Although states are no longer the primary actors in our international system, they nonetheless remain an important unit of analysis in how governance in each country determines the relationship between markets and the former; and in turn the choices each state faces are predicated on how governments choose to balance state–market relations—that is in the rules or institutions that either regulate or dictate how both function in relation to each other.

There is an implied definition of human nature in this way of looking at human activity. It assumes first that all humans have unlimited desires; second, that all humans have limited resources; third, that humans are rational in the narrow sense that they evaluate the costs and benefits of their actions; and finally, that humans are inherently self-interested. These assumptions have been contested by other social sciences, as well as within economics, but proponents argue that even if human nature does not operate strictly by these principles, models based on these principles still work at a statistical level.

This point of view is widely accepted by economists in the United States, but remains a point of debate among economists in many other parts of the world. The assumptions economists make about human behavior, operations of institutions, the creation of wealth, and other aspects of economics can be roughly grouped into three economic **paradigms** that guide economists and policymakers throughout the world. These are liberal, nationalist/mercantilist, and Marxist perspectives. Understanding the basics of all of the major different theories of political economy is important in international studies because they all remain influential, and aspects of them can be found in most economic systems. However, new dimensions that inform contemporary understanding of economics are emerging as heightened inequality along gendered lines meshes uneasily with predominant models. Feminist economics, for example employs approaches and methodologies that aim to illuminate gendered labor dynamics, reproductive labor, parity and much more. As a mode of critical inquiry, scholars of this approach question prevailing assumptions about the liberal world order and the place of gender and commodification of labor in it.

Liberal Economics

Liberal economic theory is a theory first clearly articulated during the Enlightenment in Adam Smith's *Inquiry into the Nature and Causes of the Wealth of Nations* (1776). Smith conceived of wealth as produced by a nation through the efficient division of labor and use of resources (Figure 4.1). From these roots, the science of economics took on its double role as both an academic enterprise and a useful project aimed at developing the practical foundations for the efficient production, distribution, and consumption of resources on a global level. Many theoretical variations of liberal economics have emerged with differences revolving around the relative importance of labor, the value of specific scarce resources, or the effect of changes in demand on the creation of wealth.

Liberal economic schools of thought all hold a consistent commitment to **markets** with minimal government intervention. In an absolute form, liberal economic theory assumes a perspective on human beings as "economic man," *Homo economicus*, who act to gain the highest possible well-being, or **utility**. Such individuals are rational in the sense that they seek to achieve their goals at the least possible cost. This does not mean that individuals' goals are rational or that individuals necessarily know fully what their long-term best interests are, only that they try to

Figure 4.1 Adam Smith (1723–1790) was the first to articulate a theory of liberal economics.

Source: Library of Congress.

fulfill needs and desires at minimal cost to themselves. This concept of **rationality** is fundamental to *rational choice theory*, which, in its basic form, assumes that social systems arise as the result of the actions and interactions of individual actors motivated by self-interest.

Liberal economics assumes that humans have unlimited wants and desires, thus creating **demand**, but have limited resources to fulfill them, creating **scarcity**. Trade-offs are therefore an inherent aspect of economic decision making and part of the decision to meet one set of desires requires not meeting another set of desires. Imagine a college student weighing the choice of either a concert/event ticket or a business attire for an unexpected internship opportunity on the horizon. Only one is affordable. The choice involves both objective costs (the price of the concert ticket or the business suit) and the subjective value of peer approval and a potential opportunity on the horizon. Once the choice to buy one rather than the other is made there is also the cost of the desire that is not met; buying the concert ticket comes at the cost of forgoing the suit, and vice versa. The value of demands not met is called **opportunity cost**. According to liberal economic theory, such dynamics of consumer choice are best played out where a single individual can assess these costs and benefits in a free market with free flows of information. Critics of the theory argue that the social, historical, cultural, and individual complexities of even this simple-minded example are far more complicated.

According to liberal economic theory, the best decisions about the use and transmission of wealth and resources occur without coercion. Without coercion, individuals will automatically make rational decisions about how much pleasure is obtained by each additional unit of cost for a good or service. Individuals will purchase goods/services so that the satisfaction gained equals the labor or costs invested in obtaining that satisfaction. The goal of business is to increase the point where consumer satisfaction is gained. This is called the theory of **marginal utility**, and the models derived from the theory allow for sophisticated model building on which market strategies are based.

Buyers and sellers are all trying to maximize utility. The buyers' demand can be represented by a **demand schedule** that lists the goods that buyers are willing to buy at certain prices. As the price of a good or service increases, the quantity demanded of those goods and services decreases. The **law of demand** asserts that there is an *inverse* relationship between the price of a good and the quantity demanded of that good. Price, of course, is relative not only to demand but also to the availability of money. As the income of buyers increases, so too will the demand for goods and services.

But buyers' demands for goods are not the only factor determining price in the market place. The seller's **supply** of goods also plays a role in the market price. As the price of a good increases, sellers are motivated to increase the supply of that good. According to the **law of supply**, a direct relationship exists between the price of a good and the quantity of supply of the good. In the market, the decisions of buyers interact simultaneously with those of sellers and there is a tendency for the demand to equal the supply of a good or service. When the demand for a good equals the supply of that good, the market for that good is said to be in **equilibrium**.

The place where optimal decisions about supply, demand, scarcity, utility, and the evaluation of opportunity costs can be made is in the free market. Successes in the free market abound in an increasingly globalized economy. In a free market, unrestricted by high tariffs or import quotas, Japanese car manufacturer Toyota managed to outsell US auto manufacturing giants General Motors and Ford. The loosening of impediments to optimal decision making in the international market has, from the perspective of free marketers, enhanced effective economic decisions and benefited both sellers and buyers.

From the perspective of liberal economics, the global recession actually serves as evidence that the free-market system works even as new fractures appear evident. The decade-long housing bubble, the overextension of debt, and the creation of ridiculously complex financial instruments all created a "distorted" market that was not responsive to true financial conditions. The global recession and continuing crisis were a case of the market "correcting" itself. Interventions to minimize that suffering—bank bailouts, artificially low interest rates, government investment in new businesses—may be a mistake, in this view, because they slow the market's return to balance and normalcy.

Economic Nationalism

The notion that state interventions are inherently bad sets liberal economics apart from those approaches that can be covered by the term **economic nationalism**. Economic nationalism refers to policies that are guided by the protection of national labor, production, and wealth accumulation. The fundamental principle of economic nationalism is that the economy is not independent of a country's social and political system but is an integral part of the nation-state and must be guided to perform in the nation's best interests, both domestic and international. Establishing minimum wages and setting limits on the work week, regulating manufacturing standards, policing which chemicals are allowed in foods, setting aside resources as public lands, limiting monopolies, setting terms on investments by foreign countries, and enacting tariffs and other barriers to foreign trade are examples of ways economic nationalists seek to subordinate economic activity to national interest. This contrasts with liberal economics, which views economic interests as best served by unregulated markets.

Economic nationalism has its roots in an earlier set of theories popular during the colonial era, known as mercantilism. **Mercantilism** is a theory of political economy that holds that the economic well-being of a nation is directly related to its control over the global volume of capital. In early forms of mercantilism, the volume of global trade was seen as constant and unchanging, and it was calculated in known values of precious metals held by the state. The power of the state was believed to be best improved by an economic system that appropriated as much of this constant capital as possible. This required having high quantities of exports and smaller quantities of imports. The role of government, therefore, was to enhance a positive balance of trade by enforcing **protectionist** policies, such as **tariffs** on imported goods, creating **subsidies** to protect businesses from risks, and imposing **import quotas** to prevent other nations from dumping cheap products on national markets. Protectionist policies were imposed to limit other nations' competitive advantages, because it was believed that one nation's advantage required another nation's loss. Known as a "**zero sum**" framework this approach to economics was the dominant political-economic paradigm during the emergence of the nation-state in Europe between the sixteenth and eighteenth centuries. Historically, protectionist policies gave industry time to develop their production systems and accumulate capital until they could compete in the international marketplace.

Moreover, manifestations of mercantilism were differently expressed in different countries, often on an ad hoc basis, and were not characterized by any unifying theories or models such as those found in liberal economic or Marxist paradigms. Nevertheless, there is a central idea in economic nationalism that the interests of the state are inherently tied to economic activity and that economic activity itself is subordinate to national interests. Today, this idea remains influential, and all states continue to enact forms of protectionism as means of enhancing their own economic strengths in the wake of anxieties around job security and economic dislocation. These forms can range from tax breaks or subsidies for local businesses to outright **nationalization** of industries. For example, Venezuela and Bolivia recently took steps to nationalize their petroleum and natural gas industries and appropriate larger **royalties** from multinational petrochemical corporations.

Economic nationalism is inevitably tied to ideologies of national belonging and citizenship. Nationalistic ideology focuses on the nation-state as the exclusive and essential institution, and individuals are defined according to their membership in it and their subservience to it. The nation is usually represented as a fixed homeland, with a homogeneous identity and language, a high degree of autonomy, complete sovereignty, and a unity of identity. Political elites will therefore often attempt to protect the nation from outside influences. For example, in 2005, the Chinese National Offshore Oil Corporation (CNOOC) failed in an attempt to take over the US-based multinational petroleum corporation, Unocal. The CNOOC bid met with intense lobbying efforts from the US-based petrochemical giant Chevron. The US Congress eventually forestalled the deal and the lower-bidding American company beat the higher-bidding foreign company in spite of the overall US commitment to a free-trade agenda.

China is keenly interested in acquiring oil companies because China's economic growth and its lack of petroleum reserves are contributing to increased global demands for oil, an indispensable, strategic, and finite resource. Easing China's access to petroleum to further its productive capacity may be consistent with efforts to liberalize international trade, but it is not consistent with US foreign-policy interests that see China as a potential political threat and economic rival. In this context, the policies formulated by the US Congress were meant to encourage US investments in Unocal and discourage foreign investments. These efforts were clearly motivated by American nationalist concerns.

Economic nationalism assumes a complementary relationship between national power and the nation's domestic welfare. This is at odds with liberal economic theory that would see fundamental contradictions in seeking national welfare through militarization or any form of state intervention. Liberal economists would also argue that all nations would best benefit not from protectionist or any nationalist policies but rather by instituting exactly the opposite, by opening trade between nations without restrictions or nationalist intervention. Economic nationalists see sovereign states in competition with one another and not well served by the formation of economic interdependencies.

Protection of national economic interest can become a national-security interest very quickly. When this happens, nationalism as a political philosophy gains increasing importance and is supported by judicial, police, and military power. The important issue for nationalism is therefore not mutual economic gain among the community of nations but the relative gain between nations. Global liberal economic institutions, from the World Bank to the McDonnell Douglas Corporation, however, could not have developed as they have without the support of the most powerful and self-interested liberal nation-state, the United States, whose interests are at once consistent with and at odds with nationalism. Efforts by all states to protect their economic interests are normal and recurring themes in international studies as conflicts between national industries, particularly over scarce and finite resources, become apparent in the international community.

Adherents to economic nationalist approaches, then, applaud interventions into national economic institutions and processes designed to alleviate economic hardship and minimize the collapse of banks and businesses, and strengthen employment. Economic nationalists take comparative note of the countries that suffered most and least from the global recession, and express concerns about the relative power between rival countries recovering at different rates. These concerns can, in turn, spur further efforts at market regulation and state investment.

Marxism

Marxism refers to a range of systems of economic analysis based on the notion that the value of goods and services stems not from supply and demand in a market but from the human labor, both physical and mental, required to produce it. This means that when markets set the prices of goods lower than the cost of the labor required to produce them, they may become a means of exploiting people. Based on various interpretations of the works of Karl Marx and Friedrich Engels, Marxist theories have evolved in significant ways since their basic formulations in the mid-nineteenth century. Marx's analytical approach, **historical materialism**, argued that the driving force of historical change was the relationship between people who worked to transform natural resources into goods and those who profited from this labor without contributing to it.

From the rise of river-valley agricultural civilizations to feudal systems to global capitalism, there have existed fundamental economic contradictions between laborers and the elites who enjoyed, and profited from, the goods produced by those laborers. Every era thus resulted in **class struggle**, which eventually led to a series of social transformations resulting in the emergence of a new economic system. Marx believed that the contradictions inherent in global capitalism would eventually lead to its collapse and the emergence of a utopian, classless society called **communism**.

These theories were based on Marx's observations in Germany and England in the mid-nineteenth century, where he saw extreme forms of labor exploitation, distinct class divisions, and a **political economy** that, in his view, both created and required these inequalities. Political economy can be understood as the interaction between states and markets. Marx said that what made the system structurally unequal was that some people owned the **means of production**.

They owned the means of doing business, the resources it required, the capital derived from it, and even the ideas required for it (which can be copyrighted or trademarked). They devised a political, legal, and military system to legitimize their ownership. The owners were able to accumulate **capital** without themselves contributing significantly to the actual productive process. Laborers, in his view, owned little or no capital but were responsible for actually creating the capital appropriated by the capitalist class. This happens because the working class never receives the true **value of its labor**.

Marx referred to the relations between social classes as the **relations of production**. These are the social relations that are formed by the way societies produce and reproduce their material lives. The relations of production determine how incomes, products, and assets are socially distributed, and they constitute the social structure of the society. In capitalism, according to Marx, these relations of production involve exploitation of labor and denial of basic human rights to most of the population. These Marxist perspectives gained support in the twentieth century among peasant and labor groups seeking economic and political liberty from authoritarian and oligarchic capitalist regimes in Latin America, Asia, and Africa.

Modern forms of **Marxism** can be divided into two separate movements: Marxism-Leninism and social democracy (Gilpin 1987, 30). **Marxism-Leninism** was characterized in the political economy of the Soviet Union. As a form of totalitarian state-run economy, it lost legitimacy after the USSR collapsed in 1989. **Social democracy** refers to a variety of egalitarian states that generally embrace industrial production and market systems but include governmental and social controls intended to mitigate the tendencies of market systems to exacerbate social inequalities, including partial or full state ownership of businesses or industries. Most European countries have some form of a social democracy. Countries that have instituted these social reforms have largely market-based economies that include sole proprietorships as well as multinational corporations (Saab and Ikea, in the case of Sweden, for example). In modern forms, these countries encourage private entrepreneurial activities and foster forms of capitalist industry but also offer a wide range of social safety nets, universal healthcare, and well-financed public education. As a consequence, these countries usually enjoy high life expectancies, low unemployment, low crime rates, and small national debts. The trade-off is usually higher taxes and lower overall economic growth than in countries structured by economic liberalism.

In most modern applications of Marxist theory, the goal is not to overthrow capitalism but to reform it and remove the apparent economic inequality and social injustices that, according to Marxism, are inherent in capitalism. In the *Communist Manifesto*, Marx claimed that, in capitalism, workers become a commodity. He also argued that as the drudgery of the work increases, wages decrease. This was clearly true in the nineteenth century, but over time in Europe and the United States wages generally improved and the drudgery of work decreased with technological innovation. In the less-developed world, however, and with the freeing of international trade in globalization, labor again has become increasingly commoditized. Corporations seeking increased profits have relocated their production to the developing world and emerging economies, where labor costs are far lower than in the developed world. Consequently, there has been a rise in "sweatshop labor" despite economic research suggesting that profits would not be significantly lowered if better wages and working conditions were offered (Pollin et al. 2002). US garment manufacturers like Abercrombie and Fitch, Nike, and J. Crew have been seen as particularly guilty of subcontracting to sweatshop operators in Asia while reaping huge profits. A global backlash against these manufacturers has resulted in some changes in hiring practices, but generally these conditions persist, leading to a continued interest in Marxist-inspired economic reform in many developing countries.

Political movements advocating socialist reforms have been popular in many less-developed countries but have usually drawn their inspiration more from local organizers than from Marxist theory. These movements vary considerably in their concerns, organization, and goals, and they may not identify themselves as socialist, but their basic struggle can be couched in terms of opposition to the political and economic inequalities of a capitalist economic system. These movements seek a more equitable distribution of economic resources, increases in wages, social justice, and liberty. The Occupy Wall Street movement is one such example of a clamor for wealth redistribution, corporate governance reforms and in general economic inequities from which 99 percent or the majority of society was allegedly buckling under in contrast to the 1 percent or sheltered elite.

Other kinds of Marxist-informed political ideologies have re-emerged in Bolivia, Venezuela, and other Latin American countries. They have made political economic reforms such as nationalizing domestic petroleum resources and major industries to improve social services and ease persistent and egregious levels of poverty. The Mexican rebel Subcomandante Marcos represented some of the impoverished peasant groups in southern Mexico, the Zapatistas, and the major ethnic groups of Chiapas. He denied any affiliation with socialist governments but demanded peasant rights to farm their own land, reasonable healthcare, public education, and justice. These peasants represented what is recognized as the underlying interests of social democracy, universal rights, and freedom from exploitation. As Blackman (2005, 106) points out, "very few of the Mexican peasants who joined the Zapatistas had read Marx or Engels."

For Marxist economists, the global financial crisis was the result of fundamental contradictions in the system of global capitalism, specifically the way wealth aggregates in the hands of a small percentage of the global population but from whom it is inefficiently redistributed to the rest of the world's population. Bank and corporate bailouts add to the problem by shifting debt from failing institutions to nation-states. All efforts to solve the crisis by regulation will ultimately fail, Marxist economics argues, because of another contradiction: because the markets are now global, only a global system of financial regulations can fix it. But the key players are nation-states, none of whom are willing to give up their sovereignty and national interests to an international regulatory agency (Beams 2008).

Micro and Macroeconomics

Contemporary economic analysis proceeds primarily through the construction of models of economic behavior. The field of economics is divided into two large branches: micro- and macroeconomics.

Microeconomics is concerned with studying specific market systems on a small scale, such as the economic behavior of individuals, firms, and industries, to understand the relative prices of goods and services and the alternative uses to which resources can be put in a particular market system. Microeconomics assumes that there is a host of buyers and sellers in the market, none of whom can effectively control the price structure in the market. Real-market transactions, of course, do include individuals or groups who can influence prices, and this complicates microeconomic analysis. For example, the Organization of the Petroleum Exporting Countries (OPEC) and the chaotic political climate in many oil-producing countries such as Nigeria and Iraq clearly influence the supply and cost of petroleum products. The environmental costs of using these products are increasing as well. Sophisticated models in microeconomic analysis are used to formulate business policies for a firm or industry in the context of these politically, environmentally, and economically complex marketing environments.

Macroeconomics is concerned with the study of the combined performance of all markets in a defined market system. Macroeconomics may have nation-states or global regions as its unit of analysis, and aggregate information about a nation's economy is gathered. A particularly important indicator of economic performance in this arena is **gross domestic product** (GDP), defined as the total value of all goods and services produced in a country in a year (see Map 4.1

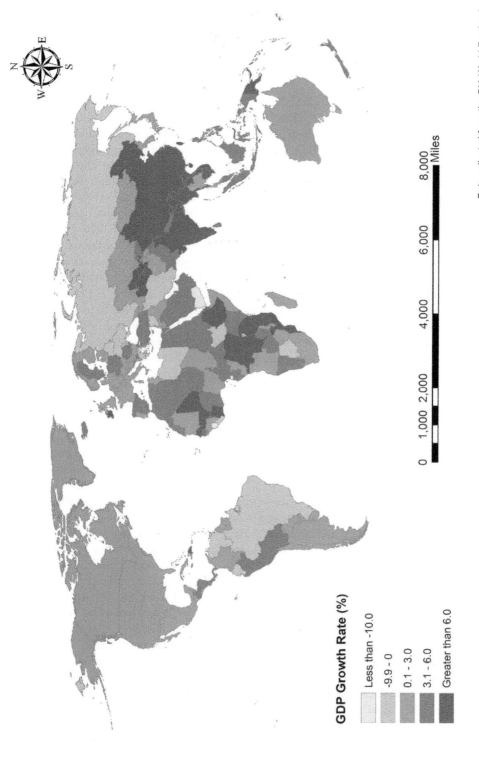

Map 4.1 GDP Growth Rate 2015.

for a snapshot of global GDP growth rates in 2015). The goal of macroeconomic analysis may include data analysis and modeling to inform government or institutional policies. The Federal Reserve Board in the United States, for example, was established in 1913 to regulate the amount of capital and credit available in the American economy. Macroeconomic analyses crucially inform the board in regulating the nation's money supply. The Federal Reserve influences the amount of Federal Reserve funds available to banks, thus controlling interest rates. "The Fed" can do this by purchasing US government securities, by increasing or decreasing the discount rate (the interest the federal government charges to banks to borrow money from the government), and by regulating the proportion of monetary reserves that banks are required to keep on hand before making loans. The higher the reserve requirement, the fewer funds are available to distribute as loans, and the availability of capital is thus adjusted.

Developmentalist Perspectives

Developmentalist perspectives study economic growth in less-developed countries. Defining *developing countries* is difficult, but the label refers to countries where standards of living are consistently low compared to the so-called First World economies in Europe, the United States, Canada, and Japan. Most of these countries are located in sub-Saharan Africa, South Asia, and Latin America, but poor countries are also found in East Asia (e.g., Vietnam), Central Asia (e.g., Kazakhstan), Eastern Europe (e.g., Romania), as well as the Middle East. The goal of economic development is to create an economic environment where people enjoy long, healthy, and creative lives. Obviously, there is more to economic development than growth in incomes, but the concept begins with developing economic structures to facilitate higher standards of living. Since World War II, there have been several policy-informing models seeking to enhance the economic development of the Third World. (The Second World consisted of the Communist bloc countries before they collapsed at the end of the 1980s.) The first such model was offered in the 1950s and 1960s by W. W. Rostow, who presented an evolutionary paradigm in his *The Stages of Economic Growth: A Non-Communist Manifesto* (1960). Rostow posited that nations pass through five consecutive stages before reaching the "stage of high mass consumption" characteristic of the United States. A central problem with early developmental theories was that they looked at how American and Western European countries became wealthy (often in idealistic ways that excluded the contributions of slavery, colonialism, and appropriation of land from Native people) and constructed idealistic "one size fits all" models that paid little or no attention to the actual ecological, social, and historical conditions of the countries they were supposed to help. International dependence theories originated in developing countries and came as a reaction to the failures of structural change policies.

Immanuel Wallerstein and Andre Gunder Frank were among those who offered critiques of Rostow's early development theories. They argued that both capitalist and Marxist economic theories were inappropriate for modeling economic development in the Third World because they were derived from Western European historical experiences. A similar perspective informed the pan-Arab movement in the 1960s and 1970s. Another critic, Arturo Escobar (1995), has laid the failures of development of many nations in the Third World at the feet of Western economic powers, arguing that development projects and economic policies based on growth-oriented, capitalist economic models that are successful with European and North American economies often fail when applied to societies that operate according to different cultural logics.

Underlying these criticisms is the empirical fact that very few development projects work as planned. Many have unexpected local consequences such as ecological depletion or disrupting traditional forms of social and political organization. Many have yet to achieve the predicted economic outcomes, with the result that recipients cannot pay off loans and thus sink even further into debt. Still other programs increase overall wealth as measured by national GDP, but the new wealth is concentrated in the hands of a few, increasing the gap between rich and poor.

Contemporary economic-development theory is associated with efforts to promote free trade and restrict government interference in economic activity. These theories, which gained popularity under Margaret Thatcher and Ronald Reagan in the 1980s, were a radical reaction to **dependency theories** and similar critiques. There are several variations of such neoliberal theory, but all advocate a free-market approach and less government intervention. The dominant model associated with the World Bank (Figure 4.2) advocates opening free markets but recognizes that

Figure 4.2 The World Bank in Washington, DC, is one of the key players in modern economic development efforts around the world.

Source: Library of Congress.

the unsophisticated financial institutions of many developing nations require some government intervention to ensure the proper evolution of industry and export markets.

Globalization and Rising Discontent

In the eighteenth century, economist Adam Smith was already considering the potential benefits of economic relations between Europe, the Americas, and the East Indies. He foresaw that "uniting, in some measure, the most distant parts of the world, by enabling them to relieve one another's wants, to increase one another's enjoyments, and to encourage one another's industry, their general tendency would seem to be beneficial" (Smith 2000, 104). Today many economists believe that a seamless system of global trade in goods and services will yield benefits to all nations and decrease the likelihood of international conflicts (Sachs 1998). But is this true? Do the benefits of globalization outweigh the costs? Economists continue to argue about this.

Globalization generally refers to the expansion of global communication and market connections, growing social and political interdependencies on a global scale, and the development of a planetary rather than national awareness among many of the world's people. In some perspectives, globalization involves consolidation and homogenization of global social relations. One of globalization's greatest champions, Thomas L. Friedman, described the phenomenon in *The Lexus and the Olive Tree: Understanding Globalization* as "the inexorable integration of markets, nation-states, and technologies to a degree never witnessed before in a way that is enabling individuals, corporations and nation-states to reach around the world farther, faster, deeper and cheaper than ever before" (Friedman 1999, 7). Certainly, globalization involves many processes, financial transactions, market expansions, electronic communications, and growing interconnections, but which of these factors is most important in understanding globalization is a matter of some contention.

There continues to be debate about when globalization began with some noting that globalization emerged several hundred years ago as empires and states emerged from warfare, trade and politics. As a form of political-economic transformation, globalization has happened so quickly that its consequences and implications for economic growth, patterns of trade, global and national transfers of currencies, and the resulting distribution of wealth in the world economy are still poorly understood. What does seem to be the case is that national economies are becoming more integrated and interdependent in several ways: through increased trade, foreign direct investment, international production, and through international treaties and legal institutions to regulate the system. However, although it is true that global trade has increased steadily since World War II, much of this is through large multinational corporations. This means that a great deal of trade and investment between countries are transactions within the same multinational company (Sachs 1998). As much as one-third of investment and its resulting trade of goods are actually shipments of component products to various production plants of the same business firm whose production processes are conducted in several different countries.

Multiple forms of globalization—economic, political, social, technological, and environmental—hold considerable impact for international development. All these forms intersect to produce complex challenges and opportunities for both state and non-state actors. Political globalization refers to dissemination of democratic principles of liberty, freedom of expression and more, as an ideal form of government that is thought to work in tandem with free trade and markets. Social globalization refers to an information revolution catalyzed by the sheer explosion of social media platforms such as Twitter, Facebook, WhatsApp that in turn shape attitudes about what is desirable for individuals including the ideal responses of governments to citizen preferences. This rapid and unprecedented flow of information around the world, especially in states with repressive policies, has produced dramatic changes in attitudes illustrating the power of Facebook in fomenting social movements and protests. The Arab spring—which began with the self-immolation of Mouamad Bouazzi and general discontent in many states in the region about economic malaise, subsidy declines/erasures, declines in living standards, and more importantly drought as part of a larger environmental challenges—spread with the help of social media platforms. Another example is Sudan in late 2018. Spurred by draconian laws that legalized child marriage, prohibited trousers for women and more, women took to the streets and their protests appeared to pay off if only temporarily. Omar Bashir, who had been president for decades, was forced from office in April of 2019 owing to sweeping protests in large part led by female demonstrators. Although the political balance has since returned to the status quo of male dominated politics, the toppling of the country's president, long a controversial figure globally, illustrates the remarkable power of social media.

Technology has long played an important role in development and thus technological globalization is a common denominator to economic, political and social globalization in providing streamlined wireless communication, faster travel, and much more. For micro, small or medium enterprises in Latin America or Africa, WhatsApp is an important tool; online banking can be done from an App on one's phone; cryptocurrency is transforming the world as we know it; and Facetime and myriad products connect us instantly with friends, family and others. As the world becomes smaller and increasingly interconnected owing to the aspects discussed above, markets have become larger and as a result new products are available at seemingly light speed. Fast fashion, "superfoods" from otherwise remote areas of the world that include fruits, vegetables and so much more are made possible by extraction and natural resources. This process is part of what we refer to as environmental globalization, which is amplified by technological developments that make **extractivism** and consumerism expand further. The logic of markets and a global appetite for expansion and development sometimes means that smaller, poorer and economically disadvantaged countries may adopt lax environmental standards for multinational corporations who choose to operate factories or plants for these purposes. Contending debates then center on how to maximize the perceived benefits of globalization and minimize what some perceive as detrimental challenges to "sustainable" development or development that continues while ensuring prosperity for future generations.

Neoliberalism is the economic theory and ideology that has served as the primary backdrop to what is commonly referred to as globalization. It is an adaptation of liberal economic theory applied to a world economy, and suspicious of many of the notions that many of the states and local communities will always be more efficient markets in managing "common good" resources (such as reserves, public lands, public schools, and hospitals) accepted by earlier schools of liberalism. Neoliberalism affirms—implicitly if not explicitly—that conflicts between market efficiency and ecological integrity should be settled in favor of the former (Scholte 2005, 12).

The goal of neoliberalism is generally to ease restrictions on trade between different countries, to free the movement of goods and services, and to maximize economic efficiency and profits. This is to be accomplished by removing controls such as tariffs, regulatory measures, and restrictions on investment, as well as relegating government services to private firms whose market orientation increases the efficiency of service delivery. During the last half of the twentieth century, deregulation of industry and privatization of government services opened economies to imports of goods as corporations seek new markets and new sources of less expensive labor than they had found in the developed world. Advances in communication and transportation of commodities reduced costs and encouraged expansion of trade and foreign investments. Moreover, advances in communication have resulted in a much more integrated system of international finance, allowing for rapid exchange of currencies. These rapid changes that include financial liquidity or the speed at which financial transfers, transactions and investments occur in milliseconds is unprecedented. Alan Greenspan, head of the Federal Reserve from 1986 until 2006, lowered interest rates, which became an important fiduciary tipping point that later precipitated the housing bubble and subsequent market crash and recession not seen since the Great Depression of 1929. In some ways financial globalization specifically viewed through the prism of the separation of commercial banking of the banking sector helped to create the conditions for the subsequent global economic crisis of 2008.

Global Economic Crisis of 2008

The global economic crisis began in the United States with a sharp decline in banking **liquidity**—the ability to pay debts when they come due without incurring unacceptable losses. Because the United States is a global financial hub, the crisis spread quickly, resulting in the collapse of giant investment firms, bank bailouts by national governments, and stock market slumps around the world. In many areas, the housing market also suffered, causing a sharp rise in evictions, foreclosures, and prolonged vacancies. The crisis led to steep declines in consumer wealth in the trillions of US dollars, ultimately leading to a severe global economic recession in 2008.

Why were so many American banks suddenly unable to pay their debts? The answer lies in 2007 with the collapse of a long-term real-estate bubble in the United States. For more than a decade, US land and housing prices had risen steadily, encouraging lenders to offer home ownership loans at increasingly higher risk; the logic was that if the borrowers were foreclosed on, the banks could recoup their loss by selling the property. When the housing bubble burst, many lending institutions found themselves holding more debt than they could manage. Similar bubbles burst in several European countries, as well as in Argentina, Australia, New Zealand, Lebanon, South Africa, Ireland, Israel, South Korea, India, Russia, Ukraine, and China.

The problem was made worse by US banking deregulation, which since the 1980s had rolled back many protections that had been put into place after the Great Depression. These reforms allowed banks and investment firms to create complicated high-risk, poorly understood new financial instruments. Thus the crisis "was not a natural disaster, but the result of high risk, complex financial products; undisclosed conflicts of interest; and the failure of regulators, the credit rating agencies, and the market itself to rein in the excesses of Wall Street," according to a 2011 US Senate report (United States Senate 2011, 1).

One of the immediate consequences was a dramatic downturn in the US stock market, which dropped from a high of 14,000 points in October 2007 to a low of 6,600 in March 2009. US market volatility was quickly reflected in stock markets in Asia and Europe. Twenty-five banks failed in 2008 and were taken over by the Federal Deposit Insurance Corporation (FDIC), including Washington Mutual Bank, the largest bank failure in US history. Another 140 failed in 2009, 158 in 2010, 92 in 2011, and 51 in 2012.

The crisis grew rapidly into a global economic shock that resulted in a number of European bank failures, falling stock indexes, and large reductions in the market value of commodity goods and equities. Beginning with the United Kingdom, governments responded with bailouts of foundering banks and large corporations to put more money in circulation, while cutting interest rates to help borrowers.

The continuing fiscal crisis in the United States affected many other countries worldwide. The US economy had been spending and borrowing at very high rates for many years, and much of the rest of the world depended on US consumers. When American borrowing and spending slowed, economic growth elsewhere was affected. Even countries that avoided the worst effects of the recession were hit by the drop in global shipping in 2009, in which, for example, exports from Taiwan dropped 42 percent, South Korea 30 percent, and Japan 27 percent.

In Europe, countries fared differently. Poland, which had imposed strict austerity measures as a result of financial problems in 2000, was the only member of the European Union to avoid a recession; the country even saw modest growth during this period. In Iceland, on the other hand, the entire international banking system collapsed, the greatest financial disaster to strike any country in modern history. The protests that followed led to the resignation of the entire ruling conservative party and its replacement by a left-leaning government.

The word **recession**, generally referring to any period of reduced economic activity, can be used in two ways. In the formal economic sense, it refers specifically to two consecutive quarters of declining economic growth. By this definition, the recession ended in the United States in the summer of 2009, and as much as six months earlier or later in most other countries. However, people often continue to use the word in a more general sense to refer to continuing high unemployment, escalating federal debt problems, inflation, rising gas and food prices, and ongoing declines in home values, leading to an increase in foreclosures and personal bankruptcies. These conditions continued in most countries well after the recession technically ended.

This recession was particularly dramatic in the **Eurozone**—those parts of Europe where the euro (€) is the common currency. In late 2009, alarm grew over the possibility of a **sovereign debt crisis**, an inability of a country to pay back its debt. Sovereign debt had increased dramatically throughout Europe as a result of the European bank bailouts, with Greece, Ireland, and Portugal seen as particularly vulnerable. The fear was that if countries like these defaulted on their debts, it would pull down countries that held their debt, like Italy and Spain. The collapse of these larger economies would in turn threaten the economies of European economic powerhouses, most importantly Germany.

In May 2010, the **International Monetary Fund (IMF)** and the Eurozone countries agreed to a €110 billion loan for Greece in exchange for harsh austerity measures including tax hikes, scaling back public benefits, and cutting pensions. This was followed by similar rescue packages for Ireland six months later and Portugal six months after that. These austerity measures led to massive public protests, and it was not clear whether or not the Greek government would fall as Iceland's had. Worse, it did not solve the problems, which resurfaced a year later over the refinancing of Greek public debts. Again in 2012, the Greek government managed to pass a new package of austerity measures, and **European Union** (EU) leaders passed a bailout package to sustain the country, but many economists began to question the viability of the European joint financial system. By 2016, Europe still had 20 million people out of work and less than 1 percent economic growth. That year, the United Kingdom voted to leave the European Union, creating greater uncertainty and instability.

Latin American states suffered during the first stage of the crisis but seemed to have successfully rebounded by 2010. Initially, stock markets became extremely volatile during the crisis, and currencies fell sharply. Except for Peru, industrial growth fell. Unemployment grew, leading to marches and protests in many countries. However, as foreign investment in Latin America declined, domestic banks, especially in Brazil, stepped in to fill the gap. The loss of US and European investments also led many countries to build stronger economic ties with China. By 2016, however, Latin America was seeing a region-wide economic downturn because of the strength of the US dollar, slowing of Chinese investment, high inflation (nearly 100 percent in Venezuela), and a recession in Brazil. Predictably, this has led to political protests and demands for change throughout the continent.

Major Asian economies experienced the same stock-market volatility and rising unemployment as the rest of the world, but while China, India, and South Korea experienced slowed growth and accompanying social and political unrest, they avoided a technical recession. Other Asian nations fared very poorly. Cambodia fell from 10 percent economic growth to nearly zero, and Bangladesh faced a sharp rise in the number of families living below the poverty line. Many Asian countries implemented strict austerity measures to try to avoid further economic problems. Cutting of benefits and pensions, rising unemployment, layoffs of public-sector workers, and wage cuts provoked strikes, protests, and riots across Asia, from Cambodia, South Korea, and Taiwan to Japan and Hong Kong.

Although oil-producing countries in the Middle East lost enormous sums in international investments, they were generally less severely affected by the crisis than many other parts of the world because of continuing high world oil prices. Iran, largely cut off from global financial markets due to US sanctions, apparently did not even sink into recession. As oil prices dropped in subsequent years, however, these countries began to cut many of the free social programs they provided to citizens, sometimes leading to rising social unrest.

Countries with less petroleum fared worse. It is no coincidence that countries with fewer petroleum reserves (such as Egypt, Syria, and Tunisia), and those in which the public enjoys a smaller share of revenues from oil sales (like Libya and Yemen), were the countries in which the so-called **Arab Spring** emerged. Already facing high unemployment and rampant government corruption, protests in these Arab countries did not decline as they did in most other parts of the world but grew dramatically, toppling apparently strong governments like that of Ben Ali in Tunisia and Hosni Mubarak in Egypt. In Libya, it turned into a full-fledged armed revolution that ousted Muammar Qaddafi, while in Syria protests escalated into civil war.

In Africa, the global economic crisis swept "away firms, mines, jobs, revenues, and livelihoods," plunging the continent into "a full blown development crisis" (AfDB 2009, 1). For more than a decade, African states and international development agencies had sought relatively strong economic growth by integrating Africa into the international financing market, but these efforts, while producing economic growth, made most African countries more vulnerable to the global economic downturn. The decline in global trade led to a drop in demand for many African commodities, such as diamonds, coffee, and rubber, which in turn led to rising unemployment. For example, in the once-prosperous Katanga province of the Democratic Republic of the Congo, 60 percent of enterprises closed and more than 300,000 people were laid off in 2009. Income from remittances by Africans living in developing countries also declined as workers faced the consequences of the global crisis in those countries. In Kenya, for example, remittances declined by 13.3 percent in late 2008 compared with the same period in 2007. Domestic investment also declined precipitously. For example, the Nigerian stock exchange lost 66 percent of its value in 2009.

The **World Trade Organization** (WTO) has been both praised and criticized as the consummate representative of globalization. The WTO was created in 1995 as part of the **General Agreement on Tariffs and Trade** (GATT), which was part of a postwar process to lower tariffs. The WTO is an international organization for negotiating, monitoring, and regulating international trade agreements. The goal of the WTO is to help producers of goods and services conduct business without fear of trade restrictions and government intervention. Consumers and producers benefit by having secure supplies of goods at low prices and having greater choices of products, raw materials, and services (Figure 4.3). Producers and exporters can predict that foreign markets will remain open to them, resulting in a more "prosperous, peaceful and accountable economic world," as the WTO's website states (WTO 2011).

In lieu of globalization's varied and sometimes ambiguous outcomes for countries endowed with either rich natural resources and poor governance or states with rampant corruption and economic inequities, increasing divides among globalization's adherents, skeptics, and pro-globalization perspectives are apparent. Noted economist Joseph E. Stiglitz in *Globalization and Its Discontents* (2002) argues that globalization, far from improving the living standards in developing countries, diminished them and heightened inequality. In contrast to perspectives that celebrated the power of markets to bring cheap goods and products to an astounding

Figure 4.3 The availability of American, British, and local goods at this mountaintop snack bar in North
    Africa demonstrates the effectiveness of global free trade in distributing market goods.

Source: Mark Allen Peterson.

number of people around the globe, Stiglitz found that economic globalization widened the gap
between rich and poor countries. In his estimation, global economic institutions like the WTO,
leave these states at the behest of powerful countries owing to little governing power since the
principles and rules are designed by rich countries who maintain a comparative advantage in
monetary and financial institutions. Stiglitz points to neoliberal financial institutions like the
International Monetary Fund and World Bank, whose policies such as structural adjustment
decimated social spending on health, education and other services for vulnerable populations
in developing states.

Critics of globalization, neoliberalism, and the WTO argue that these agreements are part of
a corporate-inspired agenda targeting any protectionist policy that might negatively influence
free trade and benefit citizens over companies. Arguments have been made that the WTO can
essentially override any law meant to protect workers or the environment if the law can be seen
as restricting the capability of corporations to trade freely. Joseph Stiglitz points out that in the
1990s, while global income rose by 2.5 percent, the number of people living in poverty increased
by 100 million and that 43 percent of the world's population lived on less than $2.00 per day.
Stiglitz criticizes the policies of global financial institutions, particularly the **World Bank** and the
International Monetary Fund (IMF), for these growing economic inequalities. One of his major
arguments is that rich nations, like the United States, became wealthy in part by protecting
their own industries when they were too immature to compete on a larger global level. Yet the

current policies of the IMF and the World Bank do not take these developmental issues into account when they authorize loans that require the borrowing nations to liberalize their markets and increase external trade rather than protect their industries. The effects of these policies are ongoing and scholars like Kwame Akonor argue that periodic non-compliance with IMF policies in African states touted for remarkable growth—such as Ghana—were the only way to sustain austerity measures, which the population bore the brunt of in myriad ways. According to Stiglitz, recent advances in economic theory demonstrate that markets only function optimally in places where people have lots of information with which to make reasonable choices, which is almost never true in developing countries.

These criticisms of neoliberal policies are not only of theoretical importance; they influence political activity at many levels. This has been readily apparent in Latin America. In 2005, the Summit of the Americas failed to establish an agreement on the Free Trade Area of the Americas (FTAA). The **Summit of the Americas** is a set of meetings held every two years between leaders of countries in North America, South America, Central America, and the Caribbean to discuss economic issues. It was established in the early 1990s to allow the leaders of the **Organization of American States** (OAS) to discuss the implementation of the principles of the **Washington Consensus**, a set of policies aimed at instituting free markets for the entire Western Hemisphere. These principles included fiscal discipline, anti-inflation policies, privatization of state enterprises, elimination of state interference in the economy, deregulation of the private sector, and liberalization of investment policies. At the first Summit of the Americas in 1994, Latin American leaders had endorsed the economic principles outlined by the Washington Consensus and began reforming their economies to conform to their policies. These reforms, however, failed to produce expected economic growth or to raise the living standards of the 50 percent of Latin Americans living in poverty. Across Latin America, people began electing governments that promised to alter or to abandon these neoliberal policies and to reinstitute social programs to mitigate growing poverty.

The election of Hugo Chavez in Venezuela in 1998, despite strong US opposition to his candidacy, became a symbol of the threat to the policies of the Washington Consensus. Chavez began his Bolivarian Revolution to replace those policies with a Latin American economic community based not on competition but on cooperation to further regional goals of increased economic and social equality. By 2005, the strains between Latin America and the United States became clear when FTAA policies were rejected. More ardent voices in this debate argued that neoliberal policies were inherently imperialist, and, with Chavez, called for a new "socialism for the 21st century."

A very different critique of classical economics has arisen in anthropology, sociology, social psychology, geography, and other humanistic sciences concerning the claim that there is a universal form of economic rationality. For states who became independent starting in the second half of the twentieth century, economic development is jagged. These states, whose economic systems emerged in the postwar period, are often termed post-colonial and are located in Asia and Africa, but primarily in the latter. Virtually all 55 African states became crippled by the consequences of imported economic and political institutions. Cobbled together by "**hegemony on a shoestring**" in which these vast territories were governed with minimal investment, their autonomy came to a halt through brutal conquest by former colonial empires that include Britain, France, Germany, Spain, Portugal and Belgium. The mechanisms that would later produce dependency in these post-colonial states reinforced a trajectory of economic development that was largely based on extraction of raw materials, natural resources and minerals as exports to developed and industrialized countries. The effects of an exclusively driven focus on primary commodity exports essentially meant little industrialization and state-led development that reflected many weaknesses such as bloated bureaucracies, nationalization of sectors like oil, or energy/utilities—which tripled external debt and exacerbated ongoing flaws—eventually leading to toppled governments in the early 1990s. The absences of key institutions to support the rule of law and accountable government in effect created a preponderance of patrimonialism in which government officials use the state as a means of personal accumulation (Oloruntoba & Falola 2020: 2). Fukuyama (2010) points to the difficulties of impersonal modern states, which in the case of African countries have been difficult to maintain. Some like Mahmood Mamdani in *Citizen and Subject* (2018) argue that these states were never emancipated owing to what Nicolas Van de Walle, Crawford Young others note are the deeply embedded mechanisms of patrimonialism and neo-patrimonialism—which are based on personal connections to a 'patron' in exchange for political favors as well as kinship or personal reciprocity.

Following the adoption of intervention packages of loans by both international financial institutions, the **World Bank** and the **International Monetary Fund (IMF)**, who acted as a lender of last resort with the second intended to support macroeconomic stability, reduce the role of the state in the economy, the price for such assistance was numerous conditionalities. Local populations, presumably the intended beneficiaries, had virtually no input in their government's decision to adopt these controversial programs which as some note were "ill-timed and grossly inappropriate for addressing the challenges facing the continent" (Mkandawire and Soudo, cited from Oloruntoba & Falola 2019). Although the first state to fall was Mexico which defaulted on its loans from the **World Bank** and **IMF**, African countries soon followed. Decades later, the structural adjustment programs (SAPS), though no longer quite in vogue owing to ambiguous outcomes and few success stories around the world, remain present in the form of the **Washington Consensus**, or a basket of policies that support privatization, export-oriented growth, minimal state subsidies and in short market-driven policies that anchor free trade. The emergence of key states and economic giants like China (who has supplanted Japan's spot as the second largest economy and the United States from its premier status as the largest) has produced a "**Beijing Consensus**." This consensus arguably functions as a counterweight to the Washington consensus, which refers to the constellation of power that stems from the World Bank, IMF and the United States at the helm. The Beijing consensus is thus named for the growing and remarkable power of China whose footprint, as some argue, has supplanted the US as a hegemon whose growing power earned it the moniker of the "rising dragon."

Sustainability

This empirical critique of economic assumptions gained some attention as global concerns arose about the sustainability of economic development. **Sustainability** refers to the capacity of a political economic system to meet the needs of present communities without reducing the ability of future generations to meet their own needs.

The debates on the universal applicability of formal rational theory led to a host of studies on economic and agricultural activities at the household and community level that seem to preserve the natural resource base. For example, Robert Netting found that relatively self-sufficient farmers in areas as diverse as Nigeria and Swiss Alpine valleys manage resources in such a way as to preserve the environment on which their economic activity depends. These resource-management activities not only constitute a form of rational utility but also provide a model for possible future forms of sustainable production. These studies provide important information on the complexity of human–environment interaction and describe forms of sustainable economic activities that are useful for creating more sustainable food production and distribution systems in an increasingly crowded and resource-scarce world. The underlying argument is that perpetual growth and pure economic efficiency is not sustainable. It cannot long continue in a world of limited resources.

This work fits well with serious criticism of the environmental consequences of unregulated liberal-economic decision making. The most famous of these early critical voices came from *The Limits to Growth* models (Meadows et al. 1972) where scientists developed computer models predicting that economic growth could not continue indefinitely due to the limited availability of natural resources, particularly oil, and the inability of the earth's systems to replenish themselves as rapidly as they were being depleted. Using then-new concepts such as **carrying capacity**, they outlined the consequences of human systems of economic growth in the context of limited and finite global resources. They argued that continuing growth-oriented economic development would lead to the exhaustion of the earth's resources and the subsequent collapse of global economic and environmental systems. These debates initiated a drive by economists to reformulate economic models to better understand ideas of valuation of natural resources.

The well-documented environmental problems often created by industrial capitalism sparked strong arguments from within the capitalist camp as well. Economists Robert Costanza, Kenneth Boulding, Herman E. Daley, and others developed the field of **ecological economics** in the early 1990s (Costanza 1991). Convinced that existing forms of economic organization were incapable of guaranteeing sustainable production or healthy ecological systems, these economists sought to include a reasonable method of explicating the value of such things as clean water, vibrant environmental systems, and future resource needs. Sustainable development goals that were formally adopted in 2015 by the United Nations General Assembly are still in progress. However, a key challenge is financing: "how to mobilize the billions of dollars required to address key goals articulated by the body with the input of individuals across the globe and member states…which will require leadership as some argue from the United States as well as China an economic and global power" (Morris & Haibing, 2017: 74).

As new markets and products for consumers proliferate, the demand for superfoods and fast fashion, for example, is expanding extractive processes that appear to have long-term consequences. This approach to accounting discounts the well-being of future generations. Ecological perspectives have begun to reconsider this narrow form of accounting and have presented accounting methods to translate the future values of environmental impacts into equivalent values in today's monetary units in order to better formulate environmental constraints in economic modeling. In 1987, a report by the Brundtland Commission made sustainable development the official principle endorsed by the United Nations. It continues to gain currency with more and more states in both the developed and developing world recognizing that resilience and adaptability in a changing world of finite resources requires innovative and transformative solutions (see Bousquet et al. 2016). Rising sea levels across global cities imply a number of challenges and as urban populations increase, the demand for services and use of resources will likely require changes that have a variety of implications for economic development and livelihood approaches. Studies by Rademaker et al. (2018) acknowledge as much. Drought and water security concerns are mounting, as is the need to address resilience strategies in places like Jharkhand in India, the world's most populous state, as a number of scholars recognize. Food security, energy access and agricultural development are also key arenas for sustainable development as global populations rise to almost 10 billion by 2050 according to the United Nations Department of Economic and Social Affairs Population division. By the end of the century, Pison (2019) predicts that the global population will number eleven billion, which is historic and unprecedented.

Conclusion

The global economic crisis led to dramatic social and political upheavals as people in many countries lost faith in their governments. In addition to those already mentioned, several waves of protests swept the world. In April 2009, protests in London over global economic policy, banking executives' salaries and bonuses following bailouts, climate change, and the war on terror were timed to coincide with the **Group of Twenty (G20)** summit. Although the majority of the protests were peaceful, many protesters were forcibly detained and there were widespread accusations of police brutality, including the death of one protester at the hands of police. The following month saw a series of international protests in conjunction with May First, International Labor Day. Traditional marches turned violent in Germany and Venezuela, and banks and shops were attacked in Turkey. May Day protests also occurred in Cuba, Hong Kong, Italy, Japan, the Philippines, Russia, and Spain. In 2011, a wave of protests swept across the United States. These included protests in Ohio and Wisconsin in the spring over state efforts to overturn union protections for public workers. Later that year, thousands turned out in New York for weeks of "Occupy Wall Street" protests, followed by sympathetic protests in Boston, Chicago, Albuquerque, New Mexico, Spokane, Washington, and Los Angeles. Figure 4.4 shows an "occupy" camp in Washington, DC. In the wake of this unrest, new political parties and projects have emerged, such as the "Abenomics" program of new Japanese Prime Minister Shinzo Abe. New social movements have emerged around the globe as groups seek to deal with deeply unpopular austerity measures, including cuts in public wages, tax hikes, and reductions in social spending. Such turbulence seems likely to grow in the near future until a new economic stability is established internationally.

The capacity for a market collapse or banking crisis in one country to cause economic problems in myriad others because of the integration of global markets demonstrates why economics is a

Figure 4.4 In the wake of the global economic downturn, anti-establishment "Occupy" movements like this one in Washington, DC, in 2011, took over public spaces in major cities around the world.

Source: Mark Allen Peterson.

crucial aspect of an interdisciplinary approach to international studies. Economics also provides insight into the ways people use resources, and exposes the pressures that create unsustainable uses of land, water, labor, and disposal of waste products. Economics maps the web of transactions across which global flows of capital, technology, and **migrant labor** flow. And it demonstrates how heightened and uneven dynamics associated with our liberal economic order and wealth can create economic disparities that produce strikes, protests, and revolutions. Close attention to economic realities is crucial to any effort at creating policies intended to improve human lives in this interconnected world.

References

AfDB (African Development Bank Group). 2009. "Impact of the Crisis on African Economies—Sustaining Growth and Poverty Reduction: African Perspectives and Recommendations to the G20." *Report from the Committee of African Finance Ministers and Central Bank Governors.* www.afdb.org/fileadmin/uploads/afdb/ Documents/Generic-Documents/impact%20of%20the%20crisis%20and%20recommendations%20 to%20the%20G20%20-%20March%2021.pdf

Beams, Nick. 2008. "The World Economic Crisis: A Marxist Analysis." The World Socialist Web Site. www.wsws.org/en/articles/2008/12/nbe1-d19.html

Blackman, Andrew. 2005. "What Is the Soul of Socialism?" *Monthly Review* 57 (3): 104–13.

Bousquet, F., A. Botta, L. Alinovi, O. Barreteau, D. Bossio, K. Brown, P. Caron, P. Cury, M. D'Errico, F. DeClerck, H. Dessard, E. Enfors Kautsky, C. Fabricius, C. Folke, L. Fortmann, B. Hubert, D. Magda, R. Mathevet, R. B. Norgaard, A. Quinlan, and C. Staver. 2016. "Resilience and Development: Mobilizing for Transformation." *Ecology and Society* 21 (3): 40.

Costanza, Robert, ed. 1991. *Ecological Economics: The Science and Management of Sustainability.* New York: Columbia University Press.

Elyachar, Julia. 2005. *Markets of Dispossession: NGOs, Economic Development and the State in Cairo.* Durham, NC: Duke University Press.

Escobar, Arturo. 1995. *Encountering Development: The Making and Unmaking of the Third World.* Princeton, NJ: Princeton University Press.

Evans, Mike. 2001. *Persistence of the Gift: Tongan Tradition in Transnational Context.* Waterloo, ON: Wilfred Laurier University Press.

Friedman, Thomas L. 1999. *The Lexus and the Olive Tree: Understanding Globalization.* New York: Farrar, Straus and Giroux.

Fukuyama, F. 2010. "Democracy's Past and Future: Transitions to the Rule of Law." *Journal of Democracy* 21 (1), 33–44.

Gilpin, Robert. 1987. *Political Economy of International Relations.* New Haven, CT: Princeton University Press.

Halperin, Rhoda H. 1994. *Cultural Economies: Past and Present.* Austin: University of Texas Press.

Hermann, Gretchen M. 1997. "Gift or Commodity: What Changes Hands in the U.S. Garage Sale?" *American Ethnologist* 24 (4): 910–30.

Kaur, N., Steinbach, D., Agarwal, A. and Manuel, C. 2017. "Building resilience to climate change: MGNREGS and climate-induced droughts in Sikkim." iied. https://pubs.iied.org/sites/default/files/pdfs/ migrate/10188IIED.pdf

Mamdani, Mahmood. 2018. *Citizen and Subject: Contemporary Africa and the Legacy of Late Colonialism.* Princeton, NJ: Princeton University Press.

Meadows, Donella H., Denise L. Meadows, Jørgen Randers, and William W. Behrens III. 1972. *The Limits to Growth.* New York: Universe Books.

Mkandawire, P. Thandika, and Charles Chukwuma Soludo. 1999. *Our Continent, Our Future: African Perspectives on Structural Adjustment.* IDRC.

Morris, S., Haibing, Z., Goodman, M., Celico, A., Elliott, D., Jin, F., ... Xijun, Z. 2017. *Parallel Perspectives on the Global Economic Order: A U.S.-China Essay Collection* (pp. 74–83, Rep.) (Remler D. & Yu Y., eds.). Center for Strategic and International Studies (CSIS). doi:10.2307/resrep23187.13

Oloruntoba, Samuel Ojo. and Falola, Toyin, eds. 2020. *The Palgrave Handbook of African Political Economy.* New York: Palgrave Macmillan.

Pison, G. 2019. "Tous les pays du monde (2019)." *Population & Societies* 569 (8), 1–8.

Pollin, Robert, Justine Burns, and James Heintz. 2002. "Global Apparel Production and Sweatshop Labor: Can Raising Retail Prices Finance Living Wages?" Political Economy Research Institute. Working Papers Series. Number 19.

Rademaker, M., Jans, K. and Verhagen, P. 2018. *Making Cities in Conflict Areas More Resilient, a Conceptual Iteration: Using the Climate Resilience and Security Monitor for Policies in Practice.* Hague: Netherlands Institute of International Relations 'Clingendael' and Center for Climate and Security.

Rostow, W. W. 1960. *The Stages of Economic Growth: A Non-Communist Manifesto.* Cambridge: Cambridge University Press.

Sachs, Jeffery. 1998. "International Economics: Unlocking the Mysteries of Globalization." *Foreign Policy* 110: 97–111.

Sahlins, Marshall. 1972. *Stone Age Economics.* Chicago: Aldine-Atherton.

Scholte, Jan Art. 2005. *Globalization: A Critical Introduction.* New York: Macmillan.

Smith, Adam. [1776] 2000. *An Inquiry Into the Nature and Causes of the Wealth of Nations.* New York: Modern Library.

Stiglitz, Joseph E. 2002. *Globalization and Its Discontents.* New York: W. W. Norton.

United States Senate. 2011. "Wall Street and the Financial Crisis: Anatomy of a Financial Collapse." http://hsgac.senate.gov/public/_files/Financial_Crisis/FinancialCrisisReport.pdf

WTO (World Trade Organization). 2011. www.wto.org

Further Reading

Books

Akonor, Kwame. 2013. *Africa and IMF Conditionality: The Unevenness of Compliance, 1983–2000.* London: Routledge.

Frieden, Jeffrey. 2007. *Global Capitalism: Its Fall and Rise in the Twentieth Century.* New York: W. W. Norton.

Gilpin, Robert. 2001. *Global Political Economy: Understanding the International Economic Order.* Princeton, NJ: Princeton University Press.

Gilpin, Robert. 1978. *The Political Economy of International Relations.* Princeton: NJ: Princeton University Press.

Marx, Karl, and Friedrich Engels. 1967. *The Communist Manifesto.* New York: Penguin Books.

Tett, Gillian. 2009. *Fool's Gold: How Unrestrained Greed Corrupted a Dream, Shattered Global Markets and Unleashed a Catastrophe.* New York: Free Press.

Varoufakis, Yanis. 1998. *Foundations of Economics: A Beginner's Companion.* London: Routledge.

Journals

Economic Affairs. onlinelibrary.wiley.com/journal/10.1111/(ISSN)1468-0270

The Economist. www.economist.com

The Financial Times. www.ft.com

International Economics and Economic Policy. link.springer.com/journal/10368

Wall Street Journal. www.wsj.com

Films

B.A.T.A.M. (2005). Liam Dalzell, Per Erik Eriksson, Johan Lindquist, directors.

Life & Debt (2001). Stephanie Black, director.

The Golf War (2000). Jen Schradie and Matt DeVries, directors.

King for a Day (2001). Alex Gabbay, director.

The Perfect Famine (2002). Steve Bradshaw and Chris Walker, directors.

Websites

Economic Policy Institute. www.epi.org

History of Economic Thought. www.hetwebsite.net/het

Political Economy Research Institute. www.peri.umass.edu

The world's first and only stand-up economist. www.standupeconomist.com

Independent: www.independent.co.uk/news/world/africa/sudan-revolution-women-uprising-democratic-transition-army-bashir-a9038786.html/

https://population.un.org/wpp/Graphs/DemographicProfiles/Line/900

Chapter 5

Political Science and International Studies

What makes political science distinct? Many of the social sciences have subfields that use the word political: Political Economy, Political Geography, Political Anthropology, and Political Psychology are all both course and textbook titles. Political Scientists clearly do not have any sort of monopoly on the study of things political. There might be a temptation to focus on the word science as what distinguishes study in that discipline from others, but all of the above are "social sciences," and it would be hard to convince most psychologists that they are less scientific than political scientists. Some of us think the use of "science" is even a little pretentious. Besides, Princeton University has a Department of Politics, and at Harvard, it is a Department of Government, so prestigious institutions leave out the science in their title and clearly do just fine.

Whatever name is given to the department at a university, political scientists focus their study of politics around the notion of power. Who has power, what is the basis of that power, how is it exercised, when is it resisted, and how is it lost? Many students assume that their political science classes will be largely about governments, and even if power is an organizing concept, it is the political power held by elected and other governmental officials that is most important. While it is fair to say that the study of politics and power in the political science discipline frequently engages public sector institutions and the theories and practice of governance from the local to global levels, political scientists produce insights on developments far removed from formal politics.

The traditional primary fields in political science are American Politics, Comparative Politics, International Relations, and Political Theory or Political Philosophy. In some places, Public Administration and Public Law may be treated as their own fields rather than subfields of American Politics. Political Economy might also be a distinct field, or potentially a subfield of American and Comparative Politics, and International Political Economy could be a subfield of International Relations. Political Scientists employ diverse methodologies and theoretical frameworks across the different fields of the discipline.

At some colleges and universities, International Studies is combined with Political Science in the same department. Many students even choose to combine the major of International Studies with that of Political Science. Comparative Politics and International Relations are the two fields in political science that receive the most attention for classes and students in International Studies. Comparative politics scholars are interested in the domestic politics of countries, typically not including the United States. Comparativists may develop single case studies in depth, they might choose to do carefully selected paired comparisons, or compare several cases up to large multi-country studies. Those studies could be as straightforward as comparing the outcomes of presidential and parliamentary systems, or they may try to determine the causal explanations for differential political economic development in any number of nation-states.

DOI: 10.4324/9781003028314-7

Much of the comparative work in political science done in the past has been by area studies specialists. A Latin Americanist or Africanist accumulates deep knowledge about a particular region of the world, and that allows them to compare Brazil and Mexican political economic development, Kenyan and Nigerian political systems, or public policy in Chile and Argentina. Traditionally, this work has been the result of lengthy field work and site visits that are not entirely dissimilar to that done by anthropologists. Other comparativists use sophisticated statistical techniques to draw conclusions about politics in large numbers of countries; their methodological approach has much in common with work done by some in economics departments.

For political "scientists," quantitative methodological approaches offered an opportunity to use mathematics-based models and statistical techniques, which would demonstrate the rigor of those in the "hard" or natural sciences. The ascendancy of quantitative work led to a backlash from those who do qualitative work. In 2000, one political scientist, calling himself "Mr. Perestroika," led a challenge to the national association of political scientists (American Political Science Association/APSA) and their flagship journal, *The American Political Science Review* (APSR). Their argument was that the discipline risked losing the valuable deep dives into the archives or field work that had produced important political science insights in the past. While the debate has not gone away, journals such as *New Political Science* and *Perspectives on Politics* were founded to provide outlets for qualitative work that some thought did not get enough access in the APSR. Two decades after Mr. Perestroika made an appearance, most political science departments seem to accept the idea that good work can be done through a number of different approaches, both qualitative and quantitative.

International Relations as a field of political science is primarily concerned with understanding events and relations that take place at the global level. Among the issues of study are the diplomatic and economic relations between nation-states, organizations trying to bring order at the global level, movements and activism by groups that extend beyond national borders, and the making of foreign policy by nation-states. The terms international studies and international relations are similar enough that for students and others they may not seem to be significantly different. As academic fields, the primary distinction is that the study of international relations takes place within the single discipline of political science, while international studies assumes an interdisciplinary approach to understanding global developments. One of those disciplines is political science, but it is no more important than several other disciplines, and even the exploration of political or diplomatic relations between countries would be interdisciplinary in International Studies classrooms.

Comparative Politics Questions

In **comparative politics**, there is the same tendency that exists in political science more generally to work in the area of institutions and political behavior as opposed to political activism, mobilization, and resistance. Democratization, political and economic development, and issues related to political systems and governmental efficacy are of particular interest in the subfield. Historically, there have been a wide range of types of government and the means by which those governments were legitimized (or not). For a long time, birth into an accepted royal family was the basis of political power and governance. We saw some evolution toward **constitutional monarchies**, in which the non-elected members of the royal family shared power with elected officials, usually operating within the parameters of a constitution. Interestingly, the constitutional monarchy of the United Kingdom still lacks a written constitution. In some cases, the divine right associated with a royal family was expanded to the idea that religious leaders themselves should rule the country as a **theocracy**, given their access to the necessary divine guidance to manage the affairs of state. Even without divine guidance or a royal family, other forms of oligarchy, or governing by the few, have emerged across the globe. One example is **military rule**, where a single or at least a small number of military leaders take control of the government and largely exclude civilians from any decision making. Map 5.1 shows types of governance.

Where royal families, religious leaders, and military officials do not have disproportionate influence over government, there are still a range of government types possible. In the twenty-first century, much of the world's population is governed by leaders who claim legitimacy by way of elections. Holding elections does not automatically make them fair, of course. In some countries, we talk about **one-party states**, or a system in which a single political party is able to monopolize political power, even if it must occasionally hold and win elections to do so. There is also considerable variation among democracies as well. The two most common systems are presidential and parliamentary. In the US, students are familiar with a **presidential system**, in which the executive is elected separately from any legislative electoral outcome, and once in office holds powers that are only somewhat circumscribed by other branches of government, including the legislature. In a **parliamentary system**, there is not the same separation of powers between the legislature and the executive. The head of government, usually a Prime Minister, is only in that position by virtue of a vote by members of the Parliament. There is a lengthy comparative politics literature on the strengths and weaknesses of the two systems. The absence of gridlock in a parliamentary system might suggest an advantage of efficiency, and the Prime Minister is more easily held accountable given the opportunity to remove them by a simple vote of no confidence in most cases. Presidential systems, such as the United States, may have an advantage in that the balance of powers puts a check on radical changes by the executive branch, or it might be that it is too difficult to enact needed legislation with a divided government. Some "strong" presidential systems, such as has been the case in Latin America, do not have the same checks on the executive as we have seen historically in the US, and that might allow for an elected leader to operate during their term with very little accountability.

Beyond the varieties of democratic systems, the process of becoming more democratic is widely studied by political scientists and provides us with a window into the work done in this subfield of the discipline. The work on democratization necessarily begins with the definition of democracy itself. Democracy is a contested concept, signifying that there are different definitions put forth by political scientists based at least in part on their ideological preferences. A minimalist definition of democracy focuses on formal democratic procedures, usually beginning with the need for fair, free, and frequent elections. The alliterative adjectives raise even more questions: would elections held every four or six years be frequent enough? Are elections fair if only candidates who can raise tens of millions of dollars have a reasonable chance to compete and win? Of course, if we look around the world and observe the sorts of undemocratic systems that exist in any number of countries, these questions may seem trivial. For lots of people, getting to choose their leaders by way of elections, even if flawed, would be a desirable move toward democracy. We might add some tests for transparency and accountability to the election question, and for many students in the United States, democracy has been adequately defined.

Other political scientists, however, would raise the stakes in their definitions of democracy. It would not be enough to say that the electoral procedures, or the processes by which elected officials are held accountable exist, but they would want to measure democratic participation. Do some groups of people vote at a higher percentage than others? That is, there may be no laws that prevent rural, indigenous Guatemalans from voting, but if their turnout is well below wealthier, lighter-skinned, urban Guatemalans, does that seem undemocratic? Or even if we look at the United States, where the growing percentage of Latinx and African American folks is more than 30 percent of the population in 2021, but there are only 9 of 100 US Senators who are from those communities, should we question the degree of democracy in our own country? If

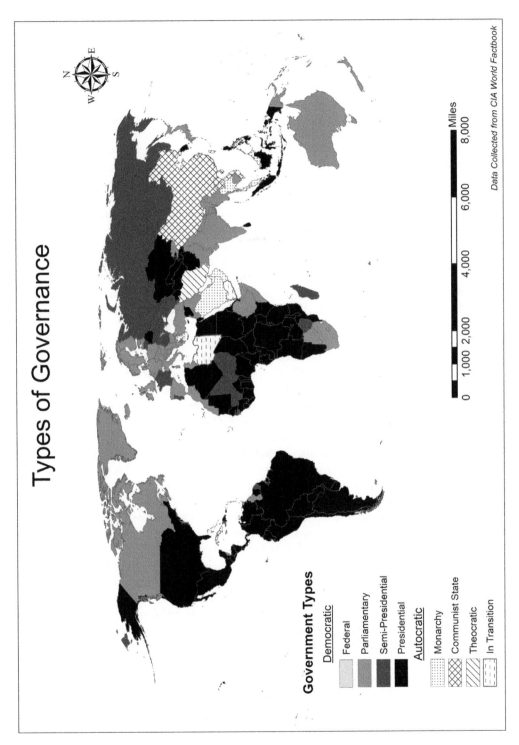

Map 5.1 Types of Governance.

women have had the vote since 1920, but no woman has ever won the presidency, does that at least raise questions about the quality of democracy in the United States?

At a time when democratic socialists are raising their profiles in the United States, we might move further along the spectrum to think about the concept of social democracy. Might there be degrees of economic inequality that are incompatible with political democracy? That is, social democrats (rather than democratic socialists) would argue that democracy requires a degree of relative economic and social inequality in society as the outcome of political processes. Is there a definition of social democracy that we might conceptualize as the goal of nation-states at the level of economic development we see in the US/Canada, Western Europe, and Japan?

Now that we have considered how complex the mere conceptualization of democracy might be, we turn to the question for comparative political scientists as to why states transition from authoritarian governments to more democratic systems. Traditionally, many in the discipline argued that it was a question of political culture. Nation-states with a democratic political culture were democracies, and those with an authoritarian political culture could not be democratic. The problem with that explanation was that it left the origin of political culture unaddressed, and it left us with a black hole of sorts in which the change to a democratic political culture was difficult to imagine. Some political scientists talked about a modernization theory, in which during capitalist economic development, a middle class came to embrace democratic values, but other political scientists provided examples of how the "middle class" was as likely to support authoritarian governments as it was changes toward democracy. That "optimistic equation" about the relationship between economic development and political development failed empirical tests across the globe.

If political culture did not explain democratization, then perhaps there were more structural variables that might be considered. The discipline returned to the focus on power, and the question of democratization became a struggle between pro-democracy forces in society and those who supported and benefited from the authoritarian government in place. That shifted the democracy protagonists from middle classes or even enlightened elites to those in society who had the most to gain from a new political system that was open to more groups and classes. In nation-states with authoritarian governments, that could be peasants, the working poor, the working class more generally, or perhaps middle classes excluded by the authoritarian governments. In that case, democracy was seen as a redistribution of political power from the elite to the rest of the population. The "middle class" might go either way in that struggle, but the strength of the working class (rural and urban) became a key variable in the democratization process. At the end of the twentieth century, students might think about Eastern European cases such as Poland, and in the early twenty-first century, Arab Spring movements to overthrow entrenched authoritarian regimes. Does the strength of the pro-democracy pressure from below versus the strength of the anti-democracy regime explain the likelihood of a transition to democracy? The strength of the pro-democracy movement is affected by variables including organization, leadership, alliances across different identities, resources, and sheer numbers.

For students of international studies, then, political science introduces questions of relative power in civil and political society to explain outcomes. There are other variables to be sure. Do international factors affect the likelihood of democratizations? The demonstration or contagion effect seems likely when we observe "waves" of democracy, and there may be cases of external forces exerting pressure that contributes to democratization. Perhaps the Pope's support of the Solidarity movement in Poland is a positive example, and global failures to respond effectively to the Arab Spring mobilization is a negative one. International studies students might consider other comparative cases as they come to their own conclusions about the variables that explain democratization. The authoritarian Soviet Union moved toward elections and other seemingly democratic processes in the late 1980s and early 1990s, while the Chinese Communist Party has continued to maintain its authoritarian control. Keeping in mind that we are not making a claim that Russia is a democracy, what explains the movement in the direction of "democratization" in the Soviet Union and then in Russia, while China has not made a significant political transition? China is not the only case, of course; one might look at North Korea or Saudi Arabia and ask the same question: why no transition from authoritarianism to more democratic processes? What variables explain the failure to become democracies?

In several countries that hold relatively fair and frequent elections, leaders described as populist have been winning lots of votes in a variety of countries in the first couple of decades of the twenty-first century. Populism is a concept that is hard to define for political scientists, in part because it is used to describe leaders on the political left such as former President Hugo Chavez in Venezuela, as well as leaders on the right such as Hungarian Prime Minister Viktor Orbán. In the United States, both Vermont Senator and former presidential candidate Bernie Sanders and former US President Donald Trump are sometimes described as populists, even as they are located pretty far apart on the political spectrum. There are some characteristics of populism that most political scientists can agree upon, even as many scholars challenge the idea that it is a useful concept in the discipline. Principally, the idea of populism is premised on a division in society between the people or the "popular" groups and classes and the "elite." The elite are found in the economic, political, and even the intellectual spheres. Those usually allied elites are seen as corrupt, self-serving, and detached from the general population. Candidates for office, then, attack elites and promise to rule in the interests of the people as a whole. The attacks may look outside the country for elites, such as foreign investors, the International Monetary Fund (IMF), or even an external government. The nationalism associated with populism may include criticism of immigrants, who while not elite, are contributing to the problems experienced by the native-born population of the country. In Europe, the populist movements have tended to be on the political right with an ethno-religious nationalism as part of the appeal. In Latin America, the populist movements have tended to be on the political left, with a critique of domestic elites and even US imperialism as part of the argument. President Jair Bolsonaro, who took office in Brazil on January 1, 2019, offers a current example of Latin American populism on the political right wing. The political spectrum cover systems both left, right and center (see Figure 5.1).

In the United Kingdom, the second decade of the twenty-first century has seen examples of both left and right populism. The Labour Party turned away from the centrism of the Tony Blair faction and elected the self-proclaimed Democratic Socialist, Jeremy Corbyn, as its leader in 2015. That same year, the Conservative Party under Prime Minister David Cameron moved forward on its promise to hold a referendum on British participation in the European Union, which was scheduled for June 2016. Faced with the straightforward question, Should the United Kingdom remain a member of the European Union or leave the union, more than 72 percent of registered voters turned out, and 51.9 percent of them cast a ballot to leave in what was seen as a "populist" movement. The political system in Britain found it very difficult to deal with the issue of Brexit after that vote. The resignation of Cameron's successor, Prime Minister Theresa May, in 2019 provided some evidence of the challenge of moving forward on the wishes of the majority of referendum voters to exit the EU. For comparativists, the question of the role of referenda such as the Brexit vote, voter behavior and populism, the effectiveness of a parliamentary

Figure 5.1 **The political spectrum.**

system, roles played by political parties, and the importance of political leadership are traditional topics of study. The various political, security, and economic relationships that member states have with the European Union provide considerable interest for international relations scholars. It is hard to imagine that any international studies student would want to try and understand the Brexit phenomenon without reference to the theories and methods of political science.

For students of international studies, developments ranging from Brexit to the Arab Spring to Occupy Wall Street to the 2019 fuel tax protests in France by the *gilets jaunes* (yellow vests), are understood by some as populist movements. The political and economic elites in the country dismiss these movements as emotional or irrational responses by segments of the population who don't know any better. As we try to understand the world in the twenty-first century, however, we need to figure out the role played by globalization, nationalism, economic insecurity, and the desire for greater political power that are manifested in the movements described as populist. For those who might be sympathetic to movements described as populist, it is interesting to think about why many people automatically assume that calling someone a populist is a criticism. Populism is difficult to define, and as a contested concept, challenging for political scientists to use in their analyses. The various movements across the globe seem indicative of a widespread dissatisfaction with the political and economic status quo felt by non-elite populations in a number of different national contexts.

Populism is a topic that comparative political scientists should be well-positioned to explain. But it is hard to imagine that we wouldn't benefit from contributions by historians, who could explain past examples of the phenomenon, or sociologists, who might be able to dig deeper into the study of individuals in their society to provide insights into the appeal of populism. For that matter, to understand the growth of populist movements in the West might require insights from the field of international relations related to the movement of people and goods from low-income to high-income countries.

Approaches to International Relations

The field of International Relations (IR) in political science is concerned with the interactions of people that cross the borders of states. In the most traditional sense, those relations took place at the level of the states. The **state** refers to the central political authority over a given territory and people who live within that physical space. As a shorthand, you might conceptualize the state as all of the institutions of government, including but not limited to, the executive branch, bureaucracy, courts, military, and internal revenue service. It is important to emphasize that the state is more than the people who may be holding office or working in these institutions at any given time. The nation is another important concept for political science, and it needs to be distinguished from the idea of a country. **Nation** refers to a given population that identifies together based on some characteristics that might include a common history, language, culture, or even set of beliefs. People might also identify with a given nation due to a shared ethnic or religious identity. In most cases, the identification as part of a nation coincides with a belief that the members of a nation should have their own system of governing. Students will sometimes see the phrase **nation-state**, which implies that the sovereign state includes only members of a single nation. In the real world, of course, there are lots of states that include people of different nations within their territorial borders. In the United States, we might think about the more than 500 Native American groupings that are federally recognized as Indian Nations. To the north, would the French-speaking population of Quebec identify as a distinct nation, whether some would prefer to remain within the Canadian state, and others seek separate state sovereignty? Looking around the world, there are any number of examples of people who see themselves as members of a nation without a (perceived legitimate) state, including Kurds, Palestinians, or the Rohingya population.

In the study of international relations, the focus is on relations among and between states, although issues of nations and nationalisms may influence the diplomacy, treaties, and agreements reached by existing states. The field of IR is also concerned with conflicts up to and including terrorism and wars. Those constitute only one part of the interactions in the field of IR. The trade of goods and services, as well as foreign investment are among the economic interactions of interest to IR scholars. The movements of people across borders, whether as migrants or tourists, as an area of study reminds us that the interactions studied can be at the level of individuals, both in government and outside.

International relations scholars talk about different levels of analysis, meaning that students may want to look at how individual actors behave, they may want to begin their analysis at the level of the global system, or they might prefer something in between. Between the individual and the system, an analysis could look at groups and classes—social movements, non-profit organizations, labor unions, peasant groups, or employer associations. Or, what is more typical, the IR study could be at the level of the state, or the institutions of government.

Traditionally, two theoretical frameworks dominated the field of International Relations: Realism and idealism (or liberalism, as it is now more widely known). As a theoretical approach, **realism** means something different than how the word is commonly used to describe pragmatism rather than naïve optimism about likely outcomes. For realists, the most important actor is the nation-state, which has as a primary goal furthering the national interest. Realists also see the world as anarchical, and all states are in continuous competition to secure as much power and influence as they can. Global governance, or any sort of cooperation among states that does not maximize the self-interest of all involved, are viewed as unrealistic goals. States, which are seen as unitary, pursue courses of action based on perceptions of relative power, and increasing power in order to maintain sovereignty becomes a primary focus of states. From this perspective, imperialism, Cold War struggles, and the emphasis for states on national security are all to be expected. The realist focus would be on preserving prosperity and security of a particular nation-state, and foreign interventions, particularly those involving the use of force, should be limited to defending vital national interests.

Beyond the realist reluctance to use force absent vital national interests to defend, they also argue that the **anarchy** of the world system incentivizes balances of power that create varying degrees of stability at different times and places. States with less military or economic power will seek alliances with major powers, or **hegemons**. The classic example was during the Cold War, when a bipolar system dominated by the United States and the Soviet Union (USSR) led a number of states to choose a hegemonic ally. During that time, although both the US and the USSR spent tremendous amounts of money on armaments, including nuclear weapons, the two countries did not use those weapons against each other directly. Countries that were allied with a hegemon did experience civil wars, revolutions, and proxy wars during the Cold War, including Korea, Vietnam, and Afghanistan. Post-revolutionary governments during this time period could choose to make alliance with a hegemon and potentially receive military and economic support (e.g., Cuba from the Soviet Union) or they could have to deal with vigorous opposition from a hegemon (Nicaragua from the United States).

Liberalism (idealism) does not see anarchy in the global system as inevitable, but rather imagines that rules, laws, and cooperation among sovereign states could produce an international community that works together toward collective interests. That is, anarchy could potentially be overcome, or at least largely mitigated. Theorists of liberalism posit that it is the institutions of the state that promote nationalism-related ideas and behavior that lead to war. Collective or multilateral efforts can produce institutional arrangements such as the United Nations (UN) or the European Union (EU) in which states cede some sovereignty to reduce the likelihood of war and other state-to-state conflict. Outside of those institutions, states may also give up some of their sovereign powers to make international agreements on trade, arms control, human rights, or the environment. Humanitarian responses to crises outside state borders or even the commitments by nation-states to respect international law would support the framework of idealism. In the case of the United States post-Cold War, foreign interventions to promote liberal democracy, spread global markets, or support liberal values in general, was part of a grand strategy described as "liberal hegemony." Unlike the realist assumption that humans are selfish and violent by nature, liberalism maintains a more optimistic view of human nature.

Early in the twentieth century, idealists such as US President Woodrow Wilson were motivated to create the League of Nations. Their argument was that such an international organization could prevent a recurrence of the devastation wrought by World War I. Idealism suffered a serious blow with the demise of the League of Nations and the breakout of World War II, but idealist approaches in international relations continued in the postwar era. Decades later, agreements that produced the European Union, **North American Free Trade Agreement** (NAFTA), and the World Trade Organization (WTO) suggested that liberalism had survived the second World War. The United Nations provided another example of multinational cooperation. The US, of course, ensured that the UN would be constrained by a Security Council that left Washington with considerable influence over the organization's actions; similarly, NAFTA was written and has been implemented in a way that does not seem to have put significant constraints on the US government's power. The United Nations Universal Declaration of Human Rights is an example of liberalism in international relations (Figure 5.2).

The European Union seemed to provide the best evidence for the liberalism argument that nation-states could choose to create entities that would produce economic and political cooperation at the transnational level, even if it meant a loss of some sovereignty for individual nation-states in the EU. The Brexit vote in 2016 that led to the negotiation about the United Kingdom's departure from the supranational organization raised questions about the permanence of the EU's economic, political, and diplomatic accomplishments. Although the United

Figure 5.2 Eleanor Roosevelt and the United Nations Universal Declaration of Human Rights.

Kingdom struggled to negotiate the terms of their departure, and the EU worked hard to make sure that other members of the EU would not see departing as an appealing option, the Brexit vote and its aftermath suggested that national interests might still transcend the liberal goal of transnational cooperation around collective interests in the twenty-first century. In the United States, President Trump's use of "America First" added more evidence to that Brexit argument from across the Atlantic.

Other Approaches to International Relations

Social constructivists argue that international norms affect state behavior in the global arena. The world is socially constructed, and while structures might shape agency, agency also influences structures. Agency, in this sense, refers to the capacity of individuals or groups to act. Constructivism argues for the importance of identities, which vary from state to state, and the norms which are associated with the different state identities.

Constructivism joins with realism and liberalism in viewing states as the fundamental actors in the international arena, and the study of international relations from those frameworks usually begins and ends with the state even if other actors are considered at some point. Alternative approaches, including Marxist and feminist analysis, offer a useful corrective to that state-centrism. For Marxist analyses, class struggle is the key driver of history at both the nation-state and international level. Traditional IR approaches assume that the greatest threats to state sovereignty are posed by other states. A Marxist perspective broadens the challenges to individual states to include actors in the global economic system. Currency traders, foreign investors, and international financial institutions can all offer challenges to state sovereignty. Marxists are also interested in how states use their power to further the interests of economic elites and contribute to the exploitation of working people by those elites. While liberalism would argue that the important aspect of global agreements on trade are that they increase cooperation and reduce the likelihood of conflict between states, Marxists would point to the influence of transnational corporations over the nature of those agreements, and how the global financial architecture furthers the power and profits on those corporate interests. When conflicts, including wars, do occur, a Marxist analysis would foreground economic interests in the search for causes. The US invasion of Iraq in 2003 was not just a question of security from weapons of mass destruction or an attempt to shape the balance of power in the Middle East, as it might appear from a realist perspective. Nor was the liberal interest in removing Saddam Hussein to install a democracy the primary motivation for Marxists. The Marxist framework would look for economic factors, whether access to oil or control over important trade routes. It is important to emphasize that a Marxist approach does not reduce the explanation for state-to-state conflict to economics, but it would argue that mainstream IR approaches suffer from the relative absence of economic variables.

Feminism offers an additional critique of the mainstream international relations theories' state-centrism. As in political science more broadly, feminists work to make the field more inclusive and sensitive to power relations at the individual and group levels. Feminist theories use gender analysis as a tool to challenge the approaches to traditional areas of study and to introduce new research questions. Feminists are also credited with introducing the gender variable into IR, and in doing so they have broadened the range of power relations that need to be addressed by IR scholars. The treatment of women workers in the global economy, the presence of prostitutes on military bases, the treatment of local women by UN peacekeepers, and even the underrepresentation of women in political leadership positions, for example, have been addressed by some IR scholars since the introduction of feminist IR. Feminists have also done work that brings to light the gendered dimensions of war and security (Sjoberg 2013).

Cynthia Enloe (2014) has made a particularly important contribution to the field of international relations by demonstrating how making diverse women visible illuminates the real workings of **international politics**. Gender analysis in political science more generally has drawn attention to those who do not seem to wield significant influence by asking not just where the women are, but also by examining the ways that race, ethnicity, and class interact with notions of masculinity and femininity. In addition to asking different questions, many feminist scholars move beyond mainstream methodologies that make claims to scientific objectivity. Furthermore, feminist scholarship does not allow the discussion of gender to be reduced to questions of cultural traditions, values, and beliefs. Rather, gender relations and the question of the role of women in feminist analysis are treated in terms of power.

Questions in international relations are not the only ones in political science that benefit from the incorporation of gender dynamics and sexuality to achieve a full understanding. Comparativists might want to look at the roles of women's movements in producing pressure from below on authoritarian governments. Those studying US politics might look at women's representation in Congress or policy outcomes in areas of women's rights. Social movement and interest group scholars should be interested in the gender dynamics at the level of organizational leadership. Scholars of the presidency have an increasing number of examples of chief executives to consider the ways that gender informs elections and performance (US excepted). Beyond the questions of gay marriage or other LGBTQ rights issues, the 2020 Democratic primary campaign featured the first serious candidate who ran as a gay man.

Globalization, Nationalism, and Political Science

Globalization has a number of different meanings. At one level, it is a description of changes in the world that have effectively compressed time and space globally. That is, information travels across borders instantaneously; goods can be transported more easily and quickly than ever; people can be immediately affected by developments that happen thousands of miles away. Globalization has an ideological component as well. That is, there are those who see economic globalization as favorable, or even "natural" and inevitable. In the US or Europe, they are sometimes called globalists in contrast to nationalists. Globalists point to benefits to investors, producers, and consumers from eliminating national borders when it comes to economic transactions. Critics on the left counter that argument with the claim that economic globalization has tended to strengthen corporations at the expense of working people, and that it has led to a more inequitable distribution of wealth within and between countries.

Among the questions that different fields in political science might help us to understand are the ways that globalization has affected the state. Does it limit the autonomy of the state? Nationalists see the loss of sovereignty, whether over immigration policy in the EU, or economic policy to the World Trade Organization (WTO). Other analysts argue that it is more accurate to say that globalization has shifted the role of the state, rather than weakening it. Economic globalization needs states that are able to check labor unions and other social movement mobilization around demands for environmental protection or preferences for buying local. That critique from the political left raised a question as to whether there is a "race to the bottom" generated by the sort of economic globalization promoted by states and their corporate allies? Race to the bottom describes the argument that the increasing mobility and leverage of foreign investors and producers will lead to downward pressure on social and economic policies, including wages and benefits for workers and environmental regulations, in order to produce a favorable investment climate. Governments will be charged with enforcing those conditions that create a favorable investment climate.

Voters who supported Brexit in the United Kingdom or those who supported a presidential candidate who promised to "make America great again" in the United States represent the nationalist counter to globalism. Nationalism as a political science concept is based on the idea that the nation and state should be congruent. The state, as we have already discussed, is the institutions of government that have sovereign control over the territory of the country. As noted earlier, nation is a more difficult concept to define, with shared characteristics ranging from history and beliefs to ethnicity and religion. In the end, the important idea is simple: that people perceive themselves as part of this "imagined community" (Anderson, 1991). All of the members of that nation should be governed by the same state, and no members of another nation should be governed by the institutions of that state. Here we can see that some of the issues posed by the movements of people across borders could lead nationalists to object. If the migrants do not share the history, culture, language, or values and beliefs of the "imagined" nation, then nationalists may respond negatively to their presence. While the movement of people across borders is not a necessary component of globalization, those migrations have increased concurrently with the movements of goods and information.

During the global Covid pandemic, the issue of nationalism came to the fore as well. Countries were not allowing citizens of other countries to cross borders, even in the European Union, where residents carry EU passports. Trade of personal protective equipment became contentious, as some governments chose to restrict businesses from exporting vital medical supplies to other countries. When vaccines became available, hoarding by some countries led to tremendous disparities in access across the world. Perhaps students will see that as "natural," but what does it mean if the relatively poor countries in the global south are denied access to masks, drugs, ventilators, or vaccines, because the wealthier countries decide to keep a reserve stockpile, just in case? Should access to immunization be determined by the accident of birthplace or current place of residency? International institutions, such as the United Nations' World Health Organization, may be stymied in their efforts to promote global cooperation by the nationalist forces, whether in China or the United States.

States and Markets

Political scientists have long been interested in the relationship between the market and the state. After the global depression of the late 1920s, political scientists in the United States sought to explain the development of New Deal social policies that suggested the need for the state to ameliorate the suffering that could be caused by the market. With the social security system, the government endeavored to provide help for the elderly, and with the Works Progress Administration (WPA), the government employed millions of people who had been cast aside by the market. In the same time period, governments in the global south moved to regulate the market, subsidize the price of necessities for poor and working people, and protect domestic industries from foreign products by way of a policy called **Import Substitution Industrialization** (ISI). Political scientists are interested in who receives benefits from the government and why. In the case of the US New Deal, were the policies the result of resistance or pressure from below by poor and working-class people; were they the product of an enlightened President Roosevelt; or were they a response to ideological shifts about what the role of the state should be in light of the economic crisis?

For a few decades following the New Deal reforms, a general Keynesian consensus existed in the US political economy that the government was a necessary actor regulating and stimulating the capitalist economy, as well as providing support to the unemployed, when necessary. In the late 1970s, economic troubles in the United States raised questions for some about the wisdom of government intervention in the market. The rise of President Ronald Reagan in the United States and Prime Minister Margaret Thatcher in the United Kingdom marked a shift toward political and economic elite consensus that government intervention was the cause of economic problems, not the appropriate response to crisis. The ideology of neoliberalism, arguing that markets make better decisions than states in the realm of the economy, spread around the globe.

Political scientists generally fell into line. In the United States, at least, the discipline was historically sympathetic to the argument that free market economics were compatible with political democracy. As neoliberal policies spread to (or were forced upon) southern countries, many political scientists offered their support for the shift from state planning to market decision making, using claims that it would increase economic efficiency and increase the likelihood of political democratization. The Cold War made that choice even easier, as did international financial institutions such as the International Monetary Fund (IMF) and the World Bank (WB). In concrete terms, neoliberalism led to a global push for governments to deregulate, reduce government subsidies that distorted the market, privatize (sell off government-owned businesses to the private sector), and to reduce any barriers to international trade or foreign investment.

The role of the state did not lessen under neoliberalism as much as it shifted from providing support for those harmed by market capitalism to providing support for capital itself. In the neoliberal era, the state strove to create a most favorable investment climate. One part of that new role was to pull back from regulations that constrained the "freedom" of businesses to operate in their home countries, put barriers in the trade of goods, and limited opportunities for foreign investors. The important point is that the state was not relegated to the sidelines as much as it took on a new role in the economic sphere. At all levels, governments may be expected to provide economic subsidies to investors, while the federal government implements agreements to facilitate the flows of capital and goods across state lines.

Social Movements, Protest, and Resistance

As the discussion above about the relationship between the state and market suggests, there is an interesting question for political scientists about how the interests of the wealthy tend to become the interests of politicians and the political system. We know that the wealthy tend to be more active in the political arena. Not only do they vote at higher percentages than those with lower incomes and wealth, but they help to fund parties and campaigns (where permitted), lobby public officials, and generally interact more often with politicians and others in government from local to federal levels. Some political scientists have studied groups of people who do not have the same easy access to the formal political system and choose to be active through social movements or protest. In some cases, such as the Arab Spring, the public rallies and demonstrations were a function of the closed political systems in those countries. The more open political systems in Europe or the United States, however, are not immune to social movement activism.

Political scientists tend to focus more of their research on formal politics—voting behavior, legislatures, executive branch decision making, the judicial system, and international diplomacy among elite actors. The discipline's focus on power makes the study of popular mobilization important as well. Whether a small protest such as the hundreds of people rallying at US state capitals demanding that the economy be reopened during the Covid-19 shelter-in-place directives or the anti-immigration rallies in places in Europe, people living in democracies make the decision that the best way to get the political outcomes they want may be through public protest. By studying these actions and movements, we might gain new insight into how politics works in different countries. Why is it that environmentalists worried about climate change are more likely to engage in rallies or demonstrations, while the fossil fuel industry confines most of their political activity to the formal arena? Study by political scientists of movements of indigenous people, women, or students mobilizing in Latin America can lead to insights about who the political systems there exclude.

Social movement activity may be transnational as well. Greta Thunberg, the Swedish teenage environmental activist was named as *Time* magazine's person of the year in 2019. Political scientists are well positioned to analyze these organizations. There is a long history of studying interest groups in democracies. Interest groups comprise any of a variety of voluntary associations of people who come together largely for the purpose of influencing policy making by the government. In the United States, these include organizations such as the National Rifle Association (NRA), American Association of Retired People (AARP), or the National Association of Manufacturers. Social movements are also voluntary, but the goals tend to go beyond a single policy, and the tactics are not as limited as those employed by interest groups.

Social movements' success relies on their ability to gain credibility and sympathy among the general public—attaining a moral authority as some have put it against opponents who have greater resources and access to political institutions and officials. Representation in the media is important, particularly since the choice of actions may be controversial to some. Walkouts, boycotts, marches, and demonstrations run the risk of backlashes. In the case of Thunberg and environmental activism, the Swede urged school climate strikes by her peers across the world, while giving widely covered public speeches of her own at the United Nations Climate Change Conference and the World Economic Forum in 2019 and 2020. The global climate strikes of fall 2019 drew millions of people into the streets around the world. She credits the students from Parkland, Florida who walked out of classes in support of new gun control laws for some of her inspiration.

Political science's interest in the idea of power—who wields it and how—means that the discipline needs to account for the potential impact by social movement activists, whether indigenous people in Bolivia, student climate activists across the globe, or anti-immigrant activists in Europe. When do these groups facilitate change—1960s civil rights movement in the United States, perhaps? When do they fail—1989 Chinese protesters at Tiananmen Square? And why? From the study of revolutions to reform, political science must be prepared to observe developments well outside the institutions of formal politics.

International Studies and the Field of American Politics

Students are clearly likely to be more familiar with the US political system than they are with politics in other countries. In looking at the institutions, procedures, and outcomes elsewhere, we have an opportunity to shed new light on the practices in our own countries. Starting at the top, are there any other countries that make use of an Electoral College-like system to elect a president? How would you explain and defend a system that allows someone who received fewer votes than their opponent to win the presidency? The US Senate, the upper house of the legislature, is populated by two representatives from each of the 50 states. Are there other countries who have the disproportionate representation in a legislative body that gives the less than 600,000 people who live in Wyoming the same number of Senators as the roughly 40 million people who live in California? In the ratification of Supreme Court justices, should the people of Wyoming be 70 times as influential as those in California? To make sure that this is not misinterpreted as a partisan argument, should the just over 600,000 residents of Vermont, who elected a self-proclaimed Democratic Socialist in Bernie Sanders, have the same influence in the Senate as nearly 30 million people of Texas? Should the 20 smallest states, in which the combined population is roughly equal to California, get 40 Senators, while the people in that state still get only 2? Once ratified, should Supreme Court justices receive life terms, or is there an approach taken by another country that might make more sense? International studies students may conclude that the US political institutions and processes are preferable to those in other countries, but that perspective should be based on deep knowledge of both their own and other political systems. The disciplinary tools of political science will be useful to them as they make comparisons between their own experiences and those in other nation-states.

For political scientists, the Covid pandemic provided considerable opportunity to test theories and ideas about how American politics works. In the United States, the relations between governments at different levels—local, state, and federal—was put to a test during the period of stay-at-home orders. Questions of federalism are important in politics, and we saw it play out with something as simple as whether beaches should be open to citizens. Should the mayor, governor, or president decide if Jacksonville, Florida should open its beaches? Are the legislative and executive branches at the national level capable of putting aside partisanship in a time of national crisis? Finally, what social and economic groups are able to persuade government officials to provide public resources that will protect them from the consequences of a crisis?

Studying Politics in the Early Twenty-first Century

In 2020, the Freedom House, which offers a yearly report on the state of democracy and freedom in the world, claimed that in 2019, for the fourteenth consecutive year, more countries had become more oppressive than freer, and that democracy and pluralism were under assault (Freedom House 2020). The Freedom House, a conservative US organization, noted setbacks in India, Myanmar, Senegal, Benin, and El Salvador, but they also saw a decline in the quality of US democracy over the last decade. That international trend invites analysis from political science. In explaining *How Democracies Die*, two political scientists focus on the election of leaders with autocratic tendencies, such as President Erdoğan in Turkey or Orbán in Hungary (Levitsky and Ziblatt 2018). Another political scientist blames "Russian Rage, Chinese Ambition, and American Complacency," in the title of his book, and argues that the threat to democracy can also come from outside countries (Diamond 2019).

The Covid pandemic shone a different light on politics across the world. In such a crisis, even democratic governments may retreat from traditional expectations in the areas of transparency, accountability, and responsiveness. Hesitation in implementing restrictions may undermine the government's legitimacy in the long term, but the attempt to control the behavior of its citizens risks a backlash as well. Officials who worry about approval polls and their prospects for re-election might give politics at least equal weight to public health concerns. More authoritarian regimes may find it easier to impose restrictions on their populations, but those public controls may also be used to further the repression of political opposition. Legitimate needs to track the spread of the virus may evolve into a permanent and systematic surveillance of a population. Authoritarian governments may also be able to cover up negative developments and mislead the public about the effectiveness of their response in the absence of an effective and independent media.

In the end, whether a pandemic or any of the other global issues discussed in an international studies classroom, political science can help to explain developments, but a comprehensive analysis would include insights from other disciplines as well. Even the making of domestic and foreign policy, clearly in the domain of political scientists, cannot be understood without reference to the work in economics, geography, anthropology, history, and other disciplines.

References

Anderson, Benedict. 1991. *Imagined Communities: Reflections on the origin and spread of Nationalism.* London: Verso Press.

Diamond, Larry. 2019. *Ill Winds: Saving Democracy from Russian Rage, Chinese Ambition, and American Complacency.* New York: Penguin Press.

Enloe, Cynthia. 2014. *Bananas, Beaches and Bases: Making Feminist Sense of International Politics.* 2nd ed. Berkeley: University of California Press,

Freedom House Report. 2020. *Freedom in the World:* https://freedomhouse.org/sites/default/files/2020-02/FIW_2020_REPORT_BOOKLET_Final.pdf

Levitsky, Steven and Daniel Ziblatt. 2018. *How Democracies Die.* New York: Crown Publishers.

Sjoberg, Laura. 2013. *Gendering Global Conflict: Toward a Feminist Theory of War.* New York: Columbia University Press.

Further Reading

Books

Aronoff, Kate, Peter Dreier, and Michael Kazin, eds. 2020. *We Own the Future: Democratic Socialism—American Style,* The New Press.

Hudson, Valerie M., Donna Lee Bowen, and Perpetua Lynne Nielsen. 2020. *The First Political Order: How Sex Shapes Governance and National Security Worldwide,* Columbia University Press.

Judis, John. 2016. *The Populist Explosion: How the Great Recession Transformed American and European Politics,* Columbia Global Reports.

Keck, Margaret and Kathryn Sikkink. 1998. *Activists Beyond Borders: Advocacy Networks in International Politics.* [Cornell University Press reprint, 2014].

Klein, Naomi. 2019. *On Fire: The (Burning) Case for a New Deal,* Simon & Schuster.

Marx, Karl and Friedrich Engels. 1848. *The Communist Manifesto.* [Vintage Classics reprint, 2018].

Steinbeck, John. 1939. *The Grapes of Wrath.* [Penguin Classics reprint, 2006].

Walt, Stephen. 2018. *The Hell of Good Intentions: America's Foreign Policy Elite and the Decline of U.S. Primacy.* [Farrar, Straus, and Giroux].

Journals

Foreign Affairs. www.foreignaffairs.com
International Studies Quarterly. https://academic.oup.com/isq
New Political Science. www.tandfonline.com/toc/cnps20/current
Perspectives on Politics. www.cambridge.org/core/journals/perspectives-on-politics
World Policy Journal. https://read.dukeupress.edu/world-policy-journal

Films

All the President's Men (1976). Director Alan J. Pakula.
Bulworth (1998). Director Warren Beatty.
Hotel Rwanda (2004). Director Terry George.
Malcolm X (1992). Director Spike Lee.
Suffragette (2015). Director Sara Gavron.
The Ides of March (2011). Director George Clooney.
V for Vendetta (2005). Director James McTeigue.
Wag the Dog (1997). Director Barry Levinson.
Zero Dark Thirty (2012). Director Kathryn Bigelow.

Websites

Congressional Quarterly Researcher: https://library.cqpress.com/cqresearcher
Fivethirtyeight: https://fivethirtyeight.com/politics/
Institute for Policy Studies: https://ips-dc.org/
International Affairs at the London School of Economics: https:/blogs.lse.ac.uk

Part Two

Interdisciplinary Approaches to Regional and International Topics

Chapter 6

North America and International Studies

At the beginning of the twenty-first century, North America—because it is home to the United States and Canada—dominates the world political and economic system. This chapter focuses on the United States and Canada (Mexico is covered in the chapter on Latin America). The United States plays a major role in international affairs, and a brief discussion of its position in the world provides illuminating comparisons with the rest of the world. The character of its people, power relationships, place, production, and the past—that is its anthropology, politics, geography, economy, and history—define North America (see Map 6.1).

A Brief History of the United States in the World

In his farewell address of 1796, US President George Washington warned the fledgling nation against involvement in the political affairs of Europe:

> Our detached and distant situation invites and enables us to pursue a different course.... . Why, by interweaving our destiny with that of any part of Europe, entangle our peace and prosperity in the toils of European ambition, rivalship, interest, humor or caprice? ... It is our true policy to steer clear of permanent alliances with any portion of the foreign world.

At the end of the eighteenth century, the United States was in no position to project its power anyway. Under Thomas Jefferson, the United States expanded its territory with the Louisiana Purchase. After a costly war with Great Britain from 1812 to 1815, the United States concentrated on westward expansion, where it rapidly overcame resistance from the indigenous peoples, who were decimated by the relentless numbers and military technologies of the United States. Until the late nineteenth century, the United States was preoccupied with North American matters, expanding to the Pacific by mid-century, and fighting a civil war from 1861 to 1865, and two territorial wars with Mexico (1846–1848) and Spain (1898). In spite of its foundational claims about the rights of free men, much of the prosperity of the US was initially built on the expropriation of land from Native peoples, and on the trade in, and the unpaid labor of, enslaved people (Figure 6.1).

Industrialization began in the late eighteenth century and by 1900 the United States had surpassed Great Britain as the world's greatest industrial power. In 1911, the country was producing over 24 million tons of steel, outstripping Germany's 14 million tons and Britain's 6.5 million tons (Hause and Maltby 1999, 757).

The United States began to wield its newfound power abroad. In 1907–1908, President Teddy Roosevelt sent the "Great White Fleet"—warships painted garishly white—around the world to show that the United States was now a power to be reckoned with. The United States built and

DOI: 10.4324/9781003028314-9

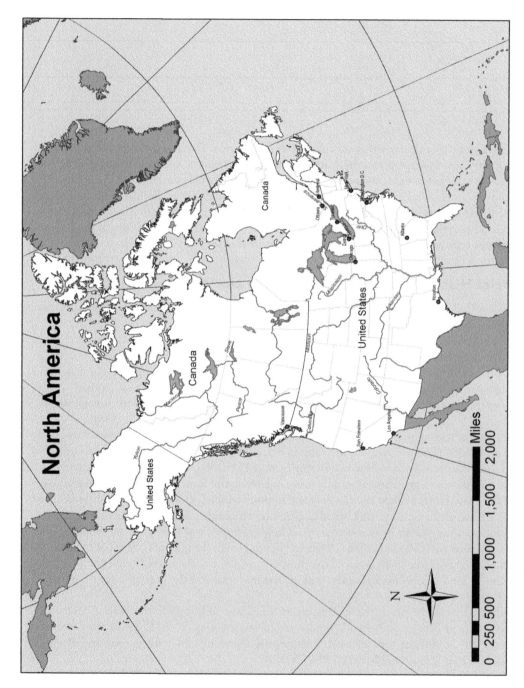

Map 6.1 North America.

Figure 6.1 Mt. Rushmore. Designed by an American immigrant with ties to the Ku Klux Klan on land in South Dakota expropriated from the Lakota Sioux, this monument memorializing four American presidents is an expression of some of the fundamental contradictions of U.S. history.

Source: S. Toops.

operated the Panama Canal (1904–1914) to allow passage for a two-ocean navy and to facilitate US trade in the Western Hemisphere and Asia.

From its inception, the United States has considered itself an exceptional country: a free, democratic republic; a beacon of righteousness far removed from the Europe of perpetual war, **monarchy**, aristocracy, and mercantilism. President Woodrow Wilson furthered this notion when he said that the United States had entered World War I to make the world safe for democracy. The United States helped defeat the Central Powers in that war and the Axis powers in World War II, confirming in American minds that the United States was an indispensable agent for freedom, peace, and prosperity. The United States emerged from the war as the world's greatest power, although for 40 years the Soviet Union was a formidable military and ideological rival.

The United States sought to establish a liberal, economic, and democratic postwar order with itself at the center. These postwar efforts birthed free-market institutions such as the **World Bank** to reconstruct the war-torn world, the **International Monetary Fund** (IMF) to regulate currency exchanges and bail out bankrupt economies, and the **General Agreement on Tariffs and Trade** (GATT), a periodic round of talks among capitalist economies to gradually lower tariffs and encourage trade. GATT evolved into the **World Trade Organization** (WTO) in 1995.

The demise of the Soviet Union in 1991 seemed to confirm that there would be no more significant challenges to this liberal economic paradigm and the political power of the United

States. By gross domestic product, the United States has the world's largest economy; the EU is second, and China third. By purchasing power parity, China is first and the US is second. The United States accounts for 8.5 percent of world exports and 17 percent of world imports (WITS 2019). The size of the US economy, as well as its dependence on trade, mandate that the United States will protect the stability of the free market global system.

Many Americans firmly believe that the United States is number one in most economic and social rankings. The high number of immigrants who want to come to the United States shows that the country is still seen as a land of opportunity. According to one study, however, on "livability" the United States comes in twenty-eighth of 163 countries. The infant mortality rate in the United States is higher than in Cuba and Canada. The Social Progress Index puts the United States forty-second in health care, forty-fourth in basic knowledge, twenty-fourth in access to clean water and sanitation, and fifty-seventh in personal safety. The US has the highest rate of incarceration in the world, seven times France's, fourteen times Japan's, and twenty-four times India's (*New York Times*, May 18, 2014) and disproportionately targets people of color.

Global Challenges for the United States

Although the United States does not face any serious existential threats, as it did from the Soviet Union in the Cold War, the increasingly globalized world has created new challenges. As the reputed "indispensable" power, Washington, DC, feels responsible to meet those challenges, whether head on or "leading from behind." The United States is the wealthiest country in the world and therefore is often seen as morally obligated to come to the aid of the needy in times of natural disasters and other humanitarian crises. The United States spends more on its military than the next 15 countries combined, providing the means necessary to intervene in any part of the world on a moment's notice. China is number two. Largest US deployments are in Japan, Germany, Middle East, and Republic of Korea. The United States maintains 800 military bases in more than 70 countries to protect its interests (Vine 2019).

Contemporary turmoil in the Middle East has the potential to draw the United States into a major war. Despite former President Barack Obama's desire to focus more attention on Asia, the wars in Iraq and Afghanistan started by his predecessor forced him to devote more resources to this region. US troops left Iraq in 2011, but the war and occupation cost nearly 4,500 American and tens of thousands of Iraqi lives. The withdrawal left Iraq in a precarious security situation. The new Iraqi regime favored the Shia south and persecuted Sunnis in the center and north of the country. The Arab Spring uprisings in Syria against the Alawite regime of Bashar al-Assad left a vacuum of power in the north of that country as well, enabling the rise of the radical Sunni Islamic State (IS), which has sought vengeance on the West for historical colonialism and contemporary interventions, often in the form of terrorist attacks on European and US targets.

Six years of brutal conflict between Syrian rebels, IS, and the al-Assad regime have left hundreds of thousands of Syrians and Iraqi dead and millions as refugees. The United States has conducted air strikes in support of the Syrian rebels and has targeted IS leaders; in 2016, US special forces aided an Iraqi Army assault on Mosul, a key IS-controlled city. Russia has continued to support the al-Assad regime with indiscriminate air strikes on Syrian rebel-held urban areas, adding to the carnage. Obama's Secretary of State, John Kerry, desperately tried to broker a ceasefire and begin peace talks, but Russia rejected any deal involving regime change in Damascus. At the end of 2016, Aleppo fell to Assad's forces, severely crippling the opposition.

The civil war in Syria and the rise of IS diverted US diplomatic efforts to resolve the half-century-old Israeli–Palestinian conflict, the most intractable in the region. In 2013, Kerry launched a new diplomatic effort to forge a final peace settlement, but Israeli Prime Minister Benjamin Netanyahu and Obama were at loggerheads over new Israeli settlements in the West

Bank and Obama's deal to limit the Iranian nuclear weapon program. Kerry's diplomatic offensive went nowhere.

In the Middle East, the US has troops deployed in Bahrain, Iraq, Israel, Jordan, Kuwait, Oman, Qatar, Saudi Arabia, Syria, and the United Arab Emirates. Bahrain has the largest base. A naval base in Diego Garcia in the Indian Ocean also supports the US military in the Middle East. Bases in Turkey, Germany, and Italy also support the US in the Persian Gulf region. Troops are also in Afghanistan but the Biden administration expects to recall combat troops from Afghanistan in 2021.

The turmoil in the Middle East sidelined US efforts to make a "pivot" to Asia, in other words, a redirection of US diplomatic and economic interests in the most populous region in the world. Japan remains Washington's main ally in the region. The US has troops and bases in Japan and South Korea. Most of these troops are there to match North Korea. South Korea and Japan are protected by the US nuclear umbrella. Ships, submarines and aircraft from US bases in Hawaii and Guam also patrol the Pacific. China's rapid economic growth has created new opportunities for US trade and investment, although China's military spending is seen by some as a threat. China is a vital partner in US efforts to denuclearize the Korean peninsula. From China's perspective, US troops in South Korea, Japan, and Afghanistan, and a defense agreement with Taiwan are not welcome. Washington also sees opportunities for cooperation with rapidly growing India.

The United States has renewed interest in Africa, and not only for economic development or humanitarian concerns. Somalia and Nigeria have seen the rise of extremist Islamic terrorist groups that threaten not only the people in these countries but neighboring countries, Europe, and the United States. In 2009, a Nigerian national linked to al Qaeda tried to blow up a US airliner, and the terrorist group Boko Haram continues to threaten the Nigerian north. In 2013, the Somali terrorist group Al-Shabaab attacked a shopping mall in Nairobi, Kenya, killing at least 70 people. US special forces and drone strikes are involved in keeping Al-Shabaab at bay.

When President George W. Bush came into office in 2001, he promised renewed efforts to increase US ties to Latin America. After the terror attack on the United States on September 11, 2001, Latin America was moved to the back burner. Bush tried to push the Free Trade Agreement of the Americas (FTAA), but rejection of neoliberalism in the region brought few results.

President Obama negotiated the Trans-Pacific Partnership (TPP) free trade agreement, which included three Latin American countries (Mexico, Peru, and Chile). The TPP was cancelled by President Trump. In 2020, the ASEAN states plus Australia, China, Japan, New Zealand and South Korea signed a new free trade agreement, the Regional Comprehensive Trade Partnership. The US was not included. This was a seismic shift in US foreign policy, which has consistently promoted more open markets.

The United States in the World Economy: Too Big to Fail

The US economy is the largest in the world in terms of Gross Domestic Product (GDP). In terms of GDP Purchasing Power Parity (PPP), China is the leader and the US is number two. GDP PPP is generally used to compare economies. US Gross Domestic Product PPP comprises 15 percent of the global GDP (the total values of all goods and services produced in the world in a year). The US manufactures about 18 percent of the world's goods, while China manufactures 20 percent and Japan manufactures 10 percent. The US is the largest importer of goods and second-largest exporter in the world (after China). It possesses the world's largest and most influential financial market, with foreign investments more than double that of any other country. Roughly 61 percent of global currency reserves are invested in US dollars,

Japanese yen, euro and Chinese yuan are increasing in shares of foreign exchange reserves. The New York Stock Exchange leads the world in number of shares traded. China (124) and US (121) are fairly close with the number of headquarters of Fortune 500 companies (CIA *World Factbook* 2020).

America's wealth derives from abundant natural resources, a well-developed infrastructure, high productivity, and a broadly mixed economy. The United States has the world's largest coal reserves and is the world's largest producer of oil and largest producer of natural gas. It also has significant holdings of copper, lead, molybdenum, phosphates, uranium, bauxite, gold, iron, mercury, nickel, potash, silver, tungsten, zinc, and timber. Heavy investment in infrastructure, both by the government and the private sector, particularly after World War II, created sophisticated water, rail, and highway transportation systems; a highly effective power grid; and a water-distribution system that together enable business growth and high quality of life. The United States is a world leader in petroleum, steel, motor vehicles, aerospace, telecommunications, chemicals, electronics, food processing, consumer goods, lumber, and mining, among other products. This highly diversified economy means that global downturns in any one major market have only minor effects on the overall US economy, as opposed to many countries that have only a handful of industries.

The American economy is a market-oriented system in which private businesses and individuals operate largely independent of the government. Corporations in the United States have greater flexibility to expand or close their businesses, dismiss workers, and develop new products than do business firms in most other nations, even strongly market-oriented economies like Germany and Japan. Overseas firms also face fewer barriers entering US markets than American firms usually do when entering foreign markets. The US is continually ranked in the top ten for countries with limitations on doing business (World Bank Group 2020).

With a few exceptions, such as the Postal Service, the Veterans Health Administration, the Corporation for Public Broadcasting, and the Federal Deposit Insurance Company, federal and state governments own and operate few businesses, contracting with private corporations for needed goods and services. An example of this is the national healthcare reform under former President Obama. Instead of creating a government healthcare system to compete with private healthcare, as most nations do, the Affordable Care Act required citizens to acquire insurance from private insurers, while mandating certain basic requirements for all insurance plans.

The United States is also the most militarily powerful country in the world. The US Department of Defense maintains more than 800 bases and other military installations overseas and is the world's largest employer, with more than 3 million employees. Combined spending on military and intelligence agencies—the departments of Defense, Veterans Affairs, and Homeland Security— accounts for 53 percent of the discretionary budget, exceeds spending on all other government agencies combined. Social Security, Medicare, and Medicaid are in a separate mandatory budget since they are derived from individual contributions (OMB 2020). Military spending, along with Medicare and Social Security costs, make up more than three-quarters of the spending of the United States, with the result that the country, in spite of its great wealth, is rarely able to balance its budget and must year after year borrow money—mostly from foreign countries like China, Japan, and UK—to pay its bills.

As the United States excelled in technological innovation, becoming a world leader in computers, medical equipment, aerospace products, and military armaments, it developed a "two-tier labor market" between professional and skilled labor and other workers (Saint-Paul 1996). Since the mid-1970s, practically all gains in household income went to those in the top 20 percent, while those without professional skills have failed to get comparable pay raises, health-insurance coverage, and other benefits. This has led to what many call "the erosion of the middle class" (Gunderson 2013; Reich 2010). Nearly 10 percent of Americans lived below the poverty level in 2019. Covid-19 and recession may increase those numbers in poverty. By the twenty-first century, the gulf between rich and poor in the United States exceeded that of many developing countries (CIA *World Factbook* 2020).

Rising debt and the weakening of the working and middle classes made the global recession of 2008 hit particularly hard. Foreclosures doubled during 2006–2008, as rising oil prices forced many families to purchase gasoline at the expense of falling behind in their mortgage payments. Soaring oil prices also caused a decline in the value of the dollar and increased the US trade deficit. Wars in Afghanistan and Iraq—totaling $900 billion in direct costs and more than four trillion in indirect costs such as veterans benefits, military pensions, homeland security, and international aid—further strained national resources, added to the budget deficit, and increased public debt (Crawford 2016). Because US revenues from taxes are lower, as a percentage of GDP, than those of most other countries, much of this war spending had to be borrowed. As a result of these pressures, in 2008, America fell into the longest and most severe economic downturn since the Great Depression of the 1930s.

The US government acted quickly to help reduce the duration and impact of the recession. In 2008, the US government invested $700 billion in local development projects and bought interests in US banks and corporations deemed **"too big to fail"** (meaning that their failure would have greater fiscal consequences than the economy could absorb). Congress authorized an additional $787-billion fiscal stimulus to be used for investment and tax cuts to create jobs. Following these measures, unemployment declined, spending by the government slowed, and the deficit shrank from 9 percent to 7.6 percent of GDP. While overall wealth, investment, and availability of credit rose in the United States faster than in other nations affected by the global recession, this recovery was slow to create new jobs, and many of the jobs created were skilled jobs requiring specialized training or education, leaving millions out of work and increasingly unhappy with the management of the US economy.

The slogan "too big to fail" was also sometimes applied to the United States as a whole to explain why foreign countries, like Japan and China, that held huge US currency reserves did not change their borrowing habits in the face of the US economic downturn. The argument was that these nations held so much US debt that they could not take any actions that might further devalue US currency, for fear of the impacts it would have on their own economies.

The American Dream

Much of what is unique about American culture can be located in a North American ethos that, through hard work, promises everyone an opportunity to build a better life than the one they were born into. Although the term **"the American Dream"** was not coined until 1931 (Adams 1931), the roots of this cultural system are expressed in the US constitution:

> We hold these truths to be self-evident: that all men are created equal, that they are endowed by their Creator with certain unalienable Rights, that among these are Life, Liberty and the pursuit of Happiness.

Articulated as a **meritocracy**—a system in which people succeed according to their own skills without regard for such social distinctions as caste, class, religion, race, ethnicity, sex, age, or kinship networks—this ethos is heavily coded into America's expressive culture, from films to games to novels to political speeches. Anthropologists who have studied contemporary North American culture have noted that the American dream entails an entire worldview that sees human life as comprising free-willed individuals whose lives are a product of the choices they make when confronted with opportunities and obstacles.

This individualistic, meritocratic view shapes America's actions in the world in three important ways. First, it shapes the division between political camps that control power in the United States. Second, it plays significantly into political, legal, and social debates about migration to the United States from elsewhere in the world and management of the cultural differences immigrants bring with them. Third, it shapes America's wider dealings with the world as it exerts power through economic aid and military force.

Many of the internal problems of US society—racism, immigration control, gender imbalances, rising costs of education—are tied to cultural contradictions in the American dream. The quint-essentially American board game *Monopoly* expresses the values of the American dream: starting from a level playing field, through luck, strategy, and skill at seizing opportunities, players acquire wealth. In real life, however, everyone does not start out with the same opportunities: some start out already owning Park Place and Boardwalk, while others have only a fistful of dollars; people get very different amounts of cash when they pass Go; and the same rules often do not apply equally to everyone.

US politics are importantly shaped by this contradiction between a worldview that emphasizes the importance of a meritocracy of individuals, on the one hand, and the inequities of everyday life for many people in the United States, on the other. American political culture has become polarized around two competing ideologies that differ largely on how the American dream is to be achieved. American political culture can be roughly divided into two strands, liberalism and civil republicanism (Sarat and Berkowitz 1998). *Liberalism* proposes that all individuals should be free to express themselves as they wish and go their own way, with civic order maintained by the state through laws (Fitzpatrick 1992). *Civil republicanism* is suspicious of the state, preferring to emphasize America as a nation, a body of people sharing a core set of common values that cross-cuts differences (Michelman 1988).

A key cultural issue that emphasizes these differences involves who is to be considered "American." Although America's origin myths emphasize its significance as a "land of immigrants," nativist discourses have also always existed. Although immigrants can achieve citizenship through a process of "naturalization," "native" citizenship is derived from birth to citizens or birth within the national boundaries of the US, so one can find both US citizens who have lived their entire lives elsewhere in the world and non-citizens who have grown up in the United States and know nothing of the countries from which their parents emigrated. Who is truly American? The person who is born in the country or the person who chooses to live there? These debates turn around a key cultural problem: does being "American" mean sharing a common cultural identity, or is it about citizenship and loyalty to the United States?

These issues are often expressed in civil republican terms through powerful cultural metaphors such as "the melting pot," through which differences are assimilated into a common, normative national character. In the early twentieth century, many liberal religious, political, and intellectual leaders began to propose an alternative to assimilationist models called the *cultural pluralism model* (subsequently renamed *multiculturalism*), which proposed that differences within society are valuable and should be preserved. Cultural pluralists have offered alternative metaphors for America's heterogeneity such as the "mosaic" (Gibbon 1938), "kaleidoscope" (Fuchs 1990), or "salad" (Chua 2007) to capture alternative ways of understanding difference in the United States. Many of these ideas spread to the United States from Canada.

Many contemporary political debates in the United States center around issues of racial, linguistic, religious, and cultural difference, in which a normative standard—hard-working, English-speaking (and traditionally white) persons who struggle to make a better life for themselves and their families—becomes a model against which other Americans are measured. This was exemplified in the 2016 presidential campaign, in which the winning candidate, Donald Trump, emphasized linguistic, cultural, and religious differences as central to immigration and security problems in the United States, while at the same time promising to transform the economy into one in which hard-working Americans could find jobs that would support their families.

The United States' exertion of power in the world has also been shaped by its desire to spread the American dream as part of a vision for global, social progress through economic aid, diplomacy, and military might (Rosenberg 1982). The idea that every country could become like the United States through democratic and liberal economic reform has long shaped US development programs (Escobar 1995). Even when expediency and national interest create partnerships that might seem to be at odds with American values—close ties with monarchs and dictators, for example—the United States generally required them to make at least a show of implementing social and political reforms in line with American values.

This may be changing. A countervailing trend—"America first"—has also always been present in US international policy. In this view, the United States should always seek to ensure that the needs of people in the United States are addressed before those of citizens in other countries. In this view, the United States should not provide aid for the poor in other countries while there are poor in the United States who need help, should not intervene in global trouble spots unless US interests—narrowly defined—are at stake, and should not support countries who are too poor to meet the financial obligations established in their alliances with the United States. Although long suppressed by favor for free global trade and an effort to create stable markets, these views enjoyed a resurgence during the presidency of Donald Trump. Trump's foreign policy was largely transactionalist, looking at foreign policies in terms of immediate benefits and eschewing affirmations even of long-term alliances such as NATO in favor of current assessments of whether the alliances benefit the US more than they cost it. This has led leaders from several European countries to South Korea and Japan, to question the reliability of the United States and its long-term commitments.

Canada and the World

In 1961, US President John F. Kennedy told the Canadian parliament: "Geography has made us neighbors. History has made us friends. Economics has made us partners. And necessity has made us allies."

Canada is often overshadowed by its bigger neighbor to the south, but it is among the most developed countries in the world, and its vast size puts it in an advantageous position for continued growth in the twenty-first century and a greater role in global affairs. Canada has the world's second-largest land area (behind Russia), although because of its proximity to the Arctic Circle, under 5 percent of the land is arable. Ninety percent of the population of 37.7 million lives within 100 miles of the US border. Access to fresh water will be a serious issue in the twenty-first century as many arid regions in the world drain off their rivers, lakes, and aquifers. Canada has the most fresh water in the world (CIA *World Factbook* 2020).

Canada is a great place to live. US News ranks Switzerland at #1 and Canada at #2 as the best country, US is #7. Canada ranks #34 in the world in per capita GDP. Unlike its neighbor to the south, Canada has a publicly funded healthcare system. Although there is also debate in Canada about the inefficiencies and quality of health delivery, Canadians are as a whole healthier than Americans. Life expectancy in Canada is 83.4 years, ranking sixth in the world, and the infant-mortality rate is among the world's lowest (CIA *World Factbook* 2020).

Canada has the eleventh-largest economy in the world and is a partner in the G7. Like most of the developed world, Canada's economy stagnated after the financial crisis of 2008. Canadian banks had followed relatively conservative financial policies, however, and the economy rebounded to average between 1.25 and 2.5 percent growth rates from 2010 to 2020.

The Covid-19 pandemic hurt the economy badly, but it recovered faster than the US, perhaps because of greater success at controlling the spread of the coronavirus pandemic. Canada has the third-largest proven oil reserves in the world; over three-fourths of Canadian exports go to the United States, much of it in gas and oil shipments. Canada's military spending is relatively low, ranking eighteenth in the world (CIA *World Factbook* 2020).

As democracies go, Canada's political parties have reached a modicum of consensus about federal fiscal policy, environmental regulation, healthcare, military spending, and social policies—issues that have caused a wide divide between the Republican and Democratic parties in the United States. In many ways, Canada has more in common with European social democracies than with the United States. Canada has no death penalty, but does have stricter gun laws, higher student test scores, a healthier population, and a higher per capita GDP than the United States.

Canada's vast size, abundant resources, and developed economy ensure that the country will play a significant role in international affairs in the twenty-first century.

Geography, Trade, and the Globalization of North America

Globalization is readily apparent in the daily lives of North Americans. On the streets of Toronto, Montreal, New York, Los Angeles, Chicago, or a small town in Ohio or Ontario, one can taste, see, and hear the global connections of market and production, culture, and politics (Figure 6.2). North Americans consume food from Latin America (orange juice made of oranges from Brazil),

Figure 6.2 Chicago. The sculpture Cloud Gate at Millennium Park.

Source: S. Toops

Africa (chocolate made of cacao from Ghana), Asia (apple juice made of apples from China), and Europe (pasta made of wheat from Italy). North American versions of tacos and burritos, pizza, and spaghetti are found in most towns. Larger cities have their forms of General Tso's chicken and aloo gobi. Musical influences such as salsa from Latin America and African-inspired jazz beats fill the airwaves and Internet. Movies from all over the world challenge the cultural power of Hollywood.

The United States and Canada combined have some 370 million residents. Yet because of buying power and trade, North America has a role in global economics far beyond the size of its population. Consumer goods, food, and popular culture from North America are diffusing across the world. The affluence of the United States and Canada derives from their **postindustrial economies**. Technology and culture combine to produce high levels of resource consumption in the United States and Canada. North American agricultural products, manufacturers, and technologies link the region to the world. Canada exports wheat from Saskatchewan to China. Nissan exports the Altima from Tennessee to the Middle East. Apple iPhones, while designed in California, are manufactured in China. Global exports include licenses for software, patents, movies, and TV shows. Travel to the United States and Canada counts as US and Canadian exports when the travelers from other countries spend money to buy goods and services.

North America is connected by the United States-Mexico-Canada (USMCA) trade agreement, signed in 2020. This agreement replaces the North American Free Trade Agreement, NAFTA, a trade bloc from the Yukon to the Yucatan. The US exports vehicles to Canada, machinery to Mexico, soybeans to China, oil to Japan, gold to the United Kingdom, and aircraft to the EU. Canada exports oil to the United States, ore to China, gems and precious metals to the United Kingdom, oil to Japan, and vegetable oil seeds to Mexico. US imports include electronics from China, oil from Canada, vehicles from Mexico, vehicles from Japan, machinery from the United Kingdom, and pharmaceuticals from Germany.

Transforming the Environment

Five hundred years ago, most of the eastern areas of the United States and Canada were forested, but today much of it is cropland. European settlers transformed the environment by cutting down forests and planting new crops. They plowed under native grasses in the Midwest and Great Plains, making way for large fields of corn, soybeans, or wheat today, none of which are native to the region or the prairie. Urbanization meant the concentration of people in metropolises such as New York, Los Angeles, and Toronto. In suburbs, people created a new landscape of shopping malls and green lawns, even in areas like southern California and Arizona where there was hardly enough water or land to do so.

Water

India and China surpass the United States' total consumption of water, but the US per capita consumption is far greater. The water footprint of the average consumer in the United States is 2,200 gallons per year, while the average consumer in China has a water footprint of 775 gallons per year. The global average is 1,002 gallons per capita (Water Calculator).

The Colorado River, which supports water users in Los Angeles, barely reaches the Gulf of California in Mexico. All of the states in the river basin (Colorado, Utah, Wyoming, New Mexico, Arizona, Nevada, and California) use the water for irrigation, residential, and industrial purposes. Population growth, as well as per capita consumption in the southwestern United States, depletes the river's flow. The United States has a desalination plant to clean the Colorado River before it reaches Mexico (Berg and Hager 2009; Rogers 2008).

Figure 6.3 Niagara Falls. Water from Lake Erie passes to Lake Ontario. Niagara Falls has the highest flow rate of any waterfall on earth.

Source: S. Toops.

The Colorado River basin is in a dry climate, but water issues also affect humid areas. Water pollution in the Great Lakes is a serious issue for Canada and the United States. Together, the five Great Lakes (Superior, Michigan, Huron, Erie, and Ontario) account for one-fifth of the world's fresh surface water. Almost 40 million people live around the Great Lakes and use the water (Figure 6.3). By the 1960s, many pollutants, including sewage, fertilizer runoff, and industrial wastes, contaminated the Great Lakes. In the 1970s, Canada and the United States began working together to clean up the lakes. They are much cleaner today, but constant development of the shoreline around the cities has resulted in a continued loss of habitat (Berg and Hager 2009, Folger 2020).

Climate Change

Most scientists agree that human activity is having a dramatic impact on the climate. Burning carbon-based fuels, such as coal and oil, puts more carbon dioxide into the atmosphere. The carbon dioxide acts as a blanket, keeping in the heat from the solar radiation reflected off the earth's surface, just like the translucent roof of a greenhouse traps the sun's heat inside the building.

Overall global temperatures are rising. What are some possible impacts in North America? Some models forecast that the Great Lakes area will become wetter by 2100, and the southwestern United States will become drier, further straining the Colorado River basin. Climate change may portend longer growing seasons along the US-Canadian border. Greater heat may also mean a drier climate in the interior. Northern Canada and Alaska will see ice melting and transformation of the tundra, with unknown ecological impacts (Fouberg and Murphy 2020).

The melting of the Antarctic and Greenland ice sheets and glaciers will result in a rise in the sea level, jeopardizing the densely populated North American coastline (Price et al. 2020). Low-lying areas in Florida, such as Miami and Tampa, would be inundated. By 2070, over \$3.5 trillion of Miami's assets would be at risk. The sea rise also means salt water would enter and affect Florida's water system. Similarly, over \$2.1 trillion of New York City's assets would be jeopardized. New York could become the Venice of the West (Folger 2013).

North America's Changing Population

In general, North America has a very mobile and affluent population, much of which lives in huge urban areas. The megalopolis from Boston to New York and Washington, DC, forms an urban corridor known as BosNyWash. Chicago to Pittsburgh, and San Francisco to Los Angeles are also great metropolitan areas. The Canadian "Main Street" runs from Montreal to Ottawa and Toronto (Figure 6.4). Canada has 37.7 million people, of which 82 percent live in urban areas. The United States has 332.6 million people, with 83 percent in cities (CIA *World Factbook* 2020).

Until the Civil War, most immigrants to the United States came from Northern Europe and from Africa through the slave trade. Immigrants came from Southern and Eastern Europe between the Civil War and World War II. Since World War II, most of the immigrant population has come from Latin America and Asia (Price et al. 2020).

The United States measures resident population by race. In the 2010 census, whites accounted for 79.5 percent of the population, blacks 12.9 percent, Asian and Pacific Islanders 4.9 percent, multiracial 1.8 percent, and Native American 1 percent, with 6.2 reporting "other." Hispanics, who can be of any race, comprise 16.3 percent (Humes, Jones and Ramirez 2011). The United States has the fifth-largest Spanish-speaking population in the world. Almost 13 percent of the population today is foreign born. Population projections show that by 2060, the United States will be 44.3 percent non-Hispanic white, 15 percent black, 9 percent Asian and Pacific Islander, and 1.7 percent Native American (multiracial may account for 6 percent of the population), with 27.5 percent of people of any race identifying as Hispanic. Foreign born will account for 17 percent (Vespa, Medina and Armstrong 2020). Because of globalization and the continued attraction of immigrants to the United States, and the higher birth rates of the non-white population, the United States will be much more diverse in 2060 (U.S. Census Bureau 2020).

Canada has fairly open migration laws. The 2016 census shows that 22 percent of the population is foreign born. The largest share of recent migrants comes from Asia (including the Middle East). Canada keeps records of the ethnic origin of people's ancestors. Forty-two percent report more than one ethnic origin. The most common are Canadian, English, French, Scottish, Irish, German, Italian, Chinese, First Nation (American Indian), Ukrainian, East Indian, Dutch, and Polish. Origins of Canadians include European 57 percent, North America 34 percent, Asia 18 percent, North America Aboriginal 6 percent, Africa 3 percent, Caribbean 2 percent, Latin America 2 percent, and Oceania 0.2 percent (Statistics Canada 2020). Canada will have a new census in 2021. Canada and the United States are globally connected not only in terms of trade but also in terms of population.

Although the US and Canadian cultural, economic, political, and historical ties are greater to Europe, North America's connections to China are becoming more and more important. For example, in 1982, one of the authors (Toops) traveled from Seattle to Vermont to continue his study of the Chinese language at Middlebury College. Air travel was cheaper in Canada in those

Figure 6.4 Toronto, Canada. Toronto is the most populous city in Canada. The CN Tower is the tallest freestanding structure in the Western Hemisphere.

Source: S. Toops.

days, so he took a flight from Vancouver, British Columbia, to Montreal, Quebec. He took an airport bus to downtown Montreal and was searching in vain for the bus station to find a bus to Middlebury, Vermont. Without French-language skills, he was fortunate to stumble upon a Chinese restaurant where he asked in Chinese for directions. North America is indeed fully globalized.

North America Matters

Covid-19, a coronavirus, was found in Wuhan, China, in December 2019. The disease has since spread around the world. East Asia was able to keep the virus under control through the use of masks. The United States has the largest number of cases and deaths, in part because masks and social distancing were not rigorously practiced. The United States may be able to produce and deliver enough vaccine but masking and distancing still need to be followed. The United States is not as poor as Brazil or India (both have a large number of cases and deaths), so the ravages of the disease may be mitigated by economic power of the United States (Pettersson et al. 2020).

The United States has the world's largest military, yet by one measure, purchasing power parity, China has surpassed the US. Together with Canada, North America is a huge geographical area with abundant arable land and water and mineral resources. Politically, the two countries have had relatively stable democratic systems for over two centuries.

The United States has inspired many of the world's political and economic systems, from the republic's constitution to the global free trade system promoted by the World Trade Organization. The US dollar is the world's most important reserve currency, and the health of the world economy is inextricably linked with the ups and downs of the US economy.

International studies largely focuses on issues beyond the borders of North America, but it is helpful to understand the politics, economics, geography, anthropology, and history of the United States and Canada to compare them to the other regions discussed in the book. North America is still a much sought-after destination for immigrants around the world for economic opportunities and political freedoms.

Timeline of Modern North American History

1821	Mexican independence from Spain.
1867	Canadian independence from Great Britain.
1898	Spanish–American War. United States acquires Puerto Rico, controls Cuba.
1903	United States takes Panama Canal Zone.
1914	Panama Canal opens.
1914, 1916	United States intervention in Mexican Revolution.
1917	United States enters the First World War.
1941	Japan bombs Pearl Harbor, Hawaii; United States enters Second World War.
1945	United States employs nuclear weapons against Japan.
1959	Cuban revolution; Castro seizes power.
1961	United States failed Bay of Pigs invasion of Cuba; United States cuts ties to Cuba.
1962	Cuban Missile Crisis.
1978	United States hosts the Camp David Accords.
1983	Reagan mines Nicaraguan harbors in support of Contras against Sandinista government; United States invades Grenada.
1986	United States amnesty for illegal immigrants.
1989	United States invades Panama.
1990–1991	First Gulf War.
1994	North American Free Trade Agreement.
1996	United States Helms-Burton Act codifies Cuban embargo into law.
1999	United States cedes Panama Canal to Panama.
1999–2013	Anti-US Hugo Chavez president of Venezuela.

2000	Election of Vincente Fox of Mexico's Alliance of Change, ending decades of PRI rule.
2001	Al-Qaeda terrorists attack New York City and Washington, DC; United States and allies invade Afghanistan.
2003	United States invades Iraq, initiating the Second Gulf War.
2008	Barack Obama elected first African American US president.
2015	Justin Trudeau appointed Prime Minister of Canada.
2016	Donald Trump elected President of the United States.
2017	President Donald Trump promises to build a wall on the US–Mexican border.
2020	United States Mexico Canada Agreement (USMCA) replaces NAFTA.
2020	Joseph Biden elected President of the United States.

References

Adams, James Truslow. 1931. *The Epic of America*. Boston: Little, Brown and Co.

Berg, Linda R., and Mary Catherine Hager. 2009. "Freshwater Resources and Water Pollution." In *Visualizing Environmental Science*, 242–68. 2nd ed. Hoboken, NJ: Wiley.

Chua, Amy. 2007. *Day of Empire: How Hyperpowers Rise to Global Dominance—and Why They Fall*. New York: Anchor Books.

CIA World Factbook. 2020. www.cia.gov/the-world-factbook/

Crawford, Neta C. 2013. "*U.S. Costs of Wars through 2013: $3.1 Trillion and Counting. Summary of Costs for the U.S. Wars in Iraq, Afghanistan and Pakistan.*" Brown University and Boston University: Costs of War Project. https://watson.brown.edu/costsofwar/files/cow/imce/papers/2016/Costs%20of%20War%20through%202016%20FINAL%20final%20v2.pdf (accessed June 23, 2013).

Escobar, Arturo. 1995. *Encountering Development: The Making and the Unmaking of the Third World*. Princeton, NJ: Princeton University Press.

Fitzpatrick, Peter. 1992. *The Mythology of Modern Law*. London: Routledge.

Folger, Tim. 2013. "Rising Seas." *National Geographic*. September. 224 (3): 30–57.

——. 2020. "North America's Greatest Resource is at Risk." *National Geographic*. December. www.nationalgeographic.com/magazine/2020/12/north-americas-most-valuable-resource-is-at-risk-feature/

Fouberg, Erin H. and Alexander B. Murphy. 2020. "The Humanized Environment." In *Human Geography: People, Place, and Culture*. 12th ed. Hoboken, NJ: Wiley.

Fuchs, Lawrence H. 1990. *The American Kaleidoscope: Race, Ethnicity, and the Civic Culture*. Middleton, CT: Wesleyan University Press.

Gibbon, John Murray. 1938. *Canadian Mosaic: The Making of a Northern Nation*. Toronto: McClelland & Stewart.

Gunderson, Steven. 2013. *The New Middle Class: Creating Wages, Wealth, and Opportunity in the 21st Century*. Austin, TX: Greenleaf Books.

Hause, Steven, and William Maltby. 1999. *Western Civilization: A History of European Society*. Belmont, CA: West/Wadsworth.

Hoekstra, Arjen Y., and Mesfin M. Mekonnen. 2012. "The Water Footprint of Humanity." *Proceedings of the National Academy of Science* 109 (9): 3232–37.

Humes, Karen, Nicholas A. Jones, and Roberto R. Ramirez. 2011. "Overview of Race and Hispanic Origin: 2010." U.S. Census Bureau. www.census.gov/prod/cen2010/briefs/c2010br-02.pdf.

Michelman, Frank. 1988. "Law's Republic." *Yale Law Journal* 97: 493–537.

OMB (Office of Management and Budget). 2020. "Outlays by Function and Subfunction: 1962–2018." www.whitehouse.gov/wp-content/uploads/2021/05/hist03z2_fy22.xlsx (accessed June 23, 2021).

Pettersson, Henrik, Byron Manley, and Sergio Hernandez. 2020. "Tracking Coronavirus Global Spread." *CNN*. www.cnn.com/interactive/2020/health/coronavirus-maps-and-cases/

Price, Marie, Martin Lewis, Wyckoff and Lester Rowntree. 2020. *Globalization and Diversity: Geography of a Changing World*. 6th ed. Upper Saddle River, NJ: Pearson Prentice Hall.

Reich, Robert B. 2010. *Aftershock: The Next Economy and America's Future*. New York: Vintage Books.

Roberts, Alasdair. 2020. "The Pandemic Exposes an Ailing US Governance Model." *Current History* 119 (820): 310–16.

Rogers, Peter. 2008. "Facing the Freshwater Crisis." *Scientific American* (August): 46–53.

Rosenberg, Emily S. 1982. *Spreading the American Dream: American Economic and Cultural Expansion 1890–1945*. New York: Hill and Wang.

Saint-Paul, Gilles. 1996. *Dual Labor Markets: A Macroeconomic Perspective*. Cambridge, MA: MIT Books.

Sarat, Austin, and Roger Berkowitz. 1998. "Disorderly Differences: Recognition, Accommodation, and American Law." In *Democracy and Ethnography: Constructing Identities in Multicultural Liberal States*, edited by Carol Greenhouse, 81–102. Albany: State University of New York Press.

Statistics Canada. 2020. www.statcan.gc.ca/eng/start

United States Census Bureau. 2020. www.census.gov/

Vespa, Jonathan, Lauren Medina, and David M. Armstrong. 2020. "Demographic Turning Points for the United States: Population Projections for 2020 to 2060." US Census Bureau. www.census.gov/content/dam/Census/library/publications/2020/demo/p25-1144.pdf

Vine, David. 2015. *Base Nation: How U.S. Military Bases Abroad Harm America and the World*. New York: Metropolitan/Henry Holt.

World Bank Group. 2020. *Doing Business 2020: Comparing Business Regulation in 190 Economies*. Washington, DC: International Bank for Reconstruction and Development.

World Integrated Trade Solutions (WITS). 2019. https://wits.worldbank.org/CountryProfile/en/Country/WLD/Year/LTST/TradeFlow/Export/Partner/by-country (accessed June 24, 2019).

World Trade Organization. www.wto.org

Further Reading

Books

Agnew, John A., and Jonathan M. Smith, eds. 2002. *American Space/American Place: Geographies of the Contemporary United States*. New York: Routledge.

Hofstadter, Richard. 1948. *The American Political Tradition: And the Men Who Made It*. New York: Knopf.

Morton, Desmond. 2001. *A Short History of Canada*. Toronto: McClelland and Stewart.

Steinbeck, John. 1939. *The Grapes of Wrath*. New York: Viking.

Williams, William Appleman. 1961. *The Contours of American History*. Cleveland, OH: World.

Journals

American Studies. https://journals.ku.edu/amsj/index

American Review of Canadian Studies. https://canam.wwu.edu/american-review-of-canadian-studies/

Canadian Review of American Studies. www.utpjournals.press/loi/cras

New York Review of Books. www.nybooks.com

Films

America: the Story of US (2010). US miniseries.

American Exceptionalism: Monopoly on Democracy (2013). Anissa Naouai, producer.

Black Robe (1991). Bruce Beresford, director.

The Canary Effect (2006). Fobin Davey, director.

Monsieur Lazhar (2011). Philippe Falardeau, director.

Websites

American Studies Association. www.theasa.net
The Atlantic. www.theatlantic.com
The Globe and Mail. www.theglobeandmail.com
Government of Canada. www.canada.ca
International Council for Canadian Studies. www.iccs-ciec.ca
The New York Times. www.nytimes.com
United States Government web portal. www.usa.gov

Chapter 7

Europe and the Modern World

In 1900, Europeans and their cultural offspring (including, for example, Americans, Canadians, and Australians) controlled nearly 85 percent of the earth's land mass. European dominance in the modern world was by no means determined five hundred years ago, but a potent mix of geographical, historical, political, cultural, and economic advantages has enabled Europe to put its stamp on global development to this day. Europeans defined the meaning of the term *modern*, which includes a rapid rise in agricultural production, currency-based trade, exchanges of goods and services over long distances, rapid improvements in industry and technology, an increase in life expectancies, lower birth rates, universal elementary education, and urbanization. **Globalization** in the late-nineteenth century was mainly a Western phenomenon.

European thinkers developed the important ideas that frame global debates today. Are democracy and human rights universally applicable to all people, regardless of ethnicity, culture, gender, or tradition? Is the capitalist, free-market economic system a model for economic development and human happiness everywhere? Does free trade best serve the interests of impoverished countries and poor people worldwide? Does the European idea of the **nation-state** have any relevance to nation-building efforts in other parts of the world?

An understanding of European political and economic development is essential to the study of international affairs today. European colonialists disseminated their political, economic, and social culture into the Western Hemisphere, Africa, and Asia. Westerners created most of the international institutions of global governance. After World War I, the Western allies formed the first global political organization to prevent war. The League of Nations failed, but following World War II the United States and Great Britain spearheaded efforts to resurrect a new United Nations, which codified the Universal Declaration on Human Rights in 1947. As the world's greatest economic power, the United States created financial and trade institutions such as the **International Monetary Fund** (IMF) and the **World Trade Organization** (WTO) to promote a stable global capitalist system. The 27 members of the **European Union** (EU) form the largest free-trade area in the world, even after the United Kingdom left it in 2020.

What Is Europe?

Europe has different and often conflicting geographic, historical, political, ethnic, and cultural definitions. The traditional **geographic definition** of the continent of Europe (Map 7.1) describes it as extending from the tip of Norway in the north to Gibraltar in the southwest and the Bosporus in the southeast, and from Iceland in the Atlantic to the Ural Mountains in central Russia. That leaves over half of Russia in Asia and puts a part of Istanbul, the largest Turkish city, in Europe.

Europe has been blessed by nature with a temperate climate, abundant rainfall, a long growing season, navigable waterways, and accessible oceans and seas. European industrialization and modernization had many causes, but its geographical advantages were significant. Europe's ample

DOI: 10.4324/9781003028314-10

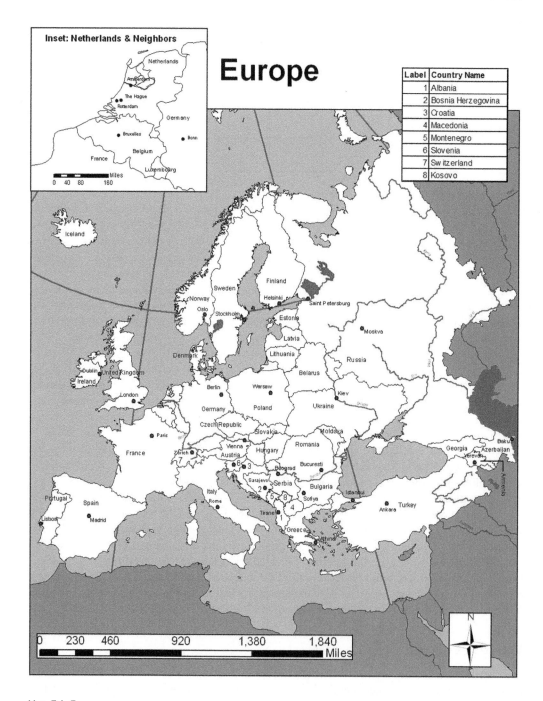

Label	Country Name
1	Albania
2	Bosnia Herzegovina
3	Croatia
4	Macedonia
5	Montenegro
6	Slovenia
7	Switzerland
8	Kosovo

Map 7.1 Europe.

timber and coal resources provided the energy necessary for early industrialization, although Europe is now largely dependent on petroleum products from outside the region.

Europe has a distinct **historical definition** as well. The Roman Empire brought the Judeo-Christian tradition to the heart of Europe in the early centuries of the first millennium CE. The Renaissance in Italy and the Reformation in Germany in the fifteenth and sixteenth centuries began an enlightened age that propelled the continent's political and economic development past the Ottoman and Chinese empires. In 1492, the powerful Spanish monarchy sent Christopher Columbus to the so-called New World, destroyed Europe's largest Jewish community, and defeated Granada, the last Muslim state in Western Europe.

European modernization was characterized by a flourishing of diverse religious, political, scientific, and technological thought. The European balance of power ensured competition among the states for the best inventors, scientists, businessmen, tradesmen, and intellects. For example, in 1697, seeing that Russia was far behind technologically, Tsar Peter the Great toured Western Europe incognito to glean innovations in sailing and weaponry.

Europe gradually acquired the military power, maritime technology, and scientific knowledge to begin its unprecedented domination of the world. It was a toxic brew that gave Europeans the power to do great harm to themselves and others. In the seventeenth and eighteenth centuries, Europeans surpassed the rest of the world in terms of modern development: relatively stable political and legal structures, standing armies, intellectual exchange, progressive social policies, industrialization, technology, urbanization, and capitalization.

The political definition of Europe has changed since World War II. The continent was divided into two camps after the war. Most West European states had democratic governments, capitalist economies, and a military alliance with the United States and Canada, forming the **North Atlantic Treaty Organization** (NATO). Six West European countries created the European **Common Market** in 1957, which has evolved into the EU. The Soviet Union's satellite states in Eastern Europe formed the **Warsaw Pact** in 1955, completing the division of Europe. Southeast European states such as Greece fell into the Western sphere, while Yugoslavia, despite its communist system, remained non-aligned. Most of Finland, Sweden, and Austria lay east of the Warsaw Pact boundary, but their neutral status and democratic systems defined them as more Western than Eastern.

After the **Iron Curtain** fell in 1989, the economic definition of Europe became nearly synonymous with membership in the EU. In 2004, the 15 members of the EU expanded to 25. With the accession of Finland, the three Baltic states (Estonia, Latvia, and Lithuania), Poland, the Czech Republic, Slovakia, Hungary, Slovenia, Cyprus, and Malta, some observers have suggested that there is a new East–West political and economic division of Europe. Bulgaria and Romania joined the EU in 2007, and Croatia in 2013, leaving Russia, Belarus, and Ukraine on the outside looking in.

The cultural definition of Europe is perhaps the most controversial. Europe traces many of its cultural influences to the Mediterranean area, from the ancient civilizations of Egypt, Palestine, Greece, and Rome. Europe is predominantly Christian, and before the Holocaust had a substantial Jewish population. The Balkan Slavs are mainly Orthodox, and their Slavic and Hungarian neighbors to the north are mostly Roman Catholic. During the Reformation, Protestantism took hold in Prussia and Saxony (northern and eastern Germany today), England, and Scandinavia. The major western Catholic countries are Italy, Spain, France, and Ireland.

But organized religion no longer plays an important role in the lives of most west Europeans. Despite the Catholic Church's conservative attitude toward birth control, Italy and Spain have among the lowest birth rates in Europe. Poles (Catholic) and the Balkan peoples (Catholic and Orthodox) tend to be more devout, and their religion remains a central element in their national identity. For example, Serbs distinguish themselves from other Yugoslavs (South Slavs) in part by their Orthodox faith.

Language is a deeper national fault line in Europe. The major Indo-European languages fall into three major groups: Germanic (English, German, and the Scandinavian languages); Romance (Spanish, French, Italian, and Romanian); and Slavic (Russian, Ukrainian, Polish, Czech, Slovak, Serbian, Slovene, Croat, Bulgarian, and Macedonian). Finnish and Hungarian belong to a distinct Finno-Ugric language group unrelated to any other European language. English is becoming the European lingua franca, but it will not replace national languages as the mother tongue in the foreseeable future.

Europe's Slow Progress Toward Liberal Democracy

The philosophical discourse about the most just and fair political systems today is informed by Europe's long evolution toward **democracy**, from the ancient Greek city-states and the laws and practices of the Roman Empire to the American and French revolutions in the late-eighteenth century. The world's first modern democracies were formed in Europe and North America.

Liberal democracy is a system of government that institutionalizes majority rule and equality under the law. Democratic institutions are characterized by free elections, an independent judiciary, a constitution or body of law, civilian control of the military, and basic civil rights such as freedom of speech, religion, assembly, and the right to trial. In theory, liberal democracies apply the law equally to all groups and guarantee the rights of the electoral minorities.

Democracies are liberal to varying degrees. Elections in and of themselves do not define liberal democracy. Many countries such as Russia and Belarus hold elections, but the outcomes are controlled by screening the candidates allowed to run for office, monopolizing the press, rigging elections, or harassing and even jailing the opposition. Constitutions can limit the rights of women and ethnic minorities and restrict civil rights. Theocracies engrave religious law into civil law. Endemic corruption is also the bane of liberal democratic rule.

In his now famous book *The End of History and the Last Man* (1992), Francis Fukuyama theorized that the fall of communism in 1989–1991 in Eastern Europe and the Soviet Union signaled the end of history. He argued that with the fall of communism and the ideological bankruptcy of Marxism, there were no other political philosophies to rival Western liberal democracy and its enlightened ideas of free political and economic thought, tolerance, and equality under the law. The inability of centrally planned Communist economies to compete with liberal-economic systems supposedly meant the end of economic history as well. **Liberal economics** is in ascendancy today, despite a growing disparity between the rich and poor classes and rich and poor countries.

Although most European countries are liberal democracies now, a short walk through modern European history should give pause to Westerners who muse about the superiority of their culture and progressive political and economic development. Europeans and their cultural offspring have made great contributions to liberal democratic thought, but their unrivaled economic and technological power over the last three centuries have enabled them to bring greater good and wreak greater havoc on the world than any other people. On the one hand, they have given the world the railroad, the automobile, the airplane, computers, constitutional law, and the protection of human rights; on the other, they have produced weapons of unparalleled lethality and have used them in war after war after war. Five million people died in the Napoleonic Wars, 600,000 in the American Civil War, and another 50 million in the two world wars. Western science produced the nuclear bomb, which the United States used to obliterate two Japanese cities to end World War II (Figure 7.1). Europeans and Americans killed and enslaved millions of Africans, and Western imperialists destroyed peoples and mangled foreign cultures. Nearly 25 million Third World peoples perished in Cold War conflicts.

Figure 7.1 Nagasaki after the atomic bomb.

Source: National Archives.

The Development of Liberal Democracy and the Threat of Nationalism

Enlightened political philosophers such as John Locke, Montesquieu, Jean-Jacques Rousseau, Voltaire, and Thomas Jefferson developed many of the liberal democratic ideas manifested in the American and French revolutions at the end of the eighteenth century. Both revolutions borrowed heavily from the Glorious Revolution of 1688 in England, when parliament asked the executive (King William III) to share power. The old regime of divine-right monarchy, aristocratic privilege, and inequality under the law came under siege in the nineteenth century when the middle and working classes, as well as oppressed nationalities, challenged the status quo.

In the late-eighteenth century, the great Prussian philosopher Immanuel Kant ([1788] /1997) wrote that "the universal and lasting establishment of peace constitutes not merely a part, but the whole final purpose and end of the science of right as viewed within the limits of reason." Current threats from terrorism, weapons of mass destruction, global warming, and genocide seem to mock Kant's optimistic vision of the ultimate reason and rationality of human beings, and his progressive view of history. But the march toward democracy in the world in the last two centuries has been inexorable, albeit with many hurdles and setbacks along the way. Liberal, democratic revolutions rocked most of the illiberal empires of Europe in 1848, but the forces of reaction prevailed. The major European states could not extinguish the fire of democratic freedom for long. Britain and France gradually broadened the franchise, the German and Austrian empires had national assemblies (Reichstag), and even the ultraconservative Russian Tsar acceded to a parliament (Duma) in 1906.

Nationalism has been the historical enemy of liberal democracy in Europe. Americans often use the terms *nation* and *state* interchangeably. A **state** is a governing political structure, while a **nation** is an imagined group of people. Nation is a loaded term, because it implies that a nation should have its own state. The definition of an ethnic group is nearly the same as nation, but the international community usually accepts the minority status of ethnic groups within a state dominated by another national group. The Kurds in Turkey, the Tibetans in China, and the **Basques** in Spain are examples.

National groups are distinguished by some of these common characteristics: language, religion, culture, an agreed-upon history, and a link to a particular piece of land. Most nations develop a historical mission, such as the defense of the nation against an alien people or the spread of the nation's way of life.

No one is born with a national identity. Nationalism is learned from the family, community, schools, and the media. Toward the end of the nineteenth century, the newly formed German Empire was one of the first states to mandate universal elementary education. Berlin sought to overcome local and regional identities with a pan-German patriotism. After World War I, the United States developed social studies courses to inculcate a distinct American national identity among its various immigrant groups. National histories often distort the truth to glorify founding fathers and heroic defenders of the nation, and raise the nation's cultural and technological achievements above those of others.

During the French Revolution, at the end of the eighteenth century, nationalism became a potent means of mobilizing the masses toward a common goal. Revolutionaries toppled the French monarchy and reduced the power of the nobility and the church, and French armies carried the people's revolution to the rest of Europe. Napoleon proclaimed himself emperor in 1804 and became a despot and conqueror rather than a liberator. German and Russian national feelings were awakened as the result of French imperialism and chauvinism, and Napoleon's crusade into central Europe and Russia in 1812 foundered in the Russian winter.

National myths appeal to emotions rather than reason. English poet Lord Byron captured the essence of romantic nationalism in his panegyric to the martyred Greeks fighting for independence from the Turks in the early nineteenth century:

> They never fail who die
> In a great cause: the block may soak their gore;
> Their heads may sodden in the sun; their limbs
> Be strung to city gates and castle walls—
> But still their spirit walks abroad. (Byron 1821)

Lord Tennyson immortalized the futile British "Charge of the Light Brigade" during the Crimean War (1854–1856) against Russia in similar romantic style. When the order was given, the soldier was to do his duty and accept a noble and heroic death on the battlefield:

> Theirs not to make reply
> Theirs not to reason why
> Theirs but to do and die
> Into the Valley of Death
> Rode the Six Hundred. (Tennyson [1854] 1964)

In the nineteenth century, European nationalism developed in tandem with industrialization, urbanization, class divisions, and increased literacy. Europeans forged further ahead in science and technology, sometimes misrepresenting science to make seemingly rational explanations for racism, anti-Semitism, and imperialism. Pseudo-sciences such as phrenology and examinations of brain sizes and facial characteristics were used to justify the superiority of one race over another.

Nationalists in the divided German and Italian states wanted to pull together their peoples into single countries, respectively, based on a common language, culture, and history. This was not necessarily a natural development for either nation. Germans were Protestant, Catholic, and Jewish, they spoke different dialects, and they were divided into 39 states with very different histories. Protestant Prussia in the north and Catholic Bavaria and Austria in the south were the largest German states, although Vienna controlled an empire with a majority of non-Germans.

A German national myth had to be developed on the basis of ostensibly superior literary, artistic, scientific, philosophical, and industrial achievements. German nationalism had a negative orientation as well, as a reaction against French political and cultural imperialism, and

Figure 7.2 Charge of the Light Brigade.

Source: Library of Congress.

German superiority over the less-developed Slavs to the east, primarily Poles and Russians. Many German nationalists considered Jews to be outside of the community of German peoples (*das Volk*). The influx of Turkish workers in the 1960s, and the new immigrants from war-torn areas of the Middle East today are testing the German sense of national unity.

There were deep cultural, economic, and historical fissures on the Italian peninsula as well, some of which persist to this day. Italian nationalists whipped up national passions by harkening back to the halcyon days of the Roman Empire, the progressive Italian city-states, and the beauty and grace of Renaissance culture. Italian unification would have to come at the expense of the Austrian Empire, which controlled two key northern Italian states, Lombardy and Venice.

The multinational Austrian Empire had the most to lose from the rise of nationalism. The empire was home to eleven different nationalities: Austrian Germans, Italians, Czechs, Slovaks, Ukrainians, Hungarians, Slovenes, Croats, Serbs, Romanians, and Poles. Russia and Prussia also possessed substantial portions of old Poland, which had been partitioned by the three eastern empires (Austria, Russia, and Prussia) in the late eighteenth century. Russia supported fellow Orthodox Slavs in the Balkans—Bulgarians and Serbs—who sought liberation from the Turkish Ottoman Empire. All of these nations have their own state today.

Conservatives in the Italian state of Piedmont-Sardinia and the German state of Prussia co-opted the nationalist appeal to the masses by promoting a **conservative nationalism** of their own, characterized by imperial conquest and loyalty to the monarchy. Piedmont-Sardinia and France defeated Austria in 1859 to begin a unification process that was completed in 1870. Prussia fought wars against Denmark (1864), Austria (1866), and France (1870) to unite the German states into the Second German Reich. The success of these unifications by war created national myths for both Italy and Germany based on what one historian termed "the armed deed" (Wandycz 1988). Unfortunately, Prussian Chancellor Otto von Bismarck put a militaristic, conservative, nationalist, and illiberal stamp on the new German state.

National pride metastasized into a martial theology of racial superiority, which would eventually become an essential element of fascist ideology. Charles Darwin's theory of the survival of the fittest in nature was transposed onto societies. "Superior" European culture, racial character, and technological achievement justified wars on other races. British imperialist Cecil Rhodes, whose name is borne by a prestigious scholarship, proclaimed that "we are the finest race in the world and the more of it we inhabit the better it is for the human race" (cited in Flint 1976, 27–28). In 1895, Teddy Roosevelt revealed his firm Darwinian belief in the invigorating benefits of war for a nation: "Let the fight [with Great Britain] come if it must. I rather hope that the fight will come soon. The clamor of the peace faction has convinced me that this country needs a war" (cited in Miller 1992, 235). When the Spanish–American War broke out in 1898, the *Washington Post* gushed with glee at the chance for the United States to prove its mettle: "Ambition, interest, land hunger, pride, the mere joy of fighting, whatever it may be, we are animated by a new sensation.... The taste of Empire is, in the mouth of the people even as the taste of blood in the jungle" (*Washington Post* 1898).

In the mid-nineteenth century, Karl Marx introduced the most threatening revolutionary idea to liberal democracy and to nationalist ideology. Marx theorized that workers in the capitalist system would never receive the value of their labor from the owners of the machines. Marx argued that the political system that protected and promoted the capitalist system had to be violently overthrown. The horrendous conditions of working-class life in early industrial Europe provided a fertile recruiting ground for the Communist parties.

Marx said that nationalism, religion, and racism were the ideological weapons of the upper classes to keep the working classes passive and obsequious. Christianity's promise of an afterlife, Marx argued, was so much hokum to keep workers from fighting the unjust order of things on earth.

National pride has proven to be the most powerful group identifier, trumping the Marxist appeal to workers' solidarity with fellow laborers on the factory floor. **Imperialism** in Africa and Asia fueled the national competition between European countries and rallied the upper, middle, and working classes behind national goals. "If you wish to avoid civil war [at home]," British empire builder Cecil Rhodes declared, "then you must become an imperialist" (cited in Lenin 1974, 256–57). When World War I erupted in 1914, the working classes and their parties again backed the national cause. Few German, British, or French workers refused to serve in the trenches or go "over the top" in futile offensives.

Political Change and the World Wars

The power of national identity was an important factor in the ultimate collapse of communism in Eastern Europe in 1989, and the failure of Marxist ideology as a whole, but nationalism is not a political system or economic program; it is an authoritarian ideology of exclusion. European governments were moving in the direction of greater liberalism in the early twentieth century, but the power of nationalism helped bring on and prolong the carnage of World War I (1914–1918). At the beginning of World War I, many Europeans were excited about the prospect of a war that could prove their country's national superiority. Over 9 million Europeans died in that war.

World War I was the catalyst for rapid and radical political change in Europe. At the end of the war, the four great Eastern empires—Germany, Austria, Russia, and Turkey—collapsed. Germany, Austria, and Turkey created republics with varying degrees of liberal democratic government. The new independent states of Finland, Estonia, Latvia, Lithuania, Hungary, Poland, Czechoslovakia, and Yugoslavia were carved out of the ruins of the old empires. All of them established democratic governments, although most were short-lived.

But liberal democracy could not survive the economic, social, and psychological damage done by World War I. Threats came from the far left and the far right. The **Bolshevik Revolution** in Russia in 1917 created the first communist state, and **Fascism** in Italy and **Nazism** in Germany emerged to meet the communist challenge to religion, nationalism, and capitalism. In contrast to liberal democracy's dilatory reaction to the economic crises and communist agitation, fascists on the far right promised action to protect national interests.

Italy created the first fascist state in 1922. Italy had allied with Britain and France in World War I but was humiliated when the Paris peacemakers denied it any significant territorial spoils of the war. Fascist leader Benito Mussolini capitalized on wounded Italian national pride to overthrow the Italian democracy. Mussolini's fascist ideology was a dynamic and spirited answer to Italian economic ills and political infighting. He promised to bring law and order to a land in profound political, economic, social, and psychological turmoil. Fascism promised to move Italy forward even if it came at the expense of Italian democracy and civil rights. The fascists glorified Italy's past, censored the press, and undermined the appeal of Marxism to workers by employing them in state works programs and by implementing controls over management–labor relations. Mussolini promised to put millions of men under arms to project Italian power abroad.

Italians were willing to go along with one-man rule as long as Mussolini stabilized the economy and ended domestic strife. This popular attraction to the promises of authoritarian rule—to bring order out of political, economic, and social chaos—remains a constant threat to liberal democracy today. Citizens in democracies have shown a dangerous tendency to sacrifice many of their civil rights for greater security and political and economic stability. For example, despite revelations in 2013 of a far-reaching personal-data-collection program run by US national-security agencies, there was little outcry from Americans fearful of terror attacks.

Adolf Hitler modeled his mass movement in Germany after Italian fascism. Nazism was the antithesis of liberal democracy. The Nazis papered over Germany's deep social and economic divisions with appeals to **anti-Semitism**, nationalism, racism, and militarism. Songs, mass rallies, symbols, creeds, marches, and messianic promises of returning Germany to first place among nations lent a fanatic religious and spiritual tone to the Nazi movement. The demonization of other groups is staple propaganda of dictatorships today, such as Iran, Syria, and North Korea, and demagoguery is always a threat to democratic rule. Hitler's rise to power is a case in point. The Nazi party garnered less than 3 percent of the German vote before the most serious depression in the history of modern capitalism hit in 1929. With millions out of work, the stress became too much for the democratic middle to save the fledgling Weimar Republic. By 1932, the Nazi Party was polling one-third of the vote, becoming the largest party in Germany. Hitler took over the chancellorship in January 1933 and quickly snuffed out any opposition to Nazi rule.

Hitler's early economic and diplomatic successes caused many skeptical Germans and Europeans to ignore his undemocratic methods and virulent anti-Semitism. Nazism was no accident, as some scholars have argued, but a logical if not predictable product of German and European modern political culture. Nineteenth-century German Marxist August Bebel called anti-Semitism "the socialism of fools." At that time, the political and economic power brokers knew that they could deflect working-class hostility from themselves onto Jews; theories proliferated about Jewish conspiracies to exploit the Christian working classes. Hitler borrowed from theories of racial superiority to argue that Jews were a threat to the purity of German blood. The mass slaughter of five and a half million Jews during World War II was the terrible result of this fanatical nationalism and racism. Although no leader since then has wanted to be labeled a fascist or a Nazi, many have established fascist dictatorships and have committed genocide, such as Pol Pot in Cambodia in the 1970s and the Hutu leaders in Rwanda in the 1990s.

Nazi nationalist and racist propaganda effectively convinced Germans to attack and subdue most of Europe in World War II and to continue fighting even when it was obvious that Germany would be defeated. Thirty-five million more Europeans died as the result of Germany's nationalist mania. Even the communists in the Soviet Union had to admit that Russian nationalism spoke to people's hearts more than class solidarity. Desperate to save the Soviet Union after Hitler's invasion in 1941, Stalin subordinated Marxist propaganda and dubbed the defense of Mother Russia "the Great Patriotic War." Stalin's compromise with nationalism foreshadowed the demise of the Soviet Union in 1991. The head of the Russian Republic, Boris Yeltsin, appealed to Russian nationalism to rescue Soviet leader Mikhail Gorbachev from a hard-liners' coup attempt in 1991. In this case, however, the strength of Russian nationalism and the bankruptcy of Soviet ideology meant the end of the communist state. Today President Vladimir Putin appeals to traditional Russian nationalism by claiming that the West is trying to undermine Russian political and economic interests, a tried and true Russian political ploy to unite the country, regardless of whether the rights of some citizens are being trampled.

Liberal democracy in Eastern Europe and Spain fared no better between the wars. **Authoritarian** nationalist dictatorships relied on support from the upper classes, large landowners, churches, and conservative elements in the armed forces. By the early thirties, every Eastern European state save Czechoslovakia had an authoritarian regime. The Spanish rebel *caudillo* Francisco Franco defeated the Spanish Republic in the bloody Spanish civil war (1936–1939). By the start of World War II in 1939, France, Belgium, the Netherlands, Luxembourg, Finland, Norway, Denmark, Sweden, and Switzerland were the only remaining democratic governments on the continent, and the Germans defeated all but the latter two neutral countries in the first year of the war. By the middle of 1940, the United States, Great Britain, Canada, and Australia were the only major liberal democratic states left. The victory of the allies over Nazi Germany in

1945 gave Europe another chance to build liberal democratic states in Western Europe, while the Soviets imposed communist systems in Eastern Europe.

From the Scourge of National Conflict to the European Union

Europe's story challenges those who argue that the world is becoming progressively more dangerous, unstable, and violent. Europe has been all of that in the twentieth century, but it has also emerged as one of the most peaceful and prosperous regions of the world. Europe has experienced a truly dramatic turnaround since those dark days of fascism, Nazi domination, and the Cold War. In the course of the world wars, the word *German* became synonymous with militarism, extreme nationalism, blind obedience, and brutality. Yet today Germany and France are fast allies.

The European Union (EU) is a liberal answer to Europe's long tradition of national conflict. There were no liberal democracies in 1900, and only about 20 after World War II (the United States was not a liberal democracy until the mid-1960s, when civil rights laws guaranteed African Americans the right to vote in the Jim Crow South). With the exception of Belarus, all of the European states have democratic systems of some sort today, although Russia and Ukraine have yet to prove their liberal democratic credentials.

Europe's exhaustion after World War II enabled the colonized peoples of Africa and Asia to demand the same right to **national self-determination** that was a theoretical hallmark of Western liberal political thought. Ho Chi Minh in Vietnam, Mohandas Gandhi in India, and Nelson Mandela in South Africa were among the many independence leaders who invoked Western political ideas to demand their countries' independence from European rulers.

The United States played an important role in the postwar unity of Western Europe. The United States emerged from World War II as the world's unparalleled economic and military power. The dynamic of the superpower confrontation and the division of Europe by the Iron Curtain from 1949 to 1989 compelled the countries of Western Europe to cooperate with the United States on the liberal democratic paradigm. The success of the American democratic and economic system along with the Soviet threat spurred transatlantic cooperation (Figure 7.3). Fascism was obviously discredited, and the crimes of Soviet leader Joseph Stalin's odious regime had been exposed. **Stalinism** held no appeal for West Europeans. All of Western Europe except Spain and Portugal developed liberal democratic political systems.

After World War II, the United States was determined not to repeat the failed economic policies of the interwar period and embarked on a **classical liberal** economic program.

European Integration

Memory of the catastrophic world wars, the Great Depression (which many scholars blame for the rise of Hitler), and the postwar communist threat were the compelling motives for European integration after World War II. The theory of **comparative advantage** also pushed the Europeans toward greater economic liberalism. The United States tried to prevent a postwar recession by creating institutions to promote free markets and international economic cooperation. The **World Bank** made loans to spur economic development, the IMF tried to keep currencies stable, and the **General Agreement on Tariffs and Trade** (GATT) provided a framework for gradually reducing barriers to freer trade between states. In 1995, GATT evolved into the WTO, which is dedicated to arbitrating international trade disputes and further lowering trade barriers. Today, the world is closer to the liberal economic model for international commerce than ever before.

In contrast to Stalin's exploitation of the East German and east European economies, the United States financed a $13 billion aid program called the **Marshall Plan** (1948–1952) to

Figure 7.3 NATO meeting in Estonia, 2010.

Source: State Department Photos.

jump-start the Western European economies. The rapid West European economic recovery in the 1950s ended any real threat from a united Communist movement. Liberal democracy in Western Europe thrived in the context of the Cold War.

The Marshall Plan was the first step toward Western European economic integration. The United States viewed economic cooperation with Western Europe as a way to bolster a community of free-market economies and liberal democracies as a counterweight to the Soviet bloc. Western Europe's economic and political stability became a strategic imperative.

Formal European economic integration began with the **European Coal and Steel Community** (ECSC) of 1951, which lowered tariffs and controlled production among France, Germany, Italy, and the Benelux countries (Belgium, the Netherlands, and Luxembourg). The ECSC was an agreement for managed trade rather than free trade, and it worked. The "Six" expanded the scope of their economic cooperation by forming the **European Economic Community** (EEC), or Common Market, in 1957, which lowered tariffs on trade as a whole and created a common external tariff. Great Britain stayed out, preferring to preserve economic ties to the empire and cultivate its special relationship with the United States. The rapid economic growth of the Common Market countries and the disintegration of the British Empire prompted a change of heart in London. Great Britain, Ireland, and Denmark joined the EEC in 1973.

The Common Market was based on liberal economic principles, but it also had important political and diplomatic objectives. The close cooperation of the two most important continental economies and former enemies—France and West Germany—promised to keep the peace. The United States supported the Common Market, even though it was an economic competitor. Washington wanted a strong Western Europe as a bulwark against the Soviet Union and its satellites in Eastern Europe.

In 1790, President George Washington predicted that one day there would be a "United States of Europe." In 1992, the European Economic Community took a major step toward achieving that goal when member states decided to form the EU and drop border controls, issue a common currency, and create a common foreign policy and defense policy. The **euro** was launched in 1999, joining the dollar and the yen as one of the world's major currencies. The Eurozone has expanded to 17 of the 27 countries in the EU. The euro makes transactions easier between the Eurozone members and for travelers; one currency provides a welcome relief from exchanging bills and coins at each European border, and having to pay an exchange fee each time. The EU's open borders have also eliminated time-consuming passport checks. Not since the heyday of the Roman Empire has Europe been so united. But unlike an empire, the EU is a voluntary union based on liberal, democratic principles.

Challenges to the European Union

Despite the union's benefits, the Greek debt crisis of the 2010s revealed that the Eurozone, and to a certain extent the EU as a whole, had pushed ahead with economic union without the requisite political legitimacy. While the Eurozone looked good on paper, not all members played by the financial rules, and there was no real means of punishing the profligate governments. When the Greek government faced default, Germany, which is the strongest economy in the EU, was forced to bail them out or risk the collapse of the Eurozone. German voters asked themselves why they should pay taxes to save Greece, a country that had, unlike Germany, spent money that it did not have. Furthermore, the Greeks' penchant for not paying their taxes also grates on the rest of those in the Eurozone who do. The future of the euro is in doubt, which would put the whole EU project in jeopardy.

The British decision to leave the EU (the "Brexit") in 2016 has also undermined the union, though it creates problems for the UK as well. Brexit could create a severe economic downturn; some economists predict that it could cost the country upwards of $80 billion a year (*USA Today*, October 12, 2016). Furthermore, British scientists fear a loss of top minds because they will no longer have access to EU research grants (*New York Times*, October 18, 2016). Worse, Britain's exit could prompt Scotland to leave the United Kingdom altogether.

The EU has fostered a common economic culture. Most European countries have systems that fall somewhere between a liberal and a command economy. European **social democracy** combines a free-market economy with extensive social benefits and substantial government regulation. All governments in the EU provide universal healthcare, generous unemployment and pension benefits, nearly free higher education, and subsidized election campaigns. Some national governments own airlines, railways, and other major industries.

However, some major continental economies such as France and Italy have struggled to maintain these generous social benefits, and suffer from chronic high unemployment. An aging population is putting strains on pension and health insurance programs in most of the EU states. When employees in a private company lose their jobs, they have little recourse. But politicians jeopardize their own positions when they try to cut government workers, and attempts to trim social welfare spending in some European countries have been met with public protests, as have changes in work rules for private firms. Greece's financial crisis has forced Athens to make draconian cuts in state spending, which has sparked repeated public demonstrations. These austerity measures have rarely worked to bring an economy out of a recession.

European states face difficult choices about the role of immigrant workers in alleviating labor shortages and about revamping welfare states to promote economic growth. The recent arrival of refugees into the EU has put further strain on social welfare systems, and they are often unfairly blamed for taking jobs from EU citizens. Extreme nationalism, Europe's old scourge, is rearing its ugly head again in the form of new political parties calling for an end to immigration.

The EU has not yet realized George Washington's prediction. The EU member states have been reluctant to give up national sovereignty on defense and foreign policy issues. The EU has decided to create a 60,000-strong Rapid Reaction Force, but has been slow to find the necessary funding. The EU's failure to act decisively to end the Yugoslav civil war in the 1990s, divisions within the community over going to war in Iraq in 2003, and the failure to find a solution to the Syrian conflict have exposed the weakness of the common EU foreign and defense policy. No European country took the lead in responding to the Syrian government's use of chemical weapons against its citizens in 2013. American policymakers have been increasingly critical of the EU's lack of defense spending, as evidenced by NATO's dependence on US weaponry in the campaign to oust Libyan dictator Muammar Qaddafi in 2011.

The EU, as some have suggested, is still a "United Europe of States." Most Europeans identify themselves as nationals first and EU citizens second. The European idea is under siege. Some Europeans describe the capital of the EU, Brussels, as representing a cold, technocratic, bureaucratic despotism—a "government of strangers." In 2005, French and Dutch voters rejected a European constitution. One anti-EU slogan in the Netherlands read, "We want to stay Dutch" (Pfaff 2005, 26). British politicians successfully lobbied for leaving the EU because they said that Britain's monetary contributions to the EU outweighed the benefits to the British economy, and that Britain wanted to regain control over immigrants coming into the country. Britain's exit from the EU puts the whole project in jeopardy. If the EU cannot achieve higher rates of economic growth and lower unemployment rates, more and more people will ask EU leaders if integration is really benefiting them. In 2016, German Chancellor Angela Merkel's Christian Democratic Party paid the price for its relatively generous immigration and refugee policies, losing several regional elections.

Open EU borders have resulted in questions about the dilution of national cultures. In the fall of 2005, widespread rioting broke out in French cities among immigrant communities, which have not been integrated into French political, economic, and cultural life. In early 2006, many European Muslims protested a Danish newspaper's publication of cartoons depicting the Prophet Muhammad in a derogatory way. Protesters in the Middle East boycotted Danish companies and attacked European embassies. The terror attacks in Paris and Brussels in 2015 and 2016 have heightened fears that Muslim immigrants present a real security threat.

As a result, more anti-immigrant, nationalist right-wing parties have sprung up in Europe, and they have been gaining in strength. The arrival of tens of thousands of refugees from the Middle East in 2016 has renewed calls for stricter EU border policies. France's Front National Party has polled about 20 percent in national elections, and has elected several mayors and deputies to the National Assembly. The party is particularly strong in the Mediterranean southeast, as a reaction against immigration there from North Africa. Germany's mainstream parties have debated banning the far-right, xenophobic National Democratic Party. In 2013, a leader from Italy's Northern League stooped to a new low when he said that a black government minister reminded him of an orangutan. In the fall of 2013, the Greek government arrested the leadership of the Golden Dawn Party, which was behind the murder of a popular anti-fascist singer, Pavlos Fyssas. Nonetheless, his party finished third in the 2015 elections. This neo-fascist demagoguery feeds on the high unemployment in some regions of the EU, where it is easy to blame foreigners and the EU for undermining national power. This was the motivation for many British when they voted in 2016 to leave the EU. Putin praised the vote, and many right-wing leaders in EU countries followed suit. Geert Wilders of the Netherlands' Freedom Party declared, "Now it's our turn" (Chrisafis 2016).

Nonetheless, Europe's contribution to liberal democratic development is undeniable. Every member of the UN has signed on to its Declaration on Human Rights. Even in times of national crisis, few leaders openly promote principles of government contrary to the declaration, such as government of and for the minority; divine or hereditary right to rule; arbitrary rather than electoral bases of power; consolidation of executive, legislative, and judicial power; government restriction of civil rights; government control over religion; restrictions on freedom of speech, the press, and the right to assemble; restrictions on economic choices; unequal treatment of women and minorities; and arbitrary imprisonment. Even authoritarian states that operate under these undemocratic principles, such as Belarus and Russia, do not trumpet their illiberal policies openly.

The Terrorist Threat in Europe

Terrorism today is mainly associated with the Middle East, but Europe has a long history of terrorist activities to demand political rights. Russian revolutionaries in the nineteenth century used terrorist tactics to oppose Tsarist rule, culminating in the assassination of Alexander II in 1881. Serbian Gavrilo Princip's assassination of the Archduke of Austria in 1914, which led to World War I, fell into a nineteenth-century tradition of national groups using terrorist methods to attack the symbols and institutions of an oppressive state. When conventional war against a stronger military and police force is impossible, nationalists often turn to so-called asymmetrical guerrilla war, or terrorist attacks on vulnerable state institutions.

Extremist Islamists conducted terrorist bombings on the transportation systems in Madrid in 2004 and in London in 2005, killing more than 100 people. But Spain and the United Kingdom have experienced terror attacks from sources even closer to home. For decades the Basque terror group **Euskadi Ta Askatasuna** (ETA) sought independence of the northern Basque region from Spain. For nearly a century, the **Irish Republican Army** (IRA) fought for the end of British rule in Northern Ireland and unification with the Republic of Ireland.

The Basque region enjoyed considerable autonomy from Madrid before the Spanish Civil War (1936–1939). The regime of Francisco Franco executed Basque nationalists, threw thousands of Basques into prison, repressed Basque cultural expression, and restricted the use of Euskera, the Basque language. After the end of Franco's dictatorship in 1975, the new constitutional monarchy of King Juan Carlos granted the Basques a measure of autonomy in 1979 that they had not enjoyed since the end of the republic in 1939. The move eventually shoved ETA onto the margins of Basque political life. There have been few attacks in the past few years, and there is little support among Basques for ETA's terrorists.

In the early twentieth century, Ireland struggled for independence from the United Kingdom. In 1914, the British government passed an Irish home rule measure, but suspended it until the end of World War I. The Irish Republic created the IRA as a defense force for the breakaway Irish government, and it began to conduct guerrilla attacks on British forces. Finally, in 1921 the British Parliament agreed to recognize the Irish Free State. Six predominantly Protestant Northern Irish provinces remained in the United Kingdom, however, and Irish nationalists have sought to unite the island of Eire ever since.

Those provinces were the source of the so-called **Troubles** that began in the 1960s, with the IRA and the Irish Catholic Nationalist community on one side and the Protestant Loyalists and the Royal Ulster Constabulary, the British army, and several Ulster paramilitary groups on the other.

By the 1990s, realism had overcome nationalism in Irish and British policy toward the Northern Ireland problem. Ireland's membership in the European Economic Community and its rapid economic growth in the late 1980s and 1990s, coupled with Northern Ireland's economic stagnation and civil strife, made the province a burden to both the Irish and British governments. Dublin had nothing to gain from inheriting the Troubles, and London wanted to rid itself of the terrorist threat and Northern Ireland's drain on the British Exchequer (treasury).

In July 2005, the IRA finally agreed to decommission, and hopes were again raised for a permanent end to the violence. In May 2007, **Sinn Fein** and the Northern Irish Loyalists agreed again to political reconciliation and self-rule.

Both ETA and the IRA have been affected by the rise of radical Islamic terrorism in the early twenty-first century. In the 1960s and 1970s, ETA and the IRA sympathized with other national liberation groups in Palestine, Latin America, and Africa. Terror groups often attack what they consider to be legitimate targets, such as the army, police, or government officials and institutions. For example, on September 11, 2001, al Qaeda attacked the World Trade Center towers and the Pentagon as symbols of American economic and military power. The IRA often called in warnings of imminent bombings to prevent collateral damage. Of course, innocent victims died anyway. The advent of suicide bombing and the wanton and deliberate killing of innocent civilians has discredited any group using terror to affect political change. After a cell of British Muslims killed over 50 people on subways and buses in the summer of 2005, the IRA renounced the use of violence to achieve its goals. Furthermore, ethnic minorities who have grievances against their national governments now have recourse in the EU. The EU has standardized civil rights among its members, and can use enormous diplomatic pressure to ensure its members' respect of those rights.

Al Qaeda is an international terrorist network formed by members of the *mujahideen*, originally guerrilla resistance fighters against the Soviet occupation of Afghanistan in the 1980s. The group was initially financed by its late leader, Osama bin Laden, who was a member of a wealthy Saudi family. Bin Laden's goals were to rid Arab lands of foreign armies, free the Muslim world from pervasive Western influence, and erect Islamic fundamentalist regimes. The September 11 terrorist attacks in the United States, and the train and bus bombings in Spain and the United Kingdom in 2004 and 2005, heightened fears of Islamic fundamentalism. Since then, the Islamic State (IS) in northern Syria and Iraq has further encouraged domestic terror in Europe, and in November 2015 attackers killed 130 people in Paris, and in March 2016, a further 32 people died in an attack in Brussels. The terror threat has contributed to the rise of anti-immigrant nationalist parties in Europe.

There are approximately 25 million Muslims living in Europe, including at least 5 million in France, 3 million in Germany, 2 million in the United Kingdom, and over a million in Italy. The challenge posed by Islamic and other non-European cultures, as well as high unemployment rates following the financial crisis of 2009, has fostered a serious debate in the EU about immigration, freedom of speech, security measures, sedition laws, and deportation of foreigners. The French Republic has been adamantly secular, and the French worry that their culture is being undermined by a devoutly religious and insular Islamic community. France passed a law in March 2004 prohibiting all religious expression in public schools. The measure was directly aimed at Islamic girls who wear the traditional North African head scarf, called a **hijab**. More recently, France banned the wearing of the face-covering **niqab** in public. Perhaps even more surprising is the backlash against immigrants in Sweden, which has been unusually tolerant in the past. The wife of a truck driver from the southern city of Malmo captured the essence of this new anti-immigrant attitude: "They do not respect Swedish people. As long as they learn the language and behave like Swedes, they are welcome. But they do not. Immigration as it is now needs to stop" (Daley 2011).

Nonetheless, Europe's experience with terrorism on the continent and in its colonies has prompted a measured response to the new threat from extremist Islamic terrorists. The EU has been critical of the United States' military approach to fighting terrorism and the idea of preventive strikes. Europe tends to view terrorism as a criminal activity to be dealt with by intelligence agencies and police forces. It is also engaged in serious debates about eliminating the causes of terrorism, which can lead to criticism of Western policies in the Middle East.

The Role of Europe in the World

Europe is one of the most healthy, well educated, and wealthy areas of the world. It is no wonder that migrants from poorer regions want to live there. As of 2014, 6.8 percent of the population of the EU came from countries outside of the organization. Life expectancy in the EU is among the highest in the world (over 80 years), as is the EU's gross national product per capita (Eurostat 2016).

The EU is the largest free-trade area in the world, with over 510 million people. The EU comprises 6.9 percent of the world's population (China has nearly 20 percent), but the EU accounts for 23.8 percent of the world's **GDP** (gross domestic product) and about 20 percent of global trade. The EU has a common internal tariff, which means that imports unloaded in Naples or Hamburg will be assessed the same duty (Eurostat 2016).

The EU has made significant efforts to increase trade with countries that have less-developed economies. In 2001, the EU instituted a program called the General System of Preference, which eliminated all tariffs on imports from the poorest 49 economies, most of which are in Africa. The EU has also launched trade and development strategies with many countries in the Caribbean, Africa, Asia, the Middle East, and Latin America.

The EU has struggled to recover from the financial crisis in the late 2000s. Unemployment hovers around 9 percent, and in some countries like Greece and Spain it is closer to 20 percent. With an aging population (only Japan has an older median age), there are worries that the welfare state that Europeans have come to expect is not sustainable in the long run.

Europe is dependent on foreign energy sources. Russia supplies over two-thirds of Europe's oil and gas supplies, and the EU has been reluctant to criticize the hemorrhaging of Russia's democracy, Putin's support of Syrian leader Bashar al-Assad, and Putin's annexation of Crimea in 2014. Despite sanctions that were imposed on Russia because of the Crimean annexation and its military meddling in eastern Ukraine, Russia is still the EU's third largest trading partner (Eurostat 2016).

The United States has always pushed the EU for lower tariffs and freer trade in general. In 2007 the US trade representative asked Europe to eliminate all tariffs of 5 percent or less. The EU balked, but tariffs on the goods exchanged between the United States and the EU still average under 3 percent, and trade disputes amount to less than 2 percent of their trade volume. The United States and the EU have maintained a close trading relationship. The United States takes in the most EU exports, while the United States ranks second in EU imports (European Commission Directorate General on Trade 2016).

The EU and the United States have tangled over subsidies for major industries and agriculture, and taxes and environmental issues. For years, the United States has accused the EU of giving Airbus, the joint European aircraft manufacturer, illegal debt relief and research-and-development monies. In 2011, the WTO ordered the EU to end the illegal subsidies to Airbus, but the practice continued. The United States charged that the subsidies continued, and in 2016 the WTO ruled in favor of Washington (*Washington Post*, September 23, 2016). The EU has countered that US-based Boeing receives indirect government subsidies through US military contracts. The EU has also brought suits against US tariffs on some European information technology imports. The WTO is adjudicating these disputes. The environmentally conscious EU states have banned meat products from hormone-injected livestock and refuse to accept US genetically modified foods (WTO 2011). In 2016, a new free trade agreement, the Transatlantic Trade Investment Partnership, foundered because of increased anti-trade and anti-immigrant sentiments among disaffected Americans and Europeans.

European and American values have diverged on social issues as well. The EU has banned the death penalty, considering it a barbaric act for the state to put a prisoner to death. Donald Trump's election as US president in 2016 gave most Europeans pause, suggesting that nationalism and xenophobia have become mainstream in US politics. Europeans are also highly critical of the role money plays in the US political system and the electoral power of right-wing Christian fundamentalists. Organized religion plays little role in mainstream Western European politics. About a third of West Europeans go to church once a month. That number is even lower in Britain. Polls vary, but at least a third of Americans go to a religious service every week.

Although former President Barack Obama's Affordable Care Act enabled millions of Americans to get health insurance, Europeans wonder about the lack of a universal healthcare system in the United States and the exorbitant cost of higher education, which seems to favor wealthier Americans. Some Europeans also decry the global influence of what they consider to be American lowbrow culture, from the Big Mac to Hollywood action films.

Europeans as a whole are much more environmentally conscious than Americans. Green parties are a strong political force in several EU countries. Europeans willingly support subsidies for environmentally friendly mass-transportation systems, and they are critical of Americans' gas-guzzling autos. Europe is responsible for approximately 25 percent of the world's carbon dioxide emissions. The United States has a smaller population but also produces about 25 percent of global carbon dioxide emissions. In March 2007, the EU agreed to cut its greenhouse gas emissions by 20 percent (compared with 1990 levels) by 2020. If non-EU states agreed to reduce emissions significantly, the EU promised to make cuts of up to 20 percent ("Europe to Cut" 2007). Chinese and United States indifference to climate change makes that target unlikely. Nonetheless, Europe is on the front line of the effort to stop global warming.

Despite these controversies, the Atlantic partnership is still strong, cemented by NATO, the G7, and many other multilateral institutions. Europe and the United States play a dominant role in world affairs. The United States and EU countries have some of the world's largest economies and the biggest and most sophisticated militaries. Western ideas still dominate the global debates on modern political and economic development.

The EU is an inspirational story for other regions of the world that have experienced ethnic strife, brutal tyranny, and devastating war. Out of the horror in the trenches of northern France and Flanders in World War I, and the bombed-out European cities and Holocaust of World War II, Europe has reconciled its ideological and national differences to enjoy unprecedented peace and prosperity. Some ethnic issues and terror threats persist, but war among the 27 members of the EU is nearly unthinkable today. The EU is, as one scholar put it, "the most progressive political development of our time" (Cohen-Tanugi 2005, 67).

Timeline of Modern European History

1914–1918	World War I. Central Powers: Germany, Austria-Hungary, Turkey, Bulgaria. Entente: Britain, France, Russia, Italy (entered in 1915).
1917	Bolshevik Revolution in Russia.
1918	German, Austrian, Turkish empires collapse. Germany creates Weimar Republic (1918–1933). New independent states formed: Finland, Estonia, Latvia, Lithuania, Poland, Czechoslovakia, Hungary, and Yugoslavia.
1919	Paris Peace Settlement. Versailles Treaty with Germany is part of this settlement.
1921	Irish Home Rule.
1922	Mussolini's fascist coup in Italy.
1929	Worldwide economic depression.

1933	Adolf Hitler's Nazis take power, end the Weimar Republic, and establish the Third Reich.
1939–1945	World War II. Axis powers: Germany, Italy, Japan. Allies: France, Britain, Soviet Union (entered in 1941), United States (entered in 1941).
1945	Victory in Europe (May).
1945	United States drops two atomic bombs on Japan; end of war in Asia (August).
1945	World Bank and International Monetary Fund created.
1945–1949	Soviet Union annexes the Baltic states and imposes communist regimes in Poland, Bulgaria, Romania, Hungary, Czechoslovakia, and East Germany.
1948–1952	European Recovery Program (Marshall Plan).
1949	North Atlantic Treaty Organization created. West Germany (liberal democracy) and East Germany (communist) created, completing the division of Europe after World War II.
1955	West Germany joins NATO. Soviet-led Warsaw Pact formed.
1957	European Economic Community (EEC or Common Market) established.
1972	Bloody Sunday massacre in Londonderry.
1973	Great Britain, Ireland, and Denmark join the EEC.
1981	Irish Republican Army prisoner Bobby Sands starves to death in prison.
1985	Mikhail Gorbachev becomes General Secretary of the Soviet Communist Party.
1989	Gorbachev allows the collapse of the communist regimes in Eastern Europe.
1990	German reunification: East Germany incorporated into West German Federal Republic.
1991	Soviet Union disintegrates after hard-liners' failed attempt to depose Gorbachev.
1991–1995	Yugoslav civil war.
1992	The Maastricht Treaty creates the European Union.
1993	Czech Republic and Slovakia declare independence.
1998	Northern Ireland Good Friday Agreement.
2002	European Monetary Union; euro adopted as new currency.
2004	Terrorist attack on Madrid trains.
2005	Terrorist attack on London transport system.
2007	Bulgaria and Romania admitted to the EU. Terrorist attack on Glasgow airport.
2011	Greek debt crisis threatens unity of Eurozone. Refugee exodus from Syrian Civil War begins.
2014	Russia annexes Crimea; Russian militias aid insurrection in Eastern Ukraine; US and EU slap sanctions on Russia for annexing Crimea and intervening in Ukraine.
2015	Greek debt crisis. Terrorist attack in Paris.
2016	Brussels suicide bombings; Terrorist truck attack in Nice. Britain votes to leave the EU. Terrorist truck attack on Berlin Christmas market.

References

Byron, George Lord. 1821. *Marino Faliero, Doge of Venice*. London: John Murray.

Chrisafis, Angelique. 2016. "European far-right hails Brexit vote." *The Guardian*, June 24. www.theguardian.com/world/2016/jun/24/european-far-right-hails-britains-brexit-vote-marine-le-pen.

Cohen-Tanugi, Laurent. 2005. "The End of Europe?" *Foreign Affairs* (November–December): 55–67.

Daley, Suzanne. 2011. "Swedes Begin to Question Liberal Migration Tenets." *New York Times*, February 26. www.nytimes.com/2011/02/27/world/europe/27sweden.html?_r=1&ref=sweden

"Europe to Cut Greenhouse Gases 20 Percent by 2020." 2007. *Environmental News Service*. March 8. www.ens-newswire.com

Eurostat. 2016. http://ec.europa.eu/eurostat/http://epp.eurostat.ec.europa.eu/statistics

Flint, John. 1976. *Cecil Rhodes*. London: Hutchinson.

Fukuyama, Francis. 1992. *The End of History and the Last Man*. New York: Penguin Books.

Kant, Immanuel. [1788] 1997. *Critique of Practical Reason*. Translated and edited by Mary Gregor. Cambridge, UK: Cambridge University Press.

Klapper, Bradley S. 2007. "WTO to Give Glimpse into Boeing-Airbus Subsidy Dispute." *Seattle Post-Intelligencer*, March 19.

Lenin, Vladimir Ilyich. 1974. "Imperialism, the Highest Stage of Capitalism." In *Collected Works*, vol. 2. Moscow: Progress Publishers.

Miller, Nathan. 1992. *Theodore Roosevelt: A Life*. New York: Morrow.

New York Times. 2016. October 18.

Pfaff, William. 2005. "What's Left of the Union?" *New York Review of Books*, July 14: 26–29.

Reuters. 2007. "EU's Mandelson Tells Russia: No Politics in Energy." *Reuters*, June 10. www.reuters.com

Rich, Norman. 1992. *Great Power Diplomacy: 1814–1914*. New York: McGraw-Hill.

Sheehan, James J. 1989. *German History: 1770–1866*. New York: Oxford University Press.

Stromberg, Roland N. 1994. *European Intellectual History since 1789*. 6th ed. Englewood Cliffs, NJ: Prentice Hall.

Tennyson, Alfred Lord. [1854] 1964. *The Charge of the Light Brigade*. New York: Golden Press.

USA Today. 2016. October 12.

USTR (Office of the U.S. Trade Representative). 2011. www.ustr.gov

Wandycz, Piotr S. 1988. "East Central Europe 1918: War and Peace, Czechoslovakia and Poland." In *Revolution and Intervention in Hungary and Its Neighboring States: 1918–1919*, edited by Peter Pastor, 397–408. Boulder, CO: Social Sciences Monograph.

Washington Post. 1898. Editorial. April 25.

Washington Post. 2016. September 23,

WTO (World Trade Organization). 2011. www.wto.org

Further Reading

Books

Bomberg, Elizabeth, John Peterson, and Alexander Stubb. 2008. *The European Union: How Does it Work?* 2nd ed. New York: Oxford.

Coogan, Tim Pat. 2002. *The IRA*. Revised ed. New York: Palgrave.

Gellner, Ernest. 1983. *Nations and Nationalism*. Ithaca, NY: Cornell University Press.

Gilbert, Felix, and David Clay Large. 2009. *The End of the European Era: 1890 to the Present*. 6th ed. New York: Norton.

Hobsbawm, Eric. 1990. *Nations and Nationalism since 1870: Programme, Myths, Reality*. Cambridge, UK: Cambridge University Press.

Hunter, Shireen T. 2002. *Islam, Europe's Second Religion: The New Social, Cultural, and Political Landscape*. Westport, CT: Praeger.

Jolly, Mette. 2007. *The European Union and the People*. New York: Oxford.

Judt, Tony. 2005. *Postwar: A History of Europe since 1945*. New York: Penguin.

Kurlansky, Mark. 2001. *The Basques in History*. New York: Penguin.

Mazower, Mark. 2000. *Dark Continent: Europe's Twentieth Century*. New York: Vintage.

Milward, Alan. 2005. *Politics and Economics in the History of the EU*. New York: Routledge.

Unwin, Tim. 1998. *A European Geography*. New York: Prentice Hall.

Wilkinson, James, and H. Stuart Hughes. 2004. *Contemporary Europe: A History*. Upper Saddle River, NJ: Pearson Prentice Hall.

Journals

Central European History. www.cambridge.org/core/journals/central-european-history

Contemporary European History. www.cambridge.org/core/journals/contemporary-european-history

European History Quarterly. journals.sagepub.com/home/ehq

Journal of European Studies. journals.sagepub.com/home/jes

Journal of Modern History. www.press.uchicago.edu/ucp/journals/journal/jmh

Films

Ashes and Diamonds (1958). Andrej Wajda, director.

Battle of Algiers (1965). Gillo Pontecorvo, director.

Bloody Sunday (2002). Paul Greengrass, director.

The Lives of Others [Das Leben der Anderen] (2006). Florian Henckel von Donners-marck, director.

No Man's Land (2001). Danis Tanovic, director.

Websites

British Broadcasting Company (BBC). www.bbc.co.uk

EU. www.europa.eu

The Financial Times. www.ft.com

NATO. www.nato.int

The Times. www.timesonline.co.uk

Chapter 8

East Asia, the Pacific, and International Studies

Demography and Development

Introduction: Why Study East Asia and the Pacific?

Several factors contribute to the significance of **East Asia** and the Pacific. First is the huge geographic scale. East Asia comprises two regions: **Northeast** and **Southeast Asia**. East Asia is the most populated region of the world's most populated continent. Thirty percent of the world's population lives in East Asia. Of the most populous countries, three are in East Asia. China has 1.4 billion people, while Indonesia has 272 million, and Japan has 126 million. Environmentally, East Asia is quite diverse, ranging from the Tibetan plateau to broad river valleys to tropical rain forests. The **monsoon** affects much of the climate of East Asia. The Pacific covers a wide expanse of territory, yet only 43 million people live in the region.

Second is the long history associated with Asian civilizations. Four to five thousand years ago, the Chinese civilization flourished along the Yellow River valley. The Great Wall is a symbol of China's history and the power of the empire (Figure 8.1). The civilizations along the Mekong, Chao Praya, and Irrawaddy are the bases of Thailand, Myanmar, Cambodia, and Vietnam today. The island countries of Japan, the Philippines, and Indonesia all took particular arcs of historical development. The continuity of these civilizations to the present day is remarkable. European colonialism broke the power of the Asian states, but the twenty-first century points toward a world where Asia will have a significant presence. While Australia was settled very early, 50,000 years ago, the islands of Polynesia were the last place on earth to be settled, in 400–800 CE.

Third is the cultural variety of East Asia. Belief systems of Buddhism and Confucian philosophies originated in Asia; Islam and Christianity came to the area by the Middle Ages. The linguistic variety is even more complex. For example, Indonesian and Chinese are both quite distinct in scripts, grammars, and vocabularies; these are just two of the many and diverse Asian languages. The Pacific Islands have a multicultural mosaic from aboriginal inhabitants and European settlers in Australia to Polynesian culture in Hawaii. Modern forces of **globalization** challenge the variety of East Asian and Pacific culture.

Fourth is the rising economic power of Asia. In terms of Gross Domestic Product Purchasing Power Parity, China is largest followed by the US, India and Japan. Japan is an economically developed power, while China is a rising star. The **newly industrialized countries (NICs)** of South Korea, Taiwan, and Singapore play a strong role in the Asian economy. At a per capita level, China's income is lower, while Japan's per capita income is quite high. Many goods and services are produced in Asia. Japanese companies play a major role in the global economy; Chinese businesses are growing strong. In the Pacific, economies range from the more-developed Australia and New Zealand to the less-developed Papua New Guinea and the Solomon Islands.

Fifth and finally, the political power and strength of Asia is of significance to the world. Asia was a major theater of World War II, and Korea and Vietnam were war zones in the Cold War. A variety of political systems uneasily coexist in Asia. Democracies such as Japan, South Korea,

DOI: 10.4324/9781003028314-11

Figure 8.1 The Great Wall of China, while not visible from space, is an important symbol of China.
Source: S. Toops.

Indonesia, and the Philippines contrast with the authoritarian regimes of China and North Korea. Myanmar was moving from an authoritarian to a democratic regime, but a military coup in 2021 returned Myanmar to an authoritarian state. Although China is the only Asian permanent member of the UN Security Council, Japan is trying to secure a permanent seat. In terms of economic and political power, East Asia is already a major player on the world stage. Political circumstances in the Pacific point to many states with strong ties to other regions. France still has colonies in the Pacific (New Caledonia and French Polynesia). Many former British Pacific colonies (Australia, Fiji, New Zealand, Papua New Guinea, etc.) are in the Commonwealth. The United States has one state (Hawaii) and several territories (Guam, American Samoa, and Northern Marianas) in the Pacific.

This chapter begins with discussions of the regional character of East Asia and the Pacific, and then focuses on demographic and development issues in East Asia, highlighting China, a rising powerhouse. The chapter closes with a discussion of East Asia's role in the twenty-first-century world.

Geographical Dimensions

Regions are mental constructs that we use to help organize the world geographically (see Chapter 2). The word *Asia* is derived from the language of the Phoenicians (ancient seagoing traders on the Mediterranean), who spoke of a region associated with the sunrise, the east. Europe was associated with the sunset in the west. This east–west distinction is still a common way to think of the world, but the historical complexities make it more reasonable to consider Asia as a variety of regions. The vast continent of Asia is usually divided into four regions: Northeast Asia, Southeast Asia, South Asia, and Central Asia. The following chapter considers South and Central Asia. The map of Asia (Map 8.1) shows the relative locations of the countries. The Pacific includes the larger island countries of Australia and New Zealand as well as the smaller island countries stretching from Papua New Guinea to French Polynesia.

Northeast Asia encompasses China, Japan, Taiwan, and North and South Korea. There are some cultural similarities here, including Mahayana Buddhism and Confucian philosophy. The languages are less interrelated, and the ethnic groups are distinct in terms of history and political identities. China and Japan are both powerful economic and political forces in the world, but with quite distinct economic and political systems. Geographically, the Koreas have acted as a bridge between China and Japan. Western China is mostly either mountains or deserts; eastern China is mostly plains, basins, and hills. A spine of mountains and hills follows the eastern segment of the Korean peninsula. South Korea has more plains than North Korea. Japan is mostly mountainous. In terms of climate, western China is either highland or dry, eastern China is mostly humid. Northern China is colder than southern China. The Koreas and Japan have a humid climate; North Korea and northern Japan have a colder climate. In terms of population, while China is the most populous country in the world, 90 percent of the settlement is in the eastern half of the country. South Korea, Japan, and eastern China are densely settled. The identities of these countries are tied up with their relative location; China has a continental influence, the Koreas are peninsular, while Japan has an island influence (Desnoyer 2020; Reischauer and Jansen 1995; Karan 2005).

Southeast Asia includes the mainland countries of Myanmar (Burma), Thailand, Vietnam, Cambodia, Laos, the peninsular countries of Malaysia and Singapore, and the island countries of Indonesia, the Philippines, Brunei, and East Timor. This region is a crossroads of influences from China and India. Islam came from South Asia to Malaysia and Indonesia in particular. Buddhism came from South Asia to Thailand, Myanmar, Cambodia, and Vietnam. Many Chinese settled in Malaysia and Singapore, as well as Indonesia, Thailand, Vietnam, and the Philippines. The highland areas of Southeast Asia in Myanmar, Laos, Vietnam and Thailand proceed down to the plains and valleys of the major river systems of the Mekong, Chao Praya, Irrawaddy, and Salween. Many of the islands of Southeast Asia have uplands with volcanoes. Overall, Southeast Asia has mostly tropical wet climates, quite warm year round. The mainland is mostly tropical savanna, while northern Vietnam and northern Laos have a humid, subtropical climate, like southern China. In contrast to Northeast Asia, Southeast Asia is more sparsely settled, particularly in the upland areas. Coastal areas and river deltas are densely settled. The densest settlement occurs on the island of Java in Indonesia because of the island's fertile soil. Indonesia is the fourth most populous country in the world.

The **Pacific** countries include several components (Map 8.2). Australia and New Zealand have some characteristics in common, given that the majority of the populations have European ancestry. **Melanesia** includes the countries of Papua New Guinea, Solomons, Vanuatu, Fiji, and the French territory of New Caledonia. **Micronesia** includes the countries of Nauru, Marshalls, Kiribati, Federated States of Micronesia, and the US territories of Guam and the Northern Marianas. **Polynesia** includes the countries of Tonga and Samoa, French Polynesia and the US territory of American Samoa, and the state of Hawaii (McKnight 1995).

There are many landform contrasts in the Pacific. Australia is mostly plateaus and lowland. New Zealand has more rugged terrain with mountains and fjords. Some Pacific Islands are high islands built by volcanoes such as in Hawaii, Samoa, Tonga, New Zealand, or New Guinea. Other Pacific Islands are low islands, atolls built up by coral such as Tuvalu, Kiribati, and the Marshalls. One significant environmental issue affecting the region is global climate change. Many of the low-lying islands, particularly Tuvalu, Kiribati, and the Marshalls, are vulnerable to

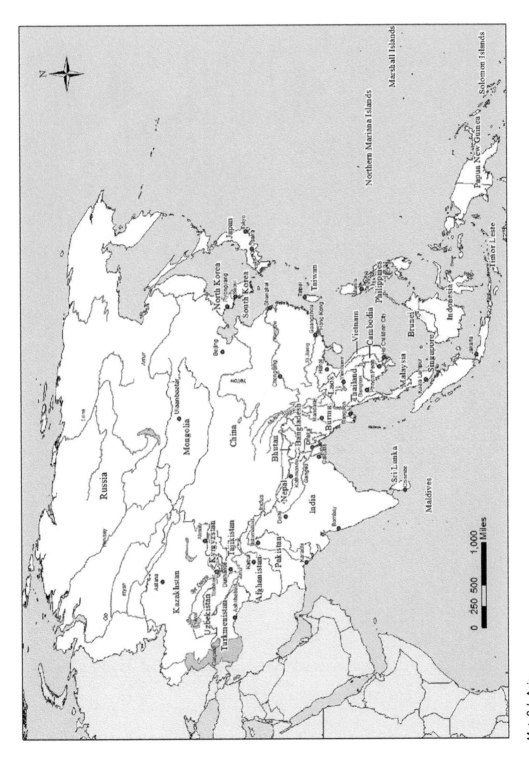

Map 8.1 Asia.

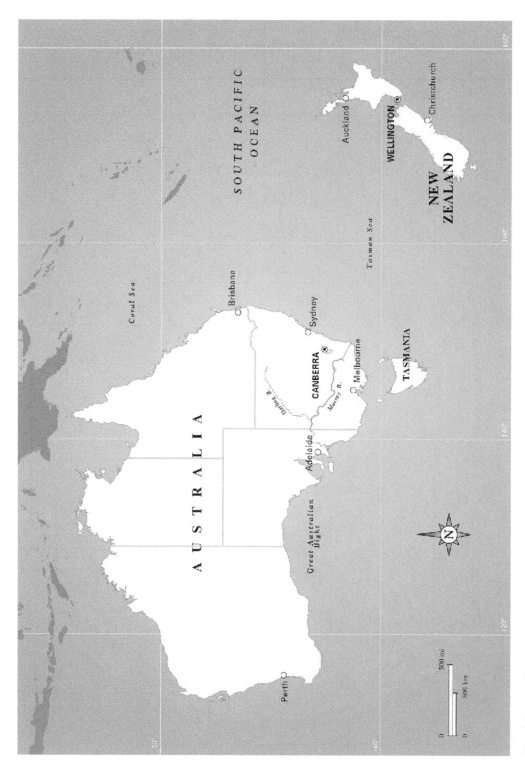

Map 8.2 Australia and New Zealand.

sea-level rise. In terms of climate, while Australia has vast tracts of desert, its coastal areas are mostly humid. New Zealand has a humid, subtropical climate. Most of the Pacific Islands have a tropical, rainy climate. High islands get more rainfall, while low islands get less rainfall.

Hazards of the natural environment include earthquakes, tsunamis, floods, and hurricanes. The western edge of the Pacific is part of the Ring of Fire, where tectonic plates collide off the coast of Japan, the Philippines, and Indonesia. The Indian Ocean tsunami of 2004 affected Thailand and Indonesia. A major earthquake damaged China in 2008; earthquakes also hit New Zealand in 2010–2012. A major earthquake and tsunami hit Japan in 2011, resulting in a nuclear disaster in Fukushima. Hurricane Haiyan devastated the Philippines in 2013. Asia Pacific countries have to deal with these damaging natural hazards.

Historical Trends

Indigenous kingdoms and empires have dominated East Asia through its long history. The ideals that guided the Chinese empires were established in the Yellow River valley in 2000 BCE. Chinese political formation remained essentially the same from 200 BCE to 1911 CE, that is, an empire built around the basic governing precepts of Confucianism formulated 2,000 years ago. The Japanese empire dates back to 50 BCE; the present-day emperor traces his line back to Japan's antiquity. Khmer, Thai, Viet, and Sri-vijaya kingdoms all controlled Southeast Asia. These very early civilizations developed by being able to produce agricultural food surpluses. These early empires were quite sophisticated culturally and possessed well-developed technologies (Desnoyer 2020; Mackerras 1995; Karan 2005).

European colonialism was very strong in Southeast Asia but less so in Northeast Asia. The Dutch secured Indonesia, the French colonized Indochina, the British colonized Malaya, and the Spanish captured the Philippines. All of the European powers gained some territorial control in China. Japan and Thailand alone escaped colonial control. At first the United States did not have a specific territory but rather sought influence and trade in many areas, but by 1898 the United States took over the Philippines from Spain (Borthwick 2014).

Resistance to European colonialism took the form of nationalism in the 1900s. Ho Chi Minh in Vietnam, Sukarno in Indonesia, and **Mao Zedong** in China were all national leaders regardless of their political philosophies. By 1949, India and Indonesia were free from **colonial rule**, and after a brutal civil war, China became a communist state. France began to withdraw from Vietnam in 1954. Fearing communist takeover of the whole country, the United States defended South Vietnam from the early sixties to 1973. Two years later, the country fell to Ho Chi Minh's communist regime.

Japan made a turn from a traditionalist to a modern state in the 1880s. Emulating the Western imperialist powers, Japan became a colonial power, taking Taiwan and Manchuria from China and colonizing Korea. In 1937 Japan invaded China, capturing Shanghai and Nanjing. The United States bombed Hiroshima with an atomic device on August 6, 1945, killing 100,000–150,000 (Figure 8.2). The Japanese then surrendered on August 15, 1945. With the end of World War II, Japan's imperial era came to a close (Brower 2005).

After World War II, the new nationalisms in East Asia meant the creation of new states in China, Korea, Vietnam, Indonesia, Malaysia, and the Philippines. The Cold War meant the divisions of China, Korea, and Vietnam into competing states. While Vietnam reunited in the 1970s, China is still divided between Taiwan and mainland China, and the demilitarized zone (DMZ) still separates North and South Korea.

Settlement in the Pacific began with the aboriginal inhabitants 50,000 years ago. Papua New Guinea was settled prior to 2500 BCE. Micronesia and the rest of Melanesia were settled by 1200 BCE. Polynesia was settled by 400–800 CE. French, British, Germans, and Americans all

Figure 8.2 Hiroshima. The City Hall ruins have been left as a memorial to the bombing.
Source: S. Toops.

had colonies in the Pacific. Australia became independent in 1901. By the 1970s, many Pacific islands became independent states. The United States and France still have dependent territories in the Pacific.

Cultural Complexities

Asia has a significant degree of diversity. Every country has its own language system for the most part. Current belief systems include Buddhism, Islam, Christianity, Daoism, and philosophies such as Confucianism. Southeast Asia has Buddhism, Islam, and Christianity, and Northeast Asia has Buddhism, Confucianism, Daoism, Shinto, and Christianity (see Map 3.1 on religions).

Both China and Japan have a combination of religious and philosophical perspectives. In China, this syncretic combination includes Daoism, Confucian philosophy, and Mahayana Buddhism. The oldest belief system is Daoism in China, which then merged with other philosophical perspectives. Daoism is rooted in nature worship and stresses spiritual harmony. Confucius was actively teaching in China in 500 BCE. Confucian philosophies permeate China, Korea, and Japan today. Confucius articulated philosophies rather than a set of religious beliefs, which pointed toward social stability based on human relationships. By 600–700 CE, Buddhism expanded into northeast Asia. In China, Japan, and Korea, the dominant Buddhist practice is Mahayana. In Mahayana Buddhism, there is less of a focus on monks or nuns to fulfill religious obligations, and adherents can also follow other belief systems. In China, most individuals practiced Buddhism, Daoism, and **Confucianism**, more as a syncretic compilation of beliefs and practices than as an organized religion. In Japan, syncretism combines Buddhism, Confucianism, and Shinto, the traditional belief system of the Japanese. Other religions practiced in China include Islam, Tibetan Buddhism, and Christianity. By 1950, Marxist atheism prevailed over traditional religions in China and North Korea (and to a lesser extent in Vietnam). Leaders in China today, particularly Communist Party members, are still required to be atheist. While technically there is freedom of religion in China, there is still state control over religious practices. In Japan today, secularism is also a feature of the cultural landscape; most Japanese have secular attitudes and only occasionally observe Buddhist rituals. South Korea and Taiwan have many adherents to Christianity.

In Southeast Asia, **Buddhism** diffused throughout the region by 1200 CE. Today, in Sri Lanka, Myanmar, Thailand, Cambodia, and Laos, adherents practice Theravada Buddhism. One structural characteristic of Theravada Buddhism is a large number of monks and nuns, who focus their lives on religious devotion. In Vietnam, people follow the Mahayana variant of Buddhism due to Chinese influence. Traders brought Islam to Malaysia and Indonesia by 1200 CE, and Indonesia is now the world's most populous Muslim country. Unlike the syncretism of Buddhism, Daoism, and Confucianism in East Asia, people in Southeast Asia practiced Islam or Buddhism exclusively. With the power of colonial administration behind them, European Christian missionaries made converts throughout Asia, with particular success in the Philippines and also parts of Indonesia.

Religious innovation and diffusion shaped the complex diversity of East Asian peoples. The challenge today is how to retain the myriad cultural identities in Asia in the midst of globalized cultural forces. Japan, South Korea, Hong Kong, and Taiwan all have capitalist cultures that respond to global influences by making the global into the local. McDonald's restaurants are everywhere, but they take on a local flavor, offering soup and tea. As China has liberalized its economy, an urban popular culture with fast food, karaoke, and theme parks has blossomed. These Chinese variations on global culture are more similar to their Korean or Japanese analogues than to American ones. South Korea and Japan are heavy innovators of cell phone, Internet, and computer technology. Access to the Internet has developed in China as well, but Internet access is monitored by the state.

East Asian culture has also spread to other parts of the world. Even in small towns in Ohio, one can find Chinese restaurants and karaoke. Chinese and Japanese movies are also available for rental, either dubbed or subtitled. Hong Kong has become one of the world's leading producers and distributors of films in the United States. Americans have begun to appreciate Chinese and Japanese culture through movies and food (Kristof and WuDunn 2000).

In the Pacific, cultural complexities vary from the aboriginal peoples of Australia to Maori culture in New Zealand. In Papua New Guinea, a great variety of local languages are spoken as well as Pijin (Pidgin English), which utilizes English vocabularies with a Melanesian grammar. Almost half of Fiji's population is South Asian in origin, and Hinduism is common there. Traditional Polynesian culture developed class-based relationships between elites and other inhabitants.

How does local culture interact with global culture? There are strong cultural variations from country to country. One model may be that of North Korea or Myanmar, both of which have resisted outside culture. Another model is that of Japan, which has accommodated itself to global culture but on its own terms. Another example is the case of China, where there are distinct global influences, but Chinese influences have also spread throughout the rest of the world. Global cultural influences go from the United States to China and back again (Borthwick 2014).

Economic Impact

The impacts of Asian economies are felt worldwide. Japan is the economic leader in terms of the size of the economy, although China has now surpassed the size of Japan. The general metaphor for Asian development has been that of a goose flock migrating, where one goose is in the lead and the others follow the leader. Japan has been that economic leader. Close behind are Singapore, Taiwan, Hong Kong, and South Korea, often referred to as the **newly industrialized countries** (NICs). The third group is composed of countries like Thailand, Malaysia, and China. Indonesia is in the fourth group. The Chinese diaspora is an important part of the Southeast Asia's economy, comprising much of the commercial class. Singapore has the most developed economy. Malaysia, Thailand, and the Philippines have lagged behind, but have experienced healthy growth rates in the past few years. Among poorer countries like Cambodia, various

Figure 8.3 Agricultural activity in Southeast Asia focuses on rice production as shown here in Vietnam.
Source: S. Toops.

factors such as conflict have severely limited the possibilities for economic growth (Frank 1998). (See Map 4.1.)

While Asia is a center of business, many still work in the agricultural sector (see Figure 8.3) or in services. Industrial production has been strong, including Japanese, Korean, and Chinese businesses. More recently, a finance and high technology sector developed after World War II.

Countries have tried various methods for economic growth. Asian governments such as Japan, South Korea, and China have been actively involved in promoting export-led industrialization as a development strategy. Asia has an important role to play in the global economy, providing numerous exports as well as imports. Of the top 15 countries in exports, six are in East Asia: China, Japan, South Korea, Singapore, Taiwan, and Hong Kong. Hong Kong, a part of China, has exports equal to that of France. The overall difficulty will be for all Asians to achieve economic satisfaction; at a local level in China, for example, there are still districts of poverty alongside high-tech districts. Global economic successes such as Japan and more recently China are set in contrast to the economic difficulties of Cambodia.

In the Pacific, Australia and New Zealand have developed economies based on the processing of primary products. Many of the other countries of the Pacific maintain a subsistence economy, including shifting cultivation or fishing. Exports include nickel from New Caledonia, phosphates from Nauru, and coconuts and fish from the Solomons. In Hawaii and French Polynesia, tourism is a significant portion of the economy (Patterson and Macintyre 2011).

Political Tensions

In an investigation into peasant activity in 1927, Mao Zedong said

> "A revolution is not a dinner party, or writing an essay, or painting a picture, or doing embroidery; it cannot be so refined, so leisurely and gentle, so temperate, kind, courteous, restrained and magnanimous. A revolution is an insurrection, an act of violence by which one class overthrows another."

This is one model of state formation in East Asia, a revolution not a dinner party, an authoritarian regime. China, in the aftermath of World War II and a civil war, became communist under Chairman Mao (Figure 8.4). Through the twenty-first century, the rise of China's global power may mirror Japan's rise in the twentieth century. At a local level, political freedoms and human rights remain issues for countries such as China, with its authoritarian regime. Hong Kong has had democracy protests against the rule of the People's Republic of China. The PRC has internment camps for Uyghurs, a Muslim minority in northwestern China (Gamer and Toops 2017).

Another model is participatory democracy. Japan, in the aftermath of World War II, became a democratic country, though more conservative than liberal. Taiwan, South Korea, and Japan all had strong authoritarian regimes before developing their democratic systems. People vote for legislators and presidents. Prime ministers are decided by the legislators. The government in these democracies are not revolutionary, but they are not dinner parties. The democracies do have political parties that represent the people.

In Southeast Asia, current political tensions are strongly related to the colonial past. Thailand and the Philippines have liberal democratic political structures. Thailand is a constitutional monarchy, but the military overthrew the prime minister in 2014. The long-reigning Thai king passed away in 2016, and the crown prince succeeded to the throne. Democracy protests continue in Thailand. Currently the president in the Philippines tends toward authoritarianism. Malaysia, Singapore, and Indonesia have democratic governments with fewer liberal credentials. Singapore is a democracy, but with a strong streak of paternalistic rule. Indonesia is

Figure 8.4 Tiananmen Square in Beijing. Chairman Mao's portrait is at the center. On the left, the banner says "10,000 years to the People's Republic of China." On the right, the banner reads "10,000 years to the great unity of the peoples of the world."

Source: S. Toops.

also a democracy, but regional issues persist in the western and eastern reaches of the country. With a military coup in 2021, Myanmar has returned to an authoritarian regime, after a brief turn to democracy. The Myanmar government has moved against the Rohingya minority near the border with Bangladesh. Vietnam and Laos have communist dictatorships. Global dimensions of politics include the development of **ASEAN**, the **Association of Southeast Asian Nations**, a supranational organization that facilitates political cooperation in the region. While ASEAN was once arrayed against Vietnam, now Vietnam and Myanmar are vital members of the association (Mackerras 1995; Friend 2003; Dixon 1991).

The Pacific has a number of political facets. Many Pacific Island states became independent in the 1960s and 1970s. While many islands are self-governing and independent, the United States and France, as well as New Zealand, control substantial territory. Indigenous land rights in Australia, New Zealand, and Hawaii are still problematic. The style of governance is democracy, with the exception of Tonga, which maintains a constitutional monarchy. According to the UN Convention on the Law of the Sea, territorial control extends 200 miles in an Exclusive Economic Zone. All of the islands therefore have economic rights, including fishing and minerals, over a large territory of ocean beyond their surface land. Many of the countries are members of the Pacific Islands Forum Secretariat, which seeks to enhance political governance and security for the region.

The political tensions in Asia reveal twin tendencies: authoritarianism and government that concerns itself with the aspirations of the people. In the modern world, this tension is between dictatorship and democracy. Asia has both, but the rising tide is toward democratic systems (Brower 2005; Kaup 2021).

Demographic Issues

Two regional issues illustrate the challenges facing Asia in the twenty-first century. This section focuses on Asia's demographic dilemma, and the next discusses Asian economic development, with an emphasis on China.

One factor of the demographic dilemma is the level of population growth. The population of Northeast Asia is about 1.6 billion; however, growth rates are relatively low (0.3 percent). Southeast Asia has a little over 660 million people, with growth rates of 1.1 percent, while the Pacific Islands total about 43 million people, with growth rates of 1 percent. (See Map 2.3.)

Asia has 60 percent of the world population, and China alone has over 1.4 billion people. In East Asia, both rural and urban densities are high, especially on the Yangtze River in China. Governments have made various choices to deal with population growth: strict family planning in China has led to a lower rate of population increase. China decided to limit the level of population growth by fiat, with only one child permitted per family, though this has recently changed. China now has a three-child policy. South Korea has a low rate of population increase as the result of modern economic development and urbanization. Japan has a negative population growth rate; the country is getting smaller and older. The government has tried some pronatal policies such as subsidies for children, but the cost of living is so high, modest economic incentives have no impact.

In Southeast Asia, Thailand has low rates of population increase due to a heavily promoted government program of family planning. Indonesia has moderate levels of population increase; the issue here is one of transmigration, as people move out of the center islands to the periphery. Singapore has a low level of population growth, so the government has embarked on a pronatalist policy, encouraging people to have more children (Population Reference Bureau 2020).

In the Pacific, there are two demographic clusters. Australia and New Zealand have larger populations, characterized by low population growth rates, high urbanization rates, and a higher percentage of population over the age of 65. In contrast, most of the other states of the Pacific have smaller populations, with high population growth rates, varying levels of urbanization, and lower percentages of the population over the age of 65.

Another demographic issue is the level of urbanization. Many people in Asia are moving from the countryside to the city. Cities are becoming quite large, including Beijing, Shanghai, Chongqing, Tokyo, Jakarta, and Manila. Overall, the level of urbanization is lower in Southeast Asia (49 percent) than Northeast Asia (64 percent). At the same time, huge cities with populations over one million are common. A city of 200,000 is a small town. Japan (92 percent urban) and South Korea (81 percent) are highly urbanized, with few people engaged in farming. In Southeast Asia, most countries have primate cities—single large urban settlements that overshadow all others. Countries such as Thailand, the Philippines, and Indonesia are encouraging the growth of secondary cities. Vietnam has two large cities, the capital, Hanoi and an economic center, Ho Chi Minh City (Figure 8.5). Singapore is essentially a city-state. In most Asian cities, planning for housing is a major issue (Karan 2004).

China's demographic predicament dwarfs that of the rest of East Asia. One way to solve a population problem is to produce more food, which was the method preferred by Mao. According to Mao, each stomach has two hands attached: the more people the better. Government policy was to keep subsistence ahead of population growth. Population growth rates approached 2.5 percent

Figure 8.5 Ho Chi Minh City. The former Saigon has long been an economic center in Vietnam.

Source: S. Toops.

in 1957. The greatest demographic disaster in China was the famine resulting from the Great Leap Forward of 1958–1960, when between 20 to 30 million people died due to poor harvests and poor planning. After the famine, birth rates soared, and a baby boom in the mid-1960s increased population (Gamer and Toops 2017).

Between 1949 and 1976, China's population had nearly doubled. The country embarked on a policy of late marriages and fewer births. In reform China, under **Deng Xiaoping**, pragmatism took hold. The government's policy of population control limited couples to one child. This policy was most effective in the cities, but in the countryside it had limited effect. By 2000, China's population growth rate was only 1 percent, an impressive feat for a developing country. Only through the centralized authoritarian government could such a policy work (Veeck et al. 2016).

Population control has been an important element of China's economic reform; without the limits on population, gains in the economy would not have registered. The impacts of population controls on society are strong. Within the space of a generation, China has shrunk its family size. Families that now have one child in the city or two children in the country became the norm. This has raised two social issues: first, how does the Chinese family adapt to having only one or two children? All the aunts and uncles, grandmothers, and grandfathers dote on that little girl or boy. Some have become quite spoiled; they are called "little emperors." Second, who will support the elderly? In traditional China, children and grandchildren supported the old (see Figure 8.6). In Maoist China, the state was responsible for retirees. In reform China, while the state looks after public-sector retirees, private-sector retirees are on their own.

Figure 8.6 This family in Shanghai has their future hope pinned on the success of their granddaughter.

Source: S. Toops.

The one child policy caused several problems, including a smaller proportion of children, an increasing proportion of elderly, and more young men than women. To alleviate these issues, a new policy in 2016 allowed all couples to have two children. Many people in urban areas will probably limit themselves to one child, but others will have two. There will be a greater proportion of the working population to solve the issue of care for the elderly; policymakers also hope that the ratio of men and women will balance out (Veeck et al. 2016). In 2021 China shifted to a three-child policy in hopes of encouraging more births.

Demographic issues pose major challenges for Asia, and there is a strong need for economic improvement. Generally speaking, changes in the economic structure, from agricultural to industrial and services, lead to greater urbanization. A demographic transition occurs when more people are urban than rural. However, a country with a large population faces greater stress in the system when moving from a rural agrarian system to an urban industrial system; China is a case in point, which will be discussed in detail later in the chapter.

Asian Economic Development

The most common type of Asian economic growth has been export-led. Most Asian economies are capitalist-market-focused economies. Japan is a good example of an economy that conforms to market pressures, and it is the most developed country in Asia (see Figure 8.7). The focus of Japan and South Korea has been big business; large corporations and most people have benefited from that development. Just as Japan and Indonesia have varieties of democracy, they also have varieties of capitalism. A contrasting example is that of China, which has a mixed-market economy, though with elements of a state-run sector.

Figure 8.7 Tokyo. Shibuya crossing, a symbol of economic development in Japan.

Source: S. Toops.

In East Asia, the general model for economic growth has been one in which the state is heavily involved in setting goals and aims for the economy (very different from the US version of capitalism). In Japan, the government bureaucracy works in tandem with integrated corporations (**keiretsu**) to build the economy. South Korea has modeled itself on the Japanese system with large industrial conglomerates (**chaebol**). In both cases, the countries have moved from exporting consumer products to heavy industry and then to high-tech goods and services. Both Japan and South Korea have built industrialized, urbanized economies (Borthwick 2014).

China has a different economic situation, in that the economy was totally controlled by the state until the 1980s, and the bulk of the population was in agriculture, with industrial activity focused on heavy industry. With the economic reforms since the 1980s, the state has encouraged a new-style economy with extensive planning, combined with a market economy. This mixed-market economy has maintained high economic growth focusing on light industry. Labor is still relatively inexpensive, so China has been able to produce many consumer goods for export. Overall, the transition from agriculture to industry to services resembles the pattern established in Japan and South Korea, although state planning is still well entrenched in China.

Southeast Asia has a mix of economies. The legacy of British, Dutch, Spanish, and French colonial control held back economic development in Southeast Asia. Economically successful countries such as Singapore, Thailand, and Malaysia have followed programs of export-led development, exporting consumer goods, similar to East Asia. Singapore is the financial hub of Southeast Asia. Indonesia, with its focus on raw materials, oil, and timber, has been less successful. Primary products such as oil and timber are exported to other countries such as Japan that derive the benefit from the raw materials. Vietnam, recovered economically from its civil wars, has recently been using a Chinese model of mixed-market economy. Economic difficulties are common in Cambodia and Laos as well as Myanmar, due to political conflicts and a lack of infrastructure. Globalized industrial production based in Southeast Asia—for example, the manufacture of DVD players or sports shoes—has meant labor-intensive production with low wages. The countries outside of this globalization are not doing as well in terms of economic growth. However, the concern is that the low-wage character of these industrial jobs does not contribute to local development (Dixon 1991; Dayley and Neher 2013).

Leaders in terms of GDP per capita are Singapore, Hong Kong, Taiwan, Japan, and South Korea. Japan's economy industrialized first during the Meiji era starting in 1868. Japan colonized Taiwan and Korea in the early 1900s. Britain had Hong Kong and Singapore as colonies. After World War II, Japan rebounded from the ashes. Singapore, Hong Kong, Taiwan, and South Korea rose economically in the 1960s and are labeled the newly industrialized countries. All of these have had strong government intervention in the business sector: government bureaucracy plans economic development. Japan, Singapore, South Korea, and Taiwan are also leaders in terms of life expectancy and literacy. At the next level are the rising economies of Thailand and Malaysia. Thailand and Malaysia have production centers that feed into the global market for consumer goods. The next set of countries are the most populous: China and Indonesia. Their large populations force the question of how to provide for all. Another issue is that of regional development; these large countries have regions of economic growth as well as regions of economic stagnation. Real poverty is entrenched in North Korea and Myanmar, but that has more to do with past and current political regimes and conflicts rather than the availability of resources (Potter et al. 1999).

In addition to GDP per capita, other measures of development include more social variables. The ability to read and the overall health of the population are two indicators of social development. Japan is a leader in life expectancy and literacy. Levels of literacy above 90 percent are common in Northeast Asia and some Southeast Asian countries. The current socialist countries have placed an emphasis on literacy. High life expectancies in Northeast Asia and some Southeast Asian countries such as Singapore and Thailand are good indicators of a better life. Countries such as Laos and Cambodia have low levels of life expectancy.

Regionally, a number of Pacific Rim countries in Asia and the Americas formed the Asia-Pacific Economic Cooperation (APEC) forum in 1989. Since then, APEC has sought to promote free trade in the region. Asian members include China, Hong Kong, Japan, Taiwan, South Korea, Brunei, Indonesia, Malaysia, Philippines, Singapore, Thailand, and Vietnam. Pacific members include Australia, New Zealand, and Papua New Guinea. American members include Canada, Chile, Mexico, Peru, and the United States. Russia is also a member. India and other Asian countries, as well as Costa Rica and Colombia, have expressed interest in admission, but the organization has limited its admissions since 1995.

In sum, whether measuring economic or social development, the Asian countries such as Japan, Singapore, the Republic of China (Taiwan), and South Korea rank high. Brunei also ranks high with its oil economy. Malaysia, People's Republic of China, and Thailand are at the next level. China has the biggest economy. Indonesia and Vietnam are at lower levels. Lowest levels of development indicators in Laos, Cambodia, and Myanmar point to major difficulties.

Development and China

Why profile China to illustrate one type of economic development in Asia? Its scale is one reason. China has 1.4 billion people in a territory the size of the United States; over 90 percent of the population is concentrated in the eastern half. China is a multicultural society, but only 8 percent of the population is not ethnic Chinese (Han). China's territory is the third largest in the world, and one-fifth of humanity speaks Chinese.

The second reason to consider China is its recent rapid economic growth. New China embarked upon a period of reform in December 1978. The government calls this "socialism with Chinese characteristics" (Gamer and Toops 2017). The Chinese economy has had growth rates of 8 to 10 percent per annum since the 1980s, with the growth rate around 6 to 7 percent as of 2020. China has the largest economy (measured in gross national product purchasing power parity) and that economy is growing fast (Veeck et al. 2016).

The third reason is China's political and cultural role in the world. China is a major voice in world affairs, and a permanent member of the UN Security Council; yet the state is an authoritarian regime controlled by the Chinese Communist Party. Chinese culture has responded to the forces of globalization. Chinese culture, food, and movies are readily available outside the country, while foreign cultures are readily visible in the urban centers of China (Gamer and Toops 2017).

In the Chinese zodiac, a dragon is the symbol of a beginning. It is part of the ceremony at the opening of a business. When the eyes of the dragon are dotted, the dragon awakes, and the new enterprise begins. Outsiders have also linked the imagery of China and the dragon. Napoleon (probably apocryphally) said, "The dragon is asleep. Let it sleep. When it awakes the world will shake" (Croll 2006, 9). China is at the dawn of a new era, an era that some suggest will be a Pacific century. Political events as well as economic realities draw the world's attention to China as a key link in Pacific Asia (Borthwick 2014).

The People's Republic of China came into being based on the peasantry. Agriculture remains a key part of the economy, especially since so many people are peasants. Under Mao, China's agricultural system rapidly changed. First, in the early 1950s through land reform, land confiscated from the landlords was given to the peasants. Then, in the mid-1950s, land was worked collectively. In 1958, Mao Zedong set up the commune system as part of the Great Leap Forward. The scale of the commune, 8,000 to 80,000 people, covering large segments of farmland, structured this Maoist landscape. The focus of production was rice and wheat to the exclusion of all else. A common slogan was "take grain as the key link." The government used the surplus produced by the peasants to stimulate industrial activity. However, when crops began to fail in the late 1950s, the commune system was disorganized and many people died during the resulting great famine (Spence 1999).

In the countryside, the change from Mao's policies came early in 1979 and took effect quickly. A return to family farming was a key feature of Deng Xiaoping's policies in reform China. Families did not own the land, but they kept the right to work the land. The scale changed— one family instead of 20,000; an acre instead of thousands. Production of most crops increased dramatically with the reforms. Grain is no longer the key link; vegetables, fruits, and other cash crops are preferred as farmers diversify. More machinery is in use. Surplus agricultural labor turns toward rural industry, construction, and transport. Farmers on the east coast have benefited most from the reforms.

China under Mao also emphasized heavy industry. The industry program followed the Soviet Union, since the Communists under Mao had more experience with the countryside than the city. To strengthen industrial expansion the government targeted increases in coal, steel, and oil production. Steel was the key link. In the 1950s, China planned to build up its industrial structure. The Great Leap Forward was a crash course in industrialization. The government promoted industry and agriculture at all scales of development. Workers had an "iron rice bowl" that could not be broken; the state guaranteed the jobs. At the end of the Maoist era, China focused on heavy and large-scale industry controlled by the state. Theoretically, all regions were to develop equally, but the north and northeast had the most developed industrial system (Borthwick 2014).

The reforms at the end of the 1970s meant much change in industry. The previous emphasis on heavy industry meant a shortage of consumer goods like bicycles or radios. Today, light industry is more favored. Cities now have a variety of factories producing many goods for local, domestic, and foreign markets. The state still runs many of the heavy-industry factories, but light industry is often run by private entrepreneurs or foreign interests. Light industry has a large domestic market and a strong export market; clothing and textiles are important products very visible in stores in the United States. Retail trade has also picked up considerably since the reforms, with the coastal region performing well.

An important part of the reforms has been the boom in trade and services. China initially relied on the Soviet Union for trade, but by 1960 the country was following a policy of self-reliance. With the reforms under Deng, China embarked on an open-door policy. Now China seeks foreign investment and trade. Exports and imports are both important to the Chinese economy. While trade and investments declined in 1989, the 1990s saw a strong resurgence. New elements of the Chinese economic landscape include the recent boom in telecommunications and tourism. Before the economic rise and the reforms, most Chinese did not have a telephone. In the coastal cities in particular, access to telephones, fax machines, microwaves, and satellite links or fiber-optic cables has now tied China into the global economy in a brand new way. In the late 1970s, China also opened its doors to international tourists. China's tourism suffered a decrease in 1989 as a result of publicity surrounding the Tiananmen Square protests, but recovered through the 2000s (Gamer and Toops 2017).

The economy is at the heart of reform in China. New railroads, new technology, new businesses, and new farming systems complete a picture of China's economic reform. The coastal region has reaped the benefits of reform, including Hong Kong, which returned to China in 1997 along with its vibrant market economy. Since 2014, however, people in Hong Kong have protested regarding the electoral system in the territory. The next step is to bring economic growth to the interior.

For China, the reform period's efforts at development are noteworthy. Millions have been brought out of poverty, and there is strong economic growth, meeting the basic definition of development (Seers 1977). With the continuation of China's changing economic reforms, many have been left unemployed, as the state sector has restructured. Inequalities are arising as well (all were equal under Communism, although some were more equal than others). The basic needs of people in China have been met, though life sustenance in China is still a major issue for the poor, who, like those in the United States (Black Hills, Appalachia, Deep South) are primarily agricultural, tilling poor soil, and far from markets. Of course, the United States, and now China, has urban poor as well. In China, as in the United States, minority ethnic groups are relatively poorer compared to the more populous and powerful elements of society. Beyond life sustenance, two elements of a broader conception of development—self-esteem and freedom—are rather more difficult to achieve (Goulet 1985; Sen 2000). Self-esteem and freedom are goals all over the world, not just in China or Asia.

Perhaps China's biggest challenge in the twenty-first century is to reconcile its rapid economic development with an authoritarian regime whose ideology is bankrupt and legitimacy is questioned. In contemporary reform China, the "expert" of technology and management has replaced the "red" of politics. Deng, a key member of the Party since the 1920s, had long been an advocate of the expert in guiding China. For reform China, the new goal is transformation into a socialist market economy, combining good elements of both communism and capitalism. At a party conference on agriculture in 1962, Deng quoted a Sichuan proverb, "It does not matter if it is a black cat or a white cat, as long as it catches mice." This pragmatism of Deng has been a hallmark of China's reform. The leaders after Deng Xiaoping have followed in his footsteps. In early 1989, students, intellectuals, and workers joined a pro-democracy movement to redress the political problems of China, calling for universal freedom. The pro-democracy movement occupied Tiananmen Square in April 1989. The government responded with violent repression under martial law on the night of June 3, 1989. The dawn of June 4 showed thousands killed by tanks and troops. Tiananmen Square was the site of a massacre; the army under the leadership of the Party had killed Chinese people. Over 30 years have passed, but the memory lingers (Gamer and Toops 2017).

The current leader of China, Xi Jinping, assumed Communist Party leadership in 2012 and rose to president of the People's Republic of China (PRC) in 2013. He has called for renewed efforts to boost the economy, rein in corruption, and consolidate political control. The new slogan is "achieve the Chinese dream," which alludes both to individual self-improvement and the revitalization of the nation. Since 2013, the government of the PRC reinvigorated its sea power and air power over the South China Sea and the East China Sea. The PRC has territorial disputes over islands with Japan and the Republic of China (on Taiwan) in the East China Sea. The South China Sea dispute with Vietnam, the Philippines, Malaysia, Brunei, and Indonesia is over the Spratly and Paracel Islands. These geopolitical disputes with surrounding countries point to a rising China in Asia. In pursuit of the "Chinese dream," the PRC landed a rover on the moon in 2013. The rover, named Jade Rabbit (Yutu), after a Chinese mythological figure, paves the way for a future manned mission to the moon. In 2020 China landed another rover and brought back 4 pounds of moon rocks to study. The rover planted the Chinese flag on the moon, the only other flag there is that of the United States (Elleman et al. 2013; Huang and Patman 2013; Myers and Chang 2020).

China's development program also has international dimensions. In 2013, the leaders of China proposed economic and geopolitical ties across Asia under the slogan "One Belt One Road." There are two parts: the Silk Road Economic Belt linking China with Central Asia, the Middle East, and Europe by land; and the Twenty-First Century Maritime Silk Road, linking China, Southeast Asia, and South Asia by sea. The policies set up China's connections with neighbors across Asia and Europe and have meant construction of infrastructural linkages such as railways and ports, as well as financial investment from Chinese agencies, banks, and companies into other countries. In 2015, Chinese President Xi spoke of the One Belt One Road Initiative as a way to encourage economic development among Asian countries; it is also a way to encourage allies in Asia and beyond (Toops 2016).

The Great Wall of China is a symbol of Chinese power. But the Wall also represents the spirit and labor of the Chinese people. The fact that the Great Wall is now on a credit card in China is emblematic of the serious challenge facing the present Chinese government to maintain its position as the economic and political power of the people grows (Gamer and Toops 2017). China is an important player in the twenty-first century.

The Role of East Asia in the World

Asia is poised to play a significant role in the global order in the twenty-first century. Asia was the center of the world economically until the 1500s and the rise of Europe. After World War II, the United States and the USSR contended for global domination. While the United States is currently the most powerful state, Europe and Asia are also formidable entities, precisely because they are not continents led by just one state. China is the strongest power in East Asia. With its long history, rising economy, large population, diverse cultures, and compelling politics, China is a model for the developing world and is on the cusp of entering the developed world. The political weight of Northeast Asia and the economic growth of Southeast Asia are both a part of Asia's future.

Asia's historical ties with the Americas, Africa, Europe, and the Middle East foreshadow developments in the twenty-first century. In ancient times, Asia was connected to Europe and to the Middle East through trade and migration. (One can argue that Europe and the Middle East are historical offshoots of Asia.) The overland trading routes of the Silk Road connected China and India to the Mediterranean. The Silk Road was a crossroads for cultural and economic communication between East and West. Trade from China reached Africa in the Middle Ages. With European colonialism, the direction of the flows began to change. Control of the flows also shifted from Asian to European hands. Spanish trading ships in the 1500s linked Asia with the Americas. Labor flows brought Asians to the Americas as well (particularly Chinese and Japanese). During the twentieth century as colonialism was lifted, Asia shifted from European imperial control to new nation-states.

East Asia's global connections have become stronger in this early segment of the twenty-first century. Descendants of Asian migrants were already vital components of communities around the world—Chinese in Australia, the United States, and Canada; Filipinos in the United States; Vietnamese in France; and Indonesians in the Netherlands are all examples of the migration of Asians around the world. Part of the process includes colonialism, but it also includes globalization as skilled engineers and scientists seek employment in the world's high-tech centers. California and New York have both become melting pots with the advent of Asian immigrants.

Transfusions of Asian culture into the global medium came along with the immigrants, including religion, film, and food. Films from China, Japan, South Korea, and Hong Kong bring enjoyment throughout the world. Ang Lee's *Crouching Tiger, Hidden Dragon* (2000) began the twenty-first century by filming in China with a starring cast from Hong Kong, Malaysia, China, and Taiwan; a director from Taiwan; writers from Taiwan, China, and the United States; and a global market. Bong Joon-ho's *Parasite*, a 2019 South Korean film, won the 2020 Academy Award for best picture and best director. *Parasite* was in Korean with subtitles and still won the Oscar. Chinese tai chi and Korean taekwondo are both popular in the West. Most towns in the United States have Chinese restaurants and many have Japanese, Korean, or Thai restaurants as well. Elements of East Asian culture are known and recognized worldwide.

Economic networks link countries and businesses. Japanese firms such as Toyota, Sanyo, and Nissan, and Korean firms such as Hyundai, Samsung, LG, and Kia, are recognizable to Western ears. Large Chinese firms such as Lenovo, Haier, and Alibaba, and Taiwanese firms such as Acer, Giant, and Tingyi are also moving onto the market. Products range from electronic goods, software, IT, automobiles, and bicycles to noodles. Asian firms have markets globally, including China's push to Africa as well as Latin America. Global transnational corporations are also heavily invested in East Asia, which offers a large skilled workforce as well as large markets. So both production and consumption in East Asia attract the global economy. The One Belt One Road Initiative links China with many Asian and European countries.

Political power and security issues also point toward the Asian connection. China is a permanent member of the UN Security Council and as such has veto power, as do Russia, the

United Kingdom, France, and the United States. Discussions of expanding the UN Security Council include consideration of India and Japan as possible members. The UN secretary general through 2016 was Ban Ki-moon from South Korea, so Asia has had an important presence at the United Nations. China has nuclear weapons, and North Korea has tested nuclear weapons. In political and security terms, East Asia is a significant component of the global system.

Covid-19, a coronavirus, was found in Wuhan, China, in December 2019. Initially the disease spread to Japan, South Korea, Thailand, Taiwan, and Vietnam. All of these countries were able to manage the disease. Probably the prevalence of mask-wearing to defend against pollution, colds, and flu in East Asia helped. Taiwan and New Zealand have had fewer cases. The disease has since spread around the world. In East Asia, Indonesia and Philippines still have a large number of cases and deaths in 2020 (Krishna 2020; Pettersson et al. 2020).

East Asia is globally connected. Asians are knowledgeable not only in the global language of business, but also in diplomacy. Asian political connections link the countries to the Americas in particular through the Asia Pacific Economic Cooperation forum, which includes all countries of the Pacific Rim. In 2020, the ASEAN states with Australia, China, Japan, New Zealand, and South Korea formed the Regional Comprehensive Economic Partnership. This free trade agreement includes all countries in East Asia with the exception of North Korea and Taiwan. Asian countries were linked with Africa during the 1955 Bandung conference of non-aligned states. The Group of 77 now includes some 130 Asian, African, Latin American, and Middle Eastern countries who work jointly to promote their interests in the United Nations. South–South communication and cooperation for development is a key part of the Group of 77's mission.

International studies, as a discipline, examines East Asia's global connections. For example, East Asia's trading connections are, of course, part of the global economic transaction. From an international studies perspective, East Asian trade has political, historical, geographic, sociological, and anthropological components. For a company, how to best market its wares in Asia depends on what country and culture it is connecting to. US political relations affect its trade with Japan and China. The spatial and temporal rhythms of trade bring in the geographical and historical components.

Beijing hosted the 2008 Olympics and made its mark on the world, just as Seoul and Tokyo did with their 1988 and 1964 Olympics, respectively. South Korea hosted the Winter Olympics in 2018, Tokyo's 2020 Summer Olympics is delayed to 2021, and Beijing will host the Winter Olympics in 2022. Market economic reforms, law-based governments, open access to technology, environmentally friendly societies, and cultural pluralism are components to a positive Asian-Pacific future. Flexibility, discipline, and drive are keys to that future.

Timeline of Modern East Asian and Pacific History

1900	Boxer Rebellion in China.
1901	Australian independence.
1905	Japanese annexation of Korea.
1911	Fall of Chinese Empire.
1912	Chinese Nationalist Party formed.
1921	Chinese Communist Party formed.
1931	Japanese invasion of Manchuria.
1932	Japan withdraws from League of Nations.
1934	"Long March" of Chinese Communists.
1937–1945	Sino–Japanese War (WWII in Asia).

1940	Japanese conquest of IndoChina.
1941	Japan attacks United States (Hawaii, Philippines) and British territories (Malaya, Singapore).
1945	Atomic bombs dropped on Hiroshima and Nagasaki, Japan surrenders. Partition of Korea.
1946	Philippine independence.
1945–1949	Civil war in China.
1946–1954	French colonial war in Indochina.
1946–1949	Dutch colonial war in East Indies.
1949	People's Republic of China on mainland, Republic of China on Taiwan.
1950	Formation of Vietnam, Cambodia, and Laos. Sukarno president of Indonesia.
1950–1953	Korean War.
1950	Chinese conquest of Tibet.
1954	French withdraw from Indochina.
1955	Creation of North and South Vietnam. Bandung Conference of non-aligned states.
1956	Japanese economic boom.
1959–1971	Tibetan revolt.
1959	Dalai Lama flees to India.
1958–1960	China's Great Leap Forward.
1963	US military aid to South Vietnam.
1964	Tokyo Olympics.
1965	US military intervention in Vietnam. Singapore forms independent state.
1966	Suharto rules Indonesia.
1966–1975	China's Cultural Revolution.
1973	US troops withdraw from Vietnam.
1975	Chairman Mao dies. Communist conquest of South Vietnam and Cambodia.
1978	End of collective farms in China.
1980	Deng Xiaoping leads China's economic boom.
1981	One-child policy in China.
1988	Seoul Olympics.
1989	Tiananmen Square incident in China, suppression of democracy movement.
1997	Deng Xiaoping dies. Asian Financial Crisis. Britain returns Hong Kong to China's control.
2004	Indian Ocean tsunami.
2008	Beijing Olympics.
2011	Japan earthquake and tsunami. Myanmar forms new nominally civilian government.
2013	Hurricane Haiyan devastates Philippines. Xi Jinping new president of People's Republic of China.
2014	Hong Kong protests.
2016	Two-child policy in China. Thai King dies, new King crowned.
2019	Covid-19 starts in China.

References

Borthwick, Mark. 2014. *Pacific Century: The Emergence of Modern Pacific Asia*. Boulder, CO: Westview Press.

Brower, Daniel R. 2005. *The World in the Twentieth-Century: From Empires to Nations*. 6th ed. Upper Saddle River, NJ: Prentice Hall.

Clayre, Alasdair. 1986. *The Heart of the Dragon*. New York: Houghton-Mifflin.

Croll, Elisabeth. 2006. *China's New Consumers: Social Development and Domestic Demand*. London: Routledge.

Dayley, Robert, and Clark D. Neher. 2013. *Southeast Asia in the New International Era*. 6th ed. Boulder, CO: Westview Press.

Deng Xiaoping. 1962. "Restore Agricultural Production." in *Selected Works of Deng Xiaoping*. Vol.1www.people.com.cn/english/dengxp/contents1.html

Desnoyers, Charles. 2020. *Patterns of East Asian History*. New York: Oxford University Press.

Dixon, Chris. 1991. *Southeast Asia in the World Economy: A Regional Geography*. Cambridge: Cambridge University Press.

Elleman, Bruce A., Stephen Kotkin, and Clive Schofield, eds. 2013. *Beijing's Power and China's Borders: Twenty Neighbors in Asia*. Armonk, NY: M. E. Sharpe.

Frank, Andre Gunder. 1998. *ReORIENT: Global Economy in the Asian Age*. Berkeley: University of California Press.

Friend, Theodore. 2003. *Indonesian Destinies*. Cambridge, MA: Harvard.

Gamer, Robert E., and Stanley Toops, eds. 2017. *Understanding Contemporary China*. Boulder, CO: Lynne Rienner.

Goscha, Christopher. 2016. *Vietnam: A New History*. New York: Basic Books.

Goulet, Denis. 1985. *The Cruel Choice: A New Concept in the Theory of Development*. Lanham, MD: University Press of America.

Huang, Xiaoming, and Robert G. Patman, eds. 2013. *China and the International System: Becoming a World Power*. New York: Routledge.

Karan, Pradyumna P. 2004. *The Non-Western World: Environment, Development, and Human Rights*. New York: Routledge.

———. 2005. *Japan in the 21st Century: Environment, Economy, and Societies*. Lexington: University of Kentucky Press.

Kaup, Katherine ed. 2021. *Understanding Contemporary Asia Pacific*. Boulder, CO: Lynne Rienner.

Krishna, Anirudh. 2020. "The Poorest After the Pandemic." *Current History* 119 (820): 291–96.

Kristof, Nicholas D., and Sheryl WuDunn. 2000. *Thunder from the East: Portrait of a Rising Asia*. New York: Knopf.

Mackerras, Colin, ed. 1995. *East and Southeast Asia: A Multidisciplinary Survey*. Boulder, CO: Lynne Reinner.

Mao Zedong. 1927. "Report on an Investigation of the Peasant Movement in Hunan." In *Selected Works of Mao Zedong*. Vol 1, p. 28. Beijing: Foreign Languages Press.

McKnight, Tom L. 1995. *Oceania: The Geography of Australia, New Zealand, and the Pacific Islands*. Upper Saddle River, NJ: Prentice Hall.

Myers, Steven and Kenneth Chang. December 16, 2020. "China Brings Moon Rocks to Earth." *New York Times*, www.nytimes.com/2020/12/16/science/china-moon-mission-rocks.html

Patterson, Mary, and Martha Macintyre, eds. 2011. *Managing Modernity in the Western Pacific*. St Lucia, Australia: University of Queensland Press.

Pettersson, Henrik, Byron Manley, and Sergio Hernandez. 2020. "Tracking Coronavirus Global Spread." *CNN*. www.cnn.com/interactive/2020/health/coronavirus-maps-and-cases/

Population Reference Bureau. 2020. *World Population Data Sheet 2020*. Washington, DC. www.prb.org/data/

Potter, Robert B, Tony Binns, Jennifer A. Elliott, and David Smith 1999. *Geographies of Development: An Introduction to Development Studies*. Harlow, UK: Pearson Education.

Price, Marie, Martin Lewis, William Wyckoff and Lester Rowntree, 2020. *Globalization and Diversity: Geography of a Changing World.* 6th ed. Upper Saddle River, NJ: Prentice Hall.

Reischauer, Edwin O., and Marius B. Jansen. 1995. *The Japanese Today: Change and Continuing.* Cambridge, MA: Harvard.

Sen, Amartya. 2000. *Development as Freedom.* New York: Anchor Books.

Seers, Dudley. 1969. "The Meaning of Development." *International Development Review,* 9 (4): 2–6.

———. 1977. "The Meaning of Development." *International Development Review,* 17 (3): 2–7.

Spence, Jonathan D. 1999. *The Search for Modern China.* New York: Norton.

Toops, Stanley. 2016. "Reflections on China's Belt and Road Initiative." *Area Development and Policy* 1 (3): 352–60. doi:10.1080/23792949.2016.1233072

Veeck, Gregory, Clifton W. Pannell, Christopher J. Smith, Youqin Huang. 2016. *China's Geography: Globalization and the Dynamics of Political, Economic, and Social Change.* 3rd ed. Lanham, MD: Rowman and Littlefield.

Further Reading

Books

Barr, Michael D. 2019. *Singapore: A Modern History.* London: I.B. Tauris.

Chang, Jung, 1991. *Wild Swans: Three Daughters of China.* New York: Simon & Schuster.

Diamond, Jared M. 2019. *Upheaval: Turning Points for Nations in Crisis.* New York: Little, Brown and Company.

Gifford, Rob. 2007. *China Road: A Journey into the Future of a Rising Power.* New York: Random House.

Hayton, Bill. 2010. *Vietnam: Rising Dragon.* New Haven, CT: Yale University Press.

Kingston, Jeff. 2019. *Japan.* Newark, NJ: Polity Press.

Rickard, John. 2017. *Australia: A Cultural History.* Clayton, Victoria: Monash University Publishing.

Schell, Orville, and John Delury. 2013. *Wealth and Power: China's Long March to the Twenty-First Century.* New York: Random House.

Wasserstrom, Jeffrey N. 2010. *China in the 21st Century: What Everyone Needs to Know.* New York: Oxford University Press.

Zha, Jianying. 2011. *Tide Players: The Movers and Shakers of a Rising China.* New York: New Press.

Journals

Asian Affairs. www.tandfonline.com/loi/raaf20

China Quarterly. www.cambridge.org/core/journals/china-quarterly

East Asia: An International Quarterly. link.springer.com/journal/12140

Journal of Southeast Asian Studies. www.cambridge.org/core/journals/journal-of-southeast-asian-studies

The Pacific Review. www.tandfonline.com/loi/rpre20

Films

Crouching Tiger, Hidden Dragon (2000). Ang Lee, Director. Sony Pictures Classics and Columbia Pictures Film Production Asia (China).

Infernal Affairs (2002). Andrew Lau, producer. Andrew Lau & Alan Max, directors. Miramax Films, Media Asia Films presents a Basic Pictures production (Hong Kong).

Parasite (2019) Bong Joon-ho, Director. Barunson (South Korea).

Pacific Century (1992). Written and produced by Alex Gibney, directed by Christopher Ralling. A co-production of PBI/Jigsaw Productions in association with NHK-Japan, KCTS/Seattle, and Antelope Films, Ltd. S. Burlington, VT: Annenberg/CPB Project.

Sunset at Chaophraya (1996). Euthana Mukdasanit, director (Thailand).

Websites

Asia Society. asiasociety.org
Asia-Pacific Economic Cooperation. www.apec.org
Association of Southeast Asian Nations. https://asean.org
UN Economic and Social Commission for Asia and the Pacific. www.unescap.org
Virtual Library Asian Studies. vlib.org/AsianStudies

Chapter 9

South and Central Asia and International Studies

Environment and Population

In 2020 the United States unveiled an economic plan to build economic and trade ties that would connect Central Asia to markets in South Asia and Europe. This was part of a US plan to improve prospects for peace in Afghanistan, which American troops invaded in 2011 but also was a counter to China's ambitious Belt and Road initiative, which seeks to link China, South and Central Asia and Iran into a single economic trade route akin to the medieval Silk Road. Currently, **South** and **Central Asia** are among the least well-integrated of the areas discussed in this textbook. China, Europe, and the United States all foresee major economic prospects in these regions if they can be economically linked. Against these prospects are the ongoing war in Afghanistan, the decades long mistrust between Pakistan and India, and violent border disputes between India and China.

Although most of the area's states are relatively new—India and Pakistan were formed in 1947 and the Central Asian states achieved independence after the Fall of the Soviet Union in 1991—the region has an ancient history. Five thousand years ago, the Harappan civilization flourished along the Indus valley. Along with China, Mesopotamia, and Egypt, this is generally considered the beginnings of civilization. The roots of today's societies in South Asia lie in this Indus Valley civilization.

South and Central Asia have a vast geographic scale to match their long history (see Map 8.1). The region accounts for 26 percent of the world's population. Three very large countries populate the region: India has 1.4 billion people, Pakistan has 221 million, and Bangladesh 170 million. Projections indicate that by 2030, India will have 1.5 billion people, thus surpassing China as the world's most populous country. In terms of the environment, the region varies from the world's highest mountain range of the Himalayas, to the tropics of Sri Lanka, to the landlocked deserts of Uzbekistan. The summer monsoon brings life-giving rain to much of South Asia.

The region is one of great cultural complexity. **Hinduism** and **Buddhism** originated in South Asia, and **Islam** came to the region by the Middle Ages. Today Islam predominates in Central Asia, Pakistan, and Bangladesh, while Hinduism is most common in India, and Buddhism in Sri Lanka and Mongolia. In terms of language, Hindi and other north Indian languages vary considerably from the Dravidian languages of South India. Turkic languages include Kazakh, Uzbek, and Kyrgyz. Tajik is related to Persian. Urdu in Pakistan is like Hindi, but is written in a modified Persian script. Global forces have changed the cultures in South and Central Asia since ancient times, and they continue to do so through the Internet and satellite television.

South Asia's economic power is growing. Following economic reforms in the 1990s, India became a rising economic star, although the new wealth is largely held by the urban middle class, with rural poverty continuing to plague India, and the whole region. Many goods and services are produced, consumed, and transferred in South Asia. Indian companies play a major role in the global economy. India is one of the BRICS (Brazil, Russia, India, China, and South Africa)

DOI: 10.4324/9781003028314-12

countries that have jump-started their economies. With the exception of Kazakhstan and its oil economy, Central Asia is relatively poor.

In terms of political power, South Asia does not yet reach the levels of East Asia, but the region includes the world's largest democracy (India), the nuclear power of India and Pakistan, the ongoing presence of al Qaeda and the Taliban in Afghanistan and Pakistan, and the political struggles of the Central Asian countries since their independence from the Soviet Union in 1991. Many countries in the region have ambitions for regional and even global leadership.

Relations between the West and India date back to Alexander the Great, who extended his conquest to the Indus and the Ganges in 326 BCE. Waves of migrants brought Christianity, Judaism and Zoroastrianism to India, and exported Buddhism and Hinduism. The colonial connections of the British make this part of Asia especially familiar to the English-speaking world. There are many words in English of Indian origin, including *pajama, cot, bungalow, loot, khaki, shampoo, guru, curry,* and *cummerbund.* Leaders of nonviolence movements such as Dr. Martin Luther King Jr. studied the tactics of Indian independence leader Mohandas Gandhi. Gandhi's philosophy was *satyagraha,* "grasping truth." In 1919, Gandhi said "Victory attained by violence is tantamount to defeat, for it is momentary." India gained its statehood back from the British through nonviolent means and India became the world's largest democracy. Finally, technology links India and the West through science and engineering as well as call centers and communication linkages.

This chapter begins with a discussion of the regional character of South and Central Asia, considering geographic, political, historical, cultural, and economic relations. An interlude on the Silk Road links historical and contemporary realities. The next section examines population and environment in the region, focusing on India, a rising power in South Asia. The chapter closes with a discussion of the global connections of South and Central Asia in the twenty-first century.

Geographical Realities

Regions of Asia include Northeast Asia and Southeast Asia (profiled in the previous chapter) and South and Central Asia (profiled in this chapter). These regions can overlap; for example, Central Asia is often categorized with the Middle East. Straddling the two regions is Afghanistan, sometimes considered part of Central Asia and sometimes part of South Asia. Because Pakistan is a Muslim-majority state playing a significant role in the US-sponsored "war on terror," the country is sometimes included in definitions of Central Asia (Karan 2004; Weightman 2011).

South Asia includes India, Pakistan, Bangladesh, Nepal, Sri Lanka, and two small states, Bhutan and Maldives. In terms of terrain, the world's highest mountains stretch along northern Pakistan, northern India, and across Nepal. Out of the Himalayas spring the massive river systems of the Indus and Ganges, forming vast plains. The historical center is the Indus River (Figure 9.1); today's center of activity is the Ganges River. The Brahmaputra flows out of Tibet, joining the Ganges and creating a massive delta system. Fertile soils have sustained an immense population on these river systems. In southern India, the Deccan Plateau does not have as reliable a water supply or fertile soils. The island countries of Sri Lanka and the Maldives lie south of India.

The monsoon dominates climate patterns in South Asia. *Monsoon* comes from the word for "season" in Arabic. In winter, a high-pressure system forms over Asia and brings dry air to India. In summer, a low-pressure system forms as heat builds up over South Asia and the lands westward. By June, the summer monsoon brings moisture from the Bay of Bengal and the Indian Ocean, with as much as 70 inches of rain in June, July, and August. However, the pattern is not regular and, if the rain from the summer monsoons is delayed, crop failure can result. The

Figure 9.1 Pakistan. The Gilgit River (left) flows into the Indus River. The author is in the foreground.

Source: S. Toops.

south is mostly tropical savanna, with a wet summer and dry winter. The alluvial lowlands of the Ganges are subtropical, much like Florida, with hot summers. The western area near Pakistan is desert and steppe. The far north has a colder climate due to elevation (Karan 2004; Price et al. 2020).

Central Asia is a landlocked region that emerged from Soviet control after the breakup of the Soviet Union in 1991. Uzbekistan, Turkmenistan, Kazakhstan, Kyrgyzstan, and Tajikistan were former Soviet Republics. There was also strong Soviet influence in Mongolia and a Soviet presence in Afghanistan. Western China (Tibet and Xinjiang) is also a part of this region. All of the countries in this region are Muslim except Mongolia (Buddhist) and have been so since the 900s. In ethnic terms, most of their peoples are Turkic, relatives of the Turks in today's Turkey. The Mongols, Tajiks, Tibetans, and some Afghan peoples are distinct ethnic groups (Brunn et al. 2012; Hanks 2013).

In terms of terrain, the Pamir Knot, on the borders of China, Pakistan, Afghanistan, Tajikistan, and Kyrgyzstan, is at the intersection of mountains such as the Hindu Kush, the Karakoram, and the Tian Shan. Landlocked rivers such as the Tarim, the Helmand, the Amu Darya, and Syr Darya never reach the ocean. Afghanistan, Tajikistan, and Kyrgyzstan are mostly mountainous; Turkmenistan, Uzbekistan and W. Kazakhstan are mostly basins; and Mongolia and E. Kazakhstan are mostly plateaus. In terms of climate, deserts such as the Kara Kum, Kizil Kum Taklamakan, and Gobi form a belt north of the mountains. Kazakhstan and Mongolia have vast tracts of steppe grasslands. As Central Asia has a mid-latitude location in the interior of a large continent, the summers are dry and hot and the winters are dry and cold (Price et al. 2020; Lewis 1992).

Major river systems such as the Ganges-Brahmaputra, mountain systems such as the Himalayas, and deserts such as the Gobi characterize this region's geographical realities.

Historical Challenges

Indigenous kingdoms and empires dominated Asia through its long history. The Indus Valley civilization goes back to 3000 BCE. A succession of empires from the Mauryan to the Mughals ruled the subcontinent till the 1700s. Parthia and Kushan ruled the Central Asian lands, then the Persians, and then the Arabs. By 1200, the Mongols ruled over all of Central Asia. Two world empires, the Mongol and Timurid, controlled Central Asia in the Middle Ages. These very early civilizations developed by being able to produce food surpluses (mostly agricultural, with the exception of Central Asia). These early empires were quite sophisticated culturally and possessed well-developed technologies.

By the 1500s, the advent of Western empires into South Asia, then Southeast and Northeast Asia, reversed the tide of Asian power. Internal conflicts in India and China set the stage for European expansion. In the seventeenth century, the Mughal empire, comprising much of present-day India and Pakistan, was the wealthiest nation in the world, attracting Dutch, Portuguese, French and British traders. A multinational corporation, the British East India Company, eventually dominated India economically, giving way to direct political rule by the British crown in the nineteenth century. Tsarist Russia conquered Central Asia in the 1800s, and for a century, the two Western empires employed diplomacy, espionage, and military support for local political actors in and around Afghanistan. Called the "Great Game" by British authors and the "Tournament of Shadows" by Russians, this Cold War between the two empires three

Figure 9.2 The Gandhi monument shows the spinning wheel, a symbol of his movement.

Source: S. Andrus.

times exploded into proxy wars (Meyer and Brysac 1999). In the twentieth century, Soviet influence dominated the region. With the breakup of the Soviet Union in 1991, Russian control ended in Central Asia (Meyer 2003).

Western imperialism engendered Asian national movements. Dozens of resistance movements dedicated to freeing Asian lands from Western domination emerged in the late nineteenth and early twentieth centuries. The most successful was the nonviolent Quit India movement, led by Mohandas Gandhi. While Gandhi's leadership was cut short by an assassin in 1948, his legacy is crucial for India (Figure 9.2). By 1949, India was free from colonial rule (Brower 2005). Disputes over how India's large Muslim population should be represented in the new nation led to a violent division of the country. Partition in 1949 meant the creation of two new states: India and Pakistan. Pakistan was further subdivided in 1971 with the creation of Bangladesh.

Before Western colonialism, Asia was, in the words of Jawaharlal Nehru, master of its destiny. The advent of the West subjugated Asian peoples. The rising nationalism after WWII meant that Asia could once again be free. With the ascendancy of Asia, especially India, in the world today, the region is increasing in power and playing a stronger role after years of European dominance.

Cultural Complexities

The level of diversity in Central and South Asia is quite high. In contrast to the Middle East or Latin America, or even Europe, there is nothing that really unites the region culturally. Current belief systems include Hinduism, Islam, Christianity, Buddhism, Sikhism, Jainism, and Zoroastrianism in South Asia, while Central Asia has Islam, Christianity, and Lama Buddhism (see Map 3.1). Both regions also harbor pockets of local shamanistic traditions.

Hinduism is the most common religion in India and Nepal. Hinduism began in the Ganges Valley as far back as 1500 BCE with the writing of scriptures such as the Vedas. Hindus have a core of belief in the many expressions of the deity, a unity in diversity. Another common belief is reincarnation, the transmigration of souls; Hinduism has many mystical elements. Rituals at homes, temples, and festivals populate the Hindu cultural landscape.

Buddhism began as a Hindu religious reform movement. The Buddha began teaching in northern India around 500 BCE, and 250 years later, Buddhists ruled most of the subcontinent. **Buddhism** diffused through South Asia, but ironically, declined in the land of its origin. In Central Asia today, Tibetans and Mongols still practice the Tibetan variant of Buddhism. In Sri Lanka, Theravada Buddhists form the majority of the population. Theravada Buddhism developed in Sri Lanka and spread to Southeast Asia. In Theravada Buddhism, many people become monks or nuns to focus their devotion.

Islam is common in Central Asia as well as Pakistan and Bangladesh. Islam, a monotheistic religion, came to the region by 1000 CE (see Figure 9.3). The Turkic peoples of Central Asia brought Islam to South Asia. Muslim rulers of India such as the Mughal (1500s–1800s), who originated in Central Asia, dominated the region (Buddhist rulers had dominated the region previously). In the northwest and northeast, many South Asians converted to Islam. Today these areas form Pakistan and Bangladesh. Muslims and Hindus lived side by side amiably for a thousand years. People in South Asia practiced Islam or Hinduism exclusively.

Christianity is common in Southwest India, in the state of Kerala and in Northeast India, particularly in the state of Nagaland, due to missionary activity. Although Syrian Christians had reached India by 200 CE, the religion had not taken hold outside small enclaves in South Asia. European colonialism brought Christianity into the region. With the advent of Russian colonialism in the 1800s, many Russians who followed Eastern Orthodox Christianity settled in Central Asia. Russian Orthodox Christianity ranges from 10 to 25 percent of the population

Figure 9.3 A Muslim wedding ceremony in Khiva, Uzbekistan, complete with a trip to the local mosque and a wishing well.

Source: S. Toops.

in the Central Asian countries. Kazakhstan has the highest percentage due to the many ethnic Russians living there.

Marxist atheism held sway in Central Asia as many mosques (and temples in Mongolia) were closed between 1930 and 1991. Some mosques reopened as museums for atheism. This secularism still has some currents in Central Asia. Secular Marxism also influenced many intellectuals and political leaders in India, although it never took hold in the general populace.

Language diversity is high. In Central Asia, Turkic languages are dominant, including Uzbek, Kyrgyz, Kazakh, and Turkmen. All of these Turkic languages use a Cyrillic script; however, since 1992, Uzbekistan has been transitioning to a Latin script similar to Turkish. After years of Russian colonization, Russian is a common language in Central Asia. Tajik, like Dari (in Afghanistan), is a Persian-related language. In the northern parts of South Asia, Indo-European languages prevail. Hindi in India and Urdu in Pakistan are mutually intelligible but are written in Devanagari and modified Persian scripts, respectively. Bengali in Bangladesh and Sinhalese in Sri Lanka are also members of the Indo-European language family. In southern India, languages such as Tamil and Telugu belong to the Dravidian language family. Due to British colonization, English is a common tongue in many parts of South Asia.

The waves of religious innovation and diffusion created the complex cultural landscape of South and Central Asia. Elements of the various traditions influenced one another over time, and various political and cultural theories of tolerance and coexistence emerged. In the South Asian context, the challenge of **globalization** is that it increases the likelihood of people mobilizing religious differences, as part of political and economic struggles over resources. Conflicts between Islam, Hinduism, Sikhism, and Christianity began to take place during colonial rule and have continued, sometimes on a large scale, under the pressures of globalization. In Central Asia, the challenge today is whether to combine, maintain, or create new cultural identities deriving from Muslim, Turkic, or Russian cultures in the midst of globalization.

Waves of cultural innovation and diffusion have sculpted the complex layers of identity. Mobile phones, computers, and satellite television bring new worlds into South and Central Asia. During the colonial era, the British government encouraged the emigration of educated Indians to its colonies elsewhere in Asia, Africa, South America, and the Caribbean. After independence, India also became a source of educated labor for the Middle East, Europe, and North America. This South Asian diaspora has marked the world with the outflow of South Asian movies from Bollywood, Indian restaurants to the UK and United States, and Indian technology entrepreneurs to Silicon Valley. Central Asia has made less of a mark on the world. Uzbek or Afghan restaurants are much less common than Indian restaurants, for one example.

Local culture in India has been able to incorporate much of Western culture on its own terms. There are distinct global influences in India, from the use of English as a national language to India's early adoption of communication technologies like the press, film, and computers, but there is also a definite South Asian influence in the wider world because of the diaspora. In the case of Central Asia, the cultural variety is seen in the use of Russian because of the colonialism dating back to the 1800s. Central Asian communities are well adapted to Europe because of the long experience with Russia. Globalization is present in Tashkent; it has Korean and Turkish as well as Russian and Uzbek restaurants.

Economic Opportunities

The impacts of Asian economies are felt worldwide. The countries have tried various methods for economic growth. Some Asian governments have been actively involved in promoting export-led industrialization as a development strategy. Most South Asian countries have two-tiered economies. Well-developed, technologically sophisticated economies exist alongside subsistence agriculture (French 1997; Wolpert 2004). Economic **development** in Central Asia has been saddled with a difficult transition from Soviet-style command economies to market-oriented systems. Central Asia has also been troubled with a declining importance of cotton in agriculture, the rising role of the oil industry in places such as Kazakhstan, and the demise of pastoral nomadism (Shaw 1995; Megoran and Sharapova 2013). Within Central Asia, Kazakhstan has a good per capita **GDP** because of its oil economy, but it lacks the infrastructural development of the **newly industrialized countries (NICs)**. India and Sri Lanka are at a lower level. Poverty is a big problem in South and Central Asia compared with East Asia. Among poorer countries like Afghanistan and Tajikistan, various factors such as conflict have severely limited the possibilities for economic growth (Frank 1998; Sievers 2003; Engelmann and Pavlaković 2001) (see Map 4.1).

India has seen explosive economic development since it began deregulating its industries in the 1990s. India, like China, is one of the countries in the BRICS group (Brazil, Russia, India, China, and South Africa), indicating that the Indian economy is moving up the development scale. Industrial production has been a strong segment in Asia, including Indian businesses such as automobiles geared to the Indian market or medicines for worldwide consumption. The educational system of India has produced many scientists and engineers. A newer sector, developed in the 1990s, includes high technology in places like Bangalore (the Indian equivalent of Silicon Valley). International communication technologies have led to the development of call centers in India from which technical advice or customer service is dispensed to people in the United States or Britain. Science and technology are factors in this innovation, but so is India's strong national education system, with its emphasis on English competence.

Economic development is defined as the process of improving the quality of human life. Underdevelopment, in contrast, moves in the opposite direction, leading people to become worse off than before. The future of development economics needs to go beyond the examination of economic growth. A newer view is to consider development as freedom that involves human rights. So in that sense, India can be said to be more developed than China, even though India has a lower GDP per capita than China (Todaro and Smith 2012; Sen 2000). Global economic successes in India contrast with the economic difficulties of Afghanistan and Bangladesh and compare well with China and Russia (Nadkarni and Noonan 2013).

Political Risks

The political systems at work in Asia interlink with historical, geographic, cultural, and economic issues. Historically, the state in Asia, be it the Mauryan or Mughal empires of India, saw itself as responsible to its people. These issues of control and leadership interact today with the need to develop the economy. In terms of geography, given the population of India, how does one state govern a billion people? Asian politics is often expressed in terms of "Asian values," which usually refer to the strong paternalism of the state. Asian nationalisms, whether in the form expressed by Nehru in India or by Nazarbayev in Kazakhstan, have produced a variety of regimes on the continent. The variety of governmental systems is shown in Map 5.1.

In South Asia, the partition of India and Pakistan after the British colonial pullout was responsible for political tension in the area. Even after the horrors of partition, democratic rule has been the norm in India, Pakistan, and Bangladesh. India is the world's largest democracy; the country has a federal system with local governments alongside a national government that deals with foreign affairs and economic issues. Overall, India is the strongest state militarily and politically in the region. The tensions between India and Pakistan over Kashmir have led to complex and shifting relationships with China, the United States, and Russia. India and Pakistan have both developed nuclear capability. Finally, in a post-9/11 world, Pakistan has allied itself with the United States against the Taliban of Afghanistan and al Qaeda. The killing of Osama bin Laden in Pakistan by US forces, without Pakistani knowledge, in 2011, shows the complexity of the US-Pakistan relationship (DeVotta 2010; Ganguly 2016).

In Central Asia, the end of the political domination of the Soviet Union has left newly established states contending with diverse political issues. Politically the region is coming out of communist dictatorship. Many of the local governments, with the exception of Mongolia, are authoritarian. Afghanistan in particular, with a Soviet invasion, civil war, Taliban conflict, and US invasion, has suffered enormous political hardships (Shaw 1995; Megoran and Sharapova 2013). State formation and identity is one issue, as newly independent states suffer from internal cultural conflicts similar to the partition that created Pakistan in the 1940s. Tajikistan and Afghanistan have suffered under civil wars. After September 11, 2001, the United States and the UK launched a major offensive against the Taliban in Afghanistan. While there were still remnants of the Taliban and al Qaeda, Afghanistan successfully held a presidential election in 2004. Forces are still looking for Taliban and al Qaeda in the borderlands of Afghanistan and Pakistan in the midst of a US drawdown in Afghanistan (see Figure 9.4). The political transitions in the other states of Central Asia may not be as complex but the issues still are. Uzbekistan, Turkmenistan, and Kazakhstan have authoritarian regimes. Kyrgyzstan is moving toward democracy. In contrast, Mongolia has a democratic system. The political vacuum left by the collapse of the Soviet Union has meant that China, Iran, Turkey, and Pakistan, as well as the United States, have all been trying to exercise influence in the area. And although the Soviet empire no longer exists, the Russians have not yet given up aspirations in Central Asia (Meyer 2003; Davis and Azizian 2007).

Most of the political systems in South and Central Asia are democracies (see Map 5.1). A few governments are authoritarian. Uzbekistan and Kazakhstan are examples of authoritarian presidencies. In contrast, India is the world's largest democracy; every time there is a national election held in India, it sets a record for the world's biggest election. Democracy is certainly stronger in South Asia than Central Asia (Adeney and Wyatt 2010).

Figure 9.4 The Khyber Pass is on the border of Pakistan and Afghanistan.

Source: S. Toops.

The Silk Road

In 2013, the President of China, Xi Jinping, proposed a Silk Road Economic Belt and Maritime Silk Road, linking China and countries in Asia by land and by sea. This mirrors the old Silk Road. China is using the metaphor of the Silk Road to connect with countries in Asia and on to Europe. It is seeking to develop infrastructure and investment projects across Asia, recreating the Silk Road. China's Belt and Road Initiative emphasizes its connections to such countries as Kazakhstan, Kyrgyzstan, and Pakistan, along trade routes that also saw the diffusion of Buddhism and Islam (Toops 2016).

The famous **Silk Road** illustrates contemporary linkages following a historic trade artery. Westerners' search for the exotic began on the ancient Silk Road more than 700 years ago, when the chronicles of traveler Marco Polo fascinated the West with stories of faraway lands with strange customs and goods. The fall of Communism in the Soviet Union in 1991 and China's opening to the West in the 1980s reopened the Silk Road to global linkages. The Silk Road has a rich mix of cultural traditions, with Afghans, Turks, Uyghurs, Chinese, Kyrgyz, Uzbeks, and Russians living along the road. The landscape encompasses mountains and steppes, deserts and oases (Millward 2013).

The historical Silk Road was a crossroads nexus of religious, cultural, and economic communication between East and West. Trod by Rabban Bar Sauma, Ibn Battuta, Clavijo, Babur, Timur, Marco Polo, Fa Xian, and Xuan Zang, the Silk Road linked China to India, Persia, and Europe. The numerous ruins, monuments, ancient cities, Buddhist caves, temples, tombs, and garrisons of long-forgotten Uzbek, Kyrgyz, Uyghur, Iranian, Turkic, Mongol, Chinese, and Russian kingdoms, empires, and dynasties are evident in the landscape. They are an important part of the heritage of the area's people. In ancient times, Buddhism spread along the Silk Road from South Asia to Central Asia. In later times, Islam followed the Silk Road from the Middle East, to Central Asia and South Asia (Boulnois 2004).

Uzbekistan illustrates the legacy of the Silk Road. Uzbeks are agriculturalists and traders along the Amu Darya and Syr Darya (rivers). The Russians came to the region in the nineteenth century and conquered the khanates (kingdoms) of the Uzbek and Kyrgyz peoples. The Russian Tsars cultivated Orthodox Christianity in the area. After the Bolshevik Revolution in 1917, Communism brought a new political ideology to the region. After gaining their independence, following the collapse of the Soviet Union, officials in Uzbekistan have tried to create new national identities, some linked to the Silk Road. The new national hero in Uzbekistan is Timur, who ruled in Samarkand from 1370 to 1405 CE, a time when trade flowed on the Silk Road. From 1370 to 1507, the Timurid dynasty conquered the areas of Central Asia, including what is now Uzbekistan, Iran, and Iraq, and conducted military campaigns to Delhi, Izmir, Ankara, and Moscow. The current Uzbek government has put up new statues of Timur and refurbished Samarkand's monumental architecture from the Timurid period (Millward 2013) (see Figure 9.5).

The Silk Road is now used as a metaphor for globalization and trade linkages in Central and South Asia. The Silk Road Project, started by Yo-Yo Ma in 1998, brings together musicians from East Asia, Central Asia, South Asia, the Middle East, and Europe. The Project promotes contemporary arts inspired by the Silk Road (Ma 2013).

As the United States and NATO began to wind down their military activity in Afghanistan in 2014, US troops and materials left the country either through Pakistan, and thence to the Indian Ocean, or via the Northern Route, through Uzbekistan, Kyrgyzstan, and Kazakhstan, and thence to Russia. US troops in Afghanistan numbered about 8,400 in 2016. The US military airbase in Kyrgyzstan, which opened in 2001, closed in 2014. In 2020, when US troops numbered 4,500, the Trump administration planned to withdraw 2,000 more before the Biden administration began (BBC, November 18, 2020). The Biden administration plans to withdraw all troops from Afghanistan before September 11, 2021 (Cooper et al., *New York Times*, April

Figure 9.5 Samarkand. The Registan complex of Samarkand, Uzbekistan was the center of the Timurid Empire.

Source: S. Toops.

13, 2021). However, the removal of offensive troops in Afghanistan and the closure of the air-base in Kyrgyzstan do not mean the end of the US presence in the region. In 2011, Secretary of State Hillary Clinton spoke of a New Silk Road as a way of expanding a modern-day trade network across South and Central Asia. The US State Department articulates a "New Silk Road Vision" through economic connections linking Afghanistan to Central and South Asia. Military ventures could be followed by economic ventures along this New Silk Road (Millward 2013).

China also has strong interests in the Silk Road in Central Asia and South Asia. The Shanghai Cooperation Organization (SCO), first started in 1996, is composed of China, Russia, Kazakhstan, Kyrgyzstan, Tajikistan, and Uzbekistan. In recent years, the SCO has had joint exercises on counter-narcotics and counterterrorism as well as discussions on economic and cultural issues (Albert 2015). China's Belt and Road Initiative connects Asian and European countries, and the Silk Road still goes through Central Asia (Toops 2016).

Demographic Issues

Two issues illustrate some of the challenges facing South and Central Asia in the twenty-first century. This section focuses on the region's demographic concerns. The next section profiles India, as an example of the environmental problems that face South and Central Asia, and the following section considers political ecology across the region as a whole.

One factor of the demographic dilemma is the level of population growth. South Asia has over 1.9 billion people. In 2020, South Asian population growth rates ranged from Sri Lanka at 0.9 percent, India at 1.4 percent, and Bangladesh at 1.6 percent, to Pakistan at 2.2 percent, so there is definite population pressure in South Asia. As India has 1.4 billion people, Pakistan has 221 million, and Bangladesh 170 million, the absolute growth of population in South Asia is greater than that in other regions. This population growth has regional and global effects. Central Asia has smaller populations, but with similar growth rates of 1.4 to 2.7 percent. Afghanistan at 2.7 percent has the highest population growth rate (see Map 2.3). **Life expectancy** in South Asia ranges from 69 years in Pakistan to 77 years in Sri Lanka. Life expectancy in Central Asia ranges from 65 years in Afghanistan to 75 years in Uzbekistan. Globally, life expectancy averages 73 years. Women generally live longer than men (Population Reference Bureau 2020).

Asia, broadly speaking, has 60 percent of the world population. India has 1.4 billion people and, with its population growth rate of 1.4 percent, will soon be the most populous country in the world, surpassing China. South Asia's population is growing faster than that of East Asia. India and Bangladesh have had some success with family planning, while other countries, like Pakistan, have not. Long years of settlement have created very dense and very large populations in the Ganges-Brahmaputra lowland of India and Bangladesh; most land area is densely inhabited. The highest densities in Pakistan are in the Punjab and along the Indus River. In contrast, Central Asia has densely settled oases amid vacant steppes, mountains, and deserts. Compared to most counties, countries in Central Asia have low population density. In the Soviet era, birth control was quite common, so people in Central Asia have had smaller families. Population growth rates in post-Soviet Central Asia are average 1.8 percent, while Afghanistan is at 2.7 percent (Population Reference Bureau 2020).

India has had only moderate levels of success in family planning, in part because India, as a democracy, could not pass a draconian family law such as China's. Difficult policies for intensive family planning may be the only way out of this dilemma. Low-cost, culturally acceptable methods (pills, condoms, and perhaps IUDs, but not sterilization) are key to a higher usage of contraception (Bradnock and Williams 2002). Advertising campaigns selling birth control as life choice have been more successful than state campaigns emphasizing social good (Mazzarella 2003).

Another demographic issue is the level of urbanization. In South Asia, urbanization levels range from 19 percent in Sri Lanka to 37 percent in Pakistan. In Central Asia, urbanization levels range from 26 percent in Afghanistan to 68 percent in Mongolia (Population Reference Bureau 2020). Many people in South Asia are moving from the countryside to the city. Urban agglomerations are becoming quite large, including Delhi–New Delhi at 25 million, Mumbai (Bombay) at 22 million, Dhaka at 21 million, Kolkata (Calcutta) at 15 million, and Karachi at 20 million (see Figure 9.6). Only Tokyo is larger than the Delhi–New Delhi agglomeration, but by 2028, Delhi–New Delhi may be the largest by agglomeration with an anticipated population of over 37 million (Price et al. 2020). Overall, the level of urbanization is lower in South Asia than East Asia. In the cities of South Asia, difficulties with housing and squatter settlements are evident. Clean water, sanitation, and housing are major issues in South Asian cities (Karan 2004). In Central Asia, urbanization is higher, with the exception of Tajikistan and Afghanistan (probably due to civil conflict). Soviet planning created more urbanized countries.

Environmental Challenges in India

As the largest country in South and Central Asia, both in land area and population, India provides an example of the problems and possibilities facing the region. India is divided into

Figure 9.6 Kolkata (Calcutta) is one of India's largest cities.

Source: S. Andrus.

three environments: the rice-producing central and southern uplands, the alluvial lowland of the fertile Ganges and Brahmaputra valleys, and the Himalayan mountains of the North.

Southern India has a tropical savanna climate at the heart of the Deccan plateau. The rugged Western Ghats separate the narrow coast from the plateau. On both east and west coastal plains, fertile soils and abundant water support high population densities. Soil in the Deccan plateau is not so good, but the main problem is water. The Western Ghats block off rain from the west, giving the area a semi-arid climate. People rely on small reservoirs or tanks of water from the wet **monsoon** for irrigation of rice, sorghum, and cotton.

The Ganges-Brahmaputra-Indus lowlands have been created by mighty river systems with fertile alluvial soil, supporting a dense population. The Ganges, the mother river, has become a sacred river to Hindus and empties into the Bay of Bengal. The Brahmaputra comes down from Tibet and merges with the Ganges. The western area bordering Pakistan is drier and rivers here flow into the Indus. People rely on these rivers as well as the rains from the wet monsoon for irrigation. Crops include wheat and pulses in the west and rice in the east.

The northern areas of the Himalayan range are formed by the subduction of the Indian Plate under the Eurasian Plate. This northern segment is tectonically active and earthquakes are common. A severe earthquake on the Pakistan side of Kashmir resulted in the deaths of 100,000 people in 2005. A severe earthquake in Nepal resulted in 9,000 deaths in 2015 and severe economic losses. The mountains are too rugged for much settlement, although fertile valleys host communities. Nestled in these mountains, the Valley of Kashmir has a denser population (Short 2020).

Environmental issues are common in India. Flooding in the Ganges River valleys, deforestation in the Western and Eastern Ghats, and water and air pollution in cities such as Mumbai

(Bombay) and Kolkata (Calcutta) are a few of the problems. Over-irrigation, coupled with Green Revolution intensification, has led to a salinization of the soil in northwestern India (Price et al. 2020).

The combination of climate and landforms makes South Asia susceptible to global climate change. India is number three or four behind the US and China in terms of carbon dioxide emissions. India's economic growth is dependent on energy usage, much of which relies on coal-fired thermal plants, so CO_2 production may well increase. India is also increasing its production of solar energy. India has many people living in low-lying areas on the coast of the Bay of Bengal. As the world begins to warm up, the polar sea ice will melt, and 5 to 10 million people could be displaced in coastal India, Bangladesh, and Sri Lanka with a one-meter rise in sea level. The whole of the Maldives could disappear under the ocean. Global climate change will also result in the retreat of Himalayan glaciers. These glaciers are the source of the Indus, Ganges, and Brahmaputra, so water supplies could be disrupted. An increase in winter temperatures will be disastrous for the wheat crops in India and Pakistan. The summer monsoon will have increased rainfall and this would result in flooding (Short 2020).

The economic transformation of India based on industry, in particular chemicals, has also led to an increase in pollution. Industrial development near Hyderabad in the Deccan plateau has created industrial waste, which pollutes the local water supply. Delhi has seen an increase in industry with the attending pollution of sulfur dioxide and nitrous oxides into the atmosphere. Automobile exhaust is another source of air contamination. In 2014, according to the World Health Organization (WHO), 13 of the world's top 20 most polluted cities were in India. India continues to be of concern as 21 of the top 30 polluted cities are there (Regan 2020). South of Delhi, air pollution threatens the Taj Mahal, with acid rain discoloring the white marble monument of Emperor Shah Jahan and his wife. The 500 million people who live in the Ganges River Valley are also a source of solid waste, much of which flows untreated into the river. Industrial waste as well as human waste, and non-biodegradable plastics add to pollution in the Ganges, a holy river sacred to the Hindus. The Ganga Action Plan in 1985–2000 was directed at cleaning up the river, but the costs of the cleanup were very high; however, the costs of not cleaning up will be much higher. The World Bank already plans to lend India US$1 billion to work on the cleanup. Successive administrations have budgeted funds for the cleanup, but the efforts have not yet been successful (Karan 2004; Price et al. 2020).

What India has spent on environmental protection is not sufficient. The state places a high priority on economic development, which includes business, education, and scientific expansion. Environmental needs are, as in many countries, ranked behind economic growth and national-security interests. In recent years, more people in India have taken nonviolent action to protect the environment. These movements emulate Gandhi and his work against British colonialism. They advocate moving away from a Western-inspired, resource-intensive development model to one that includes sustainability. Some examples of these environmental movements are Save the Narmada and the Chipko Movement. The campaign to save the Narmada River in central India works to counteract a plan to develop the river with many large dams. The Chipko Movement in northern India began in the 1970s to combat deforestation. In this movement, to protect the livelihood of villagers, many women surrounded the trees to prevent them from being felled by loggers. This Gandhian "tree-hugging" movement wrested control of the forest from a bureaucracy focused on products for the urban market (Rangan 2000).

Biodiversity and sustainability are vital tools to mitigate the impacts of climate change. The Research Foundation for Science, Technology and Ecology, founded by Dr. Vandana Shiva, an Indian physicist and activist, established seed banks in India, which maintain a diversity of seed stocks and train farmers in sustainable agricultural practices (Shiva 2005; 2008; Jahanbegloo and Shiva 2013).

Political Ecology in South and Central Asia

How does the environment relate to development? **Political ecology** combines aspects of geography, anthropology, sociology, and political science to examine environmental issues (Robbins 2012; Rocheleau et al. 1996). Political ecology considers the human adaptation to risk and uncertainty. In the case of the monsoon in South Asia, the risk is the uncertainty of the monsoon's onset. People in villages know the natural cycle of the monsoon; they know their local ecology. They prepare by spreading risk out over the dry years, they practice water harvesting with small catchment basins and tanks, and they work collectively in water conservation efforts. So the villagers are not just at the mercy of nature, but are integrated into natural patterns to reduce risk (Robbins and Moritz 1999).

Central Asia experiences great conflict over water issues. The physical environment is composed of plateaus and mountains in Kyrgyzstan, Tajikistan, Mongolia, and western China, steppes in Kazakhstan, and desert basins in Uzbekistan and Turkmenistan. The Caspian and Aral Sea basins in Turkmenistan and Uzbekistan and Southern Kazakhstan are vast arid landscapes, with hot summers and cold winters (Price et al. 2020; Brunn et al. 2012).

Up until modern times, the Aral Sea was fed by the Syr Darya and the Amu Darya (*darya* means "river"), coming from the Tian Shan (Heavenly Mountains) in Kyrgyzstan, but today the Aral is shrinking. The lands in Uzbekistan were irrigated to produce cotton during Tsarist and Soviet times. Cotton was Tsar in Uzbekistan; the newly independent state of Uzbekistan continues to rely on cotton production for exports. Besides irrigation, cotton production uses significant amounts of fertilizer and pesticides. More water was required for cotton and rice irrigation as well in these arid landscapes. This meant more canals and, correspondingly, more evaporation of water. The canals leaked, and the underlying soil is very sandy, so much water was wasted. More irrigation has meant greater salinization of the soil. Soviet planners had encouraged the production of cotton in Uzbekistan, but cotton uses a great deal of water. Once most of the river water was diverted to the irrigated fields, there was no water left for the Aral Sea, which is now threatened by desertification (Bissell 2003; Sievers 2003; Brunn et al. 2012).

Other environmental challenges abound in South and Central Asia, including access to clean water in Bangladesh and desertification across Central Asia. Human activity, intentional or unintentional, is a major cause of these environmental issues. Bangladesh is built on the low-lying Ganges delta. Flooding in Bangladesh is a problem exacerbated by the deforestation of the Ganges headwaters. Economic growth and population pressures in Bangladesh led to settlement in the delta area. Metals including arsenic contaminate many of the aquifers used for drinking water (Price et al. 2020).

In many of these cases and others, the countries were focusing on economic growth without taking into account the ecological consequences. The drive for economic growth to the exclusion of all else has created severe environmental problems, air and water quality in particular. Yet how can a government ignore the economic needs of its people? Economic needs have to be balanced with ecological realities. The cost of fixing such environmental disasters is more than the economic benefit from production and consumption. Environmental stresses in highly populated areas, like Asia, have global ramifications.

The Future of India

India has the largest population and the biggest economy in the region, so it makes sense to examine its future prospects in detail. The brightest elements of India's future rest on (1) the huge democracy that links together India's cultural diversity and (2) the country's economic rise. The democracy of India has brought many Indians, whether Hindu or Muslim, Sikh or Christian, together. The country has a variety of official languages besides Hindi, including

English and Sanskrit. The federal system has allowed local states, as well as the national government, political power. Individuals share and contribute to a common India. Although violent outbursts between different religious, ethnic, and linguistic groups occur, overall communities are integrated together into a shared identity—India. Out of plurality comes a unity (Kux 2007; Ganguly 2006).

The economic rise of India has relied on scientific expertise and a global diaspora that places a strong value on education. However, that economic rise was also based on the new economic policy in 1991 to do away with the micromanaging of licenses and permits that confined the economy. The new economic regime embraced the market and led India to self-sustaining growth. A large domestic market, growing international market, lower wages, large scientific community, and fluency in English have brought India substantial growth in recent years, though tempered by the 2008 economic depression (Rothermund 2008).

The future challenges of India are many. In terms of development, there is a two-speed India: an area of high growth around Delhi, Mumbai, and Bangalore, and regions of low growth around Kolkata and central India. There is stark contrast between impoverished villagers and a high-tech India. Unemployment in the countryside drives people to the city where, if they are lucky, they find jobs; if not, they join the ranks of the poor and sleep on the streets or in vast slums of makeshift housing. Unemployment and underemployment are linked to population increase. As discussed earlier, environmental issues are related to the economic rise and population growth. More people leads to greater consumption of scarce resources. India has protective laws on the books, but the power of large corporations and corrupt politicians often renders these laws ineffective. Inequality between men and women shows up in their unequal treatment, notably a lack of healthcare and education for women in India. There needs to be a new emphasis on educational and economic opportunities for women. Finally, communal violence that places religious fundamentalism, whether Hindu or Muslim, above cultural and political unity, is a risky path for India to follow (Kristof and WuDunn 2009; Karan 2004; Thussu 2013).

Asia Matters: Global Connections

The historical challenges of Central Asia and the cultural complexities of South Asia are all a part of Asia's future. India is regionally dominant in South Asia. In Central Asia, Kazakhstan holds more power because of its oil industry. Even in the midst of cultural diversity and population challenges, South Asia, with its rising economy, is an important component of the world.

South Asia is globally connected. Elements of South Asian culture are known and recognized worldwide, for example, Indian yoga or Indian restaurants in US cities. Bollywood movies play in cinema houses across Asia, Africa, and the Middle East, and are entering into Europe and North America. In addition, hybrid films are emerging through global media partnerships. One such film, *Slumdog Millionaire*, made in India in the slums of Mumbai in 2008, with a British director, and Anglo and Indian actors, won Academy Awards (including Best Picture) in the United States. In Scotland, a good fast-food meal is less likely to be McDonald's than *kebab* (possibly Afghani or Pakistani) or a good curry. Gandhi started his nonviolent movement in South Africa against British repression, but his ideas have influenced the American civil-rights movement and the Arab Spring. South Asian migration of Indian, Pakistani, or Bangladeshis to all corners of the world followed the path of the British Commonwealth to Canada, South Africa, Kenya, and of course to Britain. Pakistanis in the United Kingdom, Indians in the United States, Trinidad, Kenya, and Guyana are all examples of the migration of the South Asian diaspora (Luce 2007).

Central Asia has global connections as well, but they occur through past histories and contemporary geographies. Uzbeks, Kyrgyz, and Kazakhs were part of the Russian Empire and then the Soviet Union for so long that the Russian language became a common tongue among the various ethnic groups in Central Asia. Connections in Central Asia link through Russia to Europe. The other global connection in Central Asia is through Islam and Turkey to the Middle East. Most of the Central Asian languages are varieties of Turkish, albeit with a heavy Arab, Persian, and Russian vocabulary written in various Cyrillic-style scripts (Sengupta 2009).

Global transnational corporations have their production centers in South Asia. Indian firms such as Infosys, Tata, and Wipro represent the new wave of entrepreneurialism in Asia. The information technology sector in India has grown rapidly because of the country's large scientific community. Innovation in software, medical technology, and international films are growth areas. The liberalization of the Indian economy in 1991 points toward an India that is a global producer. By contrast, Central Asia has focused its resources on primary products such as oil (Kazakhstan), natural gas (Uzbekistan, Turkmenistan), and cotton (Uzbekistan). In 2015, Kazakhstan, Russia, and Belarus began a Eurasian Economic Union, solidifying Kazakhstan's economic connections with Russia.

Covid-19, a coronavirus, was found in Wuhan, China, in December 2019. The disease has since spread around the world. India has the second largest number of cases and third largest number of deaths due to Covid-19. The US has the largest number of cases and deaths. While India has a large number of deaths, the death rate per capita is not so high. Some Covid-19 deaths in India are not necessarily identified as being due to Covid-19. People in South Asia, Bangladesh and Pakistan are also affected. In India the virus may have spread through the country as during the spring lockdown, millions of laborers were sent to their rural homes of origins from their laboring jobs in the cities. India has loans from the World Bank to deal with the coronavirus. Large cities such as Delhi, Mumbai, Kolkata, Chennai, Ahmedabad, and Pune account for half of the cases. India expects to have an economic downturn in 2020 due to Covid-19. India is not as poor as some countries and has a strong scientific community, and so may be able to weather the storm. Afghanistan is much more vulnerable if Covid-19 takes hold, since Afghanistan has poverty and lack of health care. In both India and Bangladesh those most at risk are the near poor and the informally employed (Krishna 2020; Pettersson et al. 2020; Gettleman et al. 2020).

Political power and security issues also point toward the South Asian role in the world. India has been discussed as a possible permanent member of the Security Council. After the Cold War ended in the early 1990s, India and Pakistan tested nuclear weapons in 1998. The rise of the Taliban in Afghanistan and Pakistan and the death of Osama bin Laden in Pakistan maintained a global focus on South Asia. Politically and economically, India has become a regional power in Asia and by extension a global power. Some observers think that India will surpass China's economic development in this century because of India's relative political freedom (Sen 2000).

In 2012, the shooting of Malala Yousafzai, a young girl in Swat, Pakistan, by the Taliban provoked international reaction and recognition. She was shot simply for campaigning for better rights for girls in Pakistan, including being able to go to school. Some areas of Pakistan are still under the domain of the Taliban. Luckily, she was able to get medical care and has now moved to the United Kingdom. She has since co-authored a book, I Am Malala, and has won several awards, including the European Union's Sakharov Prize and the Nobel Peace Prize in 2014. Malala's experience shows the complexities of political, economic, and cultural issues in Pakistan today (Yousafzai and Lamb 2013).

Jawaharlal Nehru, in his speech on India's independence in 1947, said

"Long ago we made a tryst with destiny, and now the time comes when we shall redeem our pledge… when we step out from the old to the new, when an age ends, and when the soul of a nation , long suppressed, finds utterance."

(Kristof and WuDunn 2000)

For South and Central Asia, that destiny is rapidly approaching . India represents the capacity of democracy to manage enormous cultural complexity and is soon to be the world's most populous country and a rising economic power. In contrast, Afghanistan is in the midst of conflict. The overall trend, on the whole, is brighter for South Asia than Central Asia. Using the metaphors of the movie *Crouching Tiger, Hidden Dragon (2000)*, India is the Tiger and China is the Dragon. The Tiger though, has leaped, and the Dragon is no longer hidden.

Timeline of Modern South and Central Asia

1876	Tsars annex Central Asia.
1880	Anglo–Afghan War.
1906	Muslim League formed in India.
1917	Russian revolution; Communists extend control to Central Asia.
1918	Secularization Campaign in Central Asia.
1919	Gandhi leads Indian National Congress; Amritsar massacre in India.
1921	Provincial Self Rule in India.
1929	National Congress for Indian Independence.
1930s	Stalin's purge of Uzbek leaders.
1933	Zahir Shah King of Afghanistan.
1935	Government of India Act.
1937	Indian National Congress wins elections.
1940	Muslim League for Independent Pakistan.
1947	Indian independence and partition; Nehru Prime Minister of India.
1947–1948	India–Pakistan war.
1950s	Cotton production campaign in Central Asia.
1951	Indian federal constitution.
1954	Virgin lands campaign in Kazakhstan, Russian in-migration.
1955	Bandung Conference of non-aligned states. Baikonur Soviet space center in Kazakhstan built.
1959	Dalai Lama flees to India.
1962	Sino–Indian War.
1964	Death of Nehru.
1966	Tashkent Earthquake.
1967	"Green Revolution" crops in India.
1971	Indo–Pakistan War, independence of Bangladesh.
1977	Military coup in Pakistan.
1979–1989	Soviet invasion of Afghanistan.
1981–1989	Pakistan aid to Afghan rebels.
1982	Sikhs rebel against India.
1984	Indira Gandhi assassinated.
1988	Benazir Bhutto Prime Minister of Pakistan.
1989	Kashmiri Muslims rebel against India. Karimov in power in Uzbekistan. Nazarbayev in power in Kazakhstan.

1990	Indian Economic Reforms.
1991	Soviet Union Collapses, formation of Central Asian States.
1995	Taliban controls Afghanistan.
1998	India and Pakistan both have nuclear tests.
1999	Military coup in Pakistan.
2001	September 11 al-Qaeda bombings in New York and DC. United States and allies invade Afghanistan. Opening of pipelines from Kazakh oil fields to Russia. Shanghai Cooperation Organization of China, Russia, Kazakhstan, Kyrgyzstan, Tajikistan and Uzbekistan.
2004	Hamid Karzai elected President of Afghanistan. Indian Ocean Tsunami.
2005	Kashmir Earthquake. Andijan killings in Uzbekistan.
2007	Benazir Bhutto assassinated in Pakistan.
2008	Asif Ali Zardari (B. Bhutto's husband) elected President of Pakistan. Mumbai terrorist attack.
2011	Osama bin Laden killed in Pakistan. US Department of State articulates "New Silk Road".
2012	Malala Yousafzai wounded.
2013	China's Silk Road Economic Belt Initiatives.
2014	NATO withdraws from Afghanistan. India Hindu nationalist Bharatiya Janata party wins parliamentary elections.
2015	Nepal earthquake. Eurasian Economic Union of Russia, Kazakhstan, and Belarus begins.
2016	Uzbekistan leader Karimov dies in office.
2019	Covid-19 starts in China. Kashmir under direct control in India.
2020	Covid-19 hits India.

References

Adeney, Katharine, and Andrew Wyatt. 2010. *Contemporary India*. Houndsmills, UK: Palgrave Macmillan.

Albert, Eleanor. 2015. "The Shanghai Cooperation Organization." *Council of Foreign Relations*, October 14.

BBC. November 18, 2020. "US Troops in Afghanistan: Allies and Republicans Alarmed at Withdrawal Plan." www.bbc.com/news/world-us-canada-54980141

Bissell, Tom. 2003. *Chasing the Sea: Lost Among the Ghosts of Empire in Central Asia*. New York: Pantheon Books.

Boulnois, Luce. 2004. *Silk Road: Monks, Warriors, and Merchants on the Silk Road*. Translated by Helen Loveday. Hong Kong: Odyssey Guide.

Bradnock, Robert, and Glyn Williams. 2002. *South Asia in a Globalising World: A Reconstructed Regional Geography*. Harlow, UK: Prentice Hall.

Brower, Daniel R. 2005. *The World in the Twentieth Century: From Empires to Nations*. 6th ed. Upper Saddle River, NJ: Prentice Hall.

Brunn, Stanley D., Stanley W. Toops, and Richard Gilbreath. 2012. *The Routledge Atlas of Central Eurasian Affairs*. London: Routledge.

Chadda, Maya. 2014. *Why India Matters*. Boulder, CO: Lynne Rienner.

Cooper, Helene, Thomas Gibbons-Neff and Eric Schmitt. 2021. "Biden to Withdraw All Combat Troops from Afghanistan by Sept. 11." *New York Times*. April 13, www.nytimes.com/2021/04/13/us/politics/biden-afghanistan-withdrawal.html

Davis, Elizabeth Van Wie, and Rouben Azizian. 2007. *Islam, Oil, and Geopolitics: Central Asia After September 11*. Lanham, MD: Rowman & Littlefield.

DeVotta, Neil. 2010. *Understanding Contemporary India*. 2nd ed. Boulder, CO: Lynne Rienner.

Engelmann, Kurt E., and Vjeran Pavlaković, eds. 2001. *Rural Development in Eurasia and the Middle East: Land Reform, Demographic Change, and Environmental Constraints*. Seattle: University of Washington.

Frank, Andre Gunder. 1998. *ReORIENT: Global Economy in the Asian Age*. Berkeley: University of California Press.

French, Patrick. 1997. *Liberty or Death: India's Journey to Independence and Division*. London: Harper Collins.

Gandhi, Mohandas, May 3, 1919. Satyagraha Leaflet, No. 13.

Ganguly, Sumit, ed. 2006. *South Asia*. New York: New York University Press.

———. 2016. *Deadly Impasse: Indo-Pakistani Relations at the Dawn of a New Century*. New York: Cambridge University Press.

Gettleman, Jeffrey, Suhasini Raj, Sameer Yasir and Karan Deep Singh. December 15, 2020. "The Virus Trains: How Lockdown Chaos Spread COVID-19 Across India." *New York Times*. www.nytimes.com/2020/12/15/world/asia/india-coronavirus-shramik-specials.html

Hanks, Reuel. 2013. "A Global Crossroads Reemerges in the Twenty-first Century: An Introduction to Central Asia." *Education About Asia* 18 (3): 5–11.

Jahanbegloo, Ramin, and Vandana Shiva. 2013. *Talking Environment: Vandana Shiva in Conversation with Ramin Jahanbegloo*. New Delhi: Oxford University Press.

Karan, Pradyumna P. 2004. *The Non-Western World: Environment, Development, and Human Rights*. New York: Routledge.

Krishna, Anirudh. 2020. "The Poorest After the Pandemic." *Current History* 119 (820): 291–96.

Kristof, Nicholas D., and Sheryl WuDunn. 2000. *Thunder from the East: Portrait of a Rising Asia*. New York: Knopf.

———. 2009. *Half the Sky: Turning Oppression into Opportunity for Women Worldwide*. New York: Knopf.

Kux, Dennis. 2007. *India at Sixty: A Positive Balance Sheet*. New York: Foreign Policy Association.

Lewis, Robert A., ed. 1992. *Geographical Perspectives on Soviet Central Asia*. London: Routledge.

Luce, Edward. 2007. *In Spite of the Gods: The Strange Rise of Modern India*. New York: Doubleday.

Ma, Yo-Yo. 2013. *The Silk Road Project*. www.silkroadproject.org. (Accessed November 10, 2013).

Mazzarella, William. 2003. *Shoveling Smoke: Advertising and Globalization in Contemporary India*. Durham, NC: Duke University Press.

Megoran, Nick, and Sevara Sharapova, eds. 2013. *Central Asia in International Relations: The Legacies of Halford Mackinder*. New York: Columbia University Press.

Meyer, Karl E. 2003. *The Dust of Empire: The Race for Mastery in the Asian Heartland*. New York: PublicAffairs.

Meyer, Karl E., and Shareen Brysac. 1999. *Tournament of Shadows: The Great Game and Race for Empire in Central Asia*. Washington, DC: Counterpoint.

Millward, James A. 2013. *The Silk Road: A Very Short Introduction*. New York: Oxford University Press.

Nadkarni, Vidya, and Norma C. Noonan, eds. 2013. *Emerging Powers in a Comparative Perspective: The Political and Economic Rise of the BRIC Countries*. New York: Bloomsbury.

Pettersson, Henrik, Byron Manley, and Sergio Hernandez. 2020. "Tracking Coronavirus Global Spread." *CNN*. www.cnn.com/interactive/2020/health/coronavirus-maps-and-cases/

Population Reference Bureau. 2020. *World Population Data Sheet 2020*. Washington, DC.

Price, Marie, Martin Lewis, William Wyckoff and Lester Rowntree, 2020. *Globalization and Diversity: Geography of a Changing World*. 6th ed. Upper Saddle River, NJ: Prentice Hall.

Rangan, Haripriya. 2000. *Of Myths and Movements: Rewriting Chipko into Himalayan History*. London: VERSO.

Regan, Helen. 2020. "21 of the World's 30 Cities with the Worst Air Pollution Are in India." *CNN*. www.cnn.com/2020/02/25/health/most-polluted-cities-india-pakistan-intl-hnk/index.html

Robbins, Paul. 2012. *Political Ecology*. 2nd ed. Oxford: Blackwell.

Robbins, Paul, and Jason Moritz. 1999. "Resourceful People and People's Resources: Teaching the Cultural Ecology of South Asia." *Education about Asia* 4 (2): 12–16.

Rocheleau, Dianne, Barbara Thomas-Slayter, and Esther Wangari. 1996. *Feminist Political Ecology: Global Issues and Local Experiences*. London: Routledge.

Rothermund, Dietmar. 2008. *India: The Rise of an Asian Giant*. New Haven, CT: Yale University Press.

Sen, Amartya. 2000. *Development as Freedom*. New York: Anchor Books.

Sengupta, Anita. 2009. *Heartlands of Eurasia: The Geopolitics of Political Space*. Lanham, MD: Lexington Books.

Shaw, D. J. B. 1995. *The Post-Soviet Republics: A Systematic Geography*. New York: Wiley.

Shiva, Vandana. 2005. *Earth Democracy: Justice, Sustainability, and Peace*. Cambridge, MA: South End Press.

———. 2008. *Soil not oil*. Cambridge, MA: South End Press.

Short, John Rennie. 2020. *World Regional Geography*. New York: Oxford University Press.

Sievers, Eric W. 2003. *The Post-Soviet Decline of Central Asia: Sustainable Development and Comprehensive Capital*. London: Routledge Curzon.

Thussu, Daya Kishan. 2013. *Communicating India's Soft Power: Buddha to Bollywood*. New York: Palgrave Macmillan.

Todaro, Michael P., and Stephen C. Smith. 2012. *Economic Development*. 11th ed. Boston: Addison Wesley.

Toops, Stanley. 2016. "Reflections on China's Belt and Road Initiative." *Area Development and Policy* 1 (3): 352–60. doi:10.1080/23792949.2016.1233072

Weightman, Barbara A. 2011. *Dragons and Tigers, A Geography of South, East and Southeast Asia*. Hoboken, NJ: John Wiley.

Wolpert, Stanley. 2004. *A New History of India*. 7th ed. New York: Oxford University Press.

Yousafzai, Malala, and Christina Lamb. 2013. *I Am Malala: The Girl Who Stood Up for Education and Was Shot by the Taliban*. New York: Little, Brown.

Further Reading

Books

Dutt, Ashok K. 1987. *An Atlas of South Asia: Fully Annotated*. Boulder, CO: Westview.

Ganguly, Sumit. 2015. *The Oxford Short Introduction to Indian Foreign Policy*. New Delhi: Oxford University Press.

Ganguly, Sumit and William R. Thompson. 2017. *Ascending India and Its State Capacity: Extraction, Violence, and Legitimacy*. New Haven, CT: Yale University Press.

Potter, Robert, Tony Binns, Jennifer A. Elliott, and David Smith. 1999. *Geographies of Development*. 2nd ed. Harlow, UK: Pearson Education Limited.

Walcott, Susan M., and Corey Johnson, eds. 2014. *Eurasian Corridors of Interconnection: From South China to the Caspian Sea*. London: Routledge.

Journals

Central Asian Survey. www.tandfonline.com/loi/ccas20

Contemporary South Asia. www.tandfonline.com/loi/ccsa20

Eurasian Geography and Economics. www.tandfonline.com/loi/rege20

Journal of Asian Studies. www.cambridge.org/core/journals/journal-of-asian-studies

Films

Earth (2000). Deepa Mehta, director. New York: New Yorker Video.

Fire (1998). Deepa Mehta, director. New York: New Yorker Video.

Monsoon Wedding (2001). Mira Nair, director (India).

Osama (2004). Siddiq Barmak, director. Santa Monica, CA: MGM Home Entertainment.

Slumdog Millionaire (2008). Danny Boyle and Loveleen Tandan, directors (India/UK).

Websites

Association for Asian Studies. www.asian-studies.org

International Institute for Asian Studies. iias.asia

Silk Road Seattle. depts.washington.edu/uwch/silkroad/index.html

South Asia Resource Access on the Internet. library.columbia.edu/locations/global/virtual-libraries/sarai.
  html

Chapter 10

Sub-Saharan Africa

Africa, a vast continent of 55 states, retains a remarkable and much debated trajectory in global and international studies. It has made considerable strides, amidst growing informal sector engagement and other economic challenges which partly stem from the continent's explosive growth. As Paul T. Zeleza notes, and data from the United Nations in 2017 shows, the continent's population was 1.26 billion people or 16.64 percent of the world's total. The same data report finds that the continent's population is expected to rise to 1.70 billion by 2030, 2.53 billion in 2050 and 4.47 billion by 2100. Africa is home to 900 million in sub-Saharan Africa.

African states have long struggled to carve out independent roles in global affairs. More than any other continent, Africa has experienced illegitimate and corrupt rule, economic exploitation, and cultural assault on a large scale. During the Cold War, African countries were important to the United States and the Soviet Union solely for geopolitical reasons and strategic raw materials. Neither side prioritized democracy, peace, or prosperity for Africa. While Africa still suffers from the legacy of **colonialism**, superpower rivalry, and governance challenges, the continent is poised to enter a new age of positive political and economic development and greater integration into the world community.

Africa's vast economic and human potential is visible in the world marketplace. Africa has about one-third of the world's primary commodities. Although growth slowed in the mid-2010s, African countries have experienced robust economic growth in the twenty-first century, and the world is fostering new commercial and political connections to the continent.

Geographical Features

Africa is more diverse than any of the other regions discussed in this book. Westerners often think of Africa as a country rather than a continent and ignore the vast differences among its 55 countries and regions (see Map 10.1). Europeans defined Africa as a continent surrounded by three great bodies of water, the Mediterranean Sea on the northern coast, the Atlantic Ocean in the west, and the Indian Ocean in the east. Africa is the second-largest continent, stretching 5,000 miles from north to south and nearly as far from West Africa to the Horn of Africa in the east. It is more than three times the size of the United States.

Western geographers arbitrarily divided Europe from Asia at the Ural Mountains, but the Sahara, which is an even greater physical barrier, was not designated as a continental divide. There is no definitive description of sub-Saharan Africa. Many African countries, such as Mali, Niger, and Chad, sit astride the Sahara and have a mix of Arab and non-Arab peoples.

There are, however, significant historical, political, climatic, and cultural differences between the areas north and south of the Sahara. North Africa stretches from Morocco in the west to Egypt in the east, and is predominantly Islamic with Arabic influence and has as many connections to the Mediterranean area and to the Middle East as to sub-Saharan Africa (see

DOI: 10.4324/9781003028314-13

Africa

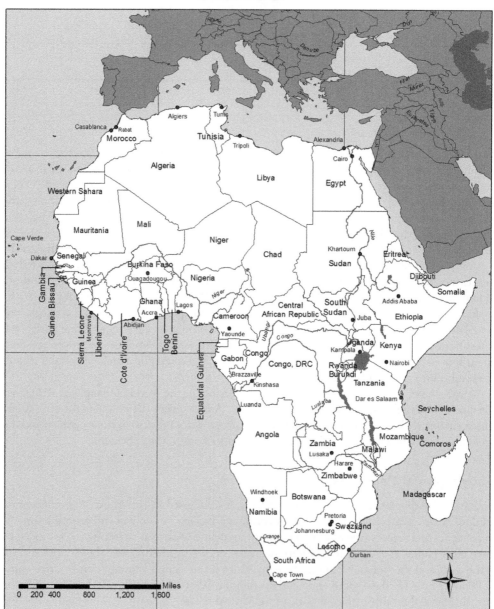

Map 10.1 Africa.

Chapter 11 on the Middle East). Fifty-five African countries are members of the UN and the **African Union** (AU); forty-five or so make up sub-Saharan Africa. Chad, Sudan, Ethiopia, and Nigeria represent the transition between the two regions.

Historically, the continent's population density was low owing to non-contiguous forms of governance among the continent in terms of diverse forms of political power over the past several centuries. Most people tend to be clustered around capital cities, coastlines, and areas of arable land. For example, only 12 percent of Niger's land can be tilled, but 90 percent of the country's 18 million people make their living from agriculture. The World Bank estimates that two-thirds of Africans are employed in the agricultural sector. In the developed world, only 1 to 2 percent of the population is engaged in agriculture. According to the UN, however, a majority of Africans will live in cities by 2025. Although infant-mortality rates are high and life expectancies are low, the birthrate in most African countries is very high, about three times that of the United States. Life expectancy is 58.6 years for sub-Saharan Africa, while the world average is 71.5. The per capita GNP is $1,630, compared to $10,400 globally (World Bank 2016).

State and Nation-Building

The UN recognizes all its members' borders as they exist today. The legitimacy of African state boundaries, however, is disputed because Africans had little role in drawing them. In the historic Berlin Conference of 1884–85, European imperial powers that include Germany, England, Portugal, France, Spain etc. carved up the continent into what noted historian Basil Davidson refers to as the "magnificent African cake" (1985). In effect, boundary lines were drawn in arbitrary ways that were a departure from existing contiguous units and ethnic groups. The lines of demarcation that would come to represent future states lumped ethnic groups together in ways that created friction and explosive dynamics that set the stage for future conflicts. British prime minister Lord Salisbury quipped that

> we have been engaged in drawing lines upon maps where no white man's feet have ever trod; we have been giving away mountains and rivers and lakes to each other, only hindered by the small impediments that we never knew exactly where the mountains and rivers and lakes were.

Salisbury might have added African peoples to his list. For the Europeans, as the old saying went, geography was about "maps not chaps" (Hargreaves 2004, 100–101). Africa, more than any other region, is a mosaic of different ethnicities, religions, cultures, and history.

Taking their cue from Great Britain—the greatest imperial power at the time—other European states began a frantic scramble for empire in Africa in the late nineteenth century (Figure 10.1). Darwin's theory of natural selection, or survival of the fittest, was now applied to nations. Even if some areas were not profitable, European states staked their claim to territories in Africa before someone else did. By the beginning of the twentieth century, the British, French, Portuguese, Italians, Spanish, Germans, and Belgians had established formal control over the entire continent, with the exception of Liberia and Ethiopia. The Berlin Conference of 1884–1885 finalized the imperial borders of Africa, most of which exist to this day.

Nation building in Africa after independence from the colonial powers was difficult because borders do not follow ethnic or physical boundaries. Traditional states such as the Ashanti in West Africa or the Bakongo in the Congo Basin included many different ethnic and linguistic groups, as did the states created by the **imperial borders**.

Post-colonialism and Independence

The end of colonial rule began in the late 1950s. Ghana, in 1957, was the first sub-Saharan country to break from British rule. When the Portuguese colonies of Mozambique and Angola gained their independence in 1975, the era of European rule in Africa was finally over. Southern

Figure 10.1 British African soldiers.

Source: Library of Congress.

Rhodesia declared independence from Britain in 1965 in order to maintain white rule, but African opposition movements forced Prime Minister Ian Smith to allow black majority rule in the country—renamed Zimbabwe—in 1980. South Africa abandoned **apartheid** and relinquished Namibia (formerly South West Africa) in 1990.

In the early 1950s, British forces executed more than 1,000 Mau Mau. The **Mau Mau rebellion** in Kenya from 1952 to 1959 was a particularly brutal conflict. The rebellion had its roots in the grievances of the Kikuyu people, whose lands had been confiscated by the British early in the twentieth century. The Kikuyu were relegated to small land reserves, which became overcrowded and impoverished. The Mau Mau were a militant Kikuyu element, many of whom were veterans of World War II. They demanded land reform and freedom for the Kikuyu. One member of the all-white Kenya Police Reserve remembered killing Mau Mau captives immediately to avoid messy trials: "Killing prisoners? Well, it's not really the same thing, is it? I mean, I'd feel an awful shit if I thought I'd been killing prisoners" (Ascherson 2005, 26). The Mau Mau responded by brutally killing and terrorizing white settlers. They coerced the general Kikuyu population into joining the rebellion as well. The British press published photos and accounts of attacks on whites, but only 32 were killed. The Mau Mau slaughtered at least 1,800 fellow Africans. The British fostered the internecine conflict by recruiting "loyalist" Kikuyu into the Kikuyu Home Guard. About a third of Kikuyu society passed through detention camps, where the British tried to re-indoctrinate them. British security forces lost about 200 people, while approximately 15,000 Kenyans, alleged to be Mau Mau, were killed. Thousands more died in the detention camps. When Kenya gained its independence in 1963, a Kikuyu moderate, Jomo Kenyatta, became president. Although the British had imprisoned Kenyatta during the rebellion, he called the Mau Mau "a disease which has been eradicated, and must never be remembered again" (Elkins 2004; Anderson 2004).

The transition to African rule went peacefully except in those countries where Europeans had settled in greater numbers, such as Kenya, Algeria, Zimbabwe, and South Africa. Yet, political governance has been fraught since the early post-colonial period. Hastily crafted institutions, myopic policies and fractious internal economic dynamics produced military regimes, and **military coups** were "Africa's revolutionary routine." Since independence, African nations have experienced over 200 coups; about 45 percent were successful (*New Africa*, November 11, 2015). About nine out of ten of these coup attempts were efforts to overthrow military regimes, which themselves had come to power through a coup (Collier 2004, 469).

The Pan-Africanist leader and Ghana's first president, Kwame Nkrumah—who inspired other African heads of state—dreamed of an all-African state that would overcome its cultural and ethnic differences to create a powerful counterpart to the rest of the world's powers. In part as a result of US and Belgian intrigue to overthrow Lumumba in Congo, 32 African states formed the **Organization of African Unity** (OAU) in 1963. The OAU hoped to maintain the independence of African states in the wake of immense Soviet and American pressure to take sides in the Cold War. It was also an attempt to find a common African bond of freedom, justice, and equality. The original charter read that it is "desirous that all African States should henceforth unite so that the welfare and well-being of their peoples can be assured" (Duiker and Spielvogel 2001, 914).

The OAU was a grouping of African states that ultimately struggled to overcome competing national and regional interests exacerbated by Cold War rivalries. After the end of the Cold War, Africa renewed efforts to create a greater continental community. In 1991, the OAU formed an African Economic Community to promote trade within the region. But lack of economic growth and protectionist policies have thwarted greater integration. Leaders of any country are loath to reduce tariff barriers or open borders to imports when so many of their own people are out of work. Although extenuating global economic factors and local political instability were often to blame for the downturn in economic fortunes, politicians had no incentive to further economic integration.

As long as Europeans maintained advantageous economic relationships with their former colonies, they did not push for greater democratic rule or equitable economic development. Western technology and modern infrastructure had been introduced by the imperialists, but most of it was relegated to urban areas and barely reached most Africans. African economies remained dependent on exports of primary resources and Western imports of technologies and manufactured goods.

The model of the European nation-state did not fit African historical, political, or cultural realities. African political elites tended to establish **neo-patrimonial** systems in which leaders funneled government largesse to their own constituencies, often to the detriment of national political and economic development. Some Westerners might label this as corruption, but African leaders often argue that they are merely taking care of their own community or ethnic group. This communal character of political identity conflicts with development of transparent, rule-bound, formal democratic institutions and common national goals. As Africanist Patrick Chabal put it, African political elites "use their official position to fulfill their unofficial obligations to their clients and to meet the demands on which their power and standing as rulers rest" (Chabal 2005, 22–24).

The new African leaders were versed in progressive Western political values, although most African countries had no well-established political parties owing to the rapid transition from colonialism to independence. The imposition of colonial rule meant that an exposure to democratic practices and economic self sufficiency as articulated in western states, was nil and this had profound consequences for African states, in the post independent period. When Belgium was forced to grant Congo its independence in 1960, Congolese held only three of the nearly 5,000 senior administrative jobs. There were only 30 eligible Congolese college graduates to fill the remaining positions (Judt 2000, 66–69; Hochschild 2005, 40). At the beginning of their independence in 1961, Tanzania had two trained engineers and nine doctors in a country of 10 million people (Best et al. 2004, 397). While the number of college graduates in African countries has dramatically increased in the last few decades, Africa lags far behind other regions of the world.

Some African leaders, in an attempt to legitimize extending their rule, have turned to rigging elections or amending their constitutions. After Kenya's presidential election of 2007, ethnic violence broke out in protest of the results. Although the election of Uhuru Kenyatta in the spring of 2013 was deemed fair, Kenyatta was indicted by the International Criminal Court (ICC) for his support of the violence in the earlier election (charges were dropped in 2015). In the spring of 2013, yet another coup in the Central African Republic continued this authoritarian political tradition. Supporters of the rebel leader, Jichel Djotodia, attacked and killed scores of people in towns backing the ousted President Francois Bozize. In 2015, coup attempts failed in Burundi and Burkina Faso, in part because of the threat of sanctions from the **African Union** (AU).

The Cold War ensured that Africa would still have the attention of the great powers, but mainly as a battleground for allegiance to the free or communist world and as a source of valuable raw materials. When the West connived to assassinate Congo leader Patrice Lumumba in 1961 because of his leftist leanings, the continent began to take sides in the Cold War. Ghana's Kwame Nkrumah, one of the leaders of the pan-African movement, became involved in undermining other pro-Western governments in the region. Fearing that Africa might be fertile ground for communist takeovers, the United States supported any leader who did not nationalize foreign assets or partner with the Soviet Union. Most Western economic aid was a reward for political loyalty and went right into the coffers of corrupt elites and their cronies. The term to describe this was **kleptocracy** and described regimes such as Mobutu Sese Seko's in Zaire. In the 1980s, anti-Communist governments such as Zaire, Liberia, Sudan, and Somalia got 80 percent of US aid to sub-Saharan Africa. Corrupt regimes siphoned off monies and failed to build infrastructure and growing economies. The United States even backed South Africa, whose white-only government ran an apartheid system that deprived black Africans of their basic human and civil rights.

Some Western scholars have called the Cold War a "long peace" because no war broke out between the superpowers, but as an old African aphorism goes, "When the elephants fight the grass suffers." Proxy wars fought in the developing countries including those in Africa led to an influx of weapons that produced fertile ground for internal struggles. Over 25 million people were killed in developing country conflicts during the Cold War. Not all of these casualties can be attributed to the Cold War directly, but the West and the Soviet bloc supplied their clients with sophisticated weapons that increased the length and lethality of civil conflicts in Ethiopia, Sudan, Somalia, Angola, and Mozambique. Furthermore, the superpowers plied African authoritarian leaders with the necessary military means to oppress their own people.

Challenges to African Political and Economic Development

During colonial rule, African trade was directed toward Europe, the home of empire, and regional commercial links languished. African countries were predominantly raw-material exporters and importers of manufactured goods and technology. These trends persist. The EU, Asia, and the United States are Africa's top trading partners (Figure 10.2). Raw materials and commodities still make up over 90 percent of Africa's exports. Africa has 54 percent of the world's cobalt, 32 percent of its bauxite, 52 percent of its manganese, and 81 percent of its chromium stocks. Eighty-four percent of the world's platinum is in South Africa. Such mineral wealth has been a curse for some African countries. Mining has not brought more jobs, and brutal wars have erupted in western and southern Africa over gold and diamonds. Sierra Leone experienced a particularly awful civil conflict over diamonds, in which child soldiers were enlisted to do the fighting. In this cruel conflict, rival militias cut the hands off many of those they captured (Beah 2006).

In the 1980s, many African countries seemed headed toward freer democratic governments and prosperous and growing economies. Military regimes collapsed, and the Cold War ended. However, a number of African countries reverted to ethnic conflict and civil war: Ethiopia, Somalia, and Sudan in East Africa; Burundi, Uganda, Rwanda, and Congo in Central Africa;

Figure 10.2 Secretary Clinton with Morgan Tsvangirai, prime minister of Zimbabwe.

Source: US Department of State. Photo: Michael Gross.

Mozambique and Angola in southern Africa; and Sierra Leone, Ivory Coast, Liberia. The political situation improved in such states as Côte d'Ivoire and Zambia, and worsened in Gambia, Uganda, the Democratic Republic of Congo, and Ethiopia (Freedom House 2016).

Unstable governments and civil conflict have taken a heavy toll. The "CNN" effect heightened by social globalization in particular has provided the means for terrorist or extremist groups to broadcast their messages and also recruit new members. Al-Shabaab is a Somalia-based terror organization, and the northern Nigerian rebel group Boko Haram has spread its terror to Niger, Chad, and Cameroon, and has pledged allegiance to the Islamic State.

Although 42 African countries are in the WTO, Africa is less connected to the global economy than any other continent. Africa accounted for less than 2 percent of world trade in 2015. The top exporters are South Africa, which ranks thirty-eighth in the world, and Nigeria fifty-second. Of the leading importers, South Africa ranks thirty-fifth and Nigeria fifty-first. The downturn in global commodity prices in the mid-2010s really hurt the region; foreign direct investment (FDI) dropped from $44.2 billion in 2014 to $31 billion in 2015 (CIA World Factbook 2016; World Bank 2016).

Some economists argue that trade barriers between African countries are the biggest cause of stunted economic growth. Tariffs within the continent are higher than external duties. For example, the WTO estimates that it costs an African country $900 to import a container from Southeast Asia, but $2,500 from another African country. Intra-African trade could reduce dependence on exports to the EU, the United States, and Japan. About two-thirds of African exports are fuels and minerals. When the economic crisis hit these developed countries in 2008 and demand dropped, African economies suffered as well (WTO 2016).

Extraction industries such as oil drilling provide few employment opportunities, and economic growth based on commodity exports is subject to price fluctuations. Most of the foreign direct investment in Africa has gone to mine diamonds, platinum, and gold, and to drill for oil. Job growth in the early twenty-first century was dependent on higher prices for these and other commodities (UNECA 2020). The severe drop in commodity prices in the mid-2010s cut into their bottom line. Regardless of the price of oil, few of the world's **petro-states** have been able to parlay oil profits into broad economic prosperity. Most African governments have not used their mineral wealth to rectify income inequalities or foster sustained economic growth. The unemployed and impoverished masses in many Middle East oil-exporting countries provide ample proof that oil reserves are no guarantee of long-term economic prosperity. Nigeria, sub-Saharan Africa's largest oil exporter, has a GDP of $6,100 per capita, ranking 159th in the world (CIA World Factbook 2016).

Until recently, the economic outlook improved in Africa in part because in the last decade the World Bank and the IMF have forgiven a significant portion of Africa's debt. In 2013, Brazil continued that trend by announcing that it was easing the $900 million debt burden on 12 African countries. Nonetheless, growth rates in Africa stagnated in the mid-2010s because of a collapse of basic commodity prices and the slowing of the Chinese economy (OECD 2016; USAID 2016). Ghana benefited from debt forgiveness, registering a huge 14.4 percent rise in GDP in 2011, but by 2015 the growth rate had dropped to 3.5 percent (Time, December 3, 2012; CIA World Factbook 2016).

African State Building and Global Economic Integration: The Cases of Nigeria and the Democratic Republic of Congo

This section focuses on two sub-Saharan African countries to illustrate some of the historical, geographical, economic, political, and cultural challenges the region faces in state building, economic development, and integration into the international community. Nigeria is an oil-rich country, but political corruption, political instability, and ethnic conflicts have stunted its growth. The Democratic Republic of Congo is another resource-rich African country whose economic progress has been blunted by a particularly onerous colonial legacy, poor leadership, civil war, and inadequate spending on infrastructure and education. Underlying these factors are what some political scientists refer to as **path dependence** which can be understood as feedback loops or mechanisms that become deeply embedded in institutions and have a way of withstanding time.

Nigeria

Despite its oil wealth, Nigeria remains mired in political conflict and economic stagnation. It is the sixth-largest oil producer in the world but has suffered the many deprivations of a country reliant on oil exports. With 186 million people, it has the largest population of the sub-Saharan countries. The British formed this huge and unwieldy state by combining Lagos and South Nigeria in 1906 and adding the northern areas in 1914. Nigeria has some 250 different ethnic groups. The four largest are the mostly Christian Yoruba in the southwest (Lagos), the Igbo in the southeast, and the Muslim Hausa and Fulani in the north; these groups comprise about two-thirds of Nigeria's population. The other ethnic groups are usually subsumed into these groups. One African scholar observes that "what people actually call the North is the Hausa-Fulani, forgetting that there are non-Hausa-Fulani people living in the North."

An uneasy coexistence of these peoples and fragile peace erupted in political and factional conflicts after Nigeria achieved independence in 1960. British administrators favored the North, and because they usually voted as a bloc, they dominated the government in Lagos. The Hausa and Fulani, who are located in the North, make up about 30 percent of the population, the Yoruba and the Igbo in the south comprise about 40 percent. About half of the population is Muslim, and 40 percent Christian. The Igbo became second-class citizens in the Muslim-run government, and their massacre at the hands of government forces prompted them to form the independent state of Biafra in 1967. At least a million Biafrans died in the fighting.

Nigeria has had repeated military coups since independence in 1960. Its governments have changed about every five years owing to its adoption of Westminster-style government or parliamentarianism. Ethnic divisions have certainly contributed to the political instability, and the failure of multiparty democracy to build the nation-state has given authoritarian leaders the excuse to run a one-party system. Nigeria's leaders tried to reconcile the country's ethnic differences in the constitutions of 1963, 1979, 1989, and 1999, but parties remain linked to ethnic groups, making consensus and compromise difficult and causing parliamentary gridlock (Bah 2005, 48–49). A decline in the standard of living, conflicts over scarce resources, ethnic favoritism, dominance of the north, and the threat of the northern Muslim leaders to impose Islamic law in the northern provinces have led to continued civil unrest. Attacks by the Islamist terrorist group Boko Haram have resulted in hundreds of deaths in the north and brutal reprisals from the Nigerian army, with civilians caught in the crossfire. "When you burn down shops and massacre civilians," said the governor of Borno State, "you are pushing them to join the camp of Boko Haram" (*New York Times*, April 30, 2013). Some kidnapped students have been rescued.

The political outlook has improved in recent years, however. The international community did not deem the April 2007 elections for a new president credible, but it was the first nonviolent transfer of power in Nigerian history. In the spring of 2011, Goodluck Jonathan defeated Muhammadu Buhari, a Muslim from the north, which sparked riots in which 800 people died.

Five years later, in a landmark election, Buhari won the presidency in free and fair elections. Nigeria had its first truly peaceful election and succession in history. Some still worry about the future of Nigerian democracy, however, because Buhari led the country in 1984–1985 as a result of a military coup, and they fear that he will privilege the north over the non-Muslim south. Vowing to tackle corruption, economic and security concerns, Muhammadu Buhari was re-elected in 2019 for a second term (BBC News, February 27, 2019).

Nigeria's economic relationship with China is representative of China's recent investment in sub-Saharan Africa. To facilitate trade with Nigeria, China is pumping billions into Nigerian infrastructure projects. The relationship has faced problems, however. Some Nigerian industries, such as textiles and clothing, have seen a dramatic drop in employment due to cheap Chinese imports. Many of these goods are of shoddy workmanship. The Nigerian government is also conducting inquiries into corruption in deals made with Chinese companies (*New York Times*, December 6, 2015).

According to the World Bank, 40 percent of Nigerians currently live below the poverty line. The World Bank also estimates that 80 percent of the oil revenues go to 1 percent of the population, and that corruption is rampant. Owing to declining refining capacity, Nigeria actually has to import gasoline. The infrastructure serving Lagos, Nigeria's largest city, is changing for the better, yet requires further investment. Roads are pockmarked, electricity blackouts are regular, and crime is rampant. The UN Human Development Index ranks Nigeria's standard of living below that of Bangladesh; life expectancy is only 52.8 years, which ranks 213th in the world (World Bank 2016; CIA *World Factbook* 2016).

Ongoing governance challenges and the expansion of disparity in wealth have exacerbated the divisions between the Muslim north and other ethnic groups in the south. The politics of extraction in what amounts to "imported institutions" during colonialism along with a country in which representation of more than 250 ethnic groups is challenging for any modern state explains the dynamics of ongoing debacles of statehood. People living in the oil-producing south and on the Niger delta have not benefited from Nigeria's oil profits owing to the well-known **resource curse** that plagues petro or resource rich states across the globe. Essentially, the discovery of oil can produce rent-seeking tendencies that produce an overriding focus on this resource to the neglect of or absent development of other lucrative economic sectors or endeavors. As a consequence, periodic unrest in the Niger-Delta area produced uprisings since the 1990s when environmental activist Ken Saro-Wiwa and others protested the government's environmental negligence and paid a dear price with their lives.

The Democratic Republic of the Congo

The history of the Democratic Republic of the Congo (DRC, formerly Zaire) illustrates the many obstacles that have stood in the way of African development and greater integration into the global economy. The DRC comprises one-thirteenth of the African landmass and possesses some of Africa's most valuable natural resources, such as oil, rubber, gold, diamonds, copper, and zinc. Belgian King Leopold II made Congo his personal property in the late-nineteenth century, and he accumulated a vast fortune from sales of ivory, rubber, and minerals. The Belgians had little regard for African lives and exploited them ruthlessly. Through forced labor, disease, and killing, scholars estimate that Congo lost nearly 50 percent of its population during Belgian colonial rule—approximately 10 million people (Hochschild 2005, 42).

Congo has confronted formidable impediments to stable, legitimate, and unified governance. It has a population of 77.3 million people who speak more than 75 different languages. The majority of the people are Bantu, but Congo has over 200 other ethnic groups. Life expectancy is 58.7 years, ranking 206th in the world. The country has 6.1 births per woman, compared to

Figure 10.3 Nixon and President Mobutu Sese Seko of Zaire meeting in the Oval Office, October 10, 1973.

Source: US National Archives and Records Administration.

2.4 worldwide. The per capita income is $800, putting it 226th in the world (World Bank 2016; CIA *World Factbook* 2016).

Patrice Lumumba was the first prime minister of Congo after it achieved independence in 1960. But his socialist leanings, and Western fears that Congo would fall into the Soviet sphere of influence, prompted the US and Belgian governments to assist the political opposition in assassinating him (see De Witte 2001). His successor, Mobutu Sese Seko, established one of the most corrupt dictatorships in Africa (Figure 10.3). Mobutu, who changed the name of Congo to Zaire, was supported by the United States and Europe during the Cold War for his staunch anti-communism. Mobutu's thievery imitated the Belgians. By the time he was forced out of office in 1997, Mobutu had homes in Switzerland and France and hundreds of millions of dollars stashed in foreign bank accounts.

Longtime opposition leader Laurent Kabila mobilized rebel forces in eastern Congo and overthrew Mobutu's government in 1997. Congo descended into what some have called Africa's First World War. Eight countries in the region became involved in the conflict. Rwanda, Burundi, and Uganda backed the opposition to Kabila, and Angola, Zimbabwe, Namibia, Chad, and Sudan sent troops to support Kabila's embattled regime and to steal the country's mineral wealth. An estimated 6 million people have died in the fighting, and over 3 million Congolese have been displaced since 2010. It is the deadliest war since World War II (French 2009, 44; BBC News, August 10, 2016; World Bank 2016).

In 2001, Kabila was assassinated and his son, Joseph Kabila, has been in power since. In late 2002, the younger Kabila was able to negotiate the withdrawal of the Rwandan Army from eastern Congo, and the warring parties in Congo agreed to a government of national unity. In November 2006, Congo held its first multiparty election in 40 years, which the international community deemed fair and impartial. Kabila won nearly 60 percent of the vote. Kabila won a second term in 2011, but riots in Kinshasa erupted in late 2016 over Kabila's apparent move to overturn the constitution's term limits and remain in power. In a 2015 Gallup poll, only 28 percent of Congolese in the DRC thought positively about their government (Gallup 2015).

Congo's civil war, weak central government, and rampant corruption have left the infrastructure in total disrepair. As one local Congolese official asked of a *New York Times* journalist, "How will you get anything to the market? There's only so much you can carry on your head." The country has a gaping divide between rich and poor. In a country with an estimated $24 trillion in mineral wealth, over 70 percent live below the poverty line.

Globalization on the African Continent: Relations with the United States, Europe, and Asia

Africa's economic potential is vast and the African Development Bank identifies infrastructure improvements as a key to improving economic opportunities. The Bank estimates that Africa spends only half of what it needs annually on infrastructure projects (WTO 2016).

Africa has been an important exporter of crude oil, holding 9 percent of the world's oil reserves. Demand from Asia and concerns about the stability of African and Middle Eastern suppliers such as Libya, Iraq, and Iran have increased the significance of the oil-rich countries of Nigeria, Chad, Angola, Sudan, Equatorial Guinea, Congo, and Gabon. China, the United States, and Canada have been the biggest importers of sub-Saharan crude oil. China gets almost a fourth of its oil imports from sub-Saharan Africa. In the mid-2010s the region suffered from a world oil glut and a drop in prices. Oil made up 53.6 percent of sub-Saharan exports in 2014, down 13 percent from the year before (World Trade Organization 2016).

Africa–U.S. Relations

The United States has steadily expanded trade through the Africa Growth and Opportunity Act (AGOA) of 2000, which gave African countries duty-free access to US markets. Through AGOA's Third Country Fabric Provision, African textile manufacturers using materials from outside of the continent can export textile products to the United States duty free. Some 6,400 items now have no tariff. US imports from sub-Saharan Africa shot up 177 percent from 2002 to 2012, although oil made up the bulk of them. US exports to the region grew 6.3 percent from 2011 to 2012, and a third of those went to South Africa. Reflecting increased oil production in North America, US imports from Africa fell from $50.1 billion in 2013 to $25.4 billion in 2015. Exports to Africa decreased from $35 billion in 2013 to $27.1 in 2015 (US Census Bureau 2016; Office of the US Trade Representative 2016).

In the 2000s, the United States pledged $15 billion for an Emergency Plan for AIDS Relief, and in 2003 launched the Millennium Challenge Corporation (MCC) for long-term economic development to those countries that displayed solid democratic practices, such as a commitment to women's rights. Twenty African countries have signed MCC agreements, and by 2016 had received nearly $8 billion for projects such as clean water, farmer training, and legal aid. In conjunction with President Obama's visit to Africa in 2013, the United States pledged $7 billion for an ambitious plan to double access to electricity in sub-Saharan Africa (www.mcc.gov; *Star Tribune*, Minneapolis, July 2, 2013).

In August 1998, the terrorist organization al Qaeda claimed responsibility for bombing two US embassies in Dar es Salaam, Tanzania, and Nairobi, Kenya, killing over 250 people and injuring another 4,000. The new US African command (AFRICOM) is part of the effort to head off these terrorist and piracy acts, to protect US economic interests, and to counter Chinese influence in the region. In the fall of 2013, Al Shabab, the Somali Islamist group, conducted a deadly terrorist attack on an upscale mall in Nairobi in retaliation for Kenya's incursion into Somalia in 2011 to support the anti-Islamist government. Over 60 people were killed. In 2015 the group killed 150 people at Kenya's Garissa University, and attacked African Union peacekeepers in Somalia.

Africa's Economic Relationship with Europe

Europe is 20 miles away from Africa, and their modern histories are inextricably linked. In 2007, the United Kingdom marked the bicentennial of the abolition of the slave trade. Britain was the first major colonial power to end the slave trade (although slavery in British colonies continued), and British Prime Minister Tony Blair invoked Britain's moral stand two centuries ago as a way to challenge the EU and the rest of the developed world to eradicate African poverty, disease, and debt.

The EU's efforts to increase trade with Africa are ongoing. It now has consular and trade offices in nearly every African capital. In 2007 the EU signed interim economic partnerships (EPAs) with several African countries that opened the EU market to African goods without tariffs. For example, textiles from Kenya and Tanzania and beef from Botswana are sold in the EU under EPAs. Africa's trade with the EU steadily increased from 2004 to 2008, but the global economic downturn in 2009 resulted in a 10 percent drop. The European Union, like the United States, imports mainly African oil. In the wake of the 2011 revolt against Libyan dictator Muammar Qaddafi and the disruption of that country's oil supplies, Nigeria and Angola stepped up their oil exports to Europe (Eurostat 2011).

Africa and Asia: South–South Cooperation

The region is rapidly becoming an important trading partner to Asia, especially India and China. India and eastern and southern Africa have centuries-old connections that are being rekindled today. Many people of Indian ancestry live in East African countries, some of whom came in the late-nineteenth century to work on construction projects such as the Kenyan–Ugandan railroad. The father of Indian independence, Mohandas Gandhi, spent many of his early years in South Africa.

At the Indian-African Partnership Conference in New Delhi in the fall of 2006, an Indian Foreign Ministry official declared that "there is a new expectation and optimism as modern India seeks to enhance its relationship with a resurgent Africa to contribute to the development of a new international order." Hundreds of African and Indian businesspeople at the conference discussed more than 300 projects worth approximately $17 billion. India's trade with Africa jumped from $37.5 billion in 2010 to $62 billion in 2014. India has surpassed the United States as the biggest importer of Nigerian oil. Nigeria, South Africa, and Angola are India's top three trading partners in sub-Saharan Africa (www.business-standard.com; Bloomberg Report, October 26, 2015).

The new Export-Import Bank of India and the Indian Africa Fund have facilitated this trade, and India has granted credits to many African countries for technology transfers, manufacturing plants, potable water facilities, and other development projects. India has also tapped Africa's energy resources. In 2003, India's largest company, the Oil and Natural Gas Corporation Ltd. (ONGC), bought a 45 percent stake in Greater Nile Petroleum Oil Company in Sudan. ONGC has also been involved in oil and natural gas deals in Ivory Coast, Gabon, and Egypt.

In 2009, China surpassed the United States as Africa's largest trade partner. China's trade with Africa doubled from 2010 to 2014, amounting to $184 billion in 2014. China wants and needs vital African raw materials, particularly oil. China has made significant investments in

African infrastructure, although almost two-thirds of its FDI has taken a loss. About 50 percent is the global average (*Forbes*, July 8, 2015). Ninety percent of China's imports from Africa are primary commodities, with fuels making up over two-thirds of that amount (African Center for Economic Transformation 2010). In the last decade, Chinese companies have signed big mining contracts in such countries as Zambia, Gabon, and the Democratic Republic of Congo. Congo has received billions for copper and cobalt mines, railways and roads, and clinics, schools, universities, and hospitals. China has invested heavily in infrastructure to extract oil and minerals from the interior of the continent. China also has granted zero-tariff treatment for many imports from more than 25 of the least-developed countries in Africa. In 2015 China's President Xi Jinping promised an additional $60 billion in development assistance (French 2009, 60–68; *New York Times*, December 6, 2015).

Western countries have expressed some alarm at China's inroads into Africa, but the amount of Chinese FDI amounts to only 3 percent of all Chinese investment. And there is some doubt about the nature of China's long-term investment given a tendency to utilize Chinese labor. One Congolese legal scholar has complained that the Chinese do not make use of local talent in management and technical positions: "They hire laborers, and that's it... . When they pack up and go, the Congo will be left with nothing, not even an upgrade in our human resources. Our earth will be dug up, emptied, and left that way" (French 2009, 60–68). In 2013 the Niger government renounced some provisions of its oil contracts with China, charging the Chinese with environmental degradation. Gabon confiscated oil areas from the Chinese and gave them to its state company. Niger's oil minister Foumakoye Gado reflects this new African concern about sustainable development: "This is all we've got... . We've got to fight to get full value for these resources ... to bring something to our people." In neighboring Chad, the oil minister halted the work of Chinese companies because they were making unprotected Chadian workers clean up excess oil they had dumped into ditches. The oil minister threw the company's local director and his assistant out of the country (*New York Times*, September 18, 2013).

In 2013, Ghanaian officials shut down gold mines run by the Chinese and jailed more than 200 for illegal mining or what is locally referred to as "galamsey," charging them with pollution and mistreatment of Ghanaian workers. In the wake of considerable investment and loans by China to the tune of some 2 billion dollars, an influx of Chinese migrants has produced politically fraught relations related to an uptick of mining and in many cases illegal mining practices.

China is also interested in the fruits of African agriculture, although the purchase of land, which constitutes sovereign wealth, is understandably a sensitive issue. China has encouraged emigration among the approximately 12 million farmers who have been displaced by China's Three Gorges Dam project. But as one scholar points out, "For many, land is at the heart of a nation's identity, and it is especially easy to raise emotions about outsiders when land is involved" (French 2009, 64; *New York Times*, January 26, 2016).

On the other hand, deepened engagement with China, as a country that has claimed solidarity with African states owing to a colonialization-free imprint, has touted South-South partnerships since the historic Bandung Conference of 1955, which brought China and African countries together. Nonetheless some argue that for all the attention on China's political machinations in terms of its emphasis on conditionality-free agreements, a key aspect of a Beijing consensus is a significant departure from the Washingtonian counterpart where political governance is deemed minimal. However, its volume of trade pales in comparison with the US: in 2015, as Zeleza notes, China's trade with Africa was just $178.8 billion, whereas in other parts of the world, its share of global trade with Europe was $696.3 billion and North America, $613.1 billion (Zeleza 2019). The volume of trade that China has with the continent, as some analysts observe, stems from commodities and what some see as considerable dependence and a legacy of colonial rule (Mshomba 2019). In many ways this is unsurprising, given the vast lands and tropical climate that are suitable for the production of crops like cocoa, coffee, cotton, etc. along with equally vast natural resources. Although the Beijing consensus appears to undercut good governance norms in states that suffer the resource curse such as Nigeria, the Democratic Republic of the Congo, Angola and others, some argue that internally, preferential trade agreements that are a part of the WTO's regulatory matrix and offered by developed countries to African states appear to have groomed them for particular roles in producing and exporting primary products (Mshomba, 2019, 3).

Africa's Prospects for Transformation

Some of the fastest growing economies on the continent are visible players that have the potential to shift a dynamic of aid dependency, which many argue is a continuous challenge for African states. Dambisa Moyo (2009) for example, argued in her book, *Dead Aid*, that far from increasing development or reducing poverty, decades of foreign aid debilitated African economies. Like Moyo, William Easterly questions the conventional wisdom about the idea that foreign aid is beneficial. In the twenty-first century, however, new perspectives on the propensity for African growth and development are emerging that suggest an "Africa rising" landscape. In this new way of thinking, scholars like Taylor (2014) and Fioramonti note how heightened investment, new business opportunities and interest in the continent's resources are replacing long-held stories of poor governance and intractable conflict. Between 2000 and 2010 Africa's real annual GDP growth was 5.4 percent; while this slowed to 3.3 percent between 2010 and 2015, it compared favorably to other world regions, and growth continued despite the global financial crisis and decline in commodity prices (Zeleza, 2019, 156). Ethiopia, Ghana, Kenya, Mozambique, Nigeria and South Africa are the fastest growing economies on the continent and impressive transformations are visible in the form of new or revamped railways and transportation systems and new manufacturing plants. Special economic zones established by Chinese companies have produced shoe factories in Ethiopia. These changes are rapidly altering what it means for African countries to operate in a globalizing world. Among these pivotal economic transmutations is that Nigeria and South Africa have emerged as key political and economic players in West Africa; despite recent ethnopolitical fractures in Ethiopia, the country's remarkable new leader, Abiy Ahmed, prime minister since 2018, is re-shaping the country as a country to watch for its rising status. Ghana, on the other hand continues to retain its status as a "model democracy" despite becoming an oil exporter a decade ago and attracting record investment from China whose massive stamp includes infrastructure projects like railways, highways, revamped buildings, mining, etc.

Other indicators point to favorable forecasts for African economic development, political stability, and full integration into the global political and economic community. The debt burden that stunted growth for two decades has eased. Increasing productivity and expanding local and regional markets are on an uptick. Africa today has more democratic regimes than ever before. Since 1990 most African leaders have left office voluntarily. Zimbabwe's despotic President Robert Mugabe, who passed away in 2018 and pummeled the country's economy into the ground, is a glaring exception. To their credit, more and more African countries are holding undemocratic leaders accountable by establishing transparent and fair political and judicial systems. A dozen countries, such as Sierra Leone and Zambia, have indicted former leaders for corruption and crimes against humanity. In 2016 the African Union (AU) oversaw the trial and conviction of former Chadian dictator Hissene Habre for crimes against humanity. It was the first time an African leader had been brought to justice in another African country.

The greatest success story is the record number of women occupying political office. In Rwanda, women occupy some 61 percent of seats in parliament/public office. Sierra Leone has been headed by two female presidents, and Malawi and other countries have had female leaders at the helm.

The end of apartheid in South Africa marked a relatively peaceful transition from white to black majority rule in 1994. The collapse of communism in Europe from 1989 to 1991 overshadowed this monumental political development. After decades of apartheid run by a seemingly intransigent white government, few scholars predicted its demise or a peaceful transition to majority rule.

The inspirational story of **Nelson Mandela** and the African National Congress attests to the importance of enlightened leadership to human progress (Figure 10.4). Mandela's courageous and peaceful opposition to apartheid eventually persuaded the white South African leadership to do the right thing. In 1990, President F. W. de Klerk released Mandela after 27 years in prison and agreed to end apartheid and to grant all South Africans full rights of citizenship.

South Africa is the richest and most industrialized country in sub-Saharan Africa. Since South African democracy emerged in 1994, the literacy rate has jumped from 82 percent to 93.7 percent today. The economy is the thirty-first largest in the world and is the engine of the region's economic expansion (World Bank 2016).

The inauguration of the African Union—a newly reconstituted body from the intergovernmental body formerly known as the Organization of African Unity in 2001—produced an economic blueprint for continental development. The **New Partnership for African Development** or NEPAD established in 2002 sought to reverse macroeconomic instability that permeated much of the continent following almost two decades of the largely failed structural adjustment programs (SAPS), which imposed stringent economic discipline on cash-strapped states that

Figure 10.4 President William J. Clinton with Nelson Mandela, Philadelphia Freedom Festival, July 4, 1993.

Source: US National Archives and Records Administration.

nonetheless required social expenditures to cushion vulnerable populations that formed the bulk of individual states. This sweeping framework sought to establish benchmarks for growth within and between member states that had suffered owing to economic malaise and poor progress and, as some would argue, persistent crises. The framework sought to reduce poverty and promote democratization, which would in turn support economic reforms and attain average growth of 5 percent continent wide (Aderemi and Agaigbe 2018). However, not much came from NEPAD for several reasons, with the most notable that people referred to NEPAD as being merely a "repackaged SAP." All the same, NEPAD has implemented an African Peer Review Mechanism to monitor government practices. Twenty-five African countries have signed on to the initiative, which mobilizes regional organizations to monitor government practices and suggest improvements. Continued political and economic progress is dependent on a freer press, incorruptible civil servants, and powerful watchdog legislatures and judiciaries (van de Walle 2005, 82). In addition, the AU's Peace and Security Council has played a key role in resolving and preventing conflicts.

Though much of Africa's development remains stained by single narratives of disease, corruption, under-development, stagnant growth and more, the twenty-first century shows promising signs of a shift in both perception about the continent and its growing strategic importance. Africa's global engagements have partly shifted from exclusively Western European and North American ties to economic partnership with the BRICs (Brazil, Russia, India and China (Zeleza 2019: 156). For example, heightened investment from China has virtually produced bilateral investment in all 55 states; and huge infrastructural development projects are changing the landscape of a continent that has longed to escape perceptions about the nature of its place in the world. Yet, among developed, post-industrialized economies, Africa's largest economic partners are the European Union, the United States, and Japan (Zeleza 2019). As the European Commission (2017) documents, the EU accounted for 35 percent of the continent's exports, followed by "Africa itself" at 18 percent, China at 11 percent, the US at 8 percent etc.

Other indicators of Africa's ongoing globalization are also evident. Its expanded engagements are reflected in diasporic connections. Paul T. Zeleza (2019) notes that the diaspora is the continent's biggest donor and that according to the World Bank, in 2017 diaspora remittances reached $69.5 billion and accounted for a significant portion of GDP in several countries. The nature of these investments have both provoked controversies about a purported scramble or neo-colonialism and raised alarms from Africans about Chinese long-term interests particularly in lieu of increasing resource extraction that includes minerals, oil and raw materials. The latter continues to unfold in some projects that observers, non-state actors and communities themselves note are mired in environmental consequences from mining activities in countries like Ghana or Angola for example, or more glaringly, manufacturing and textile industries that have been displaced owing to Chinese entry. Debates about the consequences of the world's economic giant's footprint on the vast prism of African states abound in terms of a "no strings attached" preference—which supplies vast sums of aid in multiple forms in return for investment perks and resource rights—and what this means for neo-dependency. But a number of states are emerging with remarkable trends that suggest a pivot from the status quo of malaise or stagnant development.

African governments are operating in a new and more open environment. Shenzhen zones or special economic zones that appear ubiquitous (that is areas of a country not subject to tariffs, duty free, etc., in which local populations are employed under preferential terms or an agreement) are now present in Africa and are part of the larger dynamics related to outsourcing and outflows of capital heightened by the draw of lower labor costs in developing or poor countries. These practices have drawn into sharp relief the ongoing and much contested nature of globalization in purportedly exacerbating poverty with diminished protections for the poor and working class, erosion of environmental standards that can intensify pollution in water supply when located near peri-urban or even slum dwellings that may be close to a factory.

Agenda 2063, a rather ambitious blueprint for revitalization in terms of economic and in particular sustainable development, in many ways aims to reverse commodity dependency as the primary fulcrum for growth. The agreement embodies the initial refrain following the inception of the African Union in 2001—appearing to emphasize continental jurisdiction in tendering its own prerogatives and managing its own affairs independent of external actors. In a significant development, the African Union in 2015 launched Agenda 2063, as a blueprint for transforming the continent into a global powerhouse. One overarching theme that emerged was sustainable development accompanied by targets to be met over a 50-year period, following a celebration in 2013 to commemorate the formation of the African Union at the turn of the century.

As a precursor, to this sweeping plan that aims to produce competitive industries, higher living standards and investments in local populations, the **Millennium development** goals and the challenges of fulfilling some aims inform the Agenda 2063's creation. The Millennium development goals, a specific set of some eight goals that included eradicating extreme hunger and poverty, achieving universal primary education, gender equality and female empowerment, for instance had a target date of completion by 2015. These aims were adopted and supported by 191 member states of the United Nations. In response to partial progress, African states via the African Union decided that future goals in what would later become Agenda 2063 were required (see African Commission 2015). That said, African states made progress despite not having reached the targets—indeed, poverty levels fell from 57 percent in 1990 to 41 percent in 2015 (Mshomba 2019).

One of the biggest challenges the African Union faces is in achieving economic integration, vital to the continent's socioeconomic and political transformation. Economic integration is still under 20 percent, a surprising figure for a continent with vast resources, remarkable human capital (given its population of 1.26 billion), and growing economies of scale. In fact, the share of intra-African exports increased from about 10 percent in 1995 to some 17 percent in 2017, which is comparatively low in contrast to its trade with other regions (Songwe 2019). Although good governance has long been viewed as a persistent challenge, it is important to recognize the ongoing dynamics of colonial institutions on post-colonial states—those imported institutions from former European empires whose extraction of raw materials and violent state apparatus bequeathed during the colonial period solely benefited Europeans. These factors help explain difficulties with democratic consolidation and economically robust states.

One path to finally putting behind the trail of colonial legacy on disjointed economic policies, corruption and neo-patrimonialism might be the newly constituted African Continental Free Trade Area (AfCFTA), a monetary union that aims to boost and improve economic integration. It was launched in 2018 in Kigali, Rwanda with 44 countries pledging broader integration. As a step closer to regionalism, it is a welcome development that potentially augurs well given forecasts of a new "industrial" age in Africa.

References

Aderemi, Adewale, and Faeren Agaigbe. 2018. "Challenges of Economic Development in Africa: The Dichotomy of a Debate and the Africanist View." In *The Palgrave Handbook of African Politics, Governance and Development*, edited by Samuel Ojo Oloruntoba and Toyin Falola. New York: Palgrave Macmillan.

African Center for Economic Transformation. 2010. "Looking East: China's Engagement with Africa." https://acetforafrica.org/publications/country-reports/broken-promises-a-g20-summit-report-by-global-trade-alert/

Agonafer, Mulugeta, ed. 1996. *Africa in the Contemporary International Disorder: Crises and Possibilities.* New York: University Press of America.

Anderson, David. 2004. *Histories of the Hanged: The Dirty War in Kenya and the End of Empire.* New York: Norton.

Ascherson, Neal. 2005. "The Breaking of the Mau Mau." *New York Review of Books.* April 7.

Bah, Abu Bakarr. 2005. *Breakdown and Reconstitution: Democracy, the Nation-State, and Ethnicity in Nigeria.* Lanham, MD: Lexington Books.

BBC News. 2016. August 10.

BBC News. 2019. February 27: www.bbc.com/news/world-africa-12890807

Beah, Ishmael. 2006. *A Long Way Gone: Memoirs of a Boy Soldier.* New York: Farrar, Straus and Giroux.

Best, Antony, Jussi M. Hanhimäki, Joseph A. Maiolo, and Kirsten E. Schulze. 2004. *International History of the Twentieth Century.* New York: Routledge.

Bloomberg Report. 2015. October 26.

Chabal, Patrick. 2005. "Power in Africa Reconsidered." In *The African Exception*, edited by Ulf Engel and Gorm Olsen, 17–34. Burlington, VT: Ashgate.

Christiaensen, Luc, and Shantayanan Devarajan. 2013. "Making the Most of Africa's Growth." *Current History* 112 (754): 181–87.

CIA (Central Intelligence Agency). 2016. *World Factbook.* www.cia.gov.

Collier, Paul. 2004. "Africa's Revolutionary Routine." *Foreign Policy* (May–June): 82–83.

Davidson, Basil. 1985. *The Magnificent African Cake* [Documentary Film]. London: ABC.

Devarajan, Shantayanan, and Wolfgang Fengler. 2013. "Africa's Economic Boom." *Foreign Affairs* 92 (3): 68–81.

De Witte, Ludo. 2001. *The Assassination of Lumumba.* Translated by Ann Wright and Renee Fenby. New York: Verso.

Diamond, Jared. 1999. *Guns, Germs, and Steel: The Fates of Human Societies.* New York: Norton.

Duiker, William J., and Jackson J. Spielvogel. 2001. *World History.* Belmont, CA: Wadsworth.

Easterly, William. 2010. "Foreign Aid for Scoundrels." *New York Review of Books*, November 25: 37–38.

Elkins, Caroline. 2004. *Imperial Reckoning: The Untold Story of Britain's Gulag in Kenya.* New York: Henry Holt.

Eurostat. 2011. "Africa-EU–Economic Indicators, Trade and Investment." European Union. https://ec.europa.eu/eurostat.

Fernández-Armesto, Felipe. 1995. *Millennium: A History of the Last Thousand Years.* New York: Scribner.

Forbes. 2015. July 8.

Freedom House. 2016. www.freedomhouse.org.

French, Howard W. 2009. "Kagame's Hidden War in the Congo." *New York Review of Books*, September 24: 44–47.

Gallup Poll. 2015. www.gallup.com.

———. 2010. "The Next Empire?" *The Atlantic* (May): 59–69.

———. 2010. "Africa's Forever Wars." *Foreign Policy* (March–April): 178.

Hanson, John H. 1995. "Islam and African Societies." In *Africa*, edited by Phyllis M. Martin and Patrick O'Meara, 97–114. Bloomington: Indiana University Press.

Hargreaves, J. D. 2004. "West African Boundary Making." In *Borders and Border Politics in a Globalizing World*, edited by Paul Ganster and David E. Lorey, 97–106. Wilmington, DE: Scholarly Resources.

Hochschild, Adam. 2005. "In the Heart of Darkness." *New York Review of Books* (October 6): 39–42.

———. 2010. "The Trial of Thomas Lubanga." *The Atlantic* (December): 77–82.

Houngnikpo, Mathurin. 2000. "Stuck at the Runway: Africa's Distress Call." *Africa Insight* (May): 5–12.

Judt, Tony. 2000. "The Story of Everything." *New York Review of Books.* September 21.

Karl, T.L. 1999. "The Perils of the Petro-state: Reflections on the Paradox of Plenty." *Journal of International Affairs*, 31–48.

Kennedy, Paul. 1993. *Preparing for the Twenty-first Century.* New York: Random House.

Khare, Vineet. 2013. "China and India: The Scramble for Business in Africa." *BBC News*, August 4. www.bbc.com/news/business-23225998

Lacey, Mark. 2003. "New Name, Similar Struggles for Group of African Nations." *New York Times*, February 5.

Lutulala, Bernard. 2012. "Brain Drain in Africa: State of the Issue and Possible Solutions." *Wilson Center*. www.wilsoncenter.org/publication/brain-drain-africa-state-the-issue-and-possible-solutions

Mbaye, S. 2002. "NEPAD. The Wrong Plan?" *In West Africa* Issue 4333, July 8–14, 29–31.

Moyo, Dambisa. 2009. "Why Foreign Aid Is Hurting Africa." *Wall Street Journal–Africa*, March 21. http://online.wsj.com/article/SB123758895999200083.html.

Mshomba, Richard E. 2019. "Development Trajectories in Africa." In *Oxford Encyclopedia of African Politics*, edited by Nic Cheeseman et al. Oxford: Oxford University Press.

New Africa. 2015. November 11.

New York Times. 2012. December 15.

New York Times, 2013. April 14.

New York Times, 2013. September 18.

New York Times. 2013. April 30.

New York Times. 2013. June 30.

New York Times. 2015. December 6.

New York Times. 2016. June 26.

New York Times. 2013. October 27.

New York Times. 2016. September 13.

OECD (Organisation for Economic Co-operation and Development). 2016. www.oecd.org.

Office of the U.S. Trade Representative. 2016. www.ustr.gov.

Oloruntoba, Samuel Ojo, and Falola, Toyin, eds. 2020. *The Palgrave Handbook of African Political Economy*. New York: Palgrave Macmillan.

Palgreen, Linda. 2007. "In Niger, Trees and Crops Turn Back the Desert." *New York Times*, February 11.

Pew Research Center, September 16, 2014, www.pewglobal.org.

Rush, Norman. 2006. "Exile's Return." *New York Review of Books*, April 23.

Time, 2012. December 3.

UNECA (United Nations Economic Commission for Africa). 2020. "Economic Report on Africa." https://uneca.org/era2020.

United Nations. 2016. "Millennium Development Goals Report 2016." www.un.org

United States Agency for International Development (USAID). 2016. www.usaid.gov.

United States Census Bureau. 2016. www.census.gov.

Van de Walle, Nicholas. 2005. "The Donors and the State in Africa: How Much Has Changed?" In *The African Exception*, edited by Ulf Engel and Gorm Olsen, 69–86. Burlington, VT: Ashgate.

Von Laue, Theodore H. 1987. *The World Revolution of Westernization: The Twentieth Century in Global Perspective*. New York: Oxford University Press.

World Bank (WB). 2016. www.worldbank.org/en/home.

World Trade Organization (WTO). 2016. www.wto.org.

Zartman, I. William. 2001. "Bordering on War." *Foreign Policy* (May–June): 66–67.

Zeleza, Paul, T. 2019. Africa, Internationalization and the Global Context: Making It Work. ANIE Conference.

Zeleza, P.T., 2019. "Leveraging Africa's Global Diasporas for the Continent's Development." *African Diaspora*, *11*(1–2), pp.144–61.

Further Reading

Books

Fage, J. D. 2002. *A History of Africa*. London: Routledge.

Hartman, Saidiya. 2006. *Lose Your Mother: A Journey Along the Atlantic Slave Route*. New York: Farrar, Straus, and Giroux.

Kristof, Nicholas D. 2006. "Genocide in Slow Motion." *New York Review of Books* (February 9): 14–17.

Meredith, Martin. 2005. *The Fate of Africa: From the Hopes of Freedom to the Heart of Despair*. New York: Public Affairs.

Milan, William B., and Jennifer G. Jones. 2011. "Ivory Coast: Another Asterisk for Africa's Democratization." *Current History* (May): 177–83.

Murithi, Timothy. 2005. *The African Union: Pan-Africanism, Peacebuilding and Development*. Burlington, VT: Ashgate.

Nugent, Paul. 2004. *Africa Since Independence: A Comparative History*. New York: Palgrave.

Songwe, V. 2019. "Intra-African trade: A Path to Economic Diversification and Inclusion." In *Foresight Africa: Top Priorities for the Continent 2019*, edited by Brahima S. Coulibaly. Washington, DC: Brookings Institution.

Journals

Africa Today. muse.jhu.edu/journals/at
African Affairs. afraf.oxfordjournals.org
African Studies Review. www.cambridge.org/core/journals/african-studies-review
Journal of African History. www.cambridge.org/core/journals/journal-of-african-history
Journal of Contemporary African Studies. www.tandfonline.com/loi/cjca20

Films

Blood Diamond (2006). Edward Zwick, director.
Hotel Rwanda (2004). Terry George, director.
The Last King of Scotland (2006). Kevin MacDonald, director.
Lumumba (2000). Raoul Peck, director.
A World Apart (1988). Chris Menges, director.

Websites

African News Network. allafrica.com
African Studies Association. www.africanstudies.org
African Union. www.au.int
Poverty Data, World Bank. http://povertydata.worldbank.org/poverty/country/NGA
United Nations Economic Commission for Africa. www.uneca.org
UN Women. www.unwomen.org/en/news/stories/2018/8/feature-rwanda-women-in-parliament
World Health Organization. www.who.int/topics/millennium_development_goals/about/en/.

Chapter 11

The Middle East and North Africa

In 2020 the United Arab Emirates launched *Amal* ("Hope"), an orbital spacecraft, on a scientific mission to Mars. Led by a team of Arab scientists, with assistance from US universities and space launch facilities in Japan, the effort took only six years to go from an idea to a successful launch. The goal was to remind the world—including other countries of the Middle East—that the Arab world is capable of being a technological and scientific world leader. It also was intended to help jumpstart the UAE's efforts to expand from a global business hub to a knowledge-based economy. With world oil prices in decline, many of the region's wealthiest countries were seeking ways to diversify their places in the global economy. The launch served as a powerful reminder that there is much more to the Middle East than oil, terrorism, security states and civil wars. In fact, the Middle East and North Africa (MENA) region is a complex and influential part of the global world system.

Linking Africa, Asia, and Europe, encircling half the Mediterranean Sea, the Middle East has for millennia played a crucial economic role on all three continents, dominating the trade in gold and slaves from Africa, spices and fabrics from Asia, and glass and other manufactured goods from Europe. In the twentieth century, it literally fueled globalization as the primary source of the oil that powers the ships, planes, trains, and trucks that make it possible for bananas from El Salvador or manufactured goods from China to reach the shelves of stores in Europe and the United States at astonishingly low costs.

Since the invention of agriculture, the Middle East has been the site of great empires, from the rise of Pharaonic Egypt more than six thousand years ago to the fall of the Ottoman Empire in the twentieth century. It is the birthplace of at least a half dozen world religions, from Judaism, Christianity, and Islam to Bahai, Druze, and Zoroastrianism, and dozens more that flourished for centuries or even millennia but have since passed away. Geographically, the Middle East is often conceived as a hodgepodge, an arbitrary and shifting blend of western Asia, North Africa, and parts of South and Central Asia. But the cultural, economic, and geopolitical importance of the region throughout history requires that the Middle East be considered a distinct center of global significance (Map 11.1).

The Middle of Where?

Where is the Middle East? What is it in the middle of? There is no indigenous term in Arabic or Persian or Pashtun or any other language of the region for the area stretching from the Atlantic coast of North Africa to the Iran–Afghan border that Europeans and Americans call the Middle East. North Africa, especially the Western half, is the **Maghreb**. Iran and Iraq were Persia, and the areas farther east were labeled by many different names. The term *Middle East* was created in the first years of the twentieth century by an American military historian writing in a British military journal to help label and talk about European—and later American—geopolitical

DOI: 10.4324/9781003028314-14

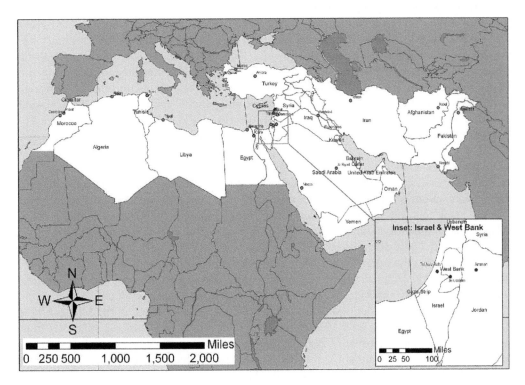

Map 11.1 The Middle East.

concerns centered in the Persian Gulf. Because of this, the geographical area constituted by the term *Middle East* changes with the changing interests of Western journalists, scholars, and politicians (Scheffler 2003). Before September 11, 2001, Afghanistan and Pakistan were usually considered South Asian countries and were rarely included in maps of the Middle East; since then, they are included in most American textbooks and maps of the region. In 2004 the G8 countries (Canada, France, Germany, Italy, Japan, Russia, the United Kingdom, and the United States) adopted the terms *Middle East*, and *Greater Middle East* to differentiate between the core of Arabic and Persian countries around the Persian Gulf and the broader range of countries from North Africa to South and Central Asia.

The borders of most contemporary Middle Eastern states are still those established by European governments more than half a century ago. With the fall of the Ottoman Empire at the end of World War I, the colonial powers of Europe divided up the Middle East and established arbitrary borders where none had previously existed. The European concern with borders exhibits a different concept of space and power than that historically held by Middle Eastern geographers. Precolonial maps drawn by Arab and Persian cartographers rarely show borders or boundaries; instead, they mapped centers—seats of power and spheres of influence. The idea of culturally distinct peoples inhabiting geographically exclusive space did not become widespread in the region until the colonial rulers brought it in.

Today, European concepts of geographical space have largely come to replace Arab and Persian concepts. People living in the region routinely use translations of the European term *Middle East* (*al-Sharq al-Awsat*) in writing and communicating with the international community. Nationalism of various kinds has become very important in local and regional politics. All of these modern nation-states have a flag, a national anthem, and a seat at the United Nations.

Yet there are also strong supernational affinities tied to linguistic, cultural, ethnic, and religious similarities that transcend borders. In the 1960s and 1970s, political leaders like Egypt's Gamel Abdel Nasser spoke of an Arab superstate linking many important Arabic-speaking lands into a single political and economic unit (Dawisha 2005). While this dream is dead as a realistic political goal in the contemporary Middle East, Arab nationalism continues to live on in the popular imagination. The Arab League is only one of several regional institutions that continue to emphasize and build common economic, cultural, and political goals among Arabic-speaking countries. The term **Arab world** is often used to describe the 22 Arabic-speaking countries of the world as a single geopolitical unit. Stretching from Morocco to Iraq, and including several sub-Saharan African countries, the combined population of this Arab world is 325 million.

Other border-crossing affinities also exist. Since its revolution in 1979, Iran has inspired two generations of political Muslims and also significantly raised the profile of Shia Islam. Although Shiites make up only about 12 percent of the world's Muslims, they are a majority in Iran and Iraq, and many countries have sizable minority Shiite communities. The rise of Iran, the fall of Saddam Hussein's Sunni-dominated government in Iraq in 2002, and the success of the militant arm of the Shiite Lebanese group Hezbollah against Israel in 2006, have led some to speak of a Shiite resurgence in the world (Nasr 2006). Shiite minorities in countries where they suffer political and economic marginalization, like Saudi Arabia, may well look to the successes of their co-religionists with greater pride and affinity than they feel for their own nations.

The largest and most encompassing of transnational identities centered in the Middle East is that of Islam. Although the ways Muslims practice their religion may differ significantly from Africa to the Arabian peninsula to Asia, most Muslims have a strong sense of themselves as members of a worldwide community of believers, or *ummah*. The term **Islamic world** is usually used to refer to the total number of the world's Muslim-majority countries in Asia, Africa, the Middle East, and Europe. Some, however, conceive of an even more encompassing concept. As the world's fastest growing religion, Islam is now the second-largest religion in most Christian majority nations. The term **Muslim world** is frequently used in a cultural sense to refer to the worldwide community of Muslims and also in a geographical and political sense to include Muslim enclaves in non-Muslim majority countries, such as Yinchuan in China, Southall in London, and Dearborn, Michigan. Although the majority of the world's Muslims live in Asia and the religion is growing fastest in Africa, the Middle East looms large in the Islamic imagination throughout the world as the geographic location of Islam's sacred historical sites, as the place toward which prayer is directed, and as the destination for the pilgrimage all Muslims seek to make during their lifetimes. These terms thus remind us that the Middle East is the center of global cultural networks as well as economic and political ones.

From Past to Present

The Middle East includes three of the world's major early river valley civilizations—the Nile, the Jordan, and the land between the Tigris and Euphrates. Together, these form what historians call the **Fertile Crescent**, a region where the invention of agriculture led to the early rise of some of the world's first cities and empires. Along this broad stretch, civilizations rose and fell, camels and horses were domesticated, and vast trading networks developed. Later European empires like those of Macedonia and Rome conquered vast stretches of North Africa and Asia Minor, where they clashed with indigenous empires like those of Egypt and Persia.

For the first thousand years following the birth of Jesus, Christianity's history is the history of the Middle East. Christianity originated in Palestine, then spread outward along trade routes throughout the Middle East and North Africa. When early Christianity came into conflict with the official religions of the Roman Empire, it was in the Middle East that most martyrdoms occurred. Even after Christianity became the state religion of the Roman Empire it continued for centuries to be considered an Eastern religion, and its influence extended into neighboring non-Christian realms. In fourth-century Sassanid Persia, for example, the emperors copied the Roman Christian model in establishing Zoroastrianism as a state religion.

By the seventh century CE, the Arabian peninsula was being squeezed between the Christian Roman Empire, based in Constantinople, and the Zoroastrian Sassanid Empire, based in Ctesiphon (now a nearly forgotten ruin located 20 kilometers south of Baghdad). Most of Arabia's wealth came from camel caravans that could transport goods across Arabia, from the Red Sea to the Gulf, more rapidly than ships could sail around the peninsula. Cities that lay along trading routes, like Mecca, grew large and wealthy. The tribes who controlled the overland trade were in continual states of warfare, however, and the cities were often divided by internal disputes and under political and military pressure from Persia and Rome.

Into this seething cauldron, Muhammad, an orphan who rose to become a successful businessman and then a prophet, brought a message of unity and egalitarianism, of a brotherhood greater than that of the tribe, and which encompasses all people who submit to God (which is what the term *Muslim* means). As his message spread, Muhammad forged the tribes of Arabia into a single community of believers, using trade agreements and political alliances as well as religious conversion.

Muhammad died in 632 CE, by which time his message had spread across trade routes, and small communities of believers had appeared in many lands. Muhammad was succeeded by a series of **caliphs**, who sent out military forces to defend Muslim communities from persecution. These expeditions rapidly turned into outright conquests. The Sassanian Empire, already beset by internal problems, fell to Muslim forces by 650 CE, as did most of the North African provinces of Rome.

The rapid expansion of Islam as both a faith and an empire brought vast wealth to the caliphs. Factionalism began to divide the Muslim community. A dispute in the seventh century over the succession to the caliphate led to a division of the Muslim community into **Shia** (or Shiites), who followed the biological descendants of the prophet (whom they called *imams*), and the majority **Sunni**, who accepted the authority of the historical caliphs. The former, who have probably never numbered more than one-fifth of the world's Muslims, settled largely in what are today Iran, Iraq, Lebanon, and India.

Under a series of caliphal dynasties, the Muslim world eventually stretched from the Atlantic coast to India and beyond. Vast mercantile networks carried the wealth of the known world from Asia to the Mediterranean, and from Africa to the Black Sea. Arab merchants profited from trade on the Red Sea and Indian Ocean trading network. Great centers of learning were established, and the region enjoyed an efflorescence of art and science. For several centuries, the Middle East seemed to be the center of the world. When Marco Polo traveled through the region at the end of the thirteenth century, it was still one of the most important in the world.

The dominance of Arabs over this center of world trade began to decline with the rise of Turkish empires in the eleventh and twelfth centuries. The first of these arose at the beginning of the eleventh century in what is today eastern Iran, Afghanistan, and Pakistan. These areas on the outskirts of the empire had increasingly been governed by slave-soldiers. Taking advantage of their positions on the outskirts of the empire, powerful slave-soldiers created semi-autonomous dynastic kingdoms. Subsequently, the Seljuk Turks from Central Asia seized much of the rest of the Middle East and defeated the Byzantine army to conquer Anatolia (in modern-day Turkey), which became their political base.

These political and economic disruptions paved the way for, and were exacerbated by, a series of invasions by foreign forces. The first series of invasions came from Western Europe, beginning in 1095 when Pope Urban II called for a crusade against Muslim domination of Christian holy places and pilgrimage routes. A series of raids by warriors from the central Asian steppes was even more devastating. Led by Hulegu Khan in the thirteenth century and Timur Leng in the fourteenth, the Mongols laid waste to entire cities, killing millions. They were finally stopped when a succession struggle back in Asia forced the splitting of their forces just as they faced unexpected resistance from the Mamluk rulers of Egypt.

In the meantime, a new power emerged in Anatolia when the Ottoman *emirs* ("commanders"), inheritors of the Seljuks, conquered Constantinople and made themselves rulers in 1453 (Figure 11.1). At the beginning of the sixteenth century, the Ottoman Turks began conquering adjoining territories. In the Middle East, they conquered Iraq in 1515, Syria in 1516, and Egypt in 1517, uniting the whole region under one rule for the first time since the reign of the Abbasid caliphs of the tenth century. In Europe, they extended their dominion to the Danube River, conquering Greece, the Balkans, and most of Hungary.

The leaders of this new Ottoman Empire took the title **sultan** (from an Arab word for "authority") and quickly established their control over almost the entire Muslim world. Under strong rulers like Suleyman the Magnificent, the Ottomans pushed their political influence into Asia and Europe, beyond the territories of the caliphal dynasties. Under weak rulers, provincial governors ruled almost as independent kings.

A century of weak administrators and a failure to keep up with changing technologies of production, transportation, and communication eventually reduced the Ottoman Empire to "the sick man of Europe," in the words of Tsar Nicholas I of Russia. From 1700 to 1900, first

Figure 11.1 After the conquest of Constantinople, the great Christian church Hagia Sophia became a mosque. Today the building is a museum.

Source: Mark Allen Peterson.

Hungary, and then Greece, Serbia, Romania, and Bulgaria, established independence from the empire. France, Italy, and Britain were able to wrest colonies in North Africa away from the Ottomans and to increase their influence in Middle Eastern provinces that remained nominally Ottoman controlled. These actions played a critical role in inducing the empire to join World War I on the side of Germany in 1914. When Germany and its allies eventually lost that war, the Ottoman Empire fell apart.

A strong leader, Mustafa Kemal Ataturk, seized control of Turkey and turned it into a Western-style nation-state. The rest of the empire was quickly divided up by the colonial powers. Great Britain created the kingdoms of Iraq and Kuwait out of the Ottoman provinces of Mosul, Baghdad, and Basra, and took control of Palestine. France assumed control of Lebanon and Syria.

Colonialism—the political, economic, and cultural domination of societies by European powers—transformed the Middle East in many ways. Increased demand for agricultural products on the world market, coupled with better medical care, led to a population explosion. International corporations were brought in to better exploit natural resources and ship them to Europe to fuel its industries. Borders between states, established by Europeans without regard for the geographies of local communities, were given force of law. Tribal, religious, ethnic, and other cultural distinctions that had often been fluid and negotiable were enumerated in laws and censuses, making them more rigid and often exacerbating tensions between groups as they competed for power and resources under colonial administrations.

World War II, however, effectively bankrupted the European colonial system. In addition, the United States pressured its European allies to abandon their colonies to reduce incentives for locals to turn to its rival, the Soviet Union, for assistance in throwing off the colonial yoke. The transition from colonies to states was difficult. In many new states, the populations had no particular sense of themselves as members of a common nation; even the names of their countries had often been imposed by foreign rulers. Local leaders seized control of administrative apparatuses, which had been designed not to govern but to rule, and to remove natural resources and sell them abroad. Whatever the original intentions of the new governments, these colonial legacies made easy the development of paternalistic central authorities and allocation states that sell their resources abroad and distribute the proceeds. These historical legacies contribute to contemporary problems in the Middle East.

Diversity and Division

One of the things that puzzles many people who have lived and worked in the region we call the Middle East is the tendency by those outside the region to imagine it as all of a piece, understanding the entire vast area in terms of a handful of stereotypes. The late critical theorist Edward Said suggested that these stereotypes originated during the colonial era as a way to justify European economic, political, and cultural domination. They have survived, he argued, because journalists, politicians, and scholars have continued to find them useful (Said 1979, 1997). Whatever the reasons, the heterogeneity of the peoples living in the Middle East often goes unrecognized. People who see Spain, France, and England as very different from one another will nonetheless often imagine Egypt, Saudi Arabia, and Iran to be much the same. Yet these countries not only differ significantly from one another in economy, social organization, and cultural practices, they also have considerable internal diversity as well.

The Middle East is a land of considerable linguistic diversity. Major languages spoken in the region include Afghan, Arabic, Aramaic, Armenian, Assyrian, Baluchi, Bari, Berber, Circassian, Coptic, English, Farsi, French, Greek, Hebrew, Hindi, Italian, Kurdish, Nubian, Pashtu, Russian, Turkic, Turkish, Turkmen, and Urdu. Some of these, like Arabic, Farsi, and Berber, are regional languages that cut across state boundaries. Others are national languages, spoken primarily within a particular country, like Turkish and Hebrew. Some, like Nubian in Egypt and Bari in the Sudan (and Bari is only one of a dozen such Hamitic-Nilotic tongues in the Sudan) are languages of minority communities within state boundaries. Others, like English, French, Italian, and Russian, are languages of political and economic elites. And still others, like Hindi in the United Arab Emirates and Urdu in Oman, are spoken by the South Asian guest workers who make up more than 15 percent of the population. A few, like Coptic in Egypt, are strictly liturgical languages.

Simply listing languages barely touches on the complexities of communication in the Middle East. Arabic is the most widely spoken language throughout the region, but how it is spoken differs dramatically. Proper Arabic, or *fusha* (pronounced foos-ha), refers to the classical Arabic of the **Quran** and of medieval literature, and to the **Modern Standard Arabic** of newspapers, television news programs, schools, and contemporary literature. Except on formal occasions, though, almost nobody speaks *fusha*. Instead, they speak a variety of dialects, some of which are mutually unintelligible. Other dialects are widely understood. Egypt itself has several different dialects, but the dialect of Cairo is widely understood throughout North Africa and the Middle East because Egypt is the center for most regional movie and television production. Even Disney films and cartoons are dubbed into Egyptian dialect.

As the language of the Quran, classical Arabic is the language of prayer for all Muslims. But Muslim religious leaders traveling from Afghanistan or Kyrgyz to Cairo or Mecca for theological training will often attend special courses in which the lectures are in English because while they can read Arabic, they cannot speak or understand it fluently. Similarly, many members of the political and economic elites across the region are illiterate in their native tongues, speaking local dialects but being more comfortable reading and writing in English, French, or Russian than literate Arabic.

Moreover, ways of using Arabic continue to evolve, for example, in computer-mediated communication. While Arabic character sets and Arabic versions of Microsoft Windows are in widespread use regionally, the vast majority of global Internet and Web tools utilize ASCII characters based on the 26 characters of the Roman alphabet. The Arabic alphabet features 28 characters, including several that represent sounds that do not occur in English. To facilitate computer-mediated communication in Arabic, many high school and college students have developed a form of ASCII-Arabic that uses standard ASCII characters to represent Arabic sounds, such as 2 for the glottal stop and 5 for the unvoiced fricative (Palfreyman and al-Khalil 2003). With this system, Arab speakers can use e-mail or instant messaging from any computer or cell phone anywhere in the world.

The region also has much greater religious diversity than many people realize. While Islam is far and away the dominant religion of the Middle East, it is by no means the only faith. The Middle East has been the birthplace of many religions, from the now extinct religions of the Sumerians, Babylonians, and Pharaonic Egyptians, to the world religions of Judaism, Christianity, Islam, and Bahai, to religions whose adherents number only a few million or less, like Zoroastrianism (India, Pakistan, Iran, and Afghanistan), Yazidism (Iraq, Syria, Turkey, Iran, Georgia, and Armenia), and Druze (Syria, Lebanon, Israel, Turkey, and Jordan). Many Middle Eastern countries have sizable Christian minorities.

Many of these religions have similar beliefs (one God, angels, devils), shared ethical values, and a common prophetic tradition. Christianity has roots in Judaism, and Islam has roots in both. Muhammad's revelation makes clear that the God of Islam is the God of the Jews and the Christians. For Muslims, Muhammad is the last of a line of prophets, beginning with Adam, who have brought God's message to humankind. Bahais agree, but teach that the line of prophets did not end with Muhammad. The Druze also emerged from a post-Muhammadan prophetic tradition. Zoroastrianism, in its long history, has both influenced and been influenced by Judaism, Christianity, and Islam. Yazidi religious traditions probably predate the Christian era, but they have clearly been influenced by Christianity, Zoroastrianism, and Islam.

Today, Islam is the dominant religion throughout the region and the second largest religion in the world after Christianity. The word **Islam** means "submission"; a Muslim is one who submits to the will of God. The message of Islam is that God is one and indivisible. God is at once great beyond human comprehension and closer to us than our jugular vein, according to the Quran.

Submitting to God begins with the *arkaan*, a set of practices sometimes called the Five Pillars of Islam, which shape people's minds and bodies into those of good Muslims. The first of these is the *shahada*, or declaration of faith: "There is no god but God, and Muhammad is his prophet." This declaration implies a commitment to the absolute priority of God and an acceptance of the authority of the revelation of Muhammad as contained in the **Quran** (the written record of Muhammad's revelation; see Figure 11.2) and the *hadith* (collected accounts of sayings and actions of the prophet and his companions). The second is prayer. Muslim prayer involves the entire body: standing, kneeling, bowing, prostrating oneself. Every Muslim is expected to pray five times each day unless circumstances make it impossible. The prayers at dawn, noon, mid-afternoon, dusk, and night are intended to break up the day, reminding Muslims that the unseen, eternal world of God takes precedence over the visible, mundane world of human activity.

The third orthodox practice is fasting. During the month of Ramadan, the entire Muslim world collectively fasts from dawn to dusk. The fourth practice is charity. Every Muslim is required each year to give 2 percent of his or her entire net worth, less the amount necessary to live at a subsistence level. Charity can be given as a personal act or it can be given to a mosque,

Figure 11.2 The Quran is the written record of God's revelation to mankind through the prophet Muhammad.

Source: Natalia Suit.

bank, or other institution for redistribution to various charities. Finally, every Muslim who is physically and financially able is expected to make a pilgrimage (*hajj*) to the city of Mecca (in modern-day Saudi Arabia) at least once in his or her life. Mecca is the city where Muhammad lived when he received his prophetic revelation, and it is believed to have been visited through history by many other prophets, including Adam and Ibrahim (Abraham). Millions of Muslims make the hajj each year, and millions more around the world celebrate the feast that culminates the event in communion with them.

In spite of the universality of these practices, Islam is not understood or practiced everywhere in the same ways. The most significant difference is between Shia and Sunni Muslims. Although they accept the orthodox principles described above, the Shia also venerate saints and make pilgrimages to their tombs, invest their clerics with special authority, and appeal to a different body of hadith in interpreting Sharia law. Other communities like the Alevis of Turkey, Syria, Iraq, and Lebanon may deviate even from the Five Pillars so that they are regarded as non-Muslims by most Sunni and Shia Muslims.

But even members of the Sunni majority do not practice their faith everywhere in the same way. There are many ways orthodox Muslims in the Middle East and around the world differ in performing even such required acts as daily prayers. The same is true of interpretations of the Quran and of the hadith. Western journalists often write of **sharia** law as if the code of law that derived from the Quran and hadith were a coherent body of rules all Muslims agree on. But it is not. Laws must be interpreted, and within orthodox Islam, there are a number of accepted schools of legal interpretation, which can differ in the ways they address everyday behavior.

Taqlid is the position that authoritative interpretation for almost any position already exists in centuries of accumulated work by theologians and jurors. Those who call themselves *salafis* believe the Quran must be interpreted only in terms of the collected sayings of Muhammad and the first three generations of Muslims. Many other Muslims, particularly in Europe and the Americas, call for *ijtihad*, the use of good judgment in applying the word of God to contemporary situations. Although they strive for consistency, different authorities may in good faith issue contradictory *fatwas*, or juridical decrees, on the same topic. In the thirteenth century, for example, debates raged over whether the newly discovered drink coffee was permitted or prohibited by the prophet's ban on intoxicants, and similar debates later emerged over tobacco. Although the view that coffee and tobacco were not forbidden won out, and both are now widely enjoyed throughout the Islamic world, some Muslims choose to follow stricter interpretations and avoid both.

Some scholars believe the current era may be a time of tremendous transformation in Islam, comparable to the Protestant Reformation in Europe in the sixteenth century. Several generations of public schooling in Islamic countries have transformed Islam from something one simply did as a member of a community to an object of scrutiny. Students around the world have begun to discover that many of the religious conventions their community took for granted were not practiced in other Muslim communities and may not be supported by the Quran or hadith. The possibility has also emerged that individuals can diverge from their community's practice on the basis of their personal study, not only of sacred texts and schoolbooks, but also of published commentaries, radio, television, cassette tape, and podcast sermons, and other sources of knowledge. The World Wide Web and other new media technologies have opened up tremendous possibilities for divergent opinions about Islam to be disseminated worldwide, not only in Arabic but in every language. People with educations in engineering, business administration, or nursing who might never dream of disagreeing with a learned sheikh or *da'wa* (religious teacher) in a traditional setting like a mosque or school often have no compunctions about authoritatively presenting their interpretations of Islam in blogs or on websites. The term **Public Islam** is being used to describe these diverse invocations of Islam by "religious scholars, self-ascribed religious authorities, secular intellectuals, Sufi orders, mothers, students, workers, engineers, consumers and many others" in public life (Eickelman and Salvatore 2006).

From Empires to Nation-States

As befits a region of such extraordinary cultural diversity, political relations in the Middle East are complex. For thousands of years, most of the Middle East was composed of communities under more-or-less loose rule by distant authorities. Outside urban centers of power, and to some extent even within them, people went about their lives with only minimal regulation by the state. Employment, marriage, banking, and living arrangements were all largely organized by informal networks of people related by blood, religion, or co-residence.

The creation of nation-states was a process that, in most cases, involved political and economic elites taking over the apparatuses of power previously held by foreign empires. Since the boundaries of the state encompassed diverse peoples with different languages, ethnicities, religious beliefs, and ways of life, it was often difficult for these myriad peoples to see themselves as forming a common nation. Instead, they continued to rely on the same informal networks they had under the empires.

One of the most important of these is tribal structure. It is often as difficult for people from nontribal societies to understand the concept of tribe as it is for oppressed or conquered people to understand patriotic sentiment for one's country. **Tribes** are large groups of people who share a common identity based on an assumption of common ancestry. They are, in a sense, extended families who may number in the tens of thousands. Common membership in a tribe can be the basis for mutual support—someone traveling to a strange city in a foreign country would certainly expect to find help from other members of their tribe who had already settled there. But tribes can also call on their members to make sacrifices for the good of the tribe, just as nations can call on their members to serve their country.

Like patriotic sentiment, people's tribal sentiments wax and wane according to personal experience and current political, social, and economic conditions. Tribal members can rely on help and protection from their tribe in the absence of external law and order. When the Taliban fell in Afghanistan in 2001, many people turned to tribal leaders for economic aid and protection. Tribal leaders moved rapidly into poppy cultivation to maximize their economic gains so they would have money to feed and house people, and to buy weapons to protect them. Likewise in Algeria, when civil society all but collapsed in the 1990s, after the government refused to accept the results of an election that would have put Islamist parties in power, ties of reciprocity and obligation organized in part around tribal identity allowed much of everyday life to continue without the assistance of police, courts, and bureaucratic structures.

Tribal organization can become the basis for state power. The classic example is Saudi Arabia, in which one tribe essentially established hegemony over most of the other tribes of the Arabian peninsula and declared a kingdom. Tribal politics can also cross-cut political organization in both democracies and dictatorships. During the reign of Saddam Hussein in Iraq (1979–2003), the dictator appointed many members of his own tribe to positions of power as a way to maximize the loyalty of those surrounding him. But tribal politics can also play a crucial role in democratization. During the legislative elections in Iraq in 2005, most of the parties were salted with tribal leaders, and many people voted as their tribal leaders recommended. In addition, some tribes had members in several parties simultaneously, ensuring that no matter which parties won, there would be tribal members in positions of power. This should not be seen only as a power grab—tribal organizations can play important roles in any political system. For example, tribal membership is a powerful way to cut across bureaucratic restrictions; the citizen who finds themselves frustrated by government bureaucracy may well be able to get their problems resolved through politicians with whom they have tribal connections.

Because the borders of many states are a colonial legacy, there is often no territorial connection between state boundaries and community tribal and ethnic identities. Sizable minorities exist in many Middle Eastern countries whose primary affiliation is not to the state but to linguistic, religious, ethnic, or tribal fellows who live in other states. These communities can number in the hundreds of thousands or even millions.

In some cases, such as that of the Kurds, these communities are spatially coherent. That is, although the Kurds live as minority communities in Iraq, Turkey, Syria, and Iran, the primary area in which they dwell is the land in which Kurds have lived for centuries. From the popular Kurdish perspective, the contemporary borders of these states arbitrarily cut up the Kurdish homeland. A majority of Kurds in these states support the creation of a new state, Kurdistan, to be carved out of pieces of each of these countries while the states themselves oppose this project.

Communities like the Kurds are often referred to as **proto-states**. Other well-known examples in the Middle East include Armenians and Palestinians. Armenians now have a state, but its borders are not what they were before it was absorbed by the Soviet Union. Armenia lays claim to sizable, mostly Christian Armenian minorities in the neighboring Muslim-majority states of Turkey and Azerbaijan and has occupied nearly one-quarter of Azerbaijan in an effort to reclaim territory Armenians see as part of their historical homeland.

The Palestinian situation is especially complex. When the region of Palestine controlled by Great Britain was divided to create the new state of Israel in 1948, hundreds of thousands of Palestinians fled from the violence of clashes between the Israelis and invading armies from Syria, Egypt, Jordan, Arabia, and Lebanon. Although a Palestinian territorial authority now exists, most of these refugees and their descendants have been refused the right to return by Israel because of fears they would fuel the violent clashes between Israelis and Palestinians that have become part of everyday life in Israel and the Palestinian territories, and fears that an Arab majority in a democratic state would cause Israel to lose its Jewish character. The result is more than 4 million exiles living mostly in the Arab states bordering Israel, whose primary allegiance is to a country many have never seen and that, in fact, no longer exists. Ironically, Israel itself is proof to the Palestinians that lost homelands can be recreated.

The Richest and the Poorest

The global economy currently runs on carbon-based fuels, which is one of the central reasons the Middle East is such an important focus in international affairs. The region possesses more than half the world's oil reserves, and more than 40 percent of the world's natural gas reserves. Problems in the Middle East therefore affect the livelihoods and economic security of billions of people around the world.

But the region's economy is complicated. Economists often divide the states of the Middle East into *production* and *allocation* states. **Production states** derive the bulk of their revenues from the labor of their citizens in agriculture, herding, manufacturing, or trade. A productive state has a centralized bureaucracy to collect taxes and other charges from the citizens. An **allocation state** does not derive its revenues by taxing its citizens but rather by directly selling key resources to the rest of the world (Luciani 1987). Most of the major oil-producing states—Saudi Arabia, Kuwait, Libya, Oman, Qatar, and the United Arab Emirates—are allocation states. Allocation states are often dependent on foreign companies and workers for everything from mining the resources to delivering services to citizens. Allocation states attract labor migration both from within the region and from elsewhere in the world. This is why in countries like Kuwait foreign workers can outnumber citizens.

The region we call the Middle East is marked by extreme economic disparities because of the irregular distribution of resources—both arable land and minerals, including oil. The region includes some states whose GDP per capita puts them among the wealthiest nations in the world. Qatar's mean average GDP per person is $124,000, and Kuwait's is $65,800. But the Middle East also includes some of the world's poorest states, like Yemen ($2,500) and Western Sahara ($2,500). Countries like Egypt ($12,700), Iran ($20,100), and Lebanon ($19,600) belong to the world's middle class. The key factor is oil—Qatar and Kuwait are oil rich, Yemen and Afghanistan have few oil reserves, and Egypt, Iran and Lebanon have mixed economies in which oil and natural gas play a large but not dominant role.

Figures indicating average GDP per capita are misleading; the hypothetical average Iranian does not earn $18,100 per year, nor does a typical resident of Qatar earn $129,700 per year. An average is just that: for every millionaire in Saudi Arabia or Syria, there must be millions of people who earn substantially less than these sums. Although Yemen has approximately 100 billionaires and 20,000 millionaires, the World Bank estimates that 54 percent of the people live in poverty and 39 percent are malnourished. Some 27 percent of the country's population is unemployed. Economic disparities are thus just as great within states as among them.

Economic disparities are exacerbated by massive population growth. For example, Egypt had a total population of about 600,000 at the dawn of the twentieth century, but had some 60 million people by the dawn of the twenty-first century. Egyptian officials estimate that a baby is born within the country's borders every three minutes.

Population growth has been accompanied by a huge upswing in urbanization. One hundred years ago, less than 10 percent of the peoples of the Middle East lived in cities. By 2000, cities accounted for more than 60 percent of the population of the region. There are many reasons for this. In some countries, there is simply insufficient arable land to create work for people living in rural communities. In some allocation states, the agricultural sector of the economy has been allowed to atrophy because of oil revenues. In yet other cases, poor agricultural planning by colonial and national rulers has led to desertification and left thousands of farmers homeless. In each case, unemployed rural peasants have sought a better life by moving to cities. Between 1800 and 2000, Cairo's population rose from about 200,000 to more than 12 million (Figure 11.3). Tehran went from about 10,000 to more than 8 million. Istanbul rose from 300,000 to more than 6 million. Casablanca had only 20,000 people in 1900, and by 2000 its population was approaching 3 million.

Unemployment and underemployment are chronic across the region. As a whole, the Middle East has the highest youth unemployment in the world, and women are twice as likely as men to be unemployed. As a result, poorer Middle Eastern nations have experienced massive labor migration across national borders. The tremendous wealth available in oil-rich countries such as Saudi Arabia, Kuwait, and Qatar attracts millions of workers. From highly trained technicians and managers to unskilled laborers to domestic servants, workers flow from the United States, Europe, India, the Philippines, and elsewhere to oil-rich countries in the Arabian peninsula. In some of these countries, such as Kuwait, foreign workers make up as much as 70 percent of the population. Arab countries are also major exporters of labor, especially Egypt and Yemen, which benefit from the cash remittances sent back into their local economies (Serageldin et al. 1983).

All these problems have been exacerbated by a half century of growing international debt and fiscal mismanagement by governments, local business elites, multinational corporations, and international agencies. In the aftermath of World War II, the United States and its allies in Western Europe, and the USSR and its allies in Eastern Europe, sought to offer economic aid to developing countries in the Middle East and elsewhere, primarily to extend their spheres of influence. Through organizations like the World Bank and the International Monetary Fund, huge loans were arranged to assist countries in developing their economic infrastructures. Often these projects failed to achieve their projected outcomes, producing low returns on investments

Figure 11.3 Under constant population pressure, cities like Cairo continue to grow even at the expense of valuable farmland.

Source: Mark Allen Peterson.

so that the recipient countries found themselves unable to pay back the loans. Additional loans, including loans to pay the interest on previous loans, led to ever-higher levels of debt. So-called **structural adjustment programs** (SAPs) imposed on recipient countries to make them abandon nonmarket practices like food subsidies often led to riots and increasingly desperate living conditions among the poor.

International investment has also sometimes contributed to economic problems. Multinational corporations have naturally preferred to partner with local elites, people who have capital to invest and knowledge of how to work with local bureaucracies. These Middle Eastern elites in return have often preferred to put their shares of profits into reliable American, Asian, or European investments, leading to **capital flight**—the tendency for wealth to leave poor countries rather than trickle down from the wealthy to the middle classes. Although foreign investments bring jobs to local economies, they are often unskilled, low-paying jobs, and foreigners are often brought in to serve as management. And they can have unforeseen consequences: in the five years leading up to the Iranian Revolution, inflation caused by foreign corporate investment caused rental prices to double every year (Beeman 2004). Allocation states are less affected by many of these problems, but they face potential dramatic economic shifts as oil and natural gas prices rise and fall.

There are many explanations offered for the failure of development strategies in the Middle East. Some have argued that the centralized, bureaucratically controlled economies of most

Middle Eastern states make it difficult for them to participate in organizations like the World Trade Organization because these institutions assume European and North American open-market philosophies. Others blame the region's colonial heritage. They argue that borders were established for administrative purposes rather than designed for national viability and that colonial economic structures were designed to extract wealth, not to nurture its growth. These legacies left a crippling burden on emergent nations as they won their freedom. Still, others have argued that the theory of development—the idea that wealthy countries can assist poor countries in becoming productive—is itself flawed. Interestingly, such critiques come from both the political left and the right. The former argues that it is simply impossible for wealthy countries to offer economic assistance to poorer countries on a for-profit or even a break-even basis since more often than not aid recipients just end up further in debt. The latter argues that the problem lies in the centralized nature of many development projects, but if bolstered by the world market, international investment, and microloans to encourage entrepreneurship, foundering Middle Eastern economies can still transform themselves.

At the dawn of the twenty-first century, all of the countries of the Middle East and North Africa face similar challenges: rapid population growth, unequal distribution of resources, economic distortions caused by the enormous flow of oil revenues into the region, international debt, poor economic management by a relatively small elite, conflicts between community identities and nation building, and often unwelcome political attention from powerful states outside the region. People survive these conditions as best they can, often relying on informal social and economic networks to get by. Such informal economies can include everything from barter to street vending to private loans to smuggling and black market activities. The International Labor Organization has estimated that the informal economies in Algeria, Morocco, Tunisia, and Egypt may exceed 4 percent of these countries' total economic activity (ILO 2002). But while they may help many people get by, informal economic activities do little to solve larger economic issues and often exacerbate them. Most people are desperate for more permanent solutions to these problems.

The Problem of Palestine

One of the most significant international issues in the Middle East is the establishment of the state of Israel in the former British colony of Palestine, and the turmoil that resulted from the wars and refugee crises that followed. The roots of this issue lie in the rise of secularism and nationalism in Europe during the seventeenth and eighteenth centuries, which transformed the ways many Jews conceived of themselves as a people. Traditionally, Jewish identity had been rooted in pre-Christian Rome's expulsion of thousands of Jews from the province of Palestine in 136 CE, following a revolt against imperial domination. The subsequent travels of these Jews and their descendants into Europe, North Africa, South and West Asia, and elsewhere is called the Jewish *diaspora*, a term used to describe transnational communities of peoples who maintain a distinct identity inside the host communities in which they settle, usually through a sense of connection to a common homeland, often one that most members of the community have never seen (Sheffer 1986).

Although Jewish communities around the world developed disparate identities and cultures, even evolving new languages like Yiddish and Ladino, their common commitment to their lost homeland was deeply embedded in shared religious doctrines and ritual practices. Jews were met with different receptions in different places and times, but Jewish communities in Europe mostly experienced prejudice and oppression. Beginning with England in 1290, many states expelled Jews from their borders from time to time. Jews who had grown wealthy under the tolerant rule of the Fatimids in Spain and Portugal found themselves forced to convert to Christianity or face losing their property after the peninsula was reconquered by Christian rulers. In other states walled communities called *ghettos* were established to seal Jews off from the larger community. Traditional religious teaching had it that someday a Messiah would come who would re-establish a Jewish kingdom centered in Jerusalem. Until then, the homeland was remembered in prayer and ritual, for example on Yom Kippur and Passover, with the traditional hopeful toast, "next year in Jerusalem."

European **nationalism**, with its ideal of the nation-state, strongly affected the ways many Jews in Europe conceived of their collective identity. Jewish intellectuals like Leo Pinsker, Moses Hess, and Theodore Herzl began to describe Jews as a nation, a distinct people united by some common origin and character. The belief that Jews constitute a sovereign people and nation and that they should have the right to establish and maintain a state in their ancestral home-land became known as **Zionism**. Zionist clubs and study groups sprang up across Europe in the 1870s and 1880s, and adventurous Jews were inspired to travel to Palestine, then a province of the Ottoman Empire, and settle there (Avineri 1981). A series of pogroms and waves of anti-Semitism in Russia and Eastern Europe between 1882 and 1914 induced another 75,000 Jews to emigrate to Palestine. A central concept of Zionism was *aliyah* (ascent), which refers to both voluntary immigration and the flight of persecuted populations of Jews to Palestine. Nonetheless, by the outbreak of World War I, only about 7 percent of Palestine's population was Jewish, smaller than its Christian Arab population and much smaller than its Muslim Arab population (Shlaim 2001).

In 1917, Great Britain, in order to obtain war loan guarantees from several Jewish banks, issued the Balfour Declaration. This was a letter from the British secretary of state to Lord Rothschild that stated that if Britain won the war and took control of Palestine from the Ottomans, the government would

> view with favour the establishment in Palestine of a national home for the Jewish people, and will use their best endeavours to facilitate the achievement of this object, it being clearly understood that nothing shall be done which may prejudice the civil and religious rights of existing non-Jewish communities in Palestine, or the rights and political status enjoyed by Jews in any other country.
>
> (Balfour, 1917)

After several initial defeats, British forces captured Palestine in December 1918, and in 1920 the newly formed League of Nations passed the British Mandate for Palestine, which gave England direct administration of the region.

More than 150,000 Jews, mostly from Russia and Eastern Europe, emigrated to Palestine over the next 17 years, sparking anti-immigrant riots in 1929 and again in 1933–1936 (Sherman 2001). Great Britain restricted immigration in response, but Jews continued to come illegally in the tens of thousands to flee the rise of Nazism in Germany. Increasingly violent Arab hostility and Jewish anger at Britain's refusal to enforce the Balfour Declaration in the way many settlers interpreted it, led to the formation of Jewish terrorist organizations like Irgun Tzvei Leumi, and the Stern Gang (Vest 2001). After World War II, European survivors of the Holocaust swelled the numbers of illegal immigrants to Palestine, and Britain established internment camps to hold those they captured while they considered where to send them.

The international community grew increasingly dissatisfied with Britain's handling of its mandate. On November 29, 1947, the United Nations voted 33 to 13 to partition Palestine into two states, one predominantly Jewish and one predominantly Muslim, in the land that had been Palestine. In order to ensure that all the Jewish majority settlements would be in Israel, a UN commission had recommended a patchwork partitioning of the country into seven interlocked sections, three controlled by Jews, three by Muslim Arabs, and one (which included Jerusalem and Bethlehem) by the United Nations. On May 14, 1948, the day set for the British mandate to expire, Israel declared its existence and independence. The following day, military forces from Egypt, Syria, Lebanon, Transjordan, and Iraq attacked the new state. In the face of this external threat, internal divisions within the Israeli independence movement vanished. Arab forces, on the other hand, were hampered by just the opposite problem: states failed to commit promised troop levels, and troops resisted following orders from commanders of other Arab states. Israel defeated the Arab armies, and an armistice was signed in 1949 (Goldschmidt and Davidson 2005). Almost simultaneously, Jordan seized a large tract of land west of the Jordan River reaching to East Jerusalem, which became known as the West Bank territory.

The establishment of the state of Israel is known to Palestinian Arabs as the *nakba*, or catastrophe, because it left the majority of them without a homeland. During the war, more than half a million Palestinian Arabs—Muslim and Christian—fled Palestine for neighboring Arab countries. Others were expelled from their homes in the early days of independence. In 1948, there were approximately 150,000 Arab Israelis, 400,000 Arabs who had become "Jordanians" through the seizure of the West Bank, and some 550,000 to 800,000 refugees. Israel refused to allow the refugees to return, claiming that they had fled under orders from the Arab high command and so abandoned any claim to Israeli citizenship. Arab countries responded by expelling Jews from their own countries. These Jews were welcomed by Israel, and today only a few Jewish communities exist in most other Middle Eastern states.

In 1956, members of this refugee community formed the Palestinian Liberation Organization (PLO), to fight for the re-establishment of a Palestinian homeland. A second organization, al-Fatah, organized along Marxist principles, was founded in 1965. Four years later they merged, and Yasir Arafat became head of the PLO. Lacking an organized, well-funded military, the PLO relied primarily on guerrilla strategies, including terrorist strategies targeting civilians. In 1972, the PLO grabbed international headlines when it killed 11 Israeli Olympic athletes in Munich, Germany, after negotiations for the return of captured PLO leaders failed. In addition to dealing with terrorist attacks by the PLO and similar groups, the state of Israel fought two more wars with its Arab neighbors: the 1967 Six-Day War, which established Israel as the pre-eminent military power in the region, and the 1973 Yom Kippur War, which had international consequences. It was settled at a peace conference in Geneva and was followed by UN recognition of the PLO as a legitimate political agency for the Palestinian diaspora. In 1979, following a visit by Egypt's president Anwar Sadat to Israel's Knesset (parliament), US president Jimmy Carter organized the historic Camp David Accord between Egypt and Israel, the first treaty to conclude with an acknowledgment of Israel's existence by an Arab state.

In fulfillment of these treaty obligations, Israel in 1982 returned lands to Egypt that it had captured in the 1967 war, most prominently the Sinai Peninsula. That same year, Israel invaded Lebanon to put an end to terrorist organizations operating out of refugee camps and to chase Arafat and the PLO out of Beirut. The occupation lasted 18 years, maintaining Israel's position as the undisputed military power in the region. However, the occupation not only failed to meet its objective of stamping out terrorists, it also produced a new anti-Israeli terrorist organization, Hezbollah, comprised primarily of Lebanese Shiites committed to resisting Israel's occupation of Lebanon. In 1987, Palestinians declared the First Intifada (resistance) against Israel. All celebrations ceased—people still married, but no parties were held. Resistance, both passive and militant, increased dramatically. The following year, the PLO said it would agree to a two-state solution—the formation of an independent Palestinian state coexisting with Israel. This has been the basis for all subsequent peace negotiations, including the ambitious Oslo Accords signed in 1993. In 1994, a government—the Palestinian Authority—was established for the Palestinian state, which did not yet exist and whose boundaries were not yet agreed upon.

Peace has proven elusive. On the Israeli side, continued construction of Israeli settlements on what was, under the treaty, supposed to become Palestinian land, led most Palestinians to doubt Israel's sincerity. Targeted assassinations of Palestinian leaders accused of terrorism, the deaths of large numbers of Palestinian noncombatants, and the refusal of Israel to consider the rights of refugees to return to their former homes or receive compensation for their losses, exacerbated tensions. On the Palestinian side, the inability of the Palestinian Authority to represent all Palestinian factions, demonstrated particularly by its incapacity to enforce cease-fire agreements or to control terrorist groups, made any negotiations unreliable at best.

In 2000, the visit of Israeli prime minister Ariel Sharon to the Dome of the Rock in Jerusalem surrounded by hundreds of police sparked riots that turned into the Second Intifada, or "uprising," a period of extended violence and noncooperation. Palestinian anger was exacerbated by Sharon's subsequent decision to build a wall separating the two states. The wall did not follow the established border, and many Palestinians saw it as a further effort by Israel to expropriate Arab land (Figure 11.4).

In 2006, the militant anti-Israeli organization Hamas was elected to lead the Palestinian Authority. The rival Fatah organization assumed power in the West Bank, and Hamas-controlled Gaza was subjected to an economic blockade that led to the suspension of an estimated 95 percent of Gaza's factories and created more than 40 percent unemployment (Oxfam 2010), which continues to this day. The Palestinian Authority remains split and thus ineffective at representing

Figure 11.4 The wall built by Israel to separate itself from the Palestinian territories—and seen by many Arabs as an effort to grab additional Palestinian land—stands as a monument to the intractable problems of just and peaceful coexistence.

Source: Brad Bailey.

the Palestinian cause as a whole, although Egypt brokered a fragile cooperation agreement in 2011. Efforts to move forward on peace talks were renewed in 2008, 2010, and 2013, but quickly foundered each time.

The Israeli–Palestinian conflict is of particular concern to the international community because Israel possesses nuclear weapons. Given the intense political, social and ideological tensions between Israel and neighboring states, Israel, the United States and European powers have intervened in the region many times to try to ensure that other Middle Eastern states do not acquire nuclear capabilities. These countries are concerned not only that the Israeli–Palestinian conflict would become a potential nuclear flashpoint, but that nuclear weapons could fall into the hands of Islamic terrorists.

Authoritarianism, Terrorism, and Political Turmoil in the Middle East

Since the collapse of European colonialism after the Second World War, the Middle East has been dominated by authoritarian regimes and security states. Some of these are patriarchal monarchies rooted in tribal politics, as in Saudi Arabia, Morocco, Qatar, and the UAE. In fact, the Middle East is home to eight of the world's ten remaining absolute monarchies. Others emerged from military coups and revolutions, such as Egypt and Syria, where regimes use the military and repressive security service to maintain control. In Iran, religious leaders control the country by supervising elections, vetoing laws approved by the parliament, and appointing high court judges. Although several countries hold elections, these elections are carefully orchestrated. For example, in Egypt's 2018 presidential election, the incumbent General Abdel Fatah al-Sisi imprisoned, intimidated, or banned every legitimate political opponent from running against him.

Authoritarianism has always produced opposition. The most significant recent anti-authoritarian movement in the Middle East took place in 2010–2011 when people in countries across the Middle East gathered in public places to demand political change. The news media named it the **Arab Spring** (although not all those taking part in the protests identify as Arabs). Popular, peaceful, and persistent in the face of violent reprisals by the government and pro-government counterdemonstrators, these uprisings shared both common techniques of civil resistance (demonstrations, marches, rallies, strikes) and the use of social media to communicate among protesters and with the outside world, circumventing attempts at censorship by the state.

The Arab Spring was the culmination of years of strikes, demonstrations, and other protest movements. These protests were driven in part by economic concerns such as rising poverty, inflation, and failing infrastructure (especially schools and public hospitals). These issues were exacerbated by a sense of helplessness in the face of autocratic governments, often supported by Western powers. Protesters complained of endemic corruption, rigged elections, and censorship of the media; they criticized police brutality, and "Emergency Laws" that rendered the police safe from reprisals.

Initially, these protests seemed to provoke real change. Tunisian president Zine El Abidine Ben Ali fled. In Egypt, President Hosni Mubarak resigned after 18 days of protests, ending a 30-year reign (Figure 11.5). Jordan, Kuwait, Lebanon, Morocco, and Oman quelled major protests by promising to implement political and economic reforms. But ten years later, none of these countries has seen any significant democratic change. New regimes replaced the old in Egypt and Tunisia; and in Libya, Syria, and Yemen, government troops met protesters with force, ultimately spiraling into civil wars.

The Syrian Civil War emerged as the most urgent international crisis in the region. Beginning as a series of peaceful protests against the regime of President Bashar al-Assad, the conflict

Figure 11.5 Protests in Egypt, inspired by an uprising in Tunisia, brought down a dictator and inspired other protests throughout the region.

Source: Malak Rouchdy.

turned into a civil war when protest groups began fighting back against military forces sent to suppress them. The al-Assad regime is a Shiite elite governing a Sunni majority and has military backing from Iran and Russia, as well as support from international insurgent organizations like Hezbollah, and many independent Shiite militias.

As the military opposition to the regime organized itself, it fractured along ideological and ethnic lines, supported by different external states, including Saudi Arabia, Qatar, Turkey, and the United States and some of its European allies. There are also multiple Sunni Islamic groups tied to al Qaeda and the Muslim Brotherhood. The Islamic State of Iraq and Lebanon (ISIL), dedicated to carving out a new **caliphate** in the region, has emerged as a powerful force not only in the Middle East but beyond, supporting and inspiring terrorist acts in the countries that back its opponents. There is also an alliance of ethnic Arab, Assyrian, Armenian, Kurdish, and Turkmen militias fighting as the Syrian Democratic Forces (SDF). Initially formed to overthrow the Assad regime and replace it with a democratic and federalist Syria, they directed most of their efforts against the Al-Nusra Front and ISIL.

By 2020 the Assad regime—with support from Iran, Russia, and the Lebanese militant group Hezbollah—had largely defeated its oppositions, but this has not increased stability in the region. More than half a million people died in the conflict. About 6.3 million people— nearly half the population—had been internally displaced, and more than 4.8 million had fled the country as refugees, mostly dispersed in Egypt, Iraq, Jordan, Lebanon, and Turkey. These displaced people are extremely vulnerable to forced labor and human sex trafficking. Moreover, the sheer numbers have created huge logistical, cultural and social problems for the countries that received them, both elsewhere in the Middle East and in Europe, and in some cases have changed the political landscapes of receiving countries by giving boosts to political parties that promise to reduce or ban refugees from the country.

But perhaps the most dangerous consequence of the Syrian civil war has been the proliferation of terrorism. Two militant Sunni fundamentalist groups—al Qaeda and the Islamic State in Syria and Iraq (ISIL)— capitalized on the instability created by the war, using extreme violence to implement their particular interpretations of Islam. At its peak in 2014, the Islamic State controlled territory across Iraq and Syria larger than the size of Great Britain. While the Islamic State has been all but eliminated as a territory-holding entity, it continues to carry out insurgent attacks in these two countries, as well as in Afghanistan, Egypt, Libya, and elsewhere around the world. Together, the Islamic State and al Qaeda have killed more than 36,000 people in the Middle East since 2002, accounting for more than 70 percent of all terrorist deaths from known groups in the region. Terrorism kills more people in the Middle East than anywhere else in the world. Eighty-three percent of the region's fatalities occurred in Iraq and Syria.

Terrorism is not new to the Middle East. It has its roots in social movements against ruling regimes dating back to the colonial era. Most European colonial powers were democracies at home but imperialists in their colonies. Resistance to this imperialism led to the emergence of many insurgent groups throughout the late nineteenth and early twentieth centuries. The most wide-ranging terrorist movement was that of the anarchists, a global network of mostly European intellectuals and militants organized into independent cells and committed to a common utopian political vision—not unlike the emergence of independent European and North American terrorists who claim inspiration from ISIL and al Qaeda (Bergesen and Han 2005). Early uses of terrorism in the Middle East developed during the late colonial era, between and after the world wars (Vest 2001), when organizations like the Muslim Brotherhood sought to reform political systems dominated by foreign powers. This organization began as an effort to meet civil society needs—such as clinics, schools, loan programs, and employment opportunities for rural migrants—that were not taken care of by the British-controlled Egyptian government. Their criticisms of the government's failures to take care of the Egyptian people led to the establishment of a political arm, and the government's periodic crackdowns on the society led to the creation of a militant arm. The outlawing of the organization was a direct result of the militant arm's role in the 1981 assassination of Egyptian president Anwar Sadat.

After World War II, inspiration for insurgent and revolutionary movements in the Middle East was drawn primarily from Marxist ideologies, in solidarity with similar groups throughout the world, drawing inspiration from Soviet models of revolution and employing terrorism as a tool. **Terrorism** is a strategy by which subnational groups, not recognized as legitimate by the states they oppose, seek to resist those states by targeting non-state actors, disrupting the flow of everyday life, and spreading generalized fear among the populations of those states. As an act of political communication, terrorism can be extremely effective. As Eqbal Ahmed points out, in 1970 Golda Meier could say "there are no Palestinians" because they had no state and Israel refused to recognize them as a people or a nation. By the 1980s, everyone acknowledged that the Palestinians existed, even if only as a "problem" (Ahmed 2001).

However, terrorism proved ineffective at achieving specific political goals. Such high-profile crimes as the murder of the Israeli Olympic athletes in 1972, the 1975 OPEC hostage taking, and the hijacking of the *Achille Lauro* in 1985 did little to advance the specific political goals of these organizations.

Instead, the first successful overthrow of a Western-backed regime was masterminded by Islamic clerics and their followers. The success of the Iranian Revolution in 1979 led to the rise of Islamic political movements. From the viewpoint of those seeking political change in the Middle East, Iran was a watershed—a relatively bloodless coup that toppled a dictatorship and put an elected parliament in place within months of the revolution. It seized US diplomats and successfully traded them after more than a year for arms with which to fight against invasion by another Western-backed dictatorship, that of Iraq. Iran inspired the rise of "political Islam."

Political Islam refers to the invocation of Islam in contemporary political and economic life, both by political actors within states and by groups opposed to existing governments. In most parts of the Middle East, this represents a new trend that has been growing since the early 1980s. For the most part, it represents a disillusionment with the secularization that has marked most Middle Eastern political economies since the end of World War II. The failure of Western economic models—socialist or capitalist—to bring about the prosperity once promised and the lack of democratization by governments who enjoy the support of the United States and European nations have led to doubts, disappointments, and anger. In the face of what many regard as a complete failure of Westernization in the region, the politicization of Islam promises new models and offers many Muslims new hope for the future. The success of Islamic parties in elections in Turkey, Tunisia, and Egypt, reflects popular support for political Islam, although the subsequent popular protests and removal of the Islamist president in Egypt demonstrate ongoing concerns about balancing religious reform with national interests.

Although political Islam is a relatively recent phenomenon, its roots can be traced back at least to the nineteenth century, to thinkers like Jama al-Afghani and Sayyid Qutb, and to groups like the Muslim Brotherhood in Egypt. Shortsighted policies by the international community have also contributed to the creation of Islamist groups. For example, the United States strongly encouraged political Islam in Afghanistan and provided strong support for the Afghans fighting a military jihad against Soviet invaders in the 1980s. Under Presidents Carter and Reagan, the United States spent over $5 billion to arm, supply, and train Afghan freedom fighters—including many of those who went on to create al Qaeda. But when the Soviets finally withdrew in 1989, the United States effectively abandoned its Afghan allies, leaving them with a collapsed economy, the second highest saturation of land mines in the world, and the highest percentage of weapons per person in the world. Power was seized by the only two groups that still had international connections—the Taliban, with ties to Pakistan, and al Qaeda, with its international financial networks. Afghanistan quickly became a training ground for terrorists. The September 11 terrorist attacks in New York were examples of what some political scientists call "blowback"—situations in which foreign policies and interventions that seem like good ideas at the time have unforeseen consequences years later.

Muslim militants often invoke the concept of *jihad*, which has come to mean "holy war" in many international contexts and especially in international news media. For Muslims, though, jihad is a much more complex concept. The term means "struggle," and Islamic scholars have long distinguished between the greater jihad of one's personal struggle to submit to God's will in the face of worldly temptations, and the lesser jihad of militant struggle against injustice—including, but not limited to, just war.

Because war is a public undertaking fraught with possibilities for abuse, theologians have devoted far more attention to working out the rules for the lesser jihad that many terrorists claim defines their actions. Most mainstream Muslim theologians of all schools denounced the September 11 attacks. "The killing of innocent men, women and children is a horrible and hideous act against all religion and against rational thinking," pronounced Sheikh Mohammed Sayyid Tantawi, grand imam of Cairo's Al-Azhar University, the world's foremost center of Islamic learning. His *fatwa* is based on traditional interpretations that limit the use of violent force to soldiers and political officials. But Tantawi, like most Muslim clerics, does not denounce Palestinian terrorism, since the right to use violence against occupiers is well testified to in Islamic jurisprudence, and the right of Israel to exist as an exclusively Jewish state on what was once Palestinian Arab land is not recognized by most theologians.

In spite of this clerical rejection of their actions, the messages the September 11 attackers left behind show that many of them saw themselves as true believers. They quoted verses from the Quran and vowed to overcome their fears of death by saying prayers and calling on God's name right to the end. Al Qaeda's justification of jihad against civilians is particularly modern since it derives from taking democracy seriously. In essence, the argument is that in a democracy, citizens govern themselves and therefore all citizens are political actors and hence subject to violent reprisals for the acts of their government. This point of view has been embraced by some other terrorist groups, such as Islamic Jihad, but rejected by many, including Hamas. The US invasion of Iraq increased sympathy for such anti-Western interpretations of jihad throughout the Islamic world. On the other hand, the callous disregard for the lives not only of collaborators but innocent bystanders in Iraq has sparked debates even within al Qaeda, IS, and other militant groups over the proper limits of military jihad.

Middle East Prospects

Located at the intersection of three continents, the Middle East remains today, as in the past, an international center of economic activity, social transformation, religious revitalization, and political struggle. The protests, insurgencies, and civil wars in the region arise from efforts by its peoples to continue to seek good governance, productive economies, and the right to live according to their own cultural systems and traditions. As always, the devil is in the details. What kinds of democracies are appropriate for these diverse peoples? How can economies become productive in the face of burdensome international debts and global market pressures? How are conflicting international alliances, political rivalries, and power struggles to be managed? Which traditions will have force of law, and how will multiple traditions coexist within states? The coming decades will see the peoples and states of this region struggle for answers, with global ramifications. A interdisciplinary lens offers our best opportunity to understand events as these struggles play out.

Timeline of Modern Middle Eastern History

1914	World War I breaks out; the Ottoman Empire enters the war on the side of Germany.
1917	Britain issues the Balfour Declaration.
1918	British forces capture Palestine.
1920	League of Nations issues British Mandate for Palestine.
1922	Mustafa Kemal Ataturk establishes an independent Turkey and abolishes the Sultanate.
1925	Reza Shah establishes the Pahlavi dynasty in Iran.
1926	Ibn Saud proclaims himself King of the Hijaz and, in 1932, proclaims the Kingdom of Saudi Arabia.
1932	Independence of Iraq.
1947	United Nations appoints the Special Commission on Palestine (UNSCOP) to deal with the fate of Palestine; UN votes for partition.
1948	Establishment of Israel; first Arab–Israeli war between Israel and its neighbors.
1953	Egypt establishes a republic.
1956	President Nasser of Egypt nationalizes the Suez Canal; Sudan, Morocco, and Tunisia become independent; Palestinian Liberation Organization formed.

1958	Iraq becomes a republic.
1962	Algeria becomes independent from France.
1965	Fatah formed.
1967	Second Arab–Israeli war (Six-Day War), between Egypt and Israel.
1971	Formation of the Union of Arab Emirates.
1973	Yom Kippur War (or October War), Israel against Syria and Egypt.
1975	Lebanese civil war begins.
1979	Iran expels the shah and declares itself an Islamic Republic; Egyptian president Anwar Sadat visits Israel; Egypt and Israel sign the Camp David Accords; Saddam Hussein seizes control of Iraq; Soviet forces invade Afghanistan.
1980–1988	Iran–Iraq War.
1982	Israel invades Lebanon; Israel will occupy southern Lebanon until 2000.
1987	First Intifada ("resistance") declared by Palestinians against Israel.
1989	Soviet troops withdraw from Afghanistan.
1990–1991	Iraq invades Kuwait, sparking the first Gulf War.
1992–2002	Algerian Civil War.
1994	Palestinian Authority established.
2000	Second Intifada (or Al-Aqsa Intifada) against Israel.
2001	Al-Qaeda terrorists attack New York City; United States and allies invade Afghanistan.
2003	United States and allies invade Iraq.
2005	Elections held in US-occupied Iraq.
2006	Israeli–Hezbollah conflict in southern Syria; Saddam Hussein executed; Hamas wins Palestinian national elections and takes control of Gaza; Israel establishes economic blockade of Gaza.
2009	Large-scale protests in Iran over alleged election fraud.
2010	Israeli commandos attack a flotilla of "freedom activists" seeking to break the Gaza embargo; nine protesters are killed and ten commandos wounded.
2010–2012	The "Arab Spring" popular revolutions in Tunisia, Egypt, Libya, Yemen, Syria, and elsewhere in the region.
2013	Syrian Civil War begins.
2014	Iraqi, Libyan, and Yemeni civil wars begin; Islamic State arises in Iraq and Syria.
2015	China, France, Germany, Russia, US, and UK sign nuclear agreement with Iran.

References

Ahmed, Eqbal. 2001. *Terrorism: Theirs and Ours*. New York: Seven Stories Press.

Avineri, Shlomo. 1981. *The Making of Modern Zionism*. New York: Basic Books.

Balfour, Arthur. 1917. The Balfour Declaration [Letter to Lord Rothschild]. WWI D.A., Official Papers.

Beeman, William O. 2004. *The "Great Satan" vs. the "Mad Mullahs": How the United States and Iran Demonize Each Other*. Westport, CT: Praeger.

Bergesen, Albert J., and Yi Han. 2005. "New Directions for Terrorism Research." *International Journal of Comparative Sociology* 46 (1–2): 133–51.

Dawisha, Adeed. 2005. *Arab Nationalism in the Twentieth Century: From Triumph to Despair*. Princeton, NJ: Princeton University Press.

Eickelman, Dale F., and Armando Salvatore. 2006. "Public Islam and the Common Good." *Etnográfica* 10 (1): 97–105.

Goldschmidt, Arthur Jr., and Lawrence Davidson. 2005. *A Concise History of the Middle East*. Boulder, CO: Westview Press.

Hitchens, Christopher. 2001. "Broadcasts." In *Blaming the Victims: Spurious Scholarship and the Palestinian Question*, edited by Edward Said and Christopher Hitchens, 73–84. London: Verso.

ILO (International Labour Organization). 2002. "*Men and Women in the Informal Economy: A Statistical Picture*." Geneva: International Labour Office. www.ilo.org/stat/Publications/WCMS_234413/lang--en/index.htm?ssSourceSiteId=addisababa

Luciani, Giacomo. 1987. "Allocation vs. Production States: A Theoretical Framework." In *The Rentier State*, edited by Hazem Beblawi and Giacomo Luciani. New York: Croom Helm.

Moubayed, Sami. 2005. "The Waxing of the Shi'ite Crescent." asiatimes.com, April 20.

Nasr, Vali. 2006. "When the Shiites Rise." *Foreign Affairs*, July/August. www.foreignaffairs.com/articles/iran/2006-07-01/when-shiites-rise

Oxfam. 2010. *The Gaza Strip: A Humanitarian Explosion*. Oxford, UK: Oxfam International.

Palfreyman, David, and Muhamed al-Khalil. 2003. "'A Funky Language for Teenzz to Use': Representing Gulf Arabic in Instant Messaging." *Journal of Computer Mediated Communication* 9 (1). doi:10.1111/j.1083-6101.2003.tb00355.x

Said, Edward W. 1979. *Orientalism*. New York: Vintage.

———. 1997. *Covering Islam: How the Media and the Experts Determine How We See the Rest of the World*. Rev. ed. New York: Vintage.

Scheffler, Thomas. 2003. "'Fertile Crescent,' 'Orient,' 'Middle East': The Changing Mental Maps of Southwest Asia." *European Review of History* 10 (2): 253–72.

Serageldin, Ismail, James A. Socknat, Stace Birks, Bob Li, and Clive A. Sinclair. 1983. *Manpower and International Labor Migration in the Middle East and North Africa*. New York: Oxford University Press.

Sheffer, Gabriel, ed. 1986. *Modern Diasporas in International Politics*. London: Croom Helm.

Sherman, A. J. 2001. *Mandate Days: British Lives in Palestine 1918–1948*. Baltimore: Johns Hopkins University Press.

Shlaim, Avi. 2001. *The Iron Wall: Israel and the Arab World*. New York: Norton.

Theodoulou, Michael. 1998. "Jews in Iran Describe a Life of Freedom Despite Anti-Israel Actions by Tehran." *Christian Science Monitor*, February 3. www.csmonitor.com/1998/0203/020398.intl.intl.3.html

Vest, Jason. 2001. "Oy McVey: From the Irv Rubin Bust to the Stern Gang: The Rich History of Jewish Terrorism." *Village Voice*, December 19–21.

Yaar, Ephraim, and Tamar S. Hermann. 2007. *The Peace Index, November 2007*. The Peace Index Project. www.peaceindex.org/files/peaceindex2007_9_3.pdf.

Further Reading

Books

Ahmed, Eqbal. 2001. *Terrorism: Theirs and Ours*. New York: Seven Stories Press.

Bowen, Donna Lee, and Evelyn A. Early, eds. 2002. *Everyday Life in the Muslim Middle East*. 2nd ed. Bloomington: Indiana University Press.

Fernea, Elizabeth. 2002. "The Veiled Revolution." In *Everyday Life in the Muslim Middle East*, edited by Donna Lee Bowen and Evelyn A. Early. Bloomington: Indiana University Press.

Ghannam, Farha. 2002. *Remaking the Modern: Space, Relocation, and the Politics of Identity in a Global Cairo*. Berkeley: University of California Press.

Halliday, Fred. 2002. *Two Hours that Shook the World: September 11, 2001: Causes and Consequences*. London: Saqi Books.

Mamdani, Mahmood. 2004. *Good Muslim, Bad Muslim*. New York: Pantheon.

Mernissi, Fatima. 2001. *Scheherazade Goes West: Different Harems, Different Customs*. New York: Washington Square Press.

Peterson, Mark Allen. 2011. *Connected in Cairo: Growing Up Cosmopolitan in the Modern Middle East*. Bloomington: Indiana University Press.
Telhami, Shibley. 2002. *The Stakes: America and the Middle East*. Boulder, CO: Westview Press.

Journals

International Journal of Middle East Studies. www.cambridge.org/core/journals/international-journal-of-middle-east-studies
Middle East Journal. www.mei.edu/middle-east-journal
Middle Eastern Studies. www.tandfonline.com/loi/fmes20
Middle East Report. www.merip.org/mer

Films

Battle of Algiers (1966). Gillo Pontecorvo, director.
Control Room (2004). Jehane Noujame, director.
The English Sheik and the Yemeni Gentleman (2000). Bader Ben Hirsi, director.
The Message: The Story of Islam (1976). Moustapha Akkad, director.
The Return to Homs (2013). Talal Derki, director.

Websites

Al-Jazeera (English edition). www.aljazeera.com
Arab Media & Society. www.arabmediasociety.com
Global Connections: The Middle East. www.pbs.org/wgbh/globalconnections/mideast/index.html
Middle East Research and Information Project. merip.org
Tabsir: Insight on Islam and the Middle East. www.tabsir.net

Chapter 12

Latin America and International Studies

What countries constitute the region of Latin America leads to a debate among those who study and teach about these countries. Are the countries of the Caribbean, for example, part of a different region than Mexico, Central America, and South America? The name Latin America has only been used to describe some countries in the Western Hemisphere since the mid-1800s. As part of an effort to legitimize its presence in the region, the French coined the phrase to refer to people in the Americas who spoke a Latin-based language. That would suggest that France had an affinity with Spanish and Portuguese speakers, while the United States, Britain, and others using Germanic languages were not natural partners of Latin America. That meant Haiti, Brazil, and Bolivia should be linked and studied together, and Mexico should be seen as part of Latin America and not North America, its continental placement. In this book, we go along with the placement of Mexico in Latin America, rather than with those in its continental location, and we also include the English-speaking countries in the Caribbean and Belize in Central America as part of an expanded region of Latin America.

The argument that all of the countries in the Western Hemisphere south of the US–Mexico border constitute a region for area studies is certainly reasonable. While the colonialisms vary, the experience of European control for three or more centuries had a lasting impact on the politics, economies, and societies in the region. After independence, the countries of Latin America gradually moved into varying degrees of subordinate roles to the Western Hemispheric hegemon, the United States. As part of the global south that experienced European colonialism before a transition to the US sphere of influence, the countries of Latin America would seem to have enough in common geographically and historically to be worthy of being a single area of study.

Others might want to emphasize the differences across the region. With more than 200 million people, is Brazil's experience in any way comparable to that of the English or Dutch-speaking micro states in the Caribbean? Does the 1804 independence for Haiti from France after a successful slave rebellion put the country in a comparable position to Jamaica, whose independence from the United Kingdom didn't come about until 1962? The region includes countries with majority European ethnicity, others that still have majority indigenous populations, and countries with large Afro populations, including Brazil with the second largest African-origin population in the world after Nigeria.

Among the differences are those of geography. Spatially, we might distinguish among the islands of the Caribbean, the region of Mexico and Central America, and South America. South America begins at the point where Panama ends and Colombia begins on the map, and there is a range of physical geography across the continent. Many will associate the area with the tropical climate of countries near the equator, which runs across Northern Brazil, Colombia, and Ecuador (the Spanish word for equator). That climate proved compatible with the production of a range of agricultural products that could not be grown as well in Europe or most of the United States (see Maps 12.1 and 12.2).

DOI: 10.4324/9781003028314-15

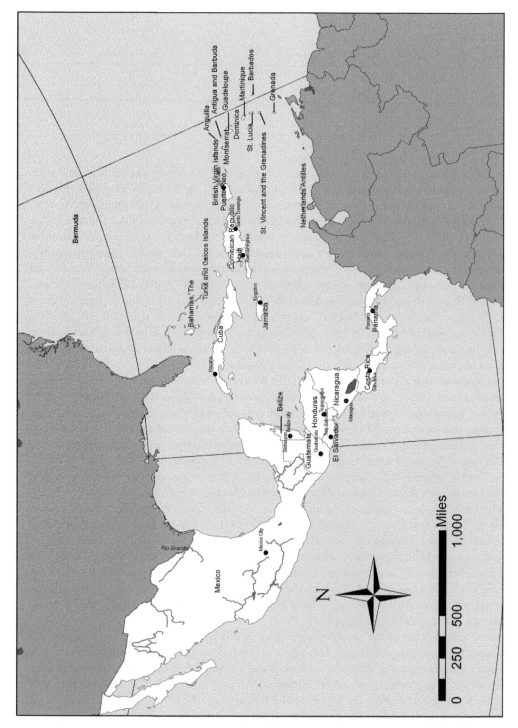

Map 12.1 Central America and Caribbean.

Map 12.2 South America.

While rainforests exist across the world, that which surrounds the Amazon River in South America is one of the largest and likely the best known to those of us in the Western Hemisphere. The Amazon river is the world's largest by volume. Protecting the rainforest, given the biodiversity present there and its role in regulating the climate, has been a central focus of environmentalists over the years. The vulnerable ecosystem is under pressure from those who see the rainforest in terms of agricultural or even industrial development. While local groups engaging in subsistence activities are responsible for some of the depletion of the rainforest, the greatest threat is from those who build roads, seek to extract oil and other minerals, or engage in commercial agriculture, including logging and cattle ranching.

The **southern cone** of the continent refers to the countries of Chile, Argentina, and Uruguay; Paraguay and even southern Brazil may be included in the cone as well. There one can find the Atacama desert in Chile, which has been declared the driest desert in the world. Many travelers are drawn to the Patagonia region that cuts through Argentina and Chile. Glaciers, whale watching, imposing mountain peaks, and national parks contribute to the appeal of a relatively undeveloped territory of more than 1 million square kilometers. The almost 5,000 kilometers of coastline in Argentina and more than 6,000 kilometers for Chile have helped to develop their export economies. The longest mountain range in the world is the **Andes**, which runs some 7,000 kilometers from the southern cone countries of Argentina and Chile to the so-called Andean countries of Ecuador, Peru, Colombia, Bolivia, and Venezuela. Those last five countries have at times worked together as the Andean group on economic trade issues.

Central America and Mexico are also geographically diverse with mountains, significant coastlines, tropical rainforests, and the Chihuahuan and Sonoran Deserts of Northern Mexico. The longest and most important river in Mexico is the Rio Bravo (Rio Grande on the US side), which runs along its northern border with parts of Texas and New Mexico. Many of the smaller rivers are in the south of the country, and some have suggested that the lack of a north-south river such as the Mississippi in the United States, may have inhibited Mexico's development. The narrowness in parts of Central American countries made them appealing routes from the Atlantic to the Pacific, and ultimately led to the important Panama Canal passage for ships. The islands of the Caribbean are known for tropical climates and beaches, which have led to an important role for tourism in their economies. The region is also particularly vulnerable to hurricanes and earthquakes in places. One division in the Caribbean has been between the Greater Antilles, including the generally larger islands of Cuba, Puerto Rico, Hispaniola (Haiti and the Dominican Republic), and Jamaica, and the Lesser Antilles, largely made up of French, English, and Dutch-speaking islands further to the southeast, such as Dominica, Grenada, and St. Lucia.

In this chapter, we explore the similarities across the region of Latin America and the Caribbean, while being careful to note the tremendous economic, political, and social diversity. One distinction that many make is between the countries of the continent of South America, those of Central America, the islands of the Caribbean, and Mexico. Others might see different historical experiences, languages, sizes of countries, or even distance from the United States as variations too great to warrant an area studies categorization. To understand the region of Latin America, we need to start the story well before the Europeans arrived to "discover" the people who were already there.

Pre-Columbian Americas

In looking at the history of the United States, many students would be hard pressed to come up with anything that happened before the arrival of Europeans that is important to understanding US politics, economics, or society today. Without passing judgment on that argument, in this chapter the contention is that Latin American students would find it much easier to do so. Material legacies from Machu Picchu in Peru to the Mexican pyramids in Teotihuacan and Chichen Itza are abundant (Figure 12.1). Anthropologists and archaeologists have found the mountain city of Machu Picchu to provide considerable evidence of the Incas' engineering accomplishments. The Aztecs were also accomplished engineers who created artificial islands and sophisticated irrigation techniques. In the areas of astronomy, medicine, language and

Figure 12.1 Machu Picchu, Peru, Inca Citadel.

Source: Alicia Gomez.

writing, the Mayans of Mesoamerica were also quite accomplished. Symbolic evidence of the importance of what happened in the region can be found in the Mexican flag. The Aztecs' hummingbird God, Huitzilopochtli, prophesied that the group should establish their city in the place where an eagle was sighted devouring a serpent coiled around a nopal cactus bush. That image serves as the coat of arms on a flag with green, white, and red stripes linked to the independence movement, the Catholic faith, and the Spaniards.

The ethnically indigenous populations of the region south of the current US–Mexico border have not disappeared. While Bolivia may be the only Latin American country that currently has a majority indigenous population, Guatemala, Peru, Ecuador, and Mexico have significant indigenous populations. In addition to those who would identify as fully indigenous, there are a large number of Latin Americans who are mestizo, or a variable mix of indigenous and European background. Some of those descendants continue to speak native languages, and they may identify with their cultural heritage rather than a post-Columbian Latin American national identity.

When the European powers, Spain and Portugal particularly, arrived in the Americas, they encountered millions of people living throughout the region. The claim "discovery" is clearly a misnomer for a region that had long been inhabited before Europeans arrived. We might think of it as an encounter or even a "collision" of cultures (Chasteen, 2016; Eakin, 2007). The conquistadores found a range of social organizations from largely nomadic, hunting groups to those who had settled in the areas of current-day Peru or Mexico City that were well-organized and administered complex societies, although pretty rigidly stratified. The Aztecs were centralized, with slaves at the bottom of the social hierarchy and a hereditary nobility that exercised near complete control. Wealth, prisoners who provided labor, and even human sacrifice were the spoils of war. Although the Incas were also administered by a small elite, their empire stretched for thousands of miles along the Andes. Terraced agriculture and a sophisticated irrigation system were among the impressive Incan accomplishments.

The Europeans arrived initially in the Caribbean, where Columbus first set foot on the island of Hispaniola. A couple of decades later, Cortés left Cuba for Mexico in 1519. An estimated force of just over 500 men, accompanied by maybe 15 horses landed, and within a little more than 2 years, the Spanish had established control over the Aztec empire. The relative ease of the conquest by such a small contingent of Spanish, although supplemented by reinforcements during that 2-year period, might seem hard to explain. Some have noted the superior technology of the Europeans, particularly in weaponry. Others have emphasized the decline of the Aztec empire at the time, and existence of rivalries with other indigenous groups who resented the Aztec power. Both the Aztecs and other groups underestimated the power and goals of the Spanish conquistadores. Finally, diseases such as smallpox devastated a population that had not yet developed immunities. In Peru, the divisions were even greater, marked by a civil war that threatened the Inca empire. The native population also underestimated the Spanish conquerors, led by Francisco Pizarro. At one point, the Spanish conquistador maneuvered to get a diplomatic encounter with the Inca leadership, which he turned into a kidnapping that allowed his fellow Spaniards to appropriate a large ransom of gold and silver from the Incas. The Incas maintained a resistance for decades, but as in Mexico, superior military technology, the use of horses, and the ability to play different groups against each other eventually led to the Spanish conquest.

Spanish Colonialism

For approximately 300 years after the conquest of Central America, the Caribbean, and South America, colonial control produced political and economic institutions that served the interests of the home countries in Europe. To maximize the benefits for the colonizer, political institutions, patterns of landholding, and economic trade relationships became entrenched from the early 1500s until at least the early 1800s, when some Latin American countries first gained independence from the European colonizers. In much of the region, the colonizers' preferred system of land ownership and control was known as the *encomienda*. Europeans were given large tracts of land, which they were expected to use in order to produce a variety of crops. In addition to the land, the *encomendero* was given the responsibility of controlling the indigenous population that had been living in that area. In this system, landowning was directly associated with power, and the landless lacked autonomy and opportunity. The unequal distribution of land would be a recurring issue in the region.

Another important economic development during colonialism was the effort to extract mineral wealth from the Americas, particularly gold and silver, to enrich the European monarchies. As one example, a silver mine in Potosi (in the country of Bolivia today) was discovered by the Spanish in the mid-1500s. For several decades that region was the largest producer of silver in the world. In order to do the mining, the indigenous people in the region were forced into hard labor that was dangerous, and in many cases led to people who could be described as having been worked to death. The situation with gold mines elsewhere was similar. The blood and sweat of the indigenous population produced the gold and silver that stimulated European industrialization and economic growth in general during these centuries of Latin American colonialism.

Labor from the indigenous population proved insufficient for a colonizer seeking to maximize the wealth that the Americas could provide in minerals and agricultural production. Enslaved

Africans were shipped to the Americas to supplement or even replace indigenous workers. Of the estimated 10 million Africans brought to the Americas during the time of slavery, roughly 4 million were sent to Brazil alone to do the work necessary for sugar and coffee production, as well as to mine gold in the Portuguese colony. Large numbers of Africans were transplanted into the various European island colonies in the Caribbean. Smaller numbers ended up in Venezuela, Colombia, Mexico and elsewhere in Latin America. Slavery first ended in Haiti, when a successful slave rebellion in 1804 forced the French to leave, and last ended when the Golden Law of 1888 finally abolished slavery in Brazil. The mixing of African, European, indigenous, and other ethnic groups throughout the region produced social and economic stratification that almost perfectly corresponded with a hierarchy from the lightest to darkest skin colors.

The ethnic and economic hierarchies of the colonial period necessitated an authoritarian political system in which force was employed by the colonial government to maintain control. In some cases, such as Mexico, the colonizer inherited existing structures of administrative control and superimposed their own rule. The first viceroyalty was established in Mexico in the 1530s, and the second in Peru in the 1540s. Viceroyalties on New Granada (roughly present-day Colombia, Venezuela, and Ecuador) and Rio de la Plata (Argentina and Chile) were formed in the early and mid-1700s respectively. Over time varying degrees of conflict developed between the local administrators, who were frequently born in the Americas (*criollos*) and the Spanish crown and those Spaniards who were born in the Iberian Peninsula and migrated to the region (*peninsulares*). In general, those born in Spain held the top positions in the administration, but the *criollos* were very influential in their own right, particularly at the local level. The primary interest of both groups of Spaniards, of course, was the maintenance of control over African, indigenous, and mestizo groups.

Brazil developed somewhat differently under their Portuguese colonizer. The relatively smaller and more scattered indigenous population meant that there was not a pre-existing administrative structure that the Europeans could use to their own benefit. Navigational skills and experience had given the Portuguese a chance to assert influence in Africa and Asia, both through the establishment of trading relationships and territorial control. The large territory of Brazil posed a different challenge and opportunity. Appearing to lack either an easily exploitable native population or abundant mineral wealth, the region did have Brazilwood (valued as a source of dye), but it wouldn't prove to be particularly profitable until it could be exploited for agricultural production. By the early 1600s, Portuguese settlers realized the opportunities available from sugar cane production. Lacking sufficient indigenous labor to exploit, the colonizer turned to Africa. As of 1810, more than 2.5 million Africans had been brought to Brazil and enslaved, and they made up roughly half the colony's population in the early nineteenth century (Smith and Green, 2019: 28).

Independence and the Nineteenth Century

The first successful struggle for independence in the region came on the island of Hispaniola, where the Haitian slave rebellion led to the 1804 departure of the French from the western part of the island. Elsewhere in the region, events in Europe played at least some role in creating more favorable conditions for independence movements. The French Revolution beginning in 1789 provided some ideological encouragement to those chafing under the control of monarchs. Napoleon's invasion of the Iberian Peninsula in the first decade of the 1800s weakened the legitimacy of the Spanish royal family. Competition between the Latin American-born creoles of Spanish heritage and those born on the Iberian Peninsula added another layer of uncertainty in the Americas. By about 1810, many areas of the Americas had seen increased anti-colonizer resistance.

In Mexico, parish priests played a leadership role in the mobilization of the indigenous population. First Father Hidalgo, himself a Creole, and later the Mestizo Father Morelos challenged the viceroyalty there. The administrators of the Peruvian viceroyalty were better prepared to fend off independence movements after having withstood the indigenous rebellion led by Tupac Amaru II in the late eighteenth century. Both Hidalgo and Morelos were captured and executed, but it became apparent that the Spanish colonizer was vulnerable, and Mexico was on the move toward an independence that came in 1821. By all accounts, however, the Mexican elite—large landholders, leaders in the Catholic church, and the military—were able to shape the outcome of independence in ways that preserved their power and privilege. The new Constitutional Republic did not upend the existing social and economic structures in an independent Mexico.

The struggles for independence in what are now described as Andean countries in Western South America took a different path. Simon Bolívar, the Liberator, was a leader of early Latin American nationalism, arguing that all of the "Americanos," regardless of ethnic heritage, should unite against the European colonizers. Bolívar succeeded in establishing Gran Colombia, which united several current South American countries for about a decade until the federation dissolved in spring of 1830. The Liberator seems to have died of tuberculosis later that year, although some have speculated that his death was not natural.

The new Constitutional Republics that were established across Latin America faced a number of challenges in the early nineteenth century. In places such as Venezuela and Mexico, the violence of the independence struggles and the resulting economic disruptions were going to be difficult to overcome. Nearly all new states lacked dependable sources of revenue. Regional identities and power structures worked against a willingness to concede to centralized power, much less provide financial support to the new governments. Large armies were still needed to maintain order in highly stratified societies, and they would either be funded locally by regional "strongmen," or the federal government would need a revenue source such as export taxes to do so. These *caudillos* were wealthy large landholders who were responsible for controlling those working that land. In many cases, the *caudillos* would privately pay for local militias to ensure their ability to maintain the necessary workforce. Certain nineteenth-century leaders, such as Juan Manuel de Rosas, who became Governor of the Province of Buenos Aires in Argentina in 1829 and (except for a short period of time in the 1830s) remained Governor until 1852, were also described as *caudillos*. Rosas's power came from both military force and a carefully developed image as the protector of the people. Over time, Rosas extended his influence into other Argentine provinces, and was the dominant force in the country during his time as Governor.

Throughout most of the nineteenth century, independent Latin American countries continued in the colonial practice of exporting commodities, both to Europe and increasingly over time to the United States. The interests of governments and large landholders were to encourage that commodity export, while importing manufactured goods from the more industrialized countries, particularly now that they were no longer limited to their Spanish or Portuguese colonizer. Already behind in manufacturing at the time of independence, Latin American countries fell further behind as they helped to provide the inputs that helped stimulate the Industrial Revolution in Europe beginning in the middle of the 1800s.

Continuity in economic stratification was largely replicated in social and racial hierarchies. In Brazil and Cuba, the African population was oppressed by the institution of slavery into the late 1880s. Indigenous populations were also discriminated against by those of European heritage in positions of economic and political power. In some cases, the *mestizo* population found new opportunities after independence breaking through the rigid caste system of colonialism. Overall, however, there was little change in a highly stratified region. In almost all cases, land ownership continued to be concentrated in a relatively small number of hands. In some countries, including Mexico, the Catholic church was the single largest landholder as well as largest money lender through the nineteenth century.

The region continued to be vulnerable to external forces, both European and the United States. Mexico provides considerable evidence of the power of outsiders to constrain their development in the nineteenth century. After the Mexican–American War, Mexico lost roughly half of the land it had claimed at independence from Spain. This loss was devastating economically and politically to the young country. From a Mexican perspective, this 1845–1848 military conflict is more accurately described as the North American Invasion of Mexico. That is, a dispute rooted in US settlers in Texas prompted the much more powerful US military to engage the Mexican military at the border, and continue on to occupy Mexico City. At that point, the Mexican government was forced to agree to the Treaty of Guadalupe Hidalgo, which gave the US the area now in the states of California, Arizona, New Mexico, Texas, and parts of a number of other western and southwestern states. The United States spread westward, and in part of that new territory the gold rush in the year following the treaty helped to stimulate US economic development and fulfill the "manifest destiny" some argued was inevitable. Mexico was invaded a little over a decade later by the French, who also occupied Mexico City and put a member of the Austrian royal family, Maximilian, into the presidency. Maximilian served in that position for a little over 3 years before being overthrown and sentenced to death by the Mexicans in 1867. For those students in the United States who might celebrate Cinco de Mayo, the origin of that holiday is in the heroic resistance by the Mexican military in the city of Puebla during the initial French invasion of the country. Since it was merely one successful battle in a losing war, it is not surprising that May 5 is not widely celebrated in Mexico itself.

By the last third of the 1800s, the ideology of liberalism had finally broken through in most countries. While liberalism contains ideas about individual rights and political freedom, in Latin America, the liberty in that ideology was primarily economic at the time. The institutions of government, some large landholders, and even the church, had generally resisted openings of markets, trade, and greater economic competition domestically and globally. The liberal idea was that trade could be a win-win situation in which all countries would export products that they could produce more cheaply than others, while importing that which another country could produce more efficiently. In many cases, the comparative advantage in Latin America continued to be in tropical agricultural products or minerals, and in that sense, liberalism reinforced existing economic priorities and practices. The increased emphasis on trade did lead to new efforts to improve infrastructure, and the openness to foreign investment increased regional access to both the capital and technology for building railroads or modernizing ports. The era of economic liberalism lasted through the 1920s.

In some countries, there were also moves to liberalize political systems during this time as well. They were generally quite limited, however, with limitations on voting and other political participation that effectively prevented any significant role for the poor, including urban and rural workers. Still, the larger countries of South America, including Argentina, Chile, and Brazil, developed legislatures, political parties, and other trappings of limited political democracy.

Latin American Economic Development

As was noted above, Latin America entered the world economy during colonialism as the exporter of primary products, including minerals and agricultural products such as sugar, cacao, tobacco, Brazilwood, and other products that were in demand among European consumers. Later, coffee, bananas, and—once shipping technology improved—even Argentine beef flowed from Latin America to US and European ports in the post-independence nineteenth century. While some industrialization took place in larger Latin American countries, the concept of comparative advantage lent credibility to the export of commodities and import of manufactured goods from the countries who had a head start in industrialization. The economic growth in the late 1800s and into the early 1900s did not benefit all sectors of Latin American society, but it did lead to the appearance of modern economic development (see Figure 12.2).

The global depression of 1929–1930 led to a region-wide reconsideration of economic liberalism. Through no apparent fault of their own, Latin American countries were faced with the consequences of a dramatic fall in the prices of the commodities they exported. As dependency theorists would argue later, decisions made outside their borders and beyond their control led to economic crises throughout the region. The reasonable response by policymakers was to shift their approach to trade by restricting the imports of some manufactured goods and promoting the production of those goods within their countries. This practice was described as Import Substitution Industrialization (ISI), and its implementation required significant government involvement in the economy. Beyond trade restrictions, the Latin American governments subsidized domestic industry and provided infrastructure to support ISI. Larger countries in the region were better able to pursue these policies, and in Brazil, Mexico, and others, the period from the late 1940s through the 1960s was characterized as an economic miracle due to the strong economic growth.

As part of the regional attempt to reclaim their independence from the global economy, a number of countries nationalized key sectors of the economy. In 1938, Mexican President Lazaro Cardenas nationalized the oil companies operating in his country and created PEMEX to administer Mexico's oil, from the drilling of crude oil to the sale of gasoline to consumers. Later Peru, Brazil, and Venezuela would do similar things with their oil. The Bolivians nationalized tin in the 1950s, and then Chileans took their copper back from US companies Kennecott and Anaconda in the early 1970s.

Figure 12.2 Poverty in some Latin American countries, washing clothes in Ecuador.

Source: ammit/123RF.

The policies of ISI and nationalization flowed naturally from a regional sense that the openings to foreign investment and trade during the period of economic liberalism had made them vulnerable to forces outside their borders and beyond their control. The shift in strategy had wide support in the region, and the accompanying economic growth in a number of countries added to its general approval.

Eduardo Galeano (1988: 112) captures the sentiment in Mexico City after the nationalization of oil:

> North of Tampico, Mexico's petroleum belongs to Standard Oil; to the south, Shell. Mexico pays dearly for its own oil, which Europe and the United States buy cheap. These companies have been looting the subsoil and robbing Mexico of taxes and salaries for thirty years—until one fine day Cárdenas decides that Mexico is the owner of Mexican oil.
>
> Since that day, nobody can sleep a wink. The challenge wakes up the country. In neverending demonstrations, enormous crowds stream into the streets carrying coffins for Standard and Shell on their backs. To a marimba beat and the tolling of bells, workers occupy wells and refineries. But the companies reply in kind: all the foreign technicians, those masters of mystery, are withdrawn. No one is left to tend the indecipherable instrument panels of management. The national flag flutters over silent towers. The drills are halted, the pipelines emptied, the fires extinguished. It is war: war against the Latin American tradition of impotence, the colonial custom of *don't know, no can do*.

In the late 1970s, many Latin American countries were faced with a more difficult challenge of deepening ISI. That is, having conquered the light ISI task of producing consumer goods such as furniture or processed food, the next stage was to domestically produce things like the machinery needed to turn the region's lumber into furniture. That heavy ISI required more investment, and Latin American governments looked to continue that process with the support of loans from European and US banks. They took those loans out with low, variable interest rates available at the time, and used the money in an effort to maintain the economic "miracles." A perfect storm of events in the early 1980s brought these Latin American government borrowers to their knees: a global drop in commodity prices, capital flight from the region to the safe harbors of northern economies, and a US Federal Reserve decision to hike interest rates. From a starting point of 6 to 8 percent, variable rates jumped to more than 20 percent. Finally, the Mexican government declared in late summer 1982 that it was unable to make even its minimal service payment, and effectively declared itself bankrupt.

To provide Mexico and soon other Latin American governments with the capacity to make their loan payments, the "lender of last resort," the International Monetary Fund (IMF) offered conditional loans. The conditions attached to those funds were described as structural adjustment policies rooted in the ideology of neoliberalism. At its essence, neoliberalism argues for the primacy of market-based solutions to problems it argues are rooted in state intervention in the economy. From the 1980s and through the end of the 1990s, the region's economies embraced neoliberal policies at the behest of the international financial institutions and Washington, and they were implemented by a new generation of technocratic Latin American politicians and bureaucrats, who seemed to be true believers.

The earliest version of these policies was seen in Chile, where under the military dictatorship of Pinochet, the so-called Chicago Boys were given relatively free rein to implement the policies being advocated by Milton Friedman, the professor for some of these technocrats when they were studying at the University of Chicago. In practice, the principal goal of reducing the state's role in the economy was achieved by a number of pro-market policies. Some of those policies were enacted to the end of deregulation of the economy. Those efforts included labor flexibilization, in effect, making it easier to hire and fire workers; weakening health, safety, and environmental rules; and simply eliminating bureaucratic obstacles to opening of new businesses. The advocacy of privatization led to the widespread selling of government-owned businesses to the private sector. To promote economic competition, trade and investment barriers were eliminated, allowing goods and capital to flow freely across national borders. The state reduced or eliminated subsidies on goods and services that distorted market prices in food, transportation, and utilities. In the case of Chile, the reduction of government spending included education and health care, as well as the privatization of the pension system. The principle to be followed was that whenever possible, the market should make decisions about production, distribution, and consumption, not the state. In Mexico, neoliberal President Salinas worked with the United States and Canada to join his country into what would be known as the North American Free Trade Agreement (NAFTA) in the early 1990s. Reducing any obstacles to the flow of goods, service, and investment between the United States and Mexico was consistent with the market-based ideology that held sway in most Latin American governments at the time.

Many students are likely to be sympathetic to this argument and the associated policies. We have heard about the inevitable inefficiencies and waste in government, and accept the assumption that businesses motivated by profit will not have those same problems. At the same time, it might also be evident that there are winners and losers associated with the ideology of neoliberalism. Some people in Latin America will have the resources that allow them to purchase publicly owned enterprises, while those who work in those sectors may see their wages and job security diminish. Eliminating subsidies of bus fares or basic foodstuffs will disproportionately affect poor and working people. Labor "flexibility" will increase the leverage of employers, while making the lives of workers more precarious. Privatization in the area of communication and infrastructure may lead to better roads and phone service, but at a price that makes them inaccessible to lots of people. The drive from Mexico City to Acapulco took maybe 7 hours in the 1980s before a private company was given a contract to build a new highway that cut the trip in half by the early 1990s. That company, however, charged tolls several times the daily minimum wage in Mexico at the time, effectively excluding all but the relatively well-off Mexicans or foreigners from the new convenience.

Similarly, with agreements such as NAFTA, there are winners and losers that seem related to one's position in the economic hierarchy. Investors and business owners now had opportunities to move industries to locations where they could be most profitable; exporters increased their access to different markets; and consumers would pay lower prices for goods imported from other countries in the region. Small businesses in Mexico that could no longer compete with the transnational corporations based in the United States, however, would go out of business, leaving their workers unemployed; small rural farming in Mexico was unable to compete with the heavily government subsidized and mechanized agricultural production in the United States, and they would have to look for alternative ways to make a living. The dislocation of perhaps 5 million Mexicans from rural areas, including both workers and family members, due to NAFTA competition played a significant role in the flow of undocumented Mexicans to the United States in the late 1990s and early 2000s. When President Trump came to office in 2017, he set about reworking NAFTA, and the resulting United States, Mexico, Canada Agreement (USMCA in English/TMEC in Spanish) took effect on July 1, 2020. Given the attacks by President Trump on NAFTA during his campaign, the changes to the agreement struck most observers as relatively minor, although there was a claim that the USMCA should lead to greater labor rights in Mexico and the return of some automobile production to the United States.

Over time, the disproportionate outcomes from these policies in Latin America led to backlashes across the region. Some have characterized protests such as that in Caracas, Venezuela in 1989 over proposed increases to the costs of transport, fuel, utilities, and food as "IMF riots," given the link of the policies to the IMF "structural adjustment" requirements for accepting money from the international financial institution. In the case of the 1989 Venezuelan protests (which came to be known as the *Caracazo*), the government responded violently with estimates of the numbers of protesters killed ranging from about 300 by the government itself to as many as 3,000. A decade after the *Caracazo*, Venezuelans elected Hugo Chavez, the first of several presidents who rose to power as part of widespread opposition to neoliberal policies. While neoliberalism did stabilize many Latin American countries and make government debt more manageable, the associated policies did not reduce poverty or inequality in the region. By the early 2000s, the shift of many governments to an anti-neoliberal left-leaning economic approach was referred to by some as a red or pink tide. The Kirchners in Argentina, Evo Morales in Bolivia, and Lula in Brazil are some examples of the shift in the region. One of the principal outcomes of the shift left was that a proposed Free Trade Area of the Americas (FTAA) that all Latin American leaders (except the absent Cuban Fidel Castro) had agreed should be enacted at the Summit of the Americas held in Miami at the end of 1994, never came to fruition. The idea was that the NAFTA model, which was implemented that year, should be extended to cover the entire region from Alaska to Argentina by January 1, 2005. Growing opposition to neoliberalism in Latin America, as well as increasing wariness about the role of the United States in the region, effectively left the FTAA for dead well before the proposed 2005 implementation.

In the second decade of the twenty-first century, the tide receded, and some of those politicians on the left were replaced by more conservative governments. That makes it more difficult to categorize the approach to economic development in Latin America in the early 2020s. President Bolsonaro in Brazil, President Duque in Colombia, and President Piñera in Chile seem committed to policies that resemble neoliberalism, even if it's hard to find a leader willing to identify specifically as a neoliberal. Mexican President López Obrador (AMLO) ran successfully on a leftist, anti-neoliberal platform, although in office it has been hard to place him on the traditional left–right Latin American spectrum. Argentine President Fernández took office in December 2019, representing the left-of-center approach that includes more significant government intervention in the economy and a goal of redistributing economic benefits more widely.

Latin American Political Development

During colonialism, Latin America was highly economically and socially stratified, and the political order reflected the need of a small group of elites to maintain their control. Large landholders in some areas maintained private militias to keep peasants under control, and officials in the centers of colonial administration took directives from Europe and implemented them without significant input from local populations. At independence then, the region was characterized by hierarchical societies and political systems that reflected that stratification, including the need for military or local militias to use force when deemed necessary. Slavery in such places as Brazil and Cuba, or indigenous folks working in virtual indentured servitude were necessarily excluded from any influence in the post-independence political systems. In nearly all Latin American countries, the same groups who had political control before independence— large landholders, the military, and the Catholic church—were able to maintain their monopoly on political power.

During the nineteenth century, there was considerable variation across the region as different countries sought to centralize political control and maintain stability. In some cases, *caudillos* such as Juan Manuel de Rosas in Argentina and Diego Portales in Chile were the forces behind state development. In Central America and Mexico, the ideological struggle between conservatives and liberals helped shape political development through much of the 1800s. In

Mexico, regional divisions and foreign interventions that included but were not restricted to the Mexican–American War, hindered the development of a strong, central state. From independence in 1821 through 1860, the country had approximately 50 different presidencies, the majority of which were led by military officials; General Santa Anna represented nine of those presidencies by himself. In most of Central America and Mexico, the liberals had won the struggle for political control by the last third of the nineteenth century. The effort to rein in the influence of the Catholic church was one of the important liberal goals that distinguished their movement from the Conservatives. Brazil was distinct from the former Spanish colonies in the Americas, as its 1822 "independence" led to a constitutional monarchy with emperors from the Portuguese ruling family in power until the end of the 1880s. Most of the Caribbean, including Spain's two remaining colonies of Cuba and Puerto Rico, continued to be politically ruled by their European colonizer.

With some notable exceptions, many of the Latin American countries added institutions and practices that increased political representation from the end of the 1800s through the early 1900s. While there were important limitations on who were granted political citizenship, parties and legislatures were operating in Argentina, Brazil, Chile, and other countries in South America. Although still not full democracies, there was evidence of political liberalization in much of the region. To emphasize, these political systems relied on the exclusion of certain groups: foreign-born workers in Argentina, indigenous populations across the region, those who couldn't meet literacy or property requirements, and women everywhere.

Mexico was an important exception to the limited, but important, political openings, with Porfirio Diaz assuming control of the government in the early 1870s and not relinquishing until the 1910 beginning of the Mexican Revolution. The countries of Central America, as well as the Caribbean cases of Cuba, Dominican Republic, and Haiti were politically constrained by the United States through the first few decades of the twentieth century. US troops were sent several times to the region, and Washington made many of the political and economic decisions for the countries.

In the wake of the global depression that began in 1929, military and other authoritarian governments established control across the region. Economic crises delegitimated some governments, and in other places led to instability that militaries saw as a reason to assume control. Prominent exceptions included Chile, which moved by the early 1930s to restore a political system with competitive and relatively fair elections until the 1973 coup by Augusto Pinochet. Mexico also continued with civilian government and impressive political stability from the 1930s for several decades. Mexico's one-party state was clearly not fully democratic, and in fact, was famously described as a "perfect dictatorship." Mexico's regular elections, the relative absence of political violence, and a military that never took power, were quite exceptional for the time in Latin America. In Central America and the Caribbean, authoritarian control meant "strongmen," such as Somoza in Nicaragua, Batista in Cuba, and Trujillo in the Dominican Republic taking power in the 1930s and keeping it for decades. Brazil and Argentina saw military coups that evolved into classic examples of populism during the rules of Getulio Vargas and Juan Perón respectively.

Conceptually, **populism** has been used to describe a political approach in which individual leaders, parties, or movements gain political power by mobilizing the masses of people against some group of elites. In Latin America, this has generally happened at times when groups and classes of people (the *popular* in Spanish) with genuine grievances have been systematically excluded from access to the political system. A leader, such as Juan Perón (1943–1954, 1973–1974) gave voice to those grievances and promised to bring their interests to the fore, if they gave him their support. Eduardo Galeano (1988: 127–28) describes Peron's rise to power:

...Perón flies swiftly along the road to the presidency with Evita, the radio actress with the feverish eyes and enticing voice; and when he gets tired, or doubtful, or scared, it is she who takes the bit in her teeth. Perón now attracts more people than all the parties put together. When they call him "agitator," he accepts the epithet as an honor. VIPs and the fashionably chic chant the name of [US] Ambassador Braden on the street corners of Buenos Aires, waving hats and handkerchiefs; but in worker barrios, the shirtless shout the name Perón. These laboring people, exiles in their own land, dumb from so much shutting up, find both a fatherland and a voice in this unusual minister who always takes their side.

Peron's popularity climbs and climbs as he shakes the dust off forgotten social laws or creates new ones. His is the law that compels respect for the rights of those who break their backs on estancias and plantations. The law does not merely remain on paper; thus the country peon, almost a thing, becomes a rural worker complete with a trade union.

Populists have defied any easy ideological categorization. Getulio Vargas in Brazil (1930–1945, 1951–1954) flexibly moved across the political spectrum during his time in office. Perón, and even more so the Peronists who followed him in Argentina, have also ruled from the political right and left. Both Perón and Vargas used corporatist institutions to help maintain their control. Corporatism in Latin American countries is characterized by state-controlled institutions that divide society according to their economic function into separate top-down organizations, initially with a stated interest in protecting or even promoting the rights of workers and peasants. The PRI in Mexico, the party that held power from the 1930s until 2000, practiced a form of corporatism as well. Peasants, workers, soldiers, and "popular" groups and classes were kept in separate sectors for the purpose of defusing class conflict and alliances, and giving the state ultimate authority to resolve conflicts.

In the mid-twentieth century and even in recent years, some populists have gained support through appeals to ethno-nationalist identities, while others have emphasized economic or even class identities. In twenty-first-century Latin America, Hugo Chavez in Venezuela was occasionally described as a leftwing populist, while Jair Bolsonaro in Brazil is a far-right populist according to some analysts. For many scholars, a conceptual category that lumps together such disparate political actors as Chavez and Bolsonaro lacks analytical usefulness. Over time a number of Latin American leaders have effectively mobilized previously excluded groups and classes to gain personalist control over the levers of government. Once in power, populist leaders have varied considerably in the extent to which they effectively respond to the mass grievances of the people who helped put them in their positions.

The Cuban Revolution in 1959 had a dramatic impact on the region and US relations with Latin America. Led by Fidel Castro, his brother Raúl, and Che Guevara among others, the Cuban revolutionaries overthrew the pro-US dictator, Fulgencio Batista and began to transform life on the island. A literacy campaign, land reform, and some nationalizations in the economy worried many in Washington, and in 1961 a CIA-backed attempt at a counter-revolution was launched by Cuban exiles. Modeled after a successful overthrow of the center-left government in Guatemala in 1954, the Bay of Pigs invasion was a disaster for the United States. Following the Cubans' successful resistance, Fidel Castro declared the revolution socialist, moved closer to the Soviet Union, and was able to consolidate the power that he held until an illness forced him to give up the presidency temporarily in 2006 and permanently in 2008. Raúl Castro succeeded his brother and held the presidency until 2018. Miguel Diaz-Canel took over at that point as the first non-Castro president in almost 60 years. Although the US and Cuba moved to normalize diplomatic relations in December 2014 by way of dramatic dual announcements by Presidents Barack Obama and Raúl Castro, the US economic embargo remains in place in the early 2020s.

Following the revolution, US policymakers became even more determined to keep **socialism** out of the rest of the hemisphere. On the one hand, there were new attempts to curry favor among populations that might be sympathetic by way of Alliance for Progress economic aid and even the formation of the Peace Corps in the early 1960s. There were also vigorous attempts to keep leftist movements and leaders from coming to power. Having failed in its effort to keep Salvador Allende from winning the election for President of Chile in 1970, Washington was once again involved in the 1973 coup to remove the democratic socialist from office. Allende was replaced by General Augusto Pinochet, who ruled over the country until 1990 (see Figure 12.3).

By the 1960s and 1970s, the absence of strong democracies in most Latin American countries, and the presence of harsh military governments in several places, needed to be explained by academics and other political analysts. To be sure, Costa Rica since 1948, and Colombia and Venezuela as of the late 1950s seemed committed to parties and elections to determine political outcomes. For some in the global north, the easy answer to explain the other authoritarian governments was that Latin American culture was not conducive to democracy. Histories of patron–client relationships, corporatism, personalist "strongmen" leaders, a willingness to accept military rule, and even the experience with a hierarchical Catholic church left the population accepting top-down political control. From that perspective, a more democratic culture needed to be developed before democracy could fully take hold in the region. Greater exposure

Figure 12.3 Street mural in Chile, Salvador Allende.

Source: Alicia Gomez.

to existing democracies such as the United States, increasing levels of education and urbanization, and enlightened leaders would help to diffuse the ideas and culture of democracy to the undemocratic masses.

Just as some were explaining economic development in Latin America by a structural dependency analysis, an alternative political explanation focused not on culture, but on power and structures as well. The point they made was that democratization is best seen as a struggle between those who would benefit from more democratic political practices and those whose interests could be threatened by more widespread political participation and greater political equality. In highly stratified Latin American societies, the relatively small group of large landholders, upper class business people, military leaders, and other elites, potentially had wealth, power, and privilege to lose if government policies were to be determined by the masses of the population. In the face of those "anti-democratic" forces and unequal economic and social structures, achieving democracy would only happen when the pro-democratic forces became stronger than those opposed. That might be usefully seen as "pressure from below." Popular organizations of indigenous people, peasants, workers, women, and others who were excluded from political influence would be the groups most likely to provide that pressure, because they had the most to gain.

In the 1980s and early 1990s, Latin America did see a series of transitions to democracy. The military government in Argentina left office abruptly in the wake of a growing economic crisis and the disastrous invasion of the Falklands Islands. Although the humiliating defeat by the navy of the United Kingdom following the Argentine attempt to take back the islands was the proximate cause of the transition back to civilians and elections, increasingly effective protests by working people and others contributed to their weakening position. The Madres de la Plaza de Mayo—women silently marching to protest the disappearances and killings of their children and husbands—were a visible representation of the pressure from below in the country. Brazil experienced a gradual transition back to democracy during the 1980s culminating in a directly elected civilian president in 1989. A variety of social movements helped to put pressure on the military government: Christian base communities, representing the Liberation Theology strain in the Catholic church, landless rural workers movements, labor unions breaking free of corporatist constraints, and women's organizations. Civil society pressure on the Pinochet government led the General to give Chileans a referendum or plebiscite to affirm the continuation of his government in late 1988. An overwhelming "no" vote led to Chile's return to democracy with a free and fair election for president in December 1989.

In the 1990s, the democratically elected leaders in Latin America continued to face the legacy of the 1980s region-wide economic crisis. In most cases, the governments continued to hew closely to the neoliberal economic model promoted by Washington, the IMF, and others. When those policies failed to deliver the goods for lots of people, the region saw a resurgence of social movements challenging elected officials. Beginning with Venezuelan voters who elected Hugo Chavez president at the end of the 1990s, there was a shift in the early 2000s to elect leaders who promised to pull back from neoliberalism and institute social and economic policies that would serve the interests of groups and classes that continued to struggle in the neoliberal period. The shift to the left was not universal. While voters in Argentina, Bolivia, Brazil, and others elected leftist presidents, Colombia, Mexico, and others largely stayed the neoliberal course.

For the most part, Latin American countries continued to hold the free, fair, and frequent elections that characterize formal democracy. Coups overthrowing leftist leaders in Venezuela (2002), Haiti (2004), and Honduras (2009) in the first decade of the twenty-first century seemed to be exceptions, and the Venezuelan coup lasted just 48 hours. In the second decade of the century, we saw what some termed "political coups," given that opposition leaders used Constitutional cover for the removal of leftist leaders such as Fernando Lugo in Paraguay (2012),

Dilma Rousseff in Brazil (2016), and even Evo Morales in Bolivia (2019), who was forced out of office and the country following a disputed vote count. Generally, however, civilians who won reasonably fair and free elections headed Latin American governments at the beginning of the 2020s.

Latin American Society

Race and ethnicity continue to be important to understanding the region. Students are frequently surprised by the range of ethnic identities in Latin America and the Caribbean. Brazil is home to more than 2 million people of Asian descent, and there are 1.5 million Asians in Peru, including one-time President Alberto Fujimori. Millions more in countries such as Brazil and Argentina are of Arab background. Other countries have significant Arab populations, including Mexico where Tacos Árabes, courtesy of Lebanese immigrants, may be the country's best street food. More often, discussions of race and ethnicity in Latin America focus on the indigenous, European, African, and mestizo populations. As referenced at the beginning of the chapter, the second largest population of African heritage people in one country is in Brazil; the largest is in Nigeria. People identifying as indigenous to the Americas make up large percentages of the current populations of Bolivia, Guatemala, Peru, and Mexico. In those countries, significant numbers in the country may not speak Spanish as a first language or even at all.

The idea of a large mestizo population may be the most challenging for US students to grasp, given a history of "one drop" classification of people as African American. Various Latin American countries have embraced the mixed-race category, including Mexico, where José Vasconcelos wrote an essay in 1925 describing the "cosmic race." In his vision, the mixing of races that took place in Latin America was producing a transcendent "race." The notion of La Raza was compelling, and it would inform even some of the Chicano and Latinx movements in the United States later in the twentieth and early twenty-first centuries.

In countries such as the Dominican Republic, the construction of racial identity has led much of the population of color to identify as Indio, even when there is some African blood in their background. In part, that is a way to distinguish themselves from the black Haitians, with whom they share the island of Hispaniola. Dominicans may add adjectives to distinguish the range of Indio: *canela* for cinnamon-colored, *trigueña* for wheat, or Indio *oscuro* for someone more dark-skinned. Many Dominicans, including some who describe their race as *blanco* while on the island, "change races" to become black when they cross the Caribbean to come to the United States.

Some Brazilians like to describe their country as a "racial democracy," due to the absence of any legal segregation or other restrictions on Afro-Brazilians since the end of slavery in the late 1880s. Like Mexico, the country promoted ideas of race-mixing as a positive thing for Brazil in the early-to-mid twentieth century, most prominently by sociologist Gilberto Freyre. The national myth of racial democracy obscures the large influence that skin color in the country has on economic status and political power. Income levels are strongly related to skin color, Afro-Brazilians are poorly represented at the top levels of business, politics, or the military, and universities are far whiter than the population as a whole.

Indigenous populations in the region have also been relegated disproportionately to lower rungs of the socioeconomic ladder. Unlike the Dominican uses of the term, being called "Indio" in many Latin American countries is meant to be derogatory. Indigenous people's movements have registered some successes in the late twentieth and early twenty-first centuries, including new rights written into Constitutions in countries such as Bolivia and Ecuador. The changes in Bolivia came during the presidency of Evo Morales, generally viewed as the country's first indigenous head of government.

The elections of several women Latin American presidents in the early 2000s might have seemed surprising in a region long seen as patriarchal and infused with a culture of machismo. That was not the first example of political agency on the part of women. Beginning with the early twentieth-century Mexican Revolution and continuing through to revolutionary activity in El Salvador and Nicaragua in the second half of the century, women were seen as increasingly important to the struggles to change political systems. The Madres de la Plaza de Mayo mentioned earlier helped challenge the Argentine military, although they did so in a way that reflected and capitalized on the cultural reverence for mothers. Some of the earliest women presidents in Latin America came to office in part or fully by virtue of their position as widows of prominent political leaders (Isabel Perón in Argentina, Violeta Chamorro in Nicaragua, and Mireya Moscoso in Panama). In the early 2000s, though, Michelle Bachelet, Cristina Fernandez de Kirchner, and Dilma Rousseff all won first elections, and then were re-elected a second time. Laura Chinchilla also served as president of Costa Rica from 2010 to 2014.

While there is plenty yet to do in the area of women's rights in Latin America, the increase in political activity from the *soldaderas* of the Mexican Revolution to the presence of several women presidents in office a century later has been a promising sign. Women are also working outside the home in increasing numbers, although the region still lags behind the global north in rates of female labor participation. A good amount of that work has been in the "**informal economy**," and there are significant wage gaps across the region. While entering the workforce is generally seen as increasing women's autonomy, when economic class is considered, the phenomenon of a new double or even "triple burden" is present. A woman working outside the home may be adding a full day of paid labor to child care and other domestic responsibilities.

Significant progress in some Latin American countries in LGBTQ rights came as a surprise to many who think of the region as rife with machismo and heavily influenced by a socially conservative Catholic church. While particularly smaller Caribbean countries lagged behind, Argentina and Uruguay led the way, with Colombia, Ecuador, and Mexico achieving considerable expansion of LGBTQ rights as well. Mexico City (2009), Argentina (2010), Uruguay (2013), and Brazil (2013) all allowed gay marriage before the United States (2015). Since then, Colombia (2016), Ecuador (2019), and Costa Rica (2020) have been added to the list. In most Latin American cases, laws protecting the rights of the LGBTQ population have gotten out ahead of overall public opinion. Brazil, for example, continues to see a very high level of hate crimes based on sexuality, and the country elected Jair Bolsonaro as president in 2018, a self-described homophobe who once said that he would rather his son die in an accident than be gay.

Looking to the Future

A number of the most important political issues in the United States in the 2020s are linked to Latin America. Immigration, drug trafficking, trade relations, and environmental policies are intermestic issues, or those that are discussed at the level of international relations and have domestic political implications in both the United States and Latin American countries. Those issues are clearly affected by the power asymmetries between the United States and the countries to its south. Mexico's economic dependence on the US affects the debate over NAFTA and trade more generally between the two countries. Central American vulnerability to US foreign policy decisions conditions those countries' responses to entreaties from the US about immigration and drug trafficking. The countries of South America seem to have attained a little more space to operate, in part due to their geographical distance from the United States, but there are still impacts based on their locations in an area where the US assumes hegemony.

The quality of Latin American democracies continues to be an issue as well. There are large countries such as Brazil, where widespread corruption and a political oligarchy that does not seem accountable to the population pose significant problems. Smaller countries such as Honduras see the façade of democracy used to marginalize the poor and maintain the power of the conservative elite. Venezuela poses a particular challenge, with some suggesting it might have been the only country in 2019–2020 with two illegitimate presidents. Under President Ortega, democracy in Nicaragua has been deteriorating for years. The legitimacy of the re-election of Evo Morales was challenged in Bolivia, and once he was forced into exile, a previously unknown legislator became the caretaker president. Upon taking the office in 2019, Jeanine Añez moved to undo much of the progress made by Morales to guarantee the rights of indigenous people and women in the country. At the end of 2020, Bolivia held a new election that was won in a landslide by Luis Arce, representing the party of Morales.

The Covid-19 pandemic has brought the region's economic inequality to the fore. Individual countries lack the economic resources needed to supply ventilators, masks, and necessary personal protective equipment to its medical personnel, even as the lack of sufficient hospital beds, doctors, and nurses were also made apparent. There are tremendous variations among and within countries in the capacity for individuals to respond to the pandemic conditions. We have also been reminded that those economically precarious Latin Americans who work in the informal sector do not have a choice to shelter-in-place, maintain social distance, or wash their hands for 20 seconds every time they would like. They are likely to lack accessible health care in many countries, and if they are unable to work, informal and other low-wage workers are unlikely to have savings or receive government checks to provide food and other necessities for families. When vaccines initially became available globally, Latin American countries were unable to procure them in significant numbers, and the region continued to be ravaged by Covid well after other parts of the world seemed on the path to recovery.

In the end, students should not leave with the idea that Latin America is a region of desperation and poverty. Nor is it simply a place of resorts, beaches, an exotic culture, and people who are friendly and glad to serve the foreign tourists looking to get away. It is a diverse and complicated place, with wealthy and poor, political instability and stability, and significant challenges to confront. In that sense, it is not so different than everywhere else early in the third decade of the twenty-first century.

Timeline of Modern Latin American History

1804	A successful slave rebellion that defeats the French colonizer makes Haiti the second country in the hemisphere, after the United States, to achieve independence.
1820s	Most Latin American countries gain independence from Spain.
1829	Beginning of prominent role for *caudillo* Juan Manuel de Rosas in Argentina that will last as a dictatorship from 1835 to 1852.
1830	Simon Bolívar dies; "The Liberator" played an important role in Latin American independence, but failed in his effort to create a unified region.
1848	Mexico loses roughly half of its territory as part of the Treaty of Guadalupe Hidalgo following the Mexican–American War.
1862	The United States recognizes Haitian independence of 1804.
1880s	Brazil abolishes slavery and completes its independence from Portugal.
1898	At the end of the Spanish–American War, the United States takes control over Cuba and Puerto Rico.
1903	Panama declares independence from Colombia, with the support of the United States, which begins to build the Panama Canal.

1910   Mexican Revolution begins and lasts nearly a decade.

1916   Argentina holds an election with universal male suffrage; Hipolito Yrigoyen is elected president.

1929   In Mexico, the National Revolutionary Party (PNR, for its initials in Spanish) is founded; in a few years, it will be renamed the Institutional Revolutionary Party (PRI) and hold power until 2000.

1932   The election of Arturo Alessandri as president of Chile marks the restoration of stability to the country and the beginning of decades of democratic elections.

1934   Fulgencio Batista leads the overthrow of the government in Cuba; he will wield power in the country for a quarter century.

1938   Mexican President Lazaro Cardenas nationalizes oil in the country, creating PEMEX.

1943   Argentina sets up a military government, with Juan Perón serving as Secretary of Labor.

1946   Juan Perón wins the election for president of Argentina; he will win re-election in 1951 and serve in office until 1955, when he is sent into exile.

1948   In Costa Rica, President Figueres abolishes the army and extends voting rights to women in the country.

1953   A national oil company, Petrobras, is formed in Brazil.

1954   A CIA-backed coup overthrows the elected leftist Jacobo Arbenz in Guatemala.

1959   Cuban Revolutionaries headed by Fidel Castro seize power.

1960   The population of Latin America and the Caribbean is approximately 220 million; half of those live in either Brazil or Mexico.

1964   A military government takes power in Brazil and will hold power for more than two decades.

1970   Chilean democratic socialist, Salvador Allende, elected president.

1973   Pressure from the United States and domestic opposition to his policies lead to a military coup in Chile, during which Salvador Allende commits suicide; General Augusto Pinochet seizes power, which he will hold until losing a plebiscite in 1988, leaving office in 1990.

1976   Isabel Perón, who took office in 1974 when her husband died after only a year in the presidency after his return from exile, is removed from office by the Argentine military beginning a "dirty war" in which thousands die, are tortured, and are "disappeared."

1979   The Sandinista Revolution in Nicaragua topples the Somoza regime.

1982   The Mexican government declares itself bankrupt, beginning the region's debt crisis, and the "lost decade" of the 1980s for the region more generally. Argentina's military government invade the Falklands Islands (Islas Malvinas) seeking to take control from the United Kingdom; Prime Minister Thatcher mobilizes her navy, and humiliates the Argentine military in taking back control of the islands.

1983   After its crushing defeat, the military junta leaves office in Argentina, and Raul Alfonsín is elected president.

1989   Brazilians elect Fernando Collor de Mello in the first direct election for the presidency since the military took power in 1964.

1990   The Sandinistas are voted out of power in Nicaragua.

1991   The trade bloc of Mercosur is established, constituted by Argentina, Brazil, Paraguay, and Uruguay.

1994	On January 1, the North American Free Trade Agreement (NAFTA) is implemented; on the same day, the Zapatistas rebel in southern Mexico, briefly taking control of the state of Chiapas. All countries of the Americas, except Cuba, agree during the Summit of the Americas in Miami, Florida to form a Free Trade Agreement of the Americas (FTAA) by January 1, 2005.
1999	President Hugo Chavez takes office in Venezuela as the first of several leftist presidents in the region, who will make up the so-called "red tide".
2000	Vicente Fox wins election to president in Mexico, the first time a non-PRI candidate has been elected since the party was formed soon after the Mexican Revolution.
2001	Argentina is devastated by an economic crisis.
2002	Lula da Silva, a former metalworker, wins the presidency of Brazil in his fourth attempt; Brazil wins its fifth World Cup.
2005	Former organizer of coca growers in Bolivia, Evo Morales wins the presidency.
2006	A member of the Chilean Socialist Party, Michelle Bachelet, becomes the country's first woman president. A seriously ill Fidel Castro cedes the presidency of Cuba temporarily to his brother Raúl; two years late, it becomes permanent.
2009	A coup in Honduras overthrows President Zelaya; the Obama administration in the United States supports the coup government's staying in power until elections later that year.
2010	Argentina becomes the first country in Latin America to legalize gay marriage. Dilma Rousseff elected as the first woman president of Brazil.
2013	Hugo Chavez dies after having supported Nicolás Maduro as his successor; Maduro wins the presidential election shortly after Chavez's death.
2014	An investigation named "Operation Car Wash," into bribery by Odebrecht, a construction firm based in Brazil, exposes corruption in that country and begins to expand across the region. President Obama and President Raúl Castro announce the normalization of relations between the US and Cuba.
2016	Negotiations lead to an agreement between the Colombian government and the FARC, a revolutionary force that has been fighting since the 1960s. In Brazil, which had hosted the World Cup in 2014, and the Olympics in 2016, President Dilma Rousseff is impeached for corruption; some term it a "political coup."
2017	Hurricane Maria sweeps through the Caribbean causing widespread devastation; the category five hurricane causes more damage to Puerto Rico than any natural disaster ever recorded.
2018	Evangelical, conservative Jair Bolsonaro wins the election for president in Brazil. In his third presidential campaign, Andres Manuel López Obrador wins the presidency of Mexico as a leftist populist in an overwhelming victory.
2019	Widespread street protests take place in Chile against the Piñera government, based specifically on a hike in subway fares and more generally on widespread social and economic inequality. Following demonstrations challenging the legitimacy of the voting process leading to his re-election, Evo Morales resigns from the presidency in Bolivia and leaves the country.
2020	The Covid-19 pandemic spreads across Latin America. Brazil is being hit hardest, although Mexico has also suffered, and the entire region seems vulnerable.

References

Chasteen, John Charles. 2016. *Born in Blood & Fire*, 4th ed. New York: W. W. Norton & Company.

Eakin, Marshall C. 2007. *The History of Latin America: Collision of Cultures*. New York: Palgrave Macmillan.

Galeano, Eduardo. 1988. *Memory of Fire: Century of Winds*. New York: Pantheon Books.

Smith, Peter H., and James N. Green. 2019. *Modern Latin America*, 9th ed. New York: Oxford University Press.

Vanden, Harry E., and Gary Prevost. 2018. *Politics of Latin America: The Power Game*, 6th ed. New York: Oxford University Press.

Further Reading

Books

Bonilla, Yarimar, and Marisol Lebrón, eds. 2019. *Aftershocks of Disaster: Puerto Rico Before and After the Storm*. Chicago: Haymarket Books.

Elsey, Brenda, and Joshua Nadel. 2019. *Futbolera: A History of Women and Sports in Latin America*. Austin: University of Texas Press.

Grandin, Greg. 2019. *From the Frontier to the Border Wall in the Mind of America*. New York: Metropolitan Books.

Jackiewicz, Edward, and Fernando Bosco, eds. 2020. *Placing Latin America: Contemporary Themes in Geography*, 4th ed. Lanham, MD: Rowman and Littlefield.

Schwarcz, Lilia Moritz and Heloisa Maria Murgel Starling. 2017. *Brazil: A Biography*. New York: Farrar, Straus, and Giroux.

Films

After Maria (2019). Director Nadia Hallgren (Netflix short).

Amores Perros (2000). Director Alejandro González Iñárritu, Mexico.

City of God (2002). Directors Fernando Meirelles and Kátia Lund, Brazil.

Even the Rain (2010). Director Icíar Bollaín, Spain.

Maria Full of Grace (2004). Director Joshua Marston, Colombia.

The Motorcycle Diaries (2004). Director Walter Moreira Salles, Argentina.

No (2012). Director Pablo Larraín, Chile.

Roma (2018). Director Alfonso Cuarón, Mexico.

Journals

Americas Quarterly. americasquarterly.org

Latin American Perspectives. journals.sagepub.com/home/lap

North America Congress on Latin America (NACLA). nacla.org

Websites

Center for Democracy in the Americas. democracyinamericas.org

Council on Hemispheric Affairs. coha.org

Latin American News Dispatch (LAND). latindispatch.com

Washington Office on Latin America. wola.org

Part Three

Contemporary Global Issues

Chapter 13

Global Climate Change

Earth Day was first celebrated in 1970. Fifty years have passed by and where are we? We are living longer. There is more food to eat. Fewer women die in childbirth. More people live longer. The population growth rate is not as high (Mann 2020). There are still global issues, climate change is one of them. Fifty years from now, where will we be?

November 2020 was the second warmest November in the 141-year record of the National Oceanic and Atmospheric Administration (di Liberto, 2020). The year 2020 was one of the top years on record for global temperature, almost equal to the record set in 2016. In December 2020, a BBC news headline read "Climate change: 2021 will be cooler but still in top six warmest." Projections indicate the earth's temperature will be 0.9 to 1.15 degrees Celsius warmer than 1850–1900. The year 2021 is slightly lower than 2019–2020 due to the La Niña event in the Pacific, which brings up colder waters from the bottom of the ocean. A BBC headline in January 2017 read, "Climate Change: Data shows 2016 to be warmest year yet." The increase over 2015 was 0.07 degrees Celsius. Fifteen of the top 16 warmest years ever recorded have been in the twenty-first century. These record temperatures were caused by human activities. Climate change is a major challenge to the world (McGrath 2017).

Human activities are closely linked to climate. Due to global climate change, all forms of life will have to make adjustments. What are the controls on climate? Solar energy comes from the sun, passing through the atmosphere. Most solar radiation is absorbed by the earth's surface, which warms the atmosphere. Some infrared radiation passes through the atmosphere into space; however, some gasses in the atmosphere absorb the infrared radiation, thus heating up the earth. Two of the gasses that absorb infrared radiation are carbon dioxide (CO_2) and methane (CH_4). This is referred to as the "greenhouse effect": these gasses trap the heat inside the atmosphere, just like a greenhouse keeps plants warm by absorbing radiation (Price et al. 2020).

What are the sources of these greenhouse gasses? Carbon dioxide is produced through the burning of fossil fuels (such as coal and oil), wood, and some other chemical reactions, such as the manufacture of cement. Concentrations of CO_2 have increased tremendously in recent years. Methane, which absorbs radiation even more efficiently, is produced through the production and transport of fossil fuels, burning vegetation, cattle effluent, organic waste decay in landfills, and pipeline leaks (U.S. EPA 2021).

In 1860, atmospheric carbon dioxide was measured at 280 parts per million (ppm). In 2015, the rate was 400 ppm (Price et al. 2020). May 2020 hit the highest CO_2 emissions ever at 417 ppm (Freeman and Mooney 2020). This increase was due to the human production of CO_2 and other gasses, such as CH_4. There is definitely more CO_2 and CH_4 in the atmosphere today, and temperatures have also risen. Temperature increases have been noted since the 1800s, with the increased industrial consumption of fossil fuels (coal and oil). As noted by Dr. Gavin Schmidt

DOI: 10.4324/9781003028314-17

of NASA, "There is no evidence that the warming trend has slowed in the past few decades" (McGrath 2016).

What are the impacts of climate change? With the increase in temperature, ice caps are melting, sea levels are rising, and more extreme weather events are occurring. Some areas are having more precipitation and flooding, while others experience a decrease in precipitation and suffer from drought. Agricultural production of corn and wheat in the United States and Canada may decline. Low-lying coastal areas such as Florida, the South Pacific Islands, and Bangladesh are affected by the rise in sea levels. Heatwaves in cities affect millions, while clean water is a problem in other areas.

Who are the major producers of greenhouse gasses? In 2020, the top 10 producers of greenhouse gasses contributed 68.9 percent of emissions. The major producers include China 26 percent, United States 13 percent, European Union (27 countries) 7.8 percent, India 6.7 percent, Russia 5.3 percent, Japan 2.7 percent, Brazil 2.3 percent, Indonesia 1.9 percent, Iran 1.7 percent, and South Korea 1.5 percent. All others produced 31.1 percent. Primary sources are fossil fuel combustion, cement manufacturing, and gas flaring. The BRICS states and the developed countries (the United States, Europe, Japan, etc.) account for a substantial portion of greenhouse gas emissions (Ge and Friedrich 2020).

International studies examines the role of the environment and space in global issues by using geography. Where are the impacts of climate change? Coastal, low-lying areas such as Bangladesh, Tuvalu, and Florida are particularly vulnerable to sea level rise. First, the sea water inundates the water table underground, then the land is covered by sea. All along Florida and the US eastern seaboard, including major cities like New York, the impact of sea-level rise is enhanced, as the eastern seaboard is subsiding at the same time. Bangladesh and Florida are vulnerable to hurricanes; the intensity of tropical storms will probably increase due to climate change. People will lose homes and be forced to move inland. Bangladesh is low-lying like Florida but has a higher density of population. People from Florida could move inland to Ohio, but where will the people of Bangladesh go? India? In the case of Tuvalu, with its low-lying islands of coral atolls, there is nowhere to go. Both Tuvalu and Bangladesh contribute little to CO_2 emissions, yet the impact of climate change is enormous in these countries (Narang 2015; Rees 2015). Yergin (2020) profiles the huge impacts of climate change on the energy mix of the United States, Russia, China and the Middle East.

International studies uses history to interpret and analyze past events. For climate change, we can analyze the rise in temperatures along with the increase in industrialization and the concomitant increase in CO_2 emissions. History also examines big ideas; for example, the history of ideas in science. The historical literature on the industrial revolution or Darwin's ideas about evolution are precursors to our understanding of climate change. How do we experience the history of climate change? The analogy is one of a frog in a vat of hot water. As the temperature is slowly increased, the frog is slowly cooked. The scale of the changes is so enormous and the amount of data to analyze climate are so huge, that scientific analysis somehow exceeds people's everyday capacities. An ignorance or distrust of science has also developed in recent years; climate change is an example of that challenge (Coen 2016).

International studies uses anthropology to understand how beliefs and values shape people's interactions. How are people's lives affected by climate change? Anthropologists studying peoples in the Arctic and Subarctic note that annual average temperatures there have increased by 2 to 3 degrees Celsius since the 1950s, or twice as much as the rest of the world. Communities there are experiencing stress on their lifestyles from climate change. In the South Pacific, as mentioned earlier, sea-level rise has affected low-lying communities such as Tuvalu, who now will make decisions on possible migration or relocation. Climate change due to anthropogenic (human-made) forces means that indigenous people in Papua New Guinea and Australia are taking up new methods to address and assess climate change in terms of both practical needs (e.g., adapting to drought events) and cosmological worldviews (Crate and Nutall 2016).

International studies considers the costs and benefits of global issues by using economics. Two policy responses to climate change are mitigation and adaptation. Mitigation responses involve ways to limit or reduce the amount of greenhouse gas emissions. Less factory production, fewer automobiles, and less burning of fossil fuels are possible methods, which have both costs and benefits. A low-carbon economy would reduce carbon output: we would need to focus on alternative energy sources such as geothermal, nuclear, solar, wind, or hydroelectric energy. Other economic or environmental costs may be associated with alternative energy. Dams for hydropower create large reservoirs, which inundate large surface areas. Nuclear power plants create nuclear waste. But these may certainly be cheaper than the costs of a global temperature increase. Adaptation is another method to live with climate change. We can move inland from the sea to higher ground, though migration costs money. We can build sea walls to protect from sea-level rise or adapt to a warmer planet by planting different crops that may be more drought resistant or saltwater tolerant. The essential issue is that only wealthy people or countries would be able to pay for such adaptations. While the rich world has caused climate change, the poor world will suffer also. In the long run, we will have to pursue both adaptation and mitigation strategies. The cost of *not* using these strategies would be larger than the cost of using them (Nunn et al. 2019; Stern 2006; Incropera 2016).

International studies uses political science to assess how power is used to manage conflict over global issues. While countries have not gone to war over climate, there are certainly political factors relevant to understanding how we can manage climate change. The debates on climate change have proceeded through several stages of international political negotiation. In 1988, two UN organizations, the World Meteorological Organization (WMO) and the United Nations Environment Programme (UNEP), set up the Intergovernmental Panel on Climate Change (IPCC), composed of scientists and practitioners. The IPCC develops reports based on current published research. (For their efforts, the IPCC won the 2007 Nobel Peace Prize, shared with former US vice president Al Gore.) The IPCC is currently working on the Sixth Assessment Report due in 2022. At the Rio Convention in 1992, countries agreed to voluntarily limit their greenhouse gas emissions. With the Kyoto Protocol in 1997, over 30 industrialized countries (including much of Europe, Japan, Australia, but not the United States) agreed to cut greenhouse gas emissions and to have penalties if emission targets were not reached. Developing countries did not have to follow this protocol, so China and India did not cut back on greenhouse gas emissions. Further negotiation in 2012–2105 led to the 2015 Paris Agreement at the United Nations Climate Change Conference (Incropera 2016). The Paris Agreement is not a treaty, so it does not need to be ratified by legislatures. The agreement covers all 195 countries, who have committed to reduce greenhouse gas emissions based on their Intended Nationally Determined Contributions (INDCs). Developed countries will contribute funds to assist poorer countries. A key element to passage of the Paris Agreement was that both China and the United States, the two largest CO_2 emitters, agreed to limit greenhouse gasses (Bradsher 2016; Faulkner 2016; Price et al. 2020). President Trump pulled out of the Paris Agreement, but President Biden rejoined the Paris Agreement (McGrath 2020; Newburger 2020). Many US states went ahead with their climate change plans during the Trump administration. John Kerry is President Biden's climate envoy—he was a lead negotiator for the United States on the Paris Agreement. The set of agreements on climate change is an example of the political theory of **idealism/liberalism** at work (see Chapter 5).

We will have more political negotiations through history, more economic cost-benefit analysis, and more geographical and anthropological analysis of climate change's impact on peoples' lands and livelihoods. In 2019 *Time* magazine chose Greta Thunberg as the Person of the Year

(Alter et al. 2019). Climate change is a significant global issue. At a Climate Action Summit at the UN, Thunberg (2019) said "We will not let you get away with this. Right here, right now is where we draw the line. The world is waking up. And change is coming, whether you like it or not."

References

Alter, Charlotte, Suyin Haynes and Justin Worland. 2019. "Time 2019 Person of the Year- Greta Thunberg." *Time*. https://time.com/person-of-the-year-2019-greta-thunberg/

Bradsher, Keith. 2016. "The Paris Agreement on Climate Change Is Official, Now What?" *The New York Times*, November 3. www.nytimes.com/2016/11/04/business/energy-environment/paris-climate-change-agreement-official-now-what.html

Coen, D. R. 2016. "Big Is a Thing of the Past: Climate Change and Methodology in the History of Ideas." *Journal of the History of Ideas* 77 (2): 305–21.

Crate, Susan A., and Mark Nuttall, eds. 2016. *Anthropology and Climate Change: From Encounters to Actions*. New York: Routledge.

Faulkner, Robert. 2016. "The Paris Agreement and the New Logic of International Climate Politics." *International Affairs* 92 (5): 1107–25.

Freeman, Andrew and Chris Mooney. June 4, 2020. "Earth's Carbon Dioxide Levels Hit Record High, Despite Coronavirus-related Emissions Drop." *Washington Post*. www.washingtonpost.com/weather/2020/06/04/carbon-dioxide-record-2020/

Ge Minpin and Johannes Friedrich. 2020. "4 Charts Explain Greenhouse Gas Emissions by Countries and Sectors." *World Resources Institute*. www.wri.org/blog/2020/02/greenhouse-gas-emissions-by-country-sector

Incropera, Frank P. 2016. *Climate Change: A Wicked Problem*. Cambridge: Cambridge University Press.

Intergovernmental Panel on Climate Change (IPCC). 2014. *Fifth Assessment Report. Climate Change 2014*. http://ipcc.ch/report/ar5/syr/

Intergovernmental Panel on Climate Change (IPCC). 2020. *AR6 Synthesis Report Climate Change 2022*. www.ipcc.ch/report/sixth-assessment-report-cycle/

di Liberto, Tony. 2020. "November 2020: The Year Is Ending as It Began, on a Hot Streak." *Climate.gov. NOAA*. www.climate.gov/news-features/understanding-climate/november-2020-year-ending-it-began-hot-streak

Mann, Charles. 2020. "Globally, Humans Are Better off Than the First Earth Day." *National Geographic*. April. www.nationalgeographic.com/magazine/2020/04/globally-humans-are-better-off-today-than-on-the-first-earth-day/

McGrath, Matt. 2017. "Climate Change: Data Shows 2016 to Be Warmest Year Yet." *BBC News*, January 18. www.bbc.com/news/science-environment-38652746

———. 2020. "Climate Change: 2021 Will Be Cooler but Still in Top Six Warmest." *BBC News*, December 18. www.bbc.com/news/science-environment-55365414

Narang, Sonali. 2015. "Imaginative Geographies of Climate Change Induced Displacements and Migration: A Case Study of Tuvalu." *Journal of Alternative Perspectives in the Social Sciences* 7 (2): 262–82.

Newburger, Emma. 2020. "Biden Will Rejoin the Paris Climate Accord." *CNBC*. www.cnbc.com/2020/11/20/biden-to-rejoin-paris-climate-accord-heres-what-happens-next-.html

Nunn, Ryan, Jimmy O'Donnell, Jay Shambaugh, Lawrence H. Goulder, Charles D. Kolstad, and Xianling Long. October 23, 2019. "Ten Facts about the Economics of Climate Change and Climate Policy." Brookings. www.brookings.edu/research/ten-facts-about-the-economics-of-climate-change-and-climate-policy/

Rees, Judith. 2015. "Geography and Climate Change: Presidential Address and Record of the Royal Geographical Society (with IBG) AGM 2015." *Geographical Journal* 181 (3): 304–10.

Price, Marie, Martin Lewis, William Wyckoff and Lester Rowntree. 2020. *Globalization and Diversity*. 6th ed. Upper Saddle River, NJ: Prentice Hall.

Stern, Nicholas. 2006. *Stern Review on the Economics of Climate Change*. http://webarchive.nationalarchives.gov.uk/ + www.hm-treasury.gov.uk/sternreview_index.htm

Thunberg, Greta 2019. "Transcript: Greta Thunberg's Speech At The U.N. Climate Action Summit." *NPR*. www.npr.org/2019/09/23/763452863/transcript-greta-thunbergs-speech-at-the-u-n-climate-action-summit

U.S. Environmental Protection Agency (EPA). 2021. "Greenhouse Gas Emissions." www.epa.gov/ghgemissions/

Yergin, Daniel. 2020. *The New Map: Energy, Climate and the Clash of Nations*. New York: Penguin.

Chapter 14

International Terrorism

In May 2020 a 17-year-old man in Toronto entered an erotic massage parlor and stabbed a female masseuse to death with a machete and injured her co-worker. The teenager was a self-identified member of the misogynistic incel movement, a group of people who profess to believe that society is sexist against men and that they are unfairly marginalized from society's "sexual economy" and seek to establish a patriarchal social order in which women are obedient and sexually accessible to men of all different backgrounds. Since 2009, individuals linked to the movement have been involved in at least 13 reported attacks in North America (Hastings, Jones and Stolte 2020). As a result, the Canadian Mounted Police charged the teenager not only with murder but with terrorism.

The sentence for terrorism is no worse than the sentence for first-degree murder in Canada, but some authorities saw this as an opportunity to test the ability of the court system to manage issues of domestic terrorism. In this, they join a rising push by politicians in many countries to establish laws that allow them to pursue domestic social movements as "terrorists." In the US, these calls have come from both the right and the left. In 2020 US President Donald Trump tweeted his intention to designate Antifa, a far-left ideological movement opposed to fascists, neo-Nazis and far-right groups, as a domestic terrorist organization and the Oklahoma County district attorney filed terrorism charges against Black Lives Matter protesters who committed vandalism. On the left, online petitions to label the racist Ku Klux Klan a terrorist organization received hundreds of thousands of signatures, and some Democratic state legislatures have promoted the creation of special police task forces targeting right-wing extremism.

Such efforts represent dramatic shifts in global terrorism over the past decade, particularly a shift to fluid networks replacing formal terrorist organizations, an increase in domestic political movements engaging in violent protests, and the rise of individual "lone wolf" terrorists.

Terrorism has emerged as one of the central global concerns of the twenty-first century. While terrorism has been an international issue since the nineteenth century, the collapse of states like Afghanistan, Iraq, Libya, and Syria created fertile ground for the rise of new transnational terrorist networks on an unprecedented scale. Americans have understandably tended to see terrorism everywhere through the lens of September 11. But understanding terrorism exclusively in terms of Islamic terrorists crossing borders to deal destruction fails to take into account either the historical depth or geographical breadth of terrorism. Worse, it creates a tendency to conflate all terrorism into a single entity against which we can imagine ourselves at war. To call for a "war on terror" is to group together such diverse terrorists as al Qaeda and the Islamic State, Chechens fighting for a separate state from Russia, the United Wa State Army in Burma, the Liberation Tigers of Tamil Eelam in Sri Lanka, Colombia's Fuerzas Armadas Revolucionarias de Colombia (FARC), Ejército del Pueblo and drug cartel militias, Peru's Sendero Luminoso, the Irish Republican Army and its successors, the Basque Euskadi Ta Askatasuna (ETA) in Spain, the Israeli Kahane Chai and Kach, the rival Palestinian groups Hamas and Fatah, the Kurdistan

DOI: 10.4324/9781003028314-18

Workers Party in Turkey, the Japanese AUM sect and Red Army, and the United States' Timothy McVeigh and the Unabomber. All these groups and individuals have used terrorism, but they believe in very different things and seek very different goals. A realistic assessment of terrorism requires consideration of the historical and contemporary political and economic conditions in which terrorism operates.

Terrorism is a strategy by which subnational groups, not recognized as legitimate by the states they oppose, seek to resist those states by targeting non-state actors, disrupting the flow of everyday life, and spreading generalized fear among the populations of those states. The Global Terrorism Database (www.start.umd.edu/gtd/) recognizes three criteria for an action to be considered "terrorism":

- The act must be aimed at attaining a political, economic, religious, or social goal.
- There must be evidence of an intention to coerce, intimidate, or convey some other message to a larger audience (or audiences) than the immediate victims.
- The action must be outside the context of legitimate warfare activities.

Terrorism is primarily a communicative act, not a strategic one. It is a technique through which groups seek to force states or other publics to acknowledge them. In many cases, terrorists seek to provoke a military or political response as a form of recognition. Terrorism may also seek to demoralize the citizens of a state and so undermine support for the regimes that the terrorists oppose. The technologies of globalization create greater opportunities for terrorists to expand those messages; for example, by posting videos to websites. Terrorism on the scale of the September 11 attacks may also inflict real damage on economic infrastructures, at least in the short run.

A great deal of misunderstanding stems from rhetorical misuses of the term *terrorism* in political speech and news reporting. The activity of terrorism—the use of violence against noncombatants and civil institutions—is often confused with terrorists' motives. In part, this is because states generally do not like to describe their allies as terrorists. For example, the British praised and supported the Malayan People's Anti-Japanese Army during World War II, even though it targeted civilian collaborators as much as Japanese occupiers. When these same groups turned on the British colonial administration of Malaya after the war, assassinating civil administrators and plantation owners, the British relabeled them terrorists. But they saw themselves as freedom fighters seeking an end to foreign rule (Bayly and Harper 2004).

An erroneous focus on motivations can lead to difficulties in recognizing and defining terrorists. Sometimes it is difficult to tell whether an organization is terrorist or engaged in a legitimate fight for freedom. In Canada, two members of the same Pakistani political organization were given completely different judgments by the country's Immigration and Refugee Board in 2007. One was declared a refugee and the other a terrorist (Humphreys 2007). "There is the famous statement: 'One man's terrorist is another man's freedom fighter.' But that is grossly leading," said Martin Rudner, director of the Canadian Centre of Intelligence and Security Studies at Ottawa's Carleton University. "It assesses the validity of the cause when terrorism is an act. One can have a perfectly beautiful cause and yet if one commits terrorist acts, it is terrorism regardless" (Humphreys 2007).

Terrorism has a long history, but it is primarily associated with the rise of colonialism. Most European colonial powers were liberal democracies at home but imperialists in their colonies. Local insurgencies arose to combat them, often targeting civilians as part of their resistance. Early uses of terrorism in the Middle East—Zionist terrorists like Irgun and the Stern Gang against British power, and Arab and Jewish groups against one another—developed at this time (Vest 2001). The most global terrorist movement of the colonial era was that of the anarchists, a network of loosely affiliated European intellectuals and militants committed to a common utopian political vision—not unlike al Qaeda today (Bergesen and Han 2005). Between the 1870s and World War I, anarchist terrorists assassinated three kings, two presidents, and two prime ministers; and they bombed cafés, railway cars, and financial districts in North America and Europe.

Since 2000, there have been more than 120,000 terrorist attacks worldwide. Total casualties exceed 200,000 people. While more than 100 countries have experienced terrorist attacks in any given year, the majority of deaths from terrorism in recent years occurred in five countries: Afghanistan, Iraq, Nigeria, Syria, and Somalia. Prior to 2002, terrorism had been on the decline; the number of terrorist incidents worldwide peaked in 1987 and had been falling. The total number of terrorist attacks in the first five years of the new millennium was less than half the total number of terrorist incidents between 1985 and 1990. The rise in terrorism since 2000 is linked to a number of factors. Wars, the collapse of the Soviet Union, and ongoing political and economic crises in Africa and West Asia have created many new states that are seen as weak and unstable, and hence vulnerable. Weak states and wars mean that more people have access to increasingly lethal weaponry.

Global economic volatility, including the 2007–2008 financial crisis and subsequent worldwide recession, the European sovereign debt crisis and the impact of Covid-19 pandemic lockdowns have exacerbated already existing problems of poverty and high unemployment, particularly among young men, who make up the primary demographic from which terrorists are recruited. Shrinking economic opportunities worldwide have also increased competition for scarce resources and exacerbated sectarian tensions. These shifts in the global economy, and ideological beliefs about the causes of these, are widely seen as reasons for the rise in far-right terrorism as well.

Finally, the use of rape, mass killing, drone strikes, assassinations, and similar measures by military forces as tactics of war has led many people in the world to call for retaliation in kind. Many experts emphasize that terrorism is closely related to activities by states: terrorists define themselves in opposition to states and exist in a dynamic relationship to oppression by those states (Lauderdale and Oliverio 2005). The contemporary use by states of retaliatory bombing, death squads, torture, and other such actions is sometimes referred to as **state terrorism**.

A classic example of state terrorism occurred in the 1970s when six Latin American governments led by Chile formed a military alliance called Operation Condor to carry out kidnappings, torture, and political assassinations against leftist opponents they deemed "terrorists." Operation Condor carried out activities not only in South America but also North America and Europe, initially with support and training from the United States (Dinges 2012). Although these states justified their actions as fighting fire with fire, many experts argue that being able to occupy a higher moral ground than their opponents is crucial for states seeking to defeat terrorism.

State terrorism should not be confused with **state-sponsored terrorism**, in which a state harbors, and sometimes supports, the terrorist enemies of another state. This concept is also highly controversial, since states rarely acknowledge that the paramilitaries and insurgents they support are terrorists. Afghanistan, Argentina, Belgium, Chile, Cuba, Iran, Iraq, Italy, Libya, Pakistan, the Palestinian Authority, South Africa, the Soviet Union, Spain, Syria, the United Kingdom, and the United States have all at various times been accused by other states of sponsoring terrorism. The United States has the distinction of being the only state to have been convicted of this offense by the World Court because of its support for the paramilitary Contras in Nicaragua in the 1980s (International Court of Justice 1986).

But state-sponsored terrorism may well be declining. Globalization has opened up unexpected new opportunities for terrorists. Global communication networks have made it easier for terrorist organizations to communicate directly with their publics, as when Iraqi insurgents have posted videos of beheadings on the Internet. In an era where a billion people every year are moving across national borders for tourism, work, or flight from disaster, the movements of a few handfuls of terrorists are relatively easy to mask.

One of the consequences of September 11 and subsequent political terrorism by Islamic groups, such as the attacks in Madrid, London, Paris, Brussels, and Nice, is that it has created a popular equation between Islam and terrorism in many parts of the world, especially North America and Europe. Previously, groups like the Palestine Liberation Organization were no more referred to as Islamic terrorists than members of the Irish Republican Army were referred to as Christian terrorists. Since September 11 there has been a growing tendency in the West to see terrorism less in political and more in religious terms. This has been exacerbated by terrorist acts carried out by Muslim citizens, immigrants, and refugees in a number of non-Muslim majority countries, including France, India, the Netherlands, the United States, and others.

Terrorism, however, is not an inherently religious act, nor is Islam, or any other religion, especially prone to producing terrorists. Atheist, Buddhist, Christian, Hindu, Jewish, and Muslim terrorists are all part of the historical record. Until very recently, the majority of terrorists in the world have been some variety of Marxist, and until the rise of the Islamic State, Marxist groups were responsible for the majority of terrorist acts. Currently, far-right terrorism has increased by more than 300 percent in Europe, North America, and the Pacific (Australia and New Zealand). More importantly, overattention to the religion or ideology of terrorist organizations can blind us to the economic and political realities that motivate many terrorists. Contemporary terrorism seems to be directly related to changes in international and intercultural relations, especially the growing integration of markets, political structures, images, technologies, and environmental concerns around the world. Globalization, in the words of one terrorism scholar, exports dreams of freedom and affluence. The failure of these dreams, and their contrast with the grim realities of global disparity, can lead to "the migration of nightmares" (Nassar 2005).

The collapse of promises of middle-class prosperity is significant for the motivations of religious terrorists. "The recruits to Islamic fundamentalist movements generally … are educated, intelligent, disillusioned men of middle and lower middle class who have been denied their place in the sun," writes anthropologist Uni Wikan (Wikan 2002, 125). They are looking for a way out of the hopelessness of what they see as unjust, corrupt, and repressive societies that they believe are immune to democratic change because they know that their governments are backed by foreign powers like the United States, Russia, European states, Qatar, or Saudi Arabia. Many turn to forms of Islam that reassure them that their souls are better than those of the wicked who prosper in this world. Some come to believe in the possibility of a political solution that would bring about a just, free, and peaceful new world order guaranteed by God. A few are willing to sacrifice their lives, and take the lives of others, to make this vision a reality.

In fact, this absence of hope that life will get better seems to be a more common denominator for terrorist motives than religion. In her conversations with Sikh militants in Asia, anthropologist Cynthia Keppley Mahmood found that economic collapse, and excessive violence by Indian national military forces seeking to combat terrorists, created a climate in which many men and women saw militancy, including terrorism, as the only meaningful option open for them (Mahmood 1996). Similarly, investigations into the motivations of captured suicide bombers in Israel suggests that the effort to escape from a hopeless present by doing something decisive and dramatic is more significant than personal faith in either religion or political ideology (Moghadam 2003). The fact that terrorism is an act by the disaffected or marginalized that seeks to draw attention to a political or ideological goal has enabled organizations like the Islamic State to use global communications networks to "inspire" acts of terror by people who are not members of the organization. Instead, these terrorists are residents, even citizens, of the states in which they commit their crimes. Terrorist groups use the intimacy of social media as a tool to recruit, inspire, and enable their followers. How, then, can states protect their citizens from terrorism?

Direct military confrontation has usually proven to be the least effective tool against terrorist groups. The amount of power states can bring against terrorist groups is considerable, and in any direct confrontation, states must win. But terrorism is a weapon of the weak, and terrorists by definition seek to avoid confrontation, to melt away, regroup, and reform. There is, moreover, considerable evidence that military confrontations provide terrorist organizations with recruitment tools.

Effective policing is one of the best ways to reduce successful terrorist attacks within states. Wealthy states usually have powerful and effective police systems and intelligence gathering. In the last few years, nearly 50 countries have passed or updated laws to help them identify and prosecute foreign terrorist fighters. In addition, many of these states form international partnerships to identify, track, and deter the travel of suspected terrorists. Efforts are also increasing to find ways to reduce terrorist attacks by citizens "inspired" by international terrorist organizations. As a result, the number of terrorist casualties in North America and Europe is generally relatively low compared to Africa and the Middle East (Bureau of Counterterrorism 2016).

When we look at how terrorist threats have historically been ended, we find the most effective solution is to transform the socioeconomic conditions that give rise to them, as World War I and the postwar changes in the global political economy ended organized anarchist terrorism. Similarly, ceasefires and cessations by separatist groups that practiced terrorism in Ireland and Spain have been created largely by changing the political landscape so that democratic alternatives to pursue change seemed plausible.

Yet implementation of effective counterterrorism policies is often challenging, especially in democratic states. Increased surveillance of communication is often strongly resisted by citizens as infringing on their rights. Efforts to rebuild **failed states** in order to prevent terrorism may seem to taxpayers to be a waste of money that could be better used at home or, worse, as rewarding terrorism. And dramatic actions by political leaders that speak to popular fears, such as bans on immigrants, have proven to be among the least effective measures in actually combatting terrorism.

A final disturbing trend of the last decade has been a rise of far-right terrorists. In Norway, a 2011 attack in Norway left 77 people dead. A mosque shooting in New Zealand in 2019 killed 51. According to a 2017 Government Accountability Office report, 73 percent of deaths from violent extremist incidents since September 12, 2001 were caused by right-wing extremist groups, including 23 killed at a Walmart in El Paso in 2019, 11 killed in a Pittsburgh synagogue in 2018, and 9 killed in a predominantly Black church in Charleston in 2015. Nine immigrants were killed in shootings at two shisha bars in Hanau, Germany in 2020. This rise of far-right terrorists is part of a larger shift from international terrorism to domestic terrorism. A problem for states seeking to control these new domestic terrorist threats is that local law enforcement is far more likely to include members of these groups than far-left terrorists (Miller-Idriss 2020).

The twenty-first century is, so far, an age of terrorism. The number of terror incidents peaked in 2014, but the geographic spread of terrorist acts and the destructive capacity of these acts remain high. The capacity of social media to increase domestic terrorism inspired and enabled by external actors poses dramatically new challenges to efforts to police terrorism within national borders. Effective policies for policing terrorism and combating specific terrorist groups continue to emerge, although terrorist organizations continue to be extremely effective at changing in response to counterterrorism efforts. The development of effective, long-lasting measures to reduce terrorism globally will require real changes in reducing global economic inequities and creating stable states that are responsive to their citizens' needs.

References

Bayly, Christopher, and Tim Harper. 2004. *Forgotten Armies: The Fall of British Asia, 1941–1945*. Cambridge, MA: Belknap Press.

Beers, Rand, and Francis X. Taylor. 2002. "Narco-Terror: The Worldwide Connection Between Drugs and Terror." Testimony before the Senate Committee on the Judiciary Subcommittee on Technology, Terrorism and Government Information. Washington, DC. March 13. https://2001-2009.state.gov/p/inl/rls/rm/8743.htm.

Bergesen, Albert J., and Yi Han. 2005. "New Directions for Terrorism Research." *International Journal of Comparative Sociology* 46 (1–2): 133–51.

Bureau of Counterterrorism and Countering Violent Extremism. 2016. *Country Reports on Terrorism 2015*. Washington, DC: United States Department of State.

Chomsky, Noam. 2001. "The United States is a Leading Terrorist State." *Monthly Review* 53 (6): 10–19.

Cragin, Kim, Peter Chalk, Sara A. Daly, and Brian A. Jackson. 2007. *Sharing the Dragon's Teeth: Terrorist Groups and Exchanges of New Technologies*. Santa Monica, CA: Rand Corporation.

Dinges, John. 2012. *The Condor Years: How Pinochet and His Allies Brought Terrorism to Three Continents*. New York: The New Press.

Enders, Walter, and Todd Sandler. 2002. "Patterns of Transnational Terrorism, 1970–1999: Alternative Time-Series Estimates." *International Studies Quarterly* 46: 145–65.

Hastings, Zoe, David Jones and Laura Stolte. 2020. *Involuntary Celibates: Background for Practitioners*. Edmonton, Canada: Organization for the Prevention of Violence. https://preventviolence.ca/wp-content/uploads/2020/09/Involuntary-Celibates-Background-for-Practitioners_webupdate.pdf

Humphreys, Adrian. 2007. "One Official's 'Refugee' Is Another's 'Terrorist': IRB Criticized for Dissimilar Rulings on Similar Cases." *National Post*, January 17. www.canada.com/nationalpost/news/story.html?id=a64f73d2-f672-4bd0-abb3-2584029db496.

International Court of Justice. 1986. "Summary of the Judgment of 27 June 1986 in the Case Concerning the Military and Paramilitary Activities in and against Nicaragua." www.icj-cij.org/public/files/case-related/70/070-19860627-JUD-01-00-EN.pdf.

Jones, Seth, Catrina Doxsee and Nicholas Harrington. 2020. "The Escalating Terrorism Problem in the United States. Center for Strategic and International Studies." www.csis.org/analysis/escalating-terrorism-problem-united-states

Lauderdale, Pat, and Annamarie Oliverio. 2005. "Critical Perspectives on Terror." *International Journal of Comparative Sociology* 46 (1–2): 3–10.

Mahmood, Cynthia Keppley. 1996. *Fighting for Faith and Nation: Dialogues with Sikh Militants*. Philadelphia: University of Pennsylvania Press.

Mamdani, Mahmood. 2004. *Good Muslim, Bad Muslim*. New York: Pantheon.

Miller-Idriss, Cynthia. 2020. *Hate in the Homeland: The New Global Far Right*. Princeton, NJ: Princeton University Press.

Moghadam, Assaf. 2003. "Palestinian Suicide Terrorism in the Second Intifada: Motivations and Organizational Aspects." *Studies in Conflict and Terrorism* 26 (1): 65–92.

Nassar, Jamal R. 2005. *Globalization and Terrorism: The Migration of Dreams and Realities*. Lanham, MD: Rowman & Littlefield.

National Consortium for the Study of Terrorism and Responses to Terrorism (START). *Global Terrorism Index 2019: Measuring the Impact of Terrorism*. Institute for Economics & Peace.

Nowrasteh, Alex. 2017. "Little National Security Benefit to Trump's Executive Order on Immigration. Cato Institute." *Cato Institute*. (Accessed February 10, 2017) www.cato.org/blog/little-national-security-benefit-trumps-executive-order-immigration.

Ruby, Charles L. 2002. "The Definitions of Terrorism." *Analysis of Social Issues and Public Policy* 2 (1): 9–14.

Stern, Jessica. 1999. *The Ultimate Terrorists*. Cambridge, MA: Harvard University Press.

United States State Department. 2002. *Patterns of Global Terrorism 2001*. https://2009-2017.state.gov/j/ct/rls/crt/2001/index.htm.

———. 2004. *Patterns of Global Terrorism 2003*, *Appendix G*. https://2009-2017.state.gov/j/ct/rls/crt/2003/33777.htm.

Vest, Jason. 2001. "Oy McVey: From the Irv Rubin Bust to the Stern Gang: The Rich History of Jewish Terrorism." *Village Voice*, December 19–25.

Wikan, Uni. 2002. "'My Son—A Terrorist?' (He was such a gentle boy)." *Anthropological Quarterly* 75 (1): 117–28.

Chapter 15

Media, Sovereignty, and Cybersecurity

Media has always been a central aspect of globalization. The term **media** refers to technologically constituted vehicles for extending human communication, from cuneiform tablets to phonograph records to newspapers to radio and television broadcasts to social media.

Intellectual Property Rights

From the eighteenth century through the first half of the twentieth century, global media was dominated by **print capitalism**, a system in which privately owned printing technologies enabled large-scale production of newspapers, books, pamphlets, sheet music and other printed materials. Entrepreneurs printed their books and media in local languages in order to maximize circulation. As a result, readers became able to build common political discourses across cultural and linguistic boundaries. Print capitalism thus helped shape the emergence of national revolutions, first in Europe and the Americas, and later in Africa and Asia.

The earliest international conflicts related to the media involved intellectual property rights. The idea of **intellectual property**—the view that intangible creations of individual human minds could be conceptualized as property and defined and protected in ways similar to physical goods—arose in the late seventeenth century, although the term itself was coined much later. New laws emerged to protect the *words* and *ideas* of creators. Under these new laws, someone who wrote a novel would have protection against others reproducing it, and later, transforming it into new media.

Originally, intellectual property laws were very limited because it was believed to be in the public interest to have books and ideas enter into the public domain as public goods. The history of intellectual property law is essentially a story of the gradual expansion of the rights of authors to profit from their work, including the capacity to sell or license those rights to other persons or corporations.

Problems arose when media creators were protected in their own countries but not internationally. Beginning with the Paris Convention in 1883, European countries—and the subordinate countries in their empires—entered into common agreements governing intellectual property. Over subsequent decades, intellectual property rights expanded and broadened. The current global agreement on intellectual property is the **Trade-Related Aspects of Intellectual Property Rights** (TRIPS) agreement, which acknowledges individual sovereignty but seeks a "one size fits all" approach. TRIPS is overseen by the **World Intellectual Property Organization** (WIPO), which was established in 1967 as an agency of the United Nations.

Intellectual property rights remains a controversial issue. Critics argue that current laws and regulations are too broad, that they give too much protection to corporations that license creative works rather than to artists and creators, and that copying is not really equivalent to property theft and should not be treated as such. Many critics also argue that current laws

DOI: 10.4324/9781003028314-19

benefit large, wealthy powerful nations like the US and Europe, and negatively impact the economic development of smaller states by restricting their access to ideas that could improve conditions.

As a result, intellectual property law is currently undergoing a "paradigm shift" from a one-size-fits-all approach to one tailored to the needs of different parts of the world (Morin 2014: 275).

Regulating the Internet

In the last three decades, all these issues were dramatically impacted by the rise of digital technologies and the Internet. Print capitalism and ideas about intellectual property were built on a system of **radial distribution**, in which media creators owned the means of media production, and their products—newspapers, movies, radio and television shows—were distributed to consumers. In socialist states, the government owned the means of media production but distribution remained radial—moving outward from a center.

This began to change with the rise of **new media**—media in which the same tools through which you consume media products become the tools through which you can create media, transform media, and distribute media. Personal computers, smartphones and related devices, combined with the rise of the Internet, completely disrupted the ways global media operated, and these technologies continue to pose new challenges.

The Internet was invented in 1969 as a means to connect academic researchers and US defense officials. The introduction of the World Wide Web in 1991 made it easier for people to connect for trade, education, information sharing and political engagement. While private corporations sold Internet services to customers, management of the Internet's organizational structure—its domains and addresses—was outsourced to a non-profit organization called the Internet Corporation for Assigned Names and Numbers (ICANN). In just decades the Internet has become a vast social and commercial platform connecting more than four billion people—and growing.

With the rise of the Internet has come the explosive growth of gigantic corporations such as Amazon, Apple, Facebook, Google, and Twitter operating Internet platforms. The convenience of common, easy-to-use technologies has enabled the emergence of digital behemoths that raise concerns both because their monopolistic economic power threatens the function of free markets, but also because they wield so much control over political communication.

However, there is little consensus about what to do about them. Some have called for governments to break up Facebook and Google. Others have called for stricter regulation to limit the ability of these companies to exploit the data they gather from users. Lawsuits accusing these companies of monopolistic behaviors have been filed in European and US courts, sometimes leading to heavy fines. These measures have been primarily used as threats to encourage these platforms to self-regulate by taking down dangerous content, curating their content more effectively, and limiting the ways they make use of data. In 2020, the European Union proposed sweeping changes that would give regulators power to sanction companies with fines up to 6 percent of their global revenues for monopolistic practices. Change is almost certainly coming, but what it will ultimately look like, and how it will change the mediascape, remains to be seen.

Cyberattacks

The growth of the Internet has introduced new concerns over data privacy, online rights and the security of digital networks. Different governments have taken different approaches to regulating the Internet, sometimes creating international conflicts. Lacking an international consensus on Internet regulation and the consequences of violating those regulations has made **cyberspace**—the conceptual environment in which communication over computer networks occurs—a dangerous place.

In 2008 a malicious computer worm was used to attack Iran's computer networks, causing substantial damage to its nuclear program. This first international cyberattack is understood to have been carried out by the US and Israel, although neither has admitted responsibility. **Cyberattacks** are assaults against single or multiple computers or networks designed to steal data, or to disable, disrupt or destroy other countries' computer systems.

Individuals, governments and corporations store vast amounts of information on the Internet. But because the Internet is built around interconnections, these connections can be "hacked" for criminal purposes, such as stealing banking information or holding computer systems hostage for financial gain.

Hacking is not limited to personal gain. Political activists such Anonymous have accessed secret information from corporate and government sites and published them in freely accessible venues as a way to increase transparency and accountability. One such site is WikiLeaks, an international non-profit organization that publishes classified media provided by anonymous sources.

Since computer networks operate everything from communication networks to power grids to banking systems, cyberattacks can potentially cause catastrophic damage in real life. In June 2017, a powerful cyberattack flooded Ukrainian computers, encrypting and overwriting computer files at airports, the national telephone service, the State Savings Bank of Ukraine, the railway network and even shutting down the radiation monitoring system at Ukraine's Chernobyl Nuclear Power Plant. It took a year for the Ukrainian government to finally secure its system against the virus.

Cyberwarfare and Cybersecurity

Cybersecurity is the effort to protect computer systems and networks from threats of damage, disruption, loss of control and information theft.

Whereas there are internationally recognized rules such as the Geneva Convention governing traditional warfare, there is no international consensus governing states' behaviors in cyberspace. No clear and consistent rules have been proposed by any international body, and it is not clear how the international community would be expected to act if a country were to break these rules if they were established.

The problem is further complicated by the fact that cyberattacks may be impossible to attribute with certainty because hackers mask their identities and locations by routing attacks through multiple servers in many different countries.

Yet even if the source of a cyberattack can be located, it may be impossible to tell if the hackers were working as agents of that government, or as agents of another government, or operating on their own. In the Ukrainian example, the vector of the attack—an update to a widely used tax preparation software—is well known. Exactly how the update became compromised, and by whom, is unknown.

While experts often distinguish in principle between **cyberwarfare**—cyberattacks carried out by states against other states—and **cyberterrorism**—cyberattacks carried out by ideologically motivated groups or individuals—the reality is that such boundaries often cannot be accurately determined. As a result, it is extremely difficult to punish cyberattacks. This means that **deterrence**—choosing not to act out of fear of retaliation—does not effectively limit cyberwarfare.

Cyber Espionage

In 2019 the cybersecurity company FireEye discovered that it had been hacked by sophisticated malware seeking data on its government clients, but also copying the hacking tools it uses to probe its customers' defenses. The vector for the attack was an update to the Orion network-monitoring software, which serves hundreds of thousands of organizations around the world, including major global corporations and many government agencies in North America, Asia, Europe, and the Middle East.

The malware does not crash systems. Instead, it opens doors for hackers to enter, locate and copy secret and proprietary information. The malware allowed hackers to impersonate system administrators at the US Departments of Treasury and Commerce, accessing e-mails and personnel records, among others.

Governments also make use of hackers to conduct **cyber espionage**, stealing other countries' sensitive information for economic or military advantage. Stolen information can sometimes be used as a political weapon. Russian agents hacked the US Democratic National Committee in 2016 and released e-mails that indicated some DNC officials were privileging one candidate over another, creating a rift in the party and potentially impacting the 2016 presidential election, which the Democrats lost.

Espionage does not violate international law. The standard technique is expelling diplomats or imposing sanctions. This becomes difficult when it cannot be proved who hacked the system. In the US, the Obama administration retaliated against Russia by expelling diplomats for its 2016 hacking. However, the Trump administration made no effort to retaliate against the 2019 violation, in part because, in the face of firm denials by Russia, the administration doubted its own intelligence agency's claims that Russia was the likely suspect.

Social Manipulation

The world has also seen efforts by states and individuals to use social media to spread disinformation and propaganda in order to manipulate public opinion and beliefs. This includes projects by Russia to influence elections and increase political polarization in European countries and the US; the role of social media platforms such as Facebook in spreading misinformation; and growing Chinese efforts to shape regional beliefs increase soft power especially in Asia, Africa and Latin America.

A 2019 report calls this **hostile social manipulation**, and defines it as "the purposeful, systematic generation and dissemination of information to produce harmful social, political, and economic outcomes in a target country by affecting beliefs, attitudes, and behavior" (Mazarr et al. 2019). While disinformation and propaganda have always been important tools of soft power, the rise of social media has dramatically increased their use and effectiveness. Often there may be no tactical or strategic goal beyond the desire to erode trust in public institutions in ways that divide the country internally and so make it a less effective international actor.

Combatting this kind of threat will require the establishment of international norms regarding the use of this kind of social manipulation. It might also demand national, or international regulation over how systems of algorithmic decision making are coded, and over the use of **deep fakes**—the use of artificial intelligence to create images of false events that are indistinguishable from actual events.

The 2020 Covid-19 pandemic increased media usage around the world, in some areas by more than 200 percent according to a Nielsen report. Media streaming, virtual meetings, e-mail, online news, social media and online gaming have become indispensable elements of life for many of the world's peoples. Yet the use of these systems creates vulnerabilities that can be exploited. Since 2003 the Center for Strategic and International Studies (CSIS) has recorded over 770 cases of cyberattacks by international actors, including more than 100 in 2020 alone—and these are only the publicly exposed cases (CSIS 2020). The study of media law, cybersecurity, and data manipulation, and the creation of policies regulating cyberspace, will continue to be significant issues in international studies for decades to come.

References

Center for Strategic and International Studies. 2020. "Significant Cyber Incidents." www.csis.org/programs/strategic-technologies-program/significant-cyber-incidents (accessed December 11, 2020).

Mazarr, Michael J., Ryan Michael Bauer, Abigail Casey, Sarah Anita Heintz, and Luke J. Matthews. 2019. *The Emerging Risk of Virtual Societal Warfare: Social Manipulation in a Changing Information Environment*. RAND Corporation. www.rand.org/pubs/research_reports/RR2714.html (accessed December 10, 2020).

Morin, Jean-Frédéric. 2014. "Paradigm Shift in the Global IP Regime: The Agency of Academics." *Review of International Political Economy* 21 (2): 275–309.

Chapter 16

Sustainable Development

A perspective on sustainable development entails development that meets the needs of the present without compromising the needs of future generations. There are political and economic dimensions to sustainable development. How do the governments proceed and plan for sustainable development? How do governments and people come together for sustainable development? The economic requirements for sustainable development go beyond economic growth for a country but also a decline of poverty and unemployment. What economic mechanisms are good for sustainable development? How are businesses, producers and consumers to work together for sustainable development? Sustainable development involves geography and a deep consideration of the environment. What is the role of people in the environment? How are we to be stewards of the environment for future generations? Sustainable development is not just for businesses and government, sustainable development is for communities and so connects with anthropology and society. How do communities of civil society work together to provide for the future? What perspectives do people from all parts of the world, not just New York or London, bring to our understanding of the complexities of sustainable development? Sustainable development is an interdisciplinary project linking people, place, power, production, and past for our future.

Historical change within human communities occurs as the people of a territory involve themselves in and interact with the world at large. After World War II, the study of such change was generally restricted to economic growth, and development was considered primarily a question of economic growth. Through the 1950s, "development" meant the ability of a national economy to sustain an annual increase in GDP of 5 percent or more (Todaro and Smith 2015).

By the 1960s, some states in the Third World were meeting this overall requirement, yet the standard of living for many people remained unchanged. To get at the real meaning of development meant to get beyond GDP and include other variables. The definition of development continued to evolve. Scholars began to view development as including not just economic growth but also a decline of inequality, unemployment, and poverty (Seers 1969).

By the 1980s, the term *development* expanded to include the achievement of political and cultural as well as social and economic goals; in short, the enrichment of the quality of human life. The good life is composed of three transcultural core values, or goals, held in common by all people. The first value is life sustenance: the provision of food, shelter, medicine, and protection to all people. The second value is self-esteem: a society's retention of dignity, worth, and respect in the midst of contact with a materially more prosperous society. The third value is freedom from servitude: an expanded range of choice, a reduction of dependence on nature, ignorance, misery, dogma, and other societies (Goulet 1985).

Without a consideration of the cultural and ethnic diversity in the human community, without putting people in their context, our understanding of development is not complete.

DOI: 10.4324/9781003028314-20

On a practical level, development projects may not come to their expected fruition without including the human factor. Development "from below" approaches, with a further consideration of the cultural dimension, have added to the wholeness of development. "Culture, not economics, technology, or politics, is the primordial dimension in development" (Goulet 1985, 272). In 1987 the UN World Commission on Environment and Development incorporated the idea of economic development and environmental preservation (Lele 2013). This new formulation leads to sustainable development: "development that meets the needs of the present without compromising the ability of future generations to meet their own needs" (UN WCED 1987).

In the 1990s a new measure for development utilized **life expectancy**, income, and education in calculating development. The United Nations Development Program put together this new Human Development Index (HDI) to include human well-being along with economic advances in development. A twenty-first-century definition points toward an organic complexity of development that goes beyond a strictly economic measure (Potter et al. 1999; Sen 2000; Todaro and Smith 2015).

In 2000, world leaders met together at the UN for the Millennium Summit. Out of this came the Millennium Development Goals, with eight goals for 2015 covering several dimensions including human capital, infrastructure and human rights. The goals were: 1. Eradicate extreme poverty and hunger, 2. Achieve universal primary education, 3. Promote gender equality and empower women, 4. Reduce child mortality, 5. Improve maternal health, 6. Combat HIV/AIDS, malaria and other diseases, 7. Ensure environmental sustainability, and 8. Global partnership for development. Governments and civil society agreed to this agenda (United Nations Millennium Goals). With goal 8, both developed and underdeveloped countries, rich and poor would be involved in the development program. By 2000, the Cold War was over and there was a general hopeful appreciation for the future of humanity in the new millennium. But by 2001, conflict again occurred with the September 11, 2001, attack on New York and Washington by al Qaeda and the subsequent war in Afghanistan. In 2003 the war was extended to Iraq. Issues associated with terrorism rather than development occupied some world leaders. Many, not all, countries still spend more on the military than on development. Still many of the Millennium Development Goals were met in 2015 and it was time for a new plan (Egelston 2013; McArthur 2013).

Sustainable development seeks to balance economic growth, social equity, and environmental protection for the long term (Potter et al. 1999; Sen 2000; Price et al. 2020). Through a series of meetings, the United Nations put together a new set of 17 Sustainable Development Goals by 2030. The sustainable development goals (in short form) are: 1. No poverty, 2. Zero hunger, 3. Good health and well-being, 4. Quality education, 5. Gender equality, 6. Clean water and sanitation, 7. Affordable and clean energy, 8. Decent work and economic growth, 9. Industry, innovation, and infrastructure, 10. Reduced inequalities, 11. Sustainable cities and communities, 12. Responsible consumption and production, 13. Climate action, 14. Life below water, 15. Life on land, 16. Peace, justice and strong institutions, 17. Partnerships for the goals. All member states of the United Nations agreed to the 17 goals. Each goal has several indicators. These efforts are seriously affected with the advent of Covid-19. Each country must devote resources to Covid-19 which may prevent completion of these goals (United Nations Sustainable Development).

Let's examine several of these goals.

"Goal 1. No poverty. End poverty in all its forms everywhere." Generally extreme poverty is considered as an adult making less than $1.90 per day. Think of what you can buy for $1.90, perhaps a cup of coffee or a soda for a dollar and maybe a hamburger for a dollar. That's it. Now consider if you have to feed dependents as well. So instead you go for free water, perhaps from a stream or a well, or collect rainwater, and some beans and rice. If there are fruits and nuts nearby, you could collect them. Ten percent of the world's people live on less than $1.90 per day. Many of the people living on $1.90 per day are in rural sub-Saharan Africa, so the needs are particularly acute in several African countries. South Asia also has a large population in poverty. With Covid-19 in 2020, the levels of poverty will probably increase rather than decrease (United Nations Sustainable Development).

"Goal 2. Zero hunger. End hunger, achieve food security and improved nutrition, and promote sustainable agriculture." About 9 percent of the world's population is hungry. About 10 percent do not have food security meaning that they may have enough to eat now but not enough for later. The largest numbers are in Asia and Africa, particularly South Asia and sub-Saharan Africa. The World Food Program has analyzed the impacts of Covid-19 and found that some 100 million people in 2020 were at risk of acute hunger due to conflicts, climate change and economic downturns. Cereal imports are down in sub-Saharan Africa and cereal production has lessened as well. People may be just above the poverty threshold, but if the cost of food goes up or food is not available because of conflict then they are at risk for hunger (United Nations Sustainable Development).

"Goal 4. Quality education. Ensure inclusive and equitable quality education and promote lifelong learning opportunities for all." Some progress has been made. However, about 20 percent of the world's children were not in school. Projections indicate that in 2030 about 60 perecent would complete secondary school. Schooling is particularly problematic in sub-Saharan Africa. Adult illiteracy is a problem in both South Asia and sub-Saharan Africa. Two-thirds of the illiterate are women. With Covid-19, many schools are closed. In developed countries there is the possibility of online learning. In some developing countries, online learning is very difficult, as there is a deep digital divide, fewer computers and laptops. Perhaps the family has a cell phone, but not a smart phone (United Nations Sustainable Development).

"Goal 5. Gender equality. Achieve gender equality and empower all women and girls." Global progress has been made, more girls are going to school and more women are in legislatures. Yet discrimination against women and girls still is a part of societies around the world. Twenty percent of women over the age of 15 have experienced violence from their partners. Just under one-quarter of people in legislatures are women. Only half of women married or in a union make their own decisions about sex or contraception. Human rights includes both men and women, boys and girls. With Covid-19, a majority of care and health workers are women in many countries. Lockdowns have increased the cases of domestic violence. Women bear the brunt of domestic and care work in the home (United Nations Sustainable Development).

"Goal 6. Clean water and sanitation. Ensure access to water and sanitation for all." Access to clean water and sanitation is a real issue for billions of people. Perhaps one-third of all people do not have clean drinking water. Hand washing prevents the spread of diseases including Covid-19, so clean water and soap is very important. In other areas water scarcity is a big problem, simply more people than local river systems and rainfall can support. Desert areas are increasing with climate change. Much of the world's wastewater is discharged into rivers or the sea without treatment. Forty percent of health care facilities worldwide do not have adequate hand washing facilities. Water is a critical element for sustainability (United Nations Sustainable Development).

"Goal 10. Reduced inequalities. Reduce inequality within and among countries." Statistical averages on a country-by-country comparison do not reveal the inequalities within a country. A gross national income of $15,000 per capita annually may seem sufficient. But that means half of the population has an income less than $15,000 and many could be under $10,000. Inequalities generally affect women, older persons, children, people with disabilities, indigenous persons and social minorities disproportionately within a country. Most of those with disabilities are in developing countries. One in ten children have disabilities. Income inequalities were declining in many countries, but with Covid-19 progress since 2015 may be eroding. The Covid-19 pandemic affects older people, people with disabilities, children, migrants and refugees, and women (United Nations Sustainable Development).

These are a few of the Sustainable Development Goals. Sustainable Development intersects with International Studies in several dimensions. The economics of sustainable development is discussed in Chapter 4 (Hanson 2017; Kumar and Managi 2009). The role of the environment in sustainable development relates to geography (Price et al. 2020). The issues for sustainable development are very much on the agenda for political systems (Sackeyfio 2017). Cultural and social conceptualizations of development connect with anthropology (Stewart and Strathern 2019). Change of human societies in sustainable development relates with the historical perspective (Egelston 2013). As Gandhi (1914) said, "We but mirror the world….If we could change ourselves, the tendencies in the world would also change." Overall, positive trends in clean water, education and health point toward improvements in the human condition (Easterly 2015).

References

Easterly, William. 2015. "The Trouble with the Sustainable Development Goals." *Current History* 114 (775): 322–24.

Egelston, Anne E. 2013. *Sustainable Development: A History*. New York: Springer.

Gandhi, Mohandas. 1914. "General Knowledge About Health XXXII: 12 Accidents Snake-Bite." *The Collected Works of Mahatma Gandhi*, Volume XII, April 1913 to December 1914.

Goulet, Denis. 1985. *The Cruel Choice: A New Concept in the Theory of Development*. Lanham, MD: University Press of America.

Hanson, Kobena T. 2017. *From Millennium Development Goals to Sustainable Development Goals: Rethinking African Development* London: Taylor and Francis.

Kumar, Surender and Shunsuke Managi. 2009. *The Economics of Sustainable Development: The Case of India*. New York: Springer.

Lele, Sharachchandra. 2013. "Rethinking Sustainable Development." *Current History* 112 (757): 311–16.

McArthur, John. 2013. "Own the Goals: What the Millennium Development Goals Have Accomplished." *Foreign Affairs* Mar/Apr, 152–62.

Meier, Gerald. M., and Joseph Stiglitz, eds. 2001. *Frontiers of Development Economics: The Future in Perspective*. Washington, DC: World Bank/Oxford University Press

Potter, Robert B., Tony Binns, Jennifer A. Elliott, and David Smith, et al. 1999. *Geographies of Development: An Introduction to Development Studies*. Harlow, UK: Pearson Education.

Price, Marie, Martin Lewis, William Wyckoff and Lester Rowntree, 2020. *Globalization and Diversity: Geography of a Changing World*. 6th ed. Upper Saddle River, NJ: Prentice Hall.

Sackeyfio, Naaborle. 2017. *Energy Politics and Rural Development: The Case of Ghana*. Cham, Switzerland: Palgrave Macmillan.

Seers, Dudley. 1969. "The Meaning of Development." *International Development Review*, 9 (4): 2–6.

———. 1977. "The Meaning of Development." *International Development Review*, 17 (3): 2–7.

Sen, Amartya. 2000. *Development as Freedom*. New York: Anchor Books.

Stewart, Pamela and Andrew Strathern. 2019. *Sustainability, Conservation, and Creativity: Ethnographic Learning from Small-Scale Practices*. London: Routledge.

Todaro, Michael P., and Stephen C. Smith. 2015. *Economic Development*. 12th ed. Boston: Pearson.

United Nations Millennium Goals. www.un.org/millenniumgoals/

United Nations Sustainable Development. www.un.org/sustainabledevelopment/
United Nation World Commission on Environment and Development. 1987. https://sustainabledevelopment.
   un.org/milestones/wced

Journals

Geography and Sustainability, Elsevier.
Sustainable Development, Wiley www.wiley.com/

Chapter 17

The Global Refugee Crisis

In 2015, the UN High Commissioner for Refugees (UNHCR) estimated that there were 65.3 million people displaced by "conflict and persecution," a population that would constitute the twenty-first largest nation in the world. Recognizing the plight of these stateless peoples, the International Olympic Committee even broke precedent when it allowed a "Refugee Team" to compete at the 2016 Rio Olympics.

Civil wars, armed insurgencies, government persecution, and dire poverty have stoked a pipeline of desperate Syrians, Iraqis, Somalis, Eritreans, Nigerians, and others trying to cross the Mediterranean to Greece and Italy. Over a million refugees poured into Europe in 2015, and another half million in 2016. Thousands have perished from drowning on the dangerous passage across the Mediterranean. The heartbreaking photo of a small Syrian boy washed up on a Turkish beach shocked the world, and yet the crisis continues. This chapter examines the historical, political, economic, geographic, and cultural aspects of the problem.

Not since World War II have so many refugees been on the move. That war cost some 35 million lives, and millions left their homes to escape the murderous Nazi occupation and the Soviet Red Army's entry into central Europe at the end of the war. In the course of the war, 60 million Europeans were displaced.

The story of British and American policy on Jewish refugees during World War II is sobering. Great Britain took in 80,000 Jews from the continent before 1939, but only 10,000 more during the war. London even cut off most Jewish immigration to Palestine. In 1939, the US Congress refused to pass the Wagner-Rogers Act, which would have allowed 20,000 Jewish children into the country above established quotas. The anti-Semitic aspect of the vote was undeniable. As the wife of the US Commissioner of Immigration infamously remarked, "20,000 charming children would all too soon grow up to be 20,000 ugly adults" (Medoff 2009). From 1933 to 1945 the United States allowed in 33,000 Jews. The bureaucratic maze that refugees had to go through was intended to keep them out and was dubbed the American "wall" (Miliband 2016, 23).

The most infamous case of the plight of Jewish refugees was the voyage of the *St. Louis*. A total of 937 Jews left Germany on the ship in 1939, only to be turned away at Cuban, US, and Canadian ports. The ship had to return to Europe, where over 250 of the passengers did not survive the Holocaust. By 1942, the Roosevelt administration was aware of the Nazi policy to annihilate Europe's Jews but did not set up a War Refugee Board until 1944.

Eight million Germans fled the Soviet Red Army at the end of the war, whose soldiers exacted terrible revenge for the barbaric Nazi policies on the eastern front. It is estimated that as the Red Army entered Germany in 1945, Russian soldiers raped hundreds of thousands of German women (Naimark 1997, 133).

When the Syrian refugee crisis began to unfold in the mid-2010s, Germany remembered the Nazi genocide and the plight of its own people at the end of World War II. Germany was among the EU countries most open to resettling refugees. Chancellor Angela Merkel has come under

DOI: 10.4324/9781003028314-21

much criticism in Germany for this open door policy, which has put a huge strain on welfare agencies and social structures. That criticism from the right sharpened after a Tunisian asylum seeker ran a truck into a Berlin Christmas market in 2016, killing 12 and injuring dozens more. He was spurred on by the Islamic State (IS) in northern Syria and Iraq, which has encouraged the use of trucks and other accessible "weapons" to attack "soft targets." Merkel bravely refused to expel the refugees.

In contrast to Germany, Great Britain and the United States have reverted back to their restrictive World War II refugee policies. The "Brexit" vote, a 2016 referendum in which the United Kingdom voted to leave the EU, was a message to the British government to protect the country's borders from foreign elements. The United States has been particularly niggardly in its resettlement policies. As of 2016, only 10,000 Syrians had been allowed in the country, and the US security agencies' vetting of the refugees has been very tight. It takes a refugee an average of 18 to 24 months to pass through the system.

The ongoing wars in Afghanistan and Iraq had generated a steady flow of refugees trying to get to Europe, but the Arab Spring of 2011 caused a mass exodus. Muammar Gaddafi's authoritarian regime in Libya was toppled, and an uprising against Bashar al-Assad in Syria resulted in a full-blown civil war. By the end of 2016, over 400,000 Syrians had been killed, and 5.5 million Syrians had fled the country.

The geographic proximity of Syria and Libya to Europe has given refugees hope that they might find a better life there. The eastern route to the EU goes through Turkey and then on boats to Greece. Most of the refugees have been Syrians and Iraqis. The western route across the Mediterranean from Libya to Sicily (Italy) is longer and more precarious, but Somalis, Eritreans, South Sudanese, and Nigerians are among those who have used the route to flee civil unrest and oppression. In 2016, over 100,000 arrived in Italy on rickety boats from Libya. The Libyan coast guard interdicted another 11,000. Over 3,000 people died on the western route in 2016 and over 400 on the eastern route (Baker and Addario 2016, 40; *New York Times* 2016).

Turkey is the historical, political, and geographic fulcrum of the Syrian refugee crisis. The collapse of the Ottoman Empire at the end of World War II enabled Britain and France to draw new boundaries in the Middle East that did not conform to the political aspirations of the ethnic groups there. Sunni Arabs in the newly created Iraq eventually ruled over a majority Shia Arab population in the south and Kurds in the north. The al-Assad regime in Syria represents a minority Shia Alawite sect in a majority Sunni country.

The 25 million Kurds in the Middle East did not get a country after World War I; they were divided between Iran, Iraq, Syria, and Turkey. Shiites and Kurds in Iraq took advantage of the toppling of President Saddam Hussein by US forces in 2003, while Syrian Kurds have provided the most reliable opposition forces to al-Assad. Ankara's adamant opposition to the Kurdistan Workers' Party complicates the Syrian Civil War. The party operates in eastern Turkey and has launched terrorist attacks against Turkish targets, so Turkey is loath to support Kurdish aspirations for autonomy in Syria and Iraq (Worth 2016).

Hundreds of thousands of Syrian refugees have fled the civil war to Lebanon and Jordan. Turkey's shared 900-kilometer border with Syria has been the biggest conduit for Syrian refugees to the West. In March 2016, the EU tried to stem the flow of refugees from Turkey by promising Ankara $6 billion to keep the refugees in Turkey and to accept many of those already in Greece. The EU also agreed to negotiate visa-free entry for Turks traveling to the EU. As of the end of 2016, the agreement was still in limbo, however. The EU has not fully funded the deal in part because it has been unable to identify Turkish agencies that serve the refugees.

Ankara wants to stay in the EU's good graces because Turkey has sought membership in the club for two decades. President Tayyip Erdoğan's increasingly authoritarian rule has worked against Turkey's case, especially after he put down a military coup in July 2016. He has imprisoned thousands and sacked some 100,000 from the military, judiciary, and educational institutions. The Syrian Civil War has further hurt Turkey's aspirations. Many Europeans once favored Turkish entry into the EU as a valuable bridge between the democratic West and the Islamic countries in the Middle East; now Turkey is seen as a pathway for a flood of refugees and potential terrorists. In November 2016, the EU suspended accession talks with Turkey.

The influx of refugees correlates with a rise in right-wing, anti-immigrant movements, most alarmingly in France and Great Britain. French National Front leader Marine Le Pen has gained popularity by railing against Muslim immigrants. The British vote in 2016 to leave the EU was a manifestation of the feeling that the EU is under threat from immigration from the Middle East. A spate of terrorist attacks in Belgium, France, and Germany has contributed to the antipathy toward Muslims in general. United States President Donald Trump played on those same fears in his successful 2016 campaign.

There are economic elements to the refugee crisis as well. The increase in the numbers of refugees is a result of the "push" of civil conflict and economic deprivation, but also the "pull" of a better life that refugees know from friends, family, the Internet, television, and movies. Many of the migrants simply leave their countries for economic reasons. As one Senegalese explained his willingness to risk the perilous Libya to Italy crossing, "I did not want to leave, but I had no choice. There is nothing for us in Senegal" (Baker and Addario 2016, 43). Even if the migrants make it to Europe, the road to integration is long. One Syrian refugee was shocked at the conditions he saw for his countrymen in Greece: "I didn't imagine I would see refugee families living here in schools and empty hotels. Refugees are everywhere" (New York Times 2016).

Smugglers prey on the hopes of people to find a better life, charging upwards of $1,500 a person to cross the Mediterranean. The smugglers overload leaky boats with refugees without any concern for their safety. Estimates put the smuggling trade on the Mediterranean at about $5 billion (Baker and Addario 2016, 41).

The advocates for Brexit propagated the myth that immigrants are bad for business. In Europe, they stereotype foreigners as the "Polish plumber" who works on the black market for below union wages. Trump suggested that Hispanic immigrants were taking away American jobs and living off of welfare. In the view of many white Americans, illegal immigrants work on the black market, undercutting opportunities and wages for the American worker. These beliefs fly in the face of studies that have found that immigration is a net advantage to an economy; one of the enduring strengths of the US economy in comparison to other developed countries is its tradition of welcoming people from other countries who work hard and make significant contributions to the US GDP.

The cultural differences between Europeans and Americans on the one hand, and the immigrants from the Middle East and Africa on the other, is another cause of the pushback against this new immigration. Some Westerners think that traditional Muslim customs, such as women's head coverings and frequent daily prayers, undermine women's rights and secular culture in Europe. Some Christian evangelicals in the United States falsely claim that Muslims are trying to impose Sharia law. The biggest fear is from radicalized Muslims, who have launched numerous terrorist attacks in Great Britain, Spain, France, Belgium, and Germany, killing hundreds. The horrific attack on New York City and Washington, DC, on September 11, 2001, amplified fears of foreign terrorism in the United States, although home-grown terrorists and homicides claim many more American lives, some 30,000 every year.

What can be done to ameliorate the refugee crisis? First, wealthy nations need to contribute more money. In 2015, the UN requested $20 billion for aid and resettlement agencies but received just $11 billion. Second, host countries need to make it easier for refugees to find a legal way to earn a living. For example, small loan programs have been successful in jumpstarting newcomers' small businesses.

Third, Europe, the United States, and other developed countries need to open their doors to more refugees. The Syrian conflict has put great strains on neighboring Lebanon, Jordan, and Turkey. Lebanon has more refugees than any other country; Syrians now comprise about a fifth of the population. The unrest in Somalia has resulted in a half-million refugees in Kenya. Germany has been by far the most receptive to refugees of the developed countries, taking in 800,000. While Germany has recognized its historical debt to refugees, Hungary has built a formidable fence on its border with Serbia to stem the flow of refugees, unmoved by memories of the 300,000 Hungarian refugees who were welcomed with open arms in the West after the Soviet Union had crushed the Hungarian Revolution in 1956 (Ruthven and Thorpe 2016, 27). Many Americans seem to have forgotten their foreign origins and Emma Lazarus's famous lines on the Statue of Liberty in New York harbor:

> Give me your tired, your poor,
> Your huddled masses yearning to breathe free,
> The wretched refuse of your teeming shore.
> Send these, the homeless, tempest-tossed, to me:
> I lift my lamp beside the golden door.

Isolated terrorist attacks have made this option politically unpopular, but courageous politicians need to make a moral case to mitigate the humanitarian disaster. Famous writer and Holocaust survivor Elie Wiesel understood what it meant for the persecuted to find a place of safety: "I am a refugee, but the word 'refugee' is not popular, but everyone likes the idea of refuge. We all need refuge" (Miliband 2016, 23).

References

Baker, Aryn and Lynsey Addario. 2016. "Between the Devil and the Deep Blue Sea." *Time*, September 12.

Medoff, Rafael. 2009. "New Evidence on FDR and the 'Voyage of the Damned.'" December. www.wymaninstitute.org.

Miliband, David. 2016. "The Best Ways to Deal with the Refugee Crisis." *New York Review of Books*, October 13.

Naimark, Norman M. 1997. *The Russians in Germany: A History of the Soviet Zone of Occupation, 1945–1949*. Cambridge, MA: Belknap Publishers.

New York Times. 2016. September 12.

New York Times. 2016. October 26.

Ruthven, Malise and Nick Thorpe. 2016. "On Today's Refugee Road." *New York Review of Books*, November 24.

Worth, Robert F. 2016. "Turkey's Hidden War." *The New York Times Magazine*, May 29.

Conclusion

How do we make the world a better place? What goals do we set? What obstacles stand in our way and how do we overcome them? What resources are needed and where will they come from? How will we measure success?

In 2000 the United Nations established a set of eight Millennium Development Goals (MDGs) to improve the future by harnessing globalization as a positive force in the world. All 189 United Nations member states committed to help achieve these goals, as did many international development agencies (see Chapter 16).

These goals ranged from eradicating extreme poverty to combating the spread of HIV/AIDS and achieving universal primary education—all by 2015 (United Nations 2007). In 2015, the UN declared that while not all goals had been met, considerable progress had been made (United Nations 2015). The number of people living in extreme poverty declined, as did the proportion of undernourished people in developing countries. The number of people lacking access to good water was cut in half, as were infant (under five) mortality rates, while maternal mortality rates declined by 45 percent. Primary school enrollment in the developing regions is at an all-time high, with a huge increase in the number of girls attending school.

In establishing the MDGs, the United Nations called on highly developed countries to commit 0.07 percent of their GNP to the needs of developing countries. While the European Union (EU) agreed to this goal, and four EU countries exceeded it, other wealthy nations set their own goals. Australia, for example, set a goal of giving 0.05 percent of GNP. Still other countries, led by the United States, balked at setting any specific targets.

The reluctance of developed countries to commit large sums to global development had been exacerbated by the global economic crisis, and social and political unrest has arisen as political parties find themselves unable to meet the economic expectations of their constituents. The complexity of the problems they address will require sustained efforts over many years. For example, achieving universal primary education requires an understanding of the historical trends, spatial organization, economic costs and benefits, political mechanisms, and cultural variables of education, both internationally and locally in each country and region. Achieving this level of understanding requires an interdisciplinary approach.

But the disciplines described in this textbook are not the only ones that can be brought to bear on understanding international problems. Other interdisciplinary approaches might include environmental studies, sociology, gender studies, comparative religions, or other disciplines in addition to, or in place of, some of those discussed in this book. What is important is developing a holistic approach that encourages us to look at the ways power, wealth, culture, and physical environments interact in complex international issues, and how these relations have changed over time so that we can begin thinking about solutions.

DOI: 10.4324/9781003028314-22

Solution-Oriented Analysis

Using interdisciplinary thinking to analyze global issues usually takes place in three basic stages. The first is identification and description of the issue, usually focused on some form of conflict between social groups; second, a description of how those concerned with the problem have tried to fix it, and why these solutions haven't worked; finally, recommendations for a way forward that might successfully overcome the obstacles that caused those earlier efforts to fail. Following these three steps can help produce analyses of issues that can be expressed in many ways, from short, 800-word op-ed pieces to 20-page reports to lengthy, detailed policy-analysis papers running to more than 75 pages.

The first step is identification of a global issue. This can be a global issue such as one of the MDGs, or an issue of international foreign policy such as Turkey's membership in the European Union, or a relatively small-scale problem of social inequity such as reducing cholera outbreaks in a Brazilian *favela* (squatter community).

Once you have identified the issue, you need to begin to unpack it, asking to whom the issue is a problem and why. You need to identify the stakeholders, and explain what rewards and risks each of them face, and how power relations are organized between them. You need to examine the wider political, cultural, and geographical contexts in which the issue is embedded.

In the second stage, you need to describe the history of the issue, paying special attention to efforts at solutions. Again, it will take interdisciplinary thinking to explore why each possible solution tried in the past has failed. Many of your sources may give different reasons for the failure of a solution based on their own disciplinary assumptions. By reading these accounts against each other, you can come to a broader, more comprehensive understanding.

The third stage requires you to define a clear goal for your solution, including the criteria used for choosing the recommended solution. A specific course of action for implementing the solution should be spelled out along with, if possible, strategies for managing those problems, and any consequences you can foresee on the basis of your analysis.

Often, as you begin to analyze a global issue, you will find that it is just too big. In this case, it is useful to pare it down to a manageable size. There are two common ways to do this. First, you can reduce the scale of the problem—instead of tackling the entire Palestinian–Israeli conflict, focus on one piece such as school parity in Jerusalem, conflict between Israeli settlers and the Palestinian villagers on whose land the new building projects encroach, or the inability of Hamas to control armed gangs within Gaza. Second, you can choose one stakeholder as your "client" and focus on the issue from their perspective—in what aspects of the problem is this group interested, and does it have agency for resolving part of the issue?

One of the biggest problems with finding solutions for global problems is that most people seek to replicate such common solutions as new regulation, specialized education, or international dialogue, envisioning top-down programs administered through national government agencies or global agencies like the World Bank or United Nations. While there is an important place for these solutions, increasingly successful solutions involve creativity and innovation.

Sources of Innovative Solutions

In 2007, a team of four undergraduates from Miami University in Ohio won an international competition open to professionals and graduate students. The Massachusetts Institute of Technology's Just Jerusalem 2050 competition challenged competitors to imagine small projects that could make a positive change toward a just and sustainable future Jerusalem. The students entered in the "economic" category and focused on the city's rapidly dwindling water resources (MIT News 2008).

Initially, every solution they imagined, from better wastewater management to water conservation regulations, had already been implemented by the Israeli state, with indifferent results. And these solutions relied on top-down implementation by the Israeli state—which risked making water a political flashpoint. At last, they began to research bottom-up strategies, water-management techniques that had worked successfully without state regulation. They found one in water harvesting—a simple technology involving the collection of rainwater by households through cisterns that could dramatically alter stress on Jerusalem's water system, and one that could be managed through training and microloans from the UN Environment Programme, which has extensive experience with the technology.

These kinds of low-cost, high-impact bottom-up solutions to manageable pieces of larger problems are increasingly the direction toward which solution-oriented analysis aims. There are many sources of innovative solutions, including leveraging inequities, fair trade, social entrepreneurship, appropriate technologies, and microfinancing.

Leveraging Inequities

In 1999, a first grader in Canada named Ryan Hreljac learned that many people in Africa do not have clean drinking water. Ryan began saving up the $2,000 it would take to pay for a well. His devotion to this cause, over several months, attracted the attention of a local newspaper, then a local television station, and soon donations came in and Ryan was able to team with an NGO then called Water Can (www.wateraidcanada.com) to build a well.

Today, as an adult, Hreljac still works with the Ryan's Well Foundation (www.ryanswell.ca), which has raised millions of dollars and helped build over 680 wells and 820 latrines bringing safe water and improved sanitation to over 723,000 people, mostly in Africa.

Hreljac's success depends on two fundamental principles. The first is that global inequities in the distribution of wealth mean that a middle-class Canadian boy has access to resources undreamed of by most adults in the world's poorest countries. In addition to the fact that money buys more in poorer countries than in wealthy ones (drilling a well in Canada would typically cost more than five times what it does in rural Africa), people in developed countries enjoy advantages of infrastructure. Access to media outlets, educational opportunities, automobile ownership, good roads, frequent flyer miles, personal computers, reliable telephone service, leisure time—can all serve as multipliers that make the work of philanthropic organizations easier and more effective.

In interviews, Hreljac has also insisted on a second lesson, which he calls "the power of one"—one person who devotes part of his or her time consistently to a cause can accomplish significant things while still leading a normal life. Hreljac himself has traveled internationally, met popes and presidents, and appeared on talk shows promoting the foundation, while also maintaining a healthy social life and extracurricular activities in school.

This principle is increasingly being used not only by philanthropies in the developed world but by people in developing countries seeking to improve conditions at home. For example, while struggling with school and the famine conditions that destroyed many families in Malawi, 14-year-old William Kamkwamba figured out how to build a windmill out of discarded engine components, PVC pipe, and bicycle parts to provide free electricity to his family's house. Teaming with philanthropists and entrepreneurs both in Africa and the developed world, he has begun working toward developing small windmills for use in his village and elsewhere in Malawi (Kamkwamba and Mealer 2009).

Fair Trade

While leveraging global inequities to fund assistance to the international poor is a classic component of philanthropic approaches, another rising approach is to transform the trade system to make it more equitable, and improve the lives of small producers within the market system. The most common example of this is **fair trade**, a system of trading partnerships that seeks to intervene in the market by setting a minimum price for paying producers of export goods. The extra cost of this minimum price is shared by the fair-trade wholesalers (using practices such as maximum wages for executives) and consumers, who often pay a small premium for fair-trade commodities.

Knowing how much they can expect to earn for their produce regardless of global market fluctuations allows local farmers in developing countries to plan ahead, expand their businesses, and take out loans. Many form cooperatives and pool their money to build schools or clinics, or create projects (like coffee roasteries) that add value to their product.

Fair trade has become a small but important part of global trade, especially in such commodities as bananas and other fresh fruits, cocoa and chocolate, coffee, cotton, flowers, handicrafts, honey, sugar, tea, and wine. As of 2010, roughly 27,000 certified fair-trade products were being sold in over 70 countries, with estimated sales amounting to $4.6 billion (FTLO 2010).

One common criticism of fair trade is that it reduces market efficiency. This is not always true. Some fair-trade practices recover efficiencies by creating more direct relationships between producers and retailers and cutting out middlemen (in the coffee trade, for example, there will sometimes be as many as seven middlemen from local bulk buyers to shippers to roasters, each adding their expenses and profit margin to the retail price). Another study argued that fair trade actually creates efficiencies by bringing exploitative conditions in developing countries more closely in line with the ideal market conditions assumed in most economic analyses (Hayes and Moore 2005).

Social Entrepreneurship

Social entrepreneurship refers to the use of entrepreneurial principles to create, organize, and manage ventures designed to produce social change. Successful entrepreneurship is understood to involve innovative, risky, solution-oriented activities that can further social and environmental goals. Social entrepreneurship is held up by advocates as a counter to the principles that get in the way of typical government and NGO-run projects: brief political cycles, demands for instant results, a desire to minimize risk and avoid blame, and an unwillingness to make difficult decisions that might be seen as unfair.

Most social entrepreneurship starts with building relationships in local communities and identifying innovative and energetic individuals who can be provided with the means to establish sustainable social projects. Once established, these ventures are operated by committed and capable teams with vested interests in the outcomes, rewarded on the basis of measurable performance (Mawson 2008).

Appropriate Technologies

Many philanthropic projects seek to improve technological access in communities with underdeveloped infrastructures so that they can use these to improve their opportunities. The One Laptop per Child trade association, a US-based non-profit organization created by faculty members of the MIT Media Lab, seeks to design, manufacture, and distribute $100 laptops so that every child in the world can have one (www.laptop.org). But artifacts like laptops assume other aspects of infrastructure—dust-free houses, reliable electricity, working telephone lines— that may not be available. And for the more than one billion people globally who live on $1 per day, even a $100 laptop may be hopelessly out of reach.

An alternative to giving people access to technologies common in the West is to develop technologies that are appropriate to different environmental and infrastructural contexts. In

Sitio Malagaya, a squatter community of brick houses with tin roofs built along a seven-mile stretch of unused railroad track in the Philippines, a man named Ilac Diaz fills soda bottles with water, seals them, and installs them on rooftops, allowing the sun's rays to shine through with nearly the brightness of a 60-watt lightbulb (literoflight.org).

Designed and developed by students from the Massachusetts Institute of Technology (MIT), the solar bottle bulb is an example of "appropriate technology"—an effort to provide simple and easily replicable technologies that address basic needs in developing communities. **Appropriate technologies** refers to using local materials to create low-cost technologies useful in specific social and environmental contexts. Bicycle-powered water pumps, self-contained solar-powered lightbulbs and streetlights, coal made from sugar cane and corn cobs, clay-pot food preservers, and many other inexpensive devices have had major impacts on people's lives, without the enormous infrastructural requirements of Western industrialization.

Microfinance

Projects in social entrepreneurship, fair trade, and appropriate technologies are sometimes funded through NGOs and philanthropies, but also often through microfinancing. **Microfinancing** involves providing small-scale financial services including loans, savings accounts, funds transfers, and insurance to low-income clients or groups, who traditionally lack access to banking services. While microfinancing is driven by ideology—efforts to alleviate poverty by enabling people to help themselves through entrepreneurship, financing educations, or facilitating savings—it is intended to be sustainable by turning a small profit on its investments.

Although microfinance can fail spectacularly, it has also provided a large number of successes. The success of microfinance seems to depend heavily on lending institutions rooted in the communities in which they provide services.

Conclusion

In 2016 the United Nations launched a new set of goals for its member states to work toward: the Sustainable Development Goals (United Nations 2016). These goals call on the nations of the world to form global partnerships to end poverty and hunger, shepherd terrestrial and water resources wisely, and pursue equal access to health care for all (Table C.1). Creating policies that will realize these goals, in large and small ways, will be the work of generations—beginning with yours.

An international studies perspective that combines geography, history, political science, anthropology, and economics (or, to phrase them in another way, population, past, power, people, and production) will be well placed to analyze and resolve these issues. International matters such as demography, information and communication technologies, war, peace, poverty, terrorism, and pollution, to name a few, demand a global integrative approach.

Our examination of the world has taken us around the globe by way of Europe, Asia, Latin America, the Middle East, and Africa. We have utilized the prisms of geography, history, political science, anthropology, and economics to scrutinize global issues such as terrorism, climate change, and refugees. We have stressed the interconnectedness of countries within regions, and regions within a global world system.

The intense cultural, economic, and political interactions among peoples and places have spread rapidly across space and time, creating ever greater levels of complexity. The last hundred years have seen incredible leaps in science and technology. Electricity lit up the Eiffel Tower at the Paris Exposition of 1900, and it still powers our computers and televisions. Electric cars may be the future of transport. Films and the escalator were also featured at the exhibition; today these technologies are ubiquitous.

Table C.1 United Nations Sustainable Development Goals

1	End poverty in all its forms everywhere
2	End hunger, achieve food security and improved nutrition, and promote sustainable agriculture
3	Ensure healthy lives and promote well-being for all at all ages
4	Ensure inclusive and equitable quality education and promote lifelong learning opportunities for all
5	Achieve gender equality and empower all women and girls
6	Ensure availability and sustainable management of water and sanitation for all
7	Ensure access to affordable, reliable, sustainable and modern energy for all
8	Promote sustained, inclusive and sustainable economic growth, full and productive employment and decent work for all
9	Build resilient infrastructure, promote inclusive and sustainable industrialization, and foster innovation
10	Reduce inequality within and among countries
11	Make cities and human settlements inclusive, safe, resilient, and sustainable
12	Ensure sustainable consumption and production patterns
13	Take urgent action to combat climate change and its impacts
14	Conserve and sustainably use the oceans, seas and marine resources for sustainable development
15	Protect, restore and promote sustainable use of terrestrial ecosystems, sustainably manage forests, combat desertification, and halt and reverse land degradation and halt biodiversity loss
16	Promote peaceful and inclusive societies for sustainable development, provide access to justice for all and build effective, accountable and inclusive institutions at all levels
17	Strengthen the means of implementation and revitalize the global partnership for sustainable development

Source: United Nations Sustainable Development (https://sdgs.un.org/goals).

People living at the beginning of the twentieth century could not have foreseen World War I, World War II, and the Cold War. Nor could they have foreseen television, computers, and the Internet. As we gaze ahead to the future from the vantage points of history, geography, political science, anthropology, and economics, we can only make educated guesses about what the world will look like in the next hundred years. As one scholar put it, "we can't predict the future, but that is not terribly significant. What is more important is that we can envision the future we want and set about making it happen" (Hammond 1999). Whatever global challenges face future generations, the interdisciplinary methodology of international studies is essential to finding solutions.

References

FTLO (Fairtrade Labeling Organizations). 2010. *Growing Stronger Together: Annual Report 2009–2010.* www.fairtrade.net/fileadmin/user_upload/content/2009/resources/FLO_Annual-Report-2009_komplett_double_web.pdf.

Hammond, Allen. 1999. "Three Global Scenarios." *The Futurist* 33 (4): 38–43.

Hayes, Mark, and Geoff Moore. 2005. *The Economics of Fair Trade: A Guide in Plain English.* Durham Business School International Workshop on the Economics of Fair Trade.

Kamkwamba, William, and Bryan Mealer. 2009. *The Boy Who Harnessed the Wind: Creating Electricity and Hope.* New York: William Morrow.

Mawson, Andrew. 2008. *The Social Entrepreneur: Making Communities Work.* London: Atlantic Books.

MIT News. 2008. "'Just Jerusalem' Competition winners announced." March 21, https://news.mit.edu/2008/just-jerusalem-competition-winners-announced.

United Nations. 2007. "UN Millennium Goals Indicators." www.un.org/millenniumgoals.

———. 2015. "The Millennium Development Goals Report 2015." www.un.org/millenniumgoals/news. shtml.

United Nations. 2016. *Transforming our World: The 2030 Agenda for Sustainable Development.* sustainabledevelopment.un.org.

Further Reading

Books

Arrillaga-Andreessen, Laura. 2011. *Giving 2.0: Transform Your Giving and Our World.* San Francisco: Jossey-Bass.

Bornstein, David. 2005. *How to Change the World: Social Entrepreneurs and the Power of New Ideas.* New York: Oxford University Press.

Eckaus, Richard S. 2009. *Appropriate Technologies for Developing Countries.* Washington, DC: National Academies.

Helms, Brigit. 2006. *Access for All: Building Inclusive Financial Systems.* Washington, DC: Consultative Group to Assist the Poor.

Schumacher, E. F. 1973. *Small Is Beautiful: A Study of Economics As If People Mattered.* London: Blond and Briggs.

Yunus, Muhammad. 2007. *Creating a World Without Poverty: Social Business and the Future of Capitalism.* New York: PublicAffairs.

Websites

Ashoka: Innovators for the Public. www.ashoka.org

AVAAZ: The World in Action. www.avaaz.org

Fair Trade International. www.fairtrade.net

Kiva: Empower People around the World for $25. www.kiva.org

The Schwab Foundation for Social Entrepreneurship. www.schwabfound.org

TED: Ideas Worth Spreading. www.ted.com

Glossary

African Continental Free Trade Area (AfCTA). Free trade area in Africa commencing in 2021.

African Union (AU). Formed in 2001, the African Union was an outgrowth of the Organization of African Unity (1963). The AU has made halting steps toward creating a larger African tariff area and establishing peacekeeping forces, watchdog organizations, and political units.

aliyah. From a Hebrew word meaning "ascent," this refers to emigration by Jews from their country of residence to Palestine and, after 1948, to Israel.

allocation state. A government that does not derive its revenues from taxation but rather by selling key resources on the world market and using the proceeds to fund governmental operations like schools, roads, and hospitals. Also called a *rentier state.*

American dream. Term describing an American worldview that proposes that all people have, or should have, opportunities to achieve material prosperity through hard work.

American politics. The branch of political science that focuses on US governmental and political institutions and behavior.

anarchy. The absence of government, the global structure within which states operate.

Andes. The dominant mountain range of western South America; the Andean region includes Ecuador, Bolivia, Peru, Colombia, and Venezuela.

anti-Semitism. For centuries, Jews in Europe faced discrimination from Christians because Jews rejected New Testament claims that Jesus was the Son of God. Modern anti-Semitism added economic and racial elements, which the Nazis exploited and used as a rationale for the Holocaust.

apartheid. Apartheid was the legal system of white rule in South Africa that denied black South Africans equal rights. It was overturned in 1990, leading to black majority rule in 1994.

appropriate technology. Technologies that are appropriate to specific local needs and infrastructures.

Arab Spring. Western media term for a series of uprisings in the Middle East that began in 2010–2011. Demands of Arab Spring protestors ranged from greater representation in government, and greater responsiveness from government, to the ousting of authoritarian regimes.

Arab world. Term used to collectively describe the 22 Arabic-speaking countries of the world, from Morocco to Iraq, as a single geopolitical unit of some 325 million people.

arbitrary. A meaning is said to be arbitrary when it relies entirely on social convention and has no natural or essential basis. Most linguistic and cultural symbols are arbitrary.

arkaan. The Five Pillars of Islam; a set of practices concerning profession of faith, along with prayer, fasting, charity, and pilgrimage that are designed to shape faithful adherents to the practices into better Muslims.

Association of Southeast Asian Nations (ASEAN). Political-economic organization of Southeast Asia.

authoritarianism.   Like fascism and Nazism, authoritarianism relies on the principle of one strong dictator to unify a country under nationalist slogans, but, unlike fascism, usually relies on support from military, business, and church elites.

balance of power.   An important concept in realist theory by which self-interested powerful states achieve a stable global system through actions that offset one another's power.

Basques.   Members of an ethnic group in northern Spain that has sought greater autonomy from the central government in Madrid. Their rights were suppressed under the dictatorship of Francisco Franco (1936–1975), breeding a terrorist organization (ETA) that sought an independent state.

behaviorism.   A methodological approach to social science that emphasizes data collection and the scientific method.

Beijing Consensus.   Economic model following China's economy and leadership rather than the Washington Consensus.

Bolshevik Revolution.   Led by Vladimir Ilyich Lenin, the Bolsheviks overthrew the Russian government in 1917, instituting nearly 75 years of Communist rule. Until the Soviet Union collapsed in 1991, Western liberal democracy was challenged by the Soviets.

Buddhism.   Religious system based on the teachings of Gautama Buddha. Divided into Mahayana in East Asia (including Zen in Japan), Theravada in Southeast Asia, and Vajrayana (or Tibetan Buddhism) in Tibet.

burqa.   Head-to-foot pleated gown with an eye screen worn by women in parts of Afghanistan and Pakistan.

caliph.   Leader of the worldwide Muslim community; political successor to Muhammad.

caliphate.   A community under the governance of a religious successor to the Prophet Muhammad.

capital.   Durable goods like cash, factories, manufacturing equipment, tools, and so forth that are used to create goods and services for exchange in a market.

capital flight.   The tendency for wealth to leave poor countries rather than trickle down from the wealthy to the middle classes.

carrying capacity.   In environmental economics, the maximum population size an environment can sustain indefinitely, given the finite resources available in the environment, the technologies people use to exploit them, and the wastes produced as a by-product.

caudillo.   Latin American military leader following independence from Spain in the early nineteenth century. The tradition of the Latin American military dictator (*caudillismo*) continued well into the twentieth century.

causation.   Historians explain historical events in different ways depending upon their theory of causation, such as political, economic, and environmental forces, ideology, or social structure.

Central Asia.   Afghanistan, Uzbekistan, and Kazakhstan are the principal countries in this region of Asia.

chaebol.   A Korean megacorporation.

class struggle.   Karl Marx theorized that historical change is driven by conflicts between classes; he called for the working classes to overthrow the capitalist classes to create a Communist system.

classical liberalism.   Enlightenment thinker Adam Smith is most remembered for the anti-mercantilist idea that economies grow and wealth is accumulated faster when the government takes a laissez-faire approach and allows the "invisible hand" of supply and demand to operate freely.

coalition.   A government or other political body that shares power among two or more political parties.

Cold War.   Battle of liberal democratic and communist ideologies and geo-strategy between the United States and the Soviet Union after World War II to the end of the 1980s.

collective security.   A system by which states ally to protect each other against external threat.

colonial rule.   European countries established formal colonial rule over most of Africa and Asia by 1885, drawing illegitimate boundaries and exploiting human and natural resources.

colonialism.   The political, economic, and cultural domination of African, American, Asian, and Middle Eastern societies by European powers.

Common Market.   *See* European Economic Community.

common sense.   The set of unstated assumptions we share with others in our community that we most rely on in making sense of the world around us. It is what we accept to be true without questioning or analyzing it.

communism.   Karl Marx's anti-capitalist theory envisioned a classless society in which the proletariat owned the means of production, and people worked according to their ability and took according to their needs. Lenin ushered in Communism into the Soviet Union in 1917, but Marxists might claim that the Soviet system was a dictatorship of the party rather than a true dictatorship of the proletariat.

comparative advantage.   This economic principle states that gains from trade follow from encouraging an economy to specialize its production. First presented by David Ricardo in 1817, if a country is *relatively* better at making one product than another, it makes sense to put more resources into that product and to use the returns from selling it to obtain those products less efficiently produced in your own economy.

comparative politics.   The branch of political science that focuses on governmental and political institutions and behaviors outside the United States. It often relies on comparative methodologies.

comparison.   By comparing the many different ways human communities solve the same problems, this anthropological perspective seeks to avoid mistakenly assuming that one set of practices or system of knowledge is natural or necessary.

complex interdependence.   A theory or situation marked by strong connections among nations and states that make these actors mutually vulnerable and sensitive.

Confucianism.   Chinese philosophical system of social order and reciprocity.

conservative nationalism.   Leaders who seek to preserve their power and the socioeconomic order use pride in nation and fear of an enemy nation as a means to unify the masses and prevent domestic unrest.

constitutional monarchy.   A king or queen from a royal family acts as the head of state, but the real political power rests with a democratically elected legislative branch.

Covid-19.   Coronavirus Disease. A virus which spread around the world starting in December 2019 causing a global pandemic.

criollos.   Latin American-born people of European descent. During the colonial period the *criollos* dominated politics and led independence movements.

cultural and social history.   The study of the history of music, food, sports, language, religion, family, gender, and other elements of culture and society.

cultural logic.   The underlying mechanism that generates meaningful human action.

cultural misunderstanding.   A failure of communication created by people or communities using different cultural logics to understand each other's speech and action.

cultural practices.   Everyday activities of people in a particular community, as well as the artifacts they employ.

culture.   A learned system of meanings by which people orient themselves in the world so that they can act in it. Culture relies on a universal human capacity to differentiate and to categorize experience.

culture shock.   The unpleasant, even traumatic, feeling people get when the rules and understandings by which they have organized their lives do not apply.

cyberattacks.   Assaults against single or multiple computers or networks designed to steal data, or to disable, disrupt or destroy other countries' computer systems.

cyber espionage. Stealing other countries' sensitive information for economic or military advantage.

cybersecurity. Organized efforts to protect computer systems and networks from threats of damage.

cyberspace. The conceptual environment in which communication over computer networks occurs.

cyberterrorism. Cyberattacks carried out by ideologically motivated groups or individuals.

cyberwarfare. Cyberattacks carried out by states against other states.

Darfur. A western region of Sudan. It has experienced a civil conflict in the first decade of the twenty-first century that has taken some 200,000 lives. Some observers accuse the Sudanese government of condoning the genocide of non-Arab peoples.

decolonization. The end of control by imperialist powers, which leads to the independence of the countries they formerly controlled as colonies.

deep fakes. Images of false events that are indistinguishable from actual events, created through the use of artificial intelligence.

demand. Demand represents the amount of a good that buyers are willing to purchase at a range of prices with the assumption that all other factors remain constant. Demand is represented in a demand curve that is almost always a downwards-sloping curve demonstrating that as the price for a good decreases, consumers will buy more of the good.

demand schedule. A list of goods that buyers are willing to buy at a certain price.

democracy. A form of governmental rule in which leaders are chosen by some form of electoral process.

Deng Xiaoping (1904–1997). Leader of China from 1978 to 1992.

dependency theory. An economic theory that finds Latin American poverty and stalled growth a product of the region's dependence on more advanced economies in the north.

determinism. The theoretical assumption that human intentions and efforts are largely irrelevant because all events are shaped by the events that preceded them, as well as by natural laws and conditions.

deterrence. The effort to prevent an action or event through instilling doubt or fear of the consequences.

development. The process of improving the quality of human life.

developmentalist perspectives. The study of economic growth in less-developed societies.

dialectic. In Marxism, the dialectic refers to the continuous contest between two social classes, the capitalists and the workers, resulting in a social transformation.

diaspora. From a Greek word for "dispersal," this term is used to describe transnational communities of peoples who maintain a distinct identity in the host communities in which they settle, often through a sense of connection to a common homeland.

diffusion. The spread of cultural practices through migration or conquest, as well as through indirect contact such as trade and mass media.

East Asia. China, Japan, North Korea, and South Korea are the principal countries of this region of Asia.

ecological economics. Branch of economics rooted in the principle that realistic economic projections need to include costs of environmental and ecological damage such as pollution and resource loss.

economic history. The study of the exchange of goods and services. Economic historians seek insight into economic trends that might inform future economic and business decisions.

economic nationalism. Economic paradigm in which economies are viewed as integrally connected to social, political, and cultural systems, and in which states should seek to intervene in markets to protect national labor, trade production, and wealth accumulation.

economics. The social science that studies, describes, models, and makes projections about flows of wealth in the process of the production, distribution, and consumption of scarce resources, by focusing on the choices made by individuals about alternative uses of scarce resources to satisfy needs and wants.

EEC.   *See* European Economic Community.

embodiment.   Cultural learning that shapes our bodies and unconscious behaviors, including such things as how we speak, how we move, how we eat, and our comfort level in relation to the proximity of other people.

empirical.   Type of knowledge derived from direct observation and careful recording of information.

enculturation.   The processes by which members of a society pass on culture to new generations.

environment.   Our physical world.

environmental determinism.   Simplistic belief that human events can be explained entirely as a result of the physical environment.

environmental history.   A field of history devoted to people's interaction with their natural surroundings, such as water usage, farming practices, food distribution, and marine and forest preservation.

environmental possibilism.   Theory that the physical environment does not determine what people attempt though it does limit what people can achieve.

equilibrium.   When the demand for a good equals the supply of that good, the market for that good is said to be in equilibrium.

ETA.   *See* Euskadi Ta Askatasuna.

euro.   Currency of the European Union.

European Coal and Steel Community (ECSC).   Created by "the Six" (West Germany, France, Italy, Belgium, Netherlands, and Luxembourg) in 1951 to regulate coal and steel production. The ECSC was so successful that its six members agreed to form the European Economic Community in 1957.

European Economic Community (EEC).   A group of six European countries (France, West Germany, Italy, and the Benelux countries) joined together in 1957 to lower tariffs on trade as a whole and create a common external tariff. Also called the Common Market. The European Economic Community evolved into the European Union.

European Union (EU).   Formed in 1992, the European Union has eliminated most borders among its 27 members and implemented currency unification (the euro). It coordinates foreign and defense policies.

Eurozone.   Area in Europe in which the common European monetary unit (the euro) is the only accepted currency.

Euskadi Ta Askatasuna (ETA).   Basque terrorist organization seeking independence from Spanish rule for the Basque territories.

evil eye.   Widespread belief in Mediterranean cultures that a look inspired by envy or anger can cause injury or bad luck for the person at whom it is directed.

evolution.   Anthropological assumption that all social and cultural systems are in a continual state of change.

exchange rate.   The value of one country's currency compared to that of another.

expressive culture.   Institutions through which a community articulates and elaborates its worldview in various symbolic forms, such as literature, art, drama, myth, ritual, and mass media.

extractivism.   Relying primarily on extracting resources from the Earth for economic growth.

failed state.   A central government that has lost control of parts of the country it governs.

fair trade.   A system of trading partnerships that intervenes in the market by setting a minimum price for export goods, protecting producers from severe economic shocks.

fascism. Benito Mussolini capitalized on Italy's wounded national pride and political and economic turmoil from World War I to overthrow the constitutional monarchy in 1922. Mussolini's fascism was a far-right mass movement that played on people's grievances.

Fertile Crescent. A region of river valleys, arcing from the Nile Valley of Egypt to Mesopotamia (modern Iraq), where the invention of agriculture led to the rise of some of the world's earliest cities and empires.

fieldwork. Collective term for a number of social science research methods that require periods of residence among the people studied.

formal learning. The acquisition of cultural knowledge that takes place within institutions specifically designed for this purpose, such as schools, apprenticeships, and on-the-job training.

formal region. A region defined by a uniformity of features.

functional region. A region defined by interaction among localities.

fusha. Pronounced foos-ha. Proper Arabic, that is, the classical Arabic of the Quran and of medieval literature. Today, it is primarily a literary language.

G7. *See* Group of Seven.

G20. *See* Group of Twenty.

GATT. *See* General Agreement on Tariffs and Trade.

GDP. *See* gross domestic product.

General Agreement on Tariffs and Trade (GATT). Provided a framework to gradually reduce barriers to freer trade between states. In 1995, GATT evolved into the World Trade Organization, which is dedicated to arbitrating international trade disputes and further lowering trade barriers.

generation of similarity. Function of social institutions and processes such as family, school, peer groups, and mass media to teach and reinforce common beliefs, values, orientations, and models for action among members of a community.

geographic definition. Boundaries of a continent, country, or other area defined by a geographic description of its borders.

geographic information system (GIS). A computerized mapping system that stores and analyzes many layers of data.

geography. Study of the interaction of physical and human phenomena at individual places and of how interactions among places form patterns and organize space.

globalization. The expansion of global communication and market connections, growing social and political interdependencies on a global scale, and the development of a planetary rather than national awareness among many of the world's people. The increasing interconnectedness around the world through economic, political, and cultural change.

Great Economic Crisis. A sharp downturn in the world economy that began in the United States in 2008 and has had devastating, worldwide consequences.

gross domestic product (GDP). A way of measuring the size of a country's economy; usually defined as the market value of all goods and services produced within a country in a given period of time.

Group of Seven (G7). The Group of Seven (G7) is an international forum for the governments of France, Japan, Italy, Germany, Canada, the United Kingdom, and the United States. These countries account for about 60 percent of the total global economic production as well as the largest proportion of global military power. Russia was a member of the Group of Eight from 1988 to 2014.

Group of Twenty (G20). A group of finance ministers and central bank governors from 20 major economies—19 countries and the European Union—that gathers annually in a summit to discuss the state of the worldwide economy.

hadith. Collected accounts of sayings and actions of the prophet Muhammad and his companions.

hegemon. A global or regional leading power whose leadership is recognized by members of the group.

hijab. A head scarf, which covers the hair and neck, worn by some Middle Eastern Muslim women.

Hinduism. The oldest religious system in Asia and the dominant religion of India.

historical definition. A country, continent, or other area that is defined by events that occurred in its history.

historical materialism. Contrasted with philosophical idealism, historical materialism is the method for studying history and social systems advocated by Karl Marx that places the material conditions of life as primary in forming social and ideological contexts.

historiography. Summary critiques of other historians' work on a particular subject.

holism. Anthropological perspective that seeks to understand human societies as complex systems with many interwoven elements.

hostile social manipulation. Efforts to affect beliefs, attitudes, and behavior through the generation and dissemination of information intended to produce harmful social, political, and economic outcomes in a target country.

human determinism. Simplistic belief that people can shape the land into any form without regard to environmental consequences.

idealism/liberalism. Theory that explains political behavior as a function of moral human decisions, institutional structures, and collective interest.

identity. The feeling a person has as a member of a group or community, as well as the set of associations others may ascribe to a person as a member of a group.

ideology. The mobilization of cultural symbols to create, sustain, or resist unequal distribution of rights, responsibilities, and control over resources in a society.

IMF. *See* International Monetary Fund.

imperial borders. European imperialists finalized the borders of Africa at the Berlin Conference in 1884–1885. The borders they drew have little relation to natural boundaries or ethnic divisions.

imperialism. Political, economic, and cultural domination of a country or area by another country.

import quotas. Limitations placed on the importation of certain goods to protect a certain segment of a country's domestic industry.

import substitution industrialization (ISI). The dominant economic model in Latin America during the 1960s and 1970s, import substitution industrialization called for national industries to provide previously imported goods.

independent Africa. Beginning with Ghana in 1956 and ending with Mozambique and Angola in 1975, all of the African states gained their independence from the European imperialists.

informal economy. Economic activity that is not monitored by a government and therefore is not taxed or included in the country's gross domestic product.

informal learning. Learning that we engage in simply by watching, listening, and participating in everyday activities.

intellectual history. Historical study of the development and influence of ideologies such as religion, nationalism, liberalism, Marxism, and feminism.

intellectual property. The idea that intangible creations of individual human minds can be defined and protected in ways similar to land or physical goods.

intercultural relations. Flows of symbols across cultural boundaries facilitated by transnational migration, new information technologies, and global markets, which can lead to creativity and innovation but also to misunderstanding and conflict.

international economics.   Focused on financial and trade relations of national economies and the effects of international trade and finance on the distribution of production, income, and wealth around the world and within nations.

International Monetary Fund (IMF).   An international organization that provides financial assistance to nations with financial problems and monitors the global financial system, observing changes in currency exchange rates and national balances of payments.

international politics.   Branch of political science that focuses on transnational political behavior.

international relations.   A subfield of political science that studies the political relationships among nations.

international studies.   An interdisciplinary field of scholarship engaged in the description and analysis of major political, economic, geographic, historic, and cultural issues that transcend national borders, often with the goal of finding policy solutions to international and global problems.

IRA.   *See* Irish Republican Army.

Irish Republican Army (IRA).   An Irish militia originally formed to protect Irish Catholics and force the British out of Ireland. After most of Ireland gained Home Rule in 1921, the Irish Republican Army evolved into a terrorist group demanding the unification of Northern Ireland with the rest of the country.

Iron Curtain.   Term used to describe the western boundary of the East European countries that fell under Soviet-friendly communist regimes after World War II (East Germany, Poland, Czechoslovakia, Hungary, Romania, and Bulgaria).

ISI.   *See* import substitution industrialization.

Islam.   The dominant religion in the Middle East, Islam is the second-largest and fastest-growing religion in the world.

Islamic world.   The total number of the world's Muslim majority countries in Asia, Africa, the Middle East, and Europe.

janjaweed.   Mostly Arab militia groups in Darfur used by the Sudanese government to massacre and intimidate the African tribes in the region.

jihad.   Islamic term for spiritual struggle. The term *greater jihad* refers to the individual's internal struggle against sin; the term *lesser jihad* refers to political and military struggle.

keiretsu.   A Japanese business conglomerate.

khimar.   A head-to-midriff covering with an oval for the face worn by some Middle Eastern and Muslim women.

kleptocracy.   A regime that loots government coffers and the national economy for the leadership's personal gain.

labor history.   Subfield of economic history that focuses on the development of working-class solidarity and worker relations with management and the government.

laissez-faire.   Minimal government intervention in a country's economy.

latifundia.   Large plantations that dominated colonial agriculture in Latin America. After independence the latifundia persisted and established a pattern of inequitable land distribution.

law of demand.   Economic theory that asserts that there is an inverse relationship between the price of a good and the quantity demanded of that good.

law of supply.   Economic theory that asserts that there is a direct relationship between the price of a good and the quantity of supply of the good.

Left, the.   The side of the political spectrum that espouses humanitarianism and idealism in world politics, and civil liberties and government responsibility in domestic politics.

liberal democracy.   A system of government that institutionalizes majority rule, has an independent judiciary, respects the rule of law, and protects the civil rights of all citizens.

liberal economic theory. Developed during the European Enlightenment, the theory emphasizes market systems that allow individuals to trade goods and services with minimal government intervention.

liberalism. The crucial tenets of liberalism in international politics include the following: (1) Humans have a capacity for good. (2) Selfish and violent behaviors come not from human nature but from institutions that promote such behavior. (3) The primary public institution leading to war is the state, because it promotes nationalism and selfishness over global welfare. (4) Multilateral action and institutions are needed to prevent war.

life expectancy. Length of life expected at birth on average.

liquidity. The capacity of an economic unit—individual, corporation, state, etc.—to pay debts when they come due without incurring unacceptable losses.

location. Where a geographic phenomenon is. Includes absolute, relative, and nominal location.

macroeconomics. The study of the combined performance of all markets in a defined market system by gathering aggregate information about nations' economies. Macroeconomics may have nation-states or global regions as its unit of analysis.

Maghreb. Arabic term for North Africa, especially the western half.

Mandela, Nelson (1918–2013). Led the African National Congress and fought apartheid in South Africa. Released after 27 years in prison, his nonviolent approach eventually brought an end to white rule in 1990. President of South Africa, 1994–1999.

Mao Zedong (1893–1976). Leader of China, 1949–1976.

map. A specialized picture of mathematical precision that expresses ideas about the world. A map is a multifaceted tool that provides a concrete understanding of the relationships that locations have with other locations.

marginal utility. Theory that the goal of business is to increase the point where consumer satisfaction is gained.

markets. Markets are a series of social arrangements for buying and selling goods. In markets, consumers gather information and participate in a voluntary exchange of goods and services, thus organizing trade.

Marshall Plan. A US-financed $13-billion aid program (1948–1952) to jumpstart the Western European economies after World War II.

Marxism. In the mid-nineteenth century, Karl Marx theorized that historical development was not a clash of ideas, as Georg Wilhelm Friedrich Hegel posited, but a struggle between classes based on their material possessions. Marx advocated violent overthrow by the working classes.

Marxism-Leninism. A form of Marxist political ideology that linked Karl Marx's economic theories to a set of political theories for the development of a communist state put forward by Vladimir Lenin.

Mau Mau rebellion. The Mau Mau were mostly Kikuyu people in Kenya who rebelled against losing their land to the British. In the 1950s, thousands of Kikuyu were killed in the rebellion.

means of production. A Marxist term that refers to the tools, knowledge, capital, and raw materials needed to produce a good.

media. Technologically constituted vehicles for extending human communication, from cuneiform tablets to phonograph records to newspapers to radio and television broadcasts to social media.

Melanesia. Region of islands in the Pacific including Papua New Guinea, the Solomon Islands, Vanuatu, and Fiji.

mercantilism. A theory of political economy that holds that the economic well-being of a nation is directly related to its degree of control over the global volume of capital.

meritocracy.   A system in which people succeed according to their own skills without regard for caste, class, religion, race, ethnicity, or kinship networks.

methodological relativism.   The principle that to be comparative, anthropology must treat all social practices as data of the same type.

microeconomics.   Area of economics that is concerned with studying specific market systems on a small scale, such as the economic behavior of individuals, firms, and industries, to understand the relative prices of goods and services and the alternative uses to which resources can be put in a particular market system.

microfinancing.   Providing small-scale loans, savings accounts, fund transfers, and other financial services to low-income clients who normally do not have access to such services.

Micronesia.   Region of islands in the Pacific including Nauru, the Marshall Islands, Guam, the Mariana Islands, and the Federated States of Micronesia.

migrant labor.   Any people who travel from their homes to work elsewhere, including migratory seasonal workers within a country.

military coup.   Military seizure of power through undemocratic means. Africa has been plagued by recurrent military coups that have undermined the continent's political stability, economic development, and evolution toward democracy.

military rule.   Rule by military leaders.

Millennium Development Project.   In 2002, the UN General Secretary created this long-range plan to eradicate poverty, hunger, and disease in the developing world.

Modern Standard Arabic.   The language of newspapers, television news programs, schools, and contemporary literature throughout the Arabic-speaking world.

monarchy.   Monarchy is an authoritarian political system in which legitimacy of the head of the government is based on royal bloodlines.

monsoon.   Seasonal climate change throughout South, Southeast, and East Asia.

Muslim world.   The worldwide community of Muslims, including Muslim enclaves in non-Muslim majority countries. See also "Islamic world."

NAFTA.   *See* North American Free Trade Agreement.

nakba.   "The Catastrophe." Common Arab term used to refer to the establishment of the state of Israel in 1948.

nation.   A people united by some common origin and character. *See also* state.

national self-determination.   The theory that every people, or nation, should have the right to determine its own political system.

nationalism.   Nationalism is a constructed bond between peoples of similar language, religion, history, and culture. Nationalism breeds a sense of being different from another national group, and often feelings of superiority and chauvinism.

nationalist histories.   Often glorified histories of a nation's past that serve as a unifier based on a common mission, culture, religion, language, and shared territory. Nationalist histories tend to elevate their nation's achievements and denigrate those of others.

nationalization.   Appropriation by nation-states of the means of production—land, factories, corporations—usually in the name of "the people" of the nation.

nation-state.   A Western idea that people with a common language and historical tradition should constitute a sovereign state. *See* nation *and* state.

NATO.   *See* North Atlantic Treaty Organization.

Nazism.   Adolf Hitler's Nazi movement borrowed from Italian fascism, adding virulent racial anti-Semitism. Hitler came to power in 1933 during the depths of the Great Depression.

neoliberalism.   The dominant economic model in most parts of the world, it professes free trade and low government intervention in the economy. It is promoted by the International Monetary Fund, World Bank, and other Western lending institutions.

neo-patrimonialism.　This patronage system is prevalent among some African leaders who use their political power to enrich members of their own ethnic group rather than act in the interests of the country as a whole.

New Imperialism.　In the late nineteenth century, European powers divided up most of the last remaining free areas of Africa and Asia. By 1900, almost 85 percent of the earth's land surface was controlled by European peoples.

new media.　Media such as personal computers, smartphones and related devices in which tools of consumption are also the tools of production and distribution.

New Partnership for Africa's Development (NEPAD).　An all-African organization formed in 2001 to examine failed political and economic policies and recommend new strategies for cooperation and development.

newly industrialized countries (NICs).　States nearing developed-world (core) status: Singapore, South Korea, and Taiwan.

niqab.　A dress that covers the entire body, accompanied by a face veil, gloves, and, in some places, an eye screen or sunglasses.

nonrenewable resources.　Materials or energy that have finite amounts, whose continued use leads to exhaustion.

North American Free Trade Agreement (NAFTA).　Agreement between the United States, Canada, and Mexico to encourage free trade by eliminating previously existing impediments to free trade.

North Atlantic Treaty Organization (NATO).　Founded in 1949, NATO is a military and political alliance formed among West European countries and the United States and Canada, mainly to protect against Soviet attack. It has 26 members today.

Northeast Asia.　China, Japan, and the Koreas are the main countries of this region of Asia.

OAS.　*See* Organization of American States.

opportunity costs.　In economics, the loss created by accepting one option over others.

Organization of African Unity (OAU).　In part as a result of US and Belgian intrigue to overthrow Patrice Lumumba in Congo, 32 African states formed the Organization of African Unity in 1963. The OAU hoped to maintain the independence of African states in the wake of immense Soviet and American pressure to take sides in the Cold War. Now called the African Union (AU).

Organization of American States (OAS).　The principal diplomatic body of the Western Hemisphere. Members include all countries in the Americas and the Caribbean, with the exception of Cuba, whose Communist government has been prevented from participation since 1962.

organization of difference.　Function of social institutions and processes to regulate behavior and reward or punish deviance.

Pacific.　Global region including the countries of Australia and New Zealand and the regions of Polynesia, Micronesia, and Melanesia.

paradigm.　Sets of practices and the associated theories and ideas that define a scientific or scholarly discipline.

parsimony.　Efficiency; a parsimonious theory is one that explains much with a few key concepts.

participant observation.　Classic anthropological research method involving relatively long-term engagements with a host community in which an anthropologist enters into the everyday life of the community insofar as his or her hosts permit.

pastoralism.　Economic system based on the raising of cattle. In the Middle East, transhuman pastoralism was common, involving nomadic herders who traveled with their flocks to take advantage of seasonal change.

path dependence.　Tendency of institutions to develop in certain ways based on structure or previous decisions.

peninsulares.   Spanish- or Portuguese-born individuals living in colonial Latin America.

petrodollars.   Funds deposited in mostly Western banks during the 1970s petroleum boom in the Middle East. Some of these funds eventually made their way into loans to Latin America and other parts of the developing world.

petro-states.   Most of the world's oil-rich states, such as Nigeria, which have not invested petroleum profits in a sustainable economic system that benefits the population as a whole.

philosophical relativism.   A position that claims, in essence, that whatever a community does is right for its members. Few, if any, anthropologists would claim to adhere wholeheartedly to this philosophy.

place.   An area and the human feelings and values attached to it.

political and diplomatic history.   Historical study concerned with the study of power and power relationships. The oldest historical tradition, political and diplomatic history is often characterized by biographies of great people. Politics, law, and foreign policy come under the purview of political history.

political ecology.   A study utilizing politics, economy, culture, and geography to analyze environmental issues.

political economy.   The interrelations of political institutions and economic systems. including markets, prices, and trade, as well as laws, governments, public opinion, and trade regulation.

political Islam.   The invocation of Islam in political and economic life, both by political actors within states and by groups opposed to existing governments. Usually advocates a political system based on some interpretation of Sharia.

political liberalism.   The philosophy concerned with civil liberty, political equality, and individual freedom to control one's own property and destiny.

political theory.   The branch of political science that focuses on philosophies of political behavior and organization.

politics.   Conflict between groups vying for power to make decisions and take action.

Polynesia.   Region of islands in the Pacific including Hawaii, Tonga, Samoa, and French Polynesia.

popular histories.   Histories written for mass consumption that compromise veracity for dramatic effect.

populism.   Authoritarian leader's appeal to the masses with nationalist slogans and government spending on the lower classes.

postindustrial economy.   An economy in which the tertiary (services) and quaternary (research) sectors are most common in employment and growth.

postmodernist history.   Postmodernists argue that all history reveals as much about the motives of the author as it does about what happened in the past. They emphasize the subjectivity of the historical record.

primary sources.   Artifacts, diaries, letters, memoirs, official documents, and other direct evidence from the past.

print capitalism.   System in which privately owned printing technologies enabled large-scale production of media such as newspapers, books, pamphlets, sheet music and other printed materials.

production state.   A state whose government derives the bulk of its revenues from taxing the wealth of its citizens.

progressivism.   German philosopher Georg Wilhelm Friedrich Hegel wrote that as new ideas challenged old traditions, a new synthesis would result to develop better political, economic, and social structures. In other words, through education and rising standards of living, people can rid society of past wrongs such as slavery, war, and inequality, and learn to live in peace and harmony.

projection.   Systematic transformation of a three-dimensional representation of the earth (a globe) to a two-dimensional representation (a map).

protectionism.   A political-economic strategy of imposing tariffs or establishing quotas on foreign imports, usually with the goal of limiting foreign industries' competition with domestic industries.

proto-state.   Communities with a historical claim to land currently under the sovereignty of one or more states.

providential.   The idea that meaning in life derives from the belief that a higher power is operating in the world, if not always in explicable ways.

public administration.   Branch of political science that focuses on applied politics, especially by local public institutions.

Public Islam.   Invocations of Islam in everyday public life, from everyday conversations to movies, blogs, and Web sites.

Quran.   The written record of Muhammad's revelation.

radial distribution.   System in which media is created in production centers and distributed outward from these production facilities.

rationality.   In economics, the assumption that human beings, and the institutions they create (organizations, corporations, states, etc.), will always act in such a way as to maximize rewards and minimize losses.

realism.   Theory that explains political behavior as a function of rational actions by self-interested states in a global system of anarchy.

realpolitik.   Another term for realism, from the German.

recession.   Any period of declining economic growth that continues beyond two consecutive quarters (i.e., six months).

refugees.   People who must flee their country of origin due to persecution, war, famine, terrorism, or natural disaster and seek asylum in a foreign country.

region.   A mental construct of an area.

relations of production.   In Marxist thought, the social relations that are necessarily formed by the way societies produce and reproduce their material lives. The relations of production determine how incomes, products, and assets are socially distributed, and they constitute the social structure of the society.

relativism.   The anthropological commitment to recognizing that humans are capable of collectively generating innumerable creative solutions to the problems that beset life, and to understanding how and why they work in a particular time and place.

renewable resource.   A resource produced by nature at rates similar to those consumed by people.

resource.   An item used to satisfy a need.

revisionist history.   Historical accounts that use new evidence to revise generally accepted or traditional versions of the past.

Right, the.   The side of the political spectrum that emphasizes national security and national interests in world politics, and individual liberties, private property, and low government involvement in domestic affairs in domestic politics.

royalties.   Payments made based on a percentage of the number of goods sold.

Salafi.   An approach to Islam that rejects centuries of Islamic theology and attempts to return to the "purity" of the earliest teachings of the faith by Muhammad and his first companions. Salafists are known for extremely rigorous ascetic practices and the belief that non-Salafists aren't true Muslims.

scale.   Relative sizes of an object on a map and in reality.

scarcity.   Scarcity results from insufficient resources to fill limitless and subjectively defined wants in a world in which not all individual desires can be fulfilled.

secondary sources.   Newspaper articles, journal articles, books, and other oral or written narratives derived from primary sources.

Sharia.   Code of law derived from the Quran and hadith.

Shia.   The largest minority sect in Islam. Members believe that authentic teaching and leadership after the prophet's death came to biological descendants of the prophet.

Silk Road.   Trade routes linking Asia, Middle East, and Europe.

Sinn Fein.   The political arm of the Irish Republican Army.

social democracy.   Most Western European states developed a social welfare system after World War II that features cooperation between labor and management, generous state pension and unemployment benefits, and universal healthcare.

social entrepreneurship.   The use of entrepreneurial principles to create, organize, and manage projects intended to produce social change.

socialism.   A variety of political doctrines or movements that endorse a political-economic system whereby property and the distribution of wealth are controlled by the community.

South Asia.   India, Pakistan, and Bangladesh are the main countries of this region of Asia.

Southeast Asia.   Thailand, Indonesia, Malaysia, and Vietnam are the main countries of this region of Asia.

Southern Cone.   The southernmost region of South America, including Uruguay, Argentina, Chile, and Paraguay.

sovereign debt crisis.   The inability of the government of a country to pay back its debt in full. Also known as *sovereign debt default*.

space.   The arrangement of geographic phenomena across the earth's surface.

spatial interaction.   The movement or flows across space.

spatial organization.   The delineation of territory.

Stalinism.   Joseph Stalin came to power in the Soviet Union after Vladimir Ilyich Lenin's death in 1924. Through random purges of the Communist Party and forced industrialization and collectivization, he killed millions as he institutionalized totalitarian rule.

state.   An international actor characterized by a defined territory, a central government, and international recognition as a legitimate sovereign entity. *See also* nation *and* nation-state.

state-sponsored terrorism.   Term for situations in which a state harbors, funds, or otherwise supports the terrorist enemies of another state.

state terrorism.   The contemporary use by states of retaliatory bombing, death squads, torture, and other such actions.

structural adjustment programs (SAPs).   Part of the neoliberal economic model, SAPs include difficult economic policies such as currency devaluation; cuts in government subsidies, jobs, and services; opening to foreign investment and trade; and privatization.

subsidies.   Forms of government financial assistance, such as tax breaks or capital payments, meant to encourage or discourage the production of a good.

sultan.   Supreme political ruler of the Ottoman Empire.

Summit of the Americas.   Established to allow the leaders of the Organization of American States to discuss the implementation of the principles of the Washington Consensus, a set of neoliberal policies aimed at instituting free markets for the entire Western Hemisphere.

Sunni.   The majority of the world's Muslims. Members accept the authority of the caliphs as successors to the prophet.

supply.   The amount of goods available for trade.

sustainability.   Offered as a criticism of liberal economic ideas of unlimited growth, sustainability refers to a political-economic system that meets the needs of present communities without reducing the ability of future generations to meet their needs.

sustainable development.   Development that meets the needs of the present without compromising the needs of future generations.

Sustainable Development Goals.   UN sponsored program in 2016 that established 17 goals to end poverty, protect the planet, and ensure that by 2030 all people enjoy peace and prosperity.

symbol.   Something that stands for something else according to a cultural convention, association, or resemblance.

tariff.   A tax placed by governments on imported goods for the purpose of protecting national industries from foreign competition.

terrorism.   A strategy by which subnational groups not recognized as legitimate by the states they oppose seek to resist those states by targeting nonstate actors, disrupting the flow of everyday life, and spreading generalized fear among the populations of those states.

theocracy.   Rule by religious leaders.

theoretical relativism.   An assumption much tested and held by most anthropologists that all human actions make rational sense when understood in their own contexts.

theories of history.   Frameworks that historians use to understand the factors that cause historical change.

"too big to fail."   A slogan that emerged during the global recession of 2008, explaining the need many governments felt to use tax monies to bail out foundering banks and corporations whose failures would have greater fiscal consequences than the economy could absorb.

totalitarianism.   Theory popularized in the West during the Cold War to equate communism with fascism. Instead of sitting at the opposite ends of the political spectrum, totalitarian theory held that the dictatorial methods used by the far Right and the far Left were similar.

Trade-Related Aspects of Intellectual Property Rights (TRIPS).   International agreement defining global intellectual property rights and regulation.

tribe.   Large groups of people who share a common identity based on an assumption of common ancestry.

Troubles, the.   Began in the 1960s with the Irish Republican Army and the Irish Catholic Nationalist community on one side and the Protestant Loyalists and the Royal Ulster Constabulary, the British army, and several Ulster paramilitary groups on the other. Spurred on by the civil-rights movement in the United States and the French student riots in 1968, Irish Catholics in Northern Ireland demanded their own equal civil and economic rights.

uniform region.   A region defined by a uniformity of features.

utility.   The attempt to gain the highest possible well-being.

United States-Mexico-Canada Agreement (USMCA).   Trade agreement between US, Mexico, and Canada in 2020 replacing NAFTA.

value of labor.   According to liberal economic theory, the value of a product is determined by consumer choices assigning values to commodities. Marxist economic theory, in contrast, argues that a product is worth the value of the work expended to produce it.

Wahhabism.   An eighteenth-century religious reform movement that became the official religion of Saudi Arabia.

Warsaw Pact.   Formed in 1955 as a military alliance of East European countries and the Soviet Union. It served as a counterweight to NATO but quickly fell apart after the collapse of the Communist regimes in 1989.

Washington Consensus.   A phrase invented by economist John Williamson, who posited ten policy recommendations for economic reform in Latin American countries plagued by fiscal irresponsibility. These recommendations included reinstitution of market economics, openness to global trade, and macroeconomic discipline.

World Bank.   An international organization responsible for providing financial assistance and advice to countries to facilitate economic development and eliminate poverty.

World Intellectual Property Organization (WIPO).   Agency of the United Nations established in 1967 to oversee the Trade-Related Aspects of Intellectual Property Rights (TRIPS) agreement.

World Trade Organization (WTO).   An international organization responsible for negotiating, monitoring, and regulating international trade agreements. Its goal is to help producers of goods and services conduct business without fear of trade restrictions and government intervention.

worldview.   The most encompassing level of cultural integration, comprising organized assumptions people have about the structure of the universe. A worldview is a model of reality that people use to orient themselves in the world.

WTO.   *See* World Trade Organization.

zero-sum approach.   Situation in which one nation's advantage requires another nation's loss.

Zionism.   The belief that Jews constitute a sovereign people and nation and that they should have the right to establish and maintain a state in their ancestral homeland.

Index